Lecture Notes in Computer Science 2622

Edited by G. Goos, J. Hartmanis, and J. van Leeuwen

W0079509

Springer
Berlin
Heidelberg
New York
Barcelona
Hong Kong
London
Milan
Paris
Tokyo

Görel Hedin (Ed.)

Compiler Construction

12th International Conference, CC 2003
Held as Part of the Joint European Conferences
on Theory and Practice of Software, ETAPS 2003
Warsaw, Poland, April 7-11, 2003
Proceedings

 Springer

Series Editors

Gerhard Goos, Karlsruhe University, Germany
Juris Hartmanis, Cornell University, NY, USA
Jan van Leeuwen, Utrecht University, The Netherlands

Volume Editor

Görel Hedin
Lund University, Department of Computer Science
Box 118, 221 00 Lund, Sweden
E-mail:gorel.hedin@cs.lth.se

Cataloging-in-Publication Data applied for

A catalog record for this book is available from the Library of Congress.

Bibliographic information published by Die Deutsche Bibliothek.
Die Deutsche Bibliothek lists this publication in the Deutsche Nationalbibliografie;
detailed bibliographic data is available in the Internet at <http://dnb.ddb.de>.

CR Subject Classification (1998): D.3.4, D.3.1, F.4.2, D.2.6, F.3, I.2.2

ISSN 0302-9743
ISBN 3-540-00904-3 Springer-Verlag Berlin Heidelberg New York

Springer-Verlag Berlin Heidelberg New York
a member of BertelsmannSpringer Science+Business Media GmbH

http://www.springer.de

© Springer-Verlag Berlin Heidelberg 2003
Printed in Germany

Typesetting: Camera-ready by author, data conversion by PTP-Berlin GmbH
Printed on acid-free paper   SPIN: 10872988   06/3142   5 4 3 2 1 0

Foreword

ETAPS 2003 was the sixth instance of the European Joint Conferences on Theory and Practice of Software. ETAPS is an annual federated conference that was established in 1998 by combining a number of existing and new conferences. This year it comprised five conferences (FOSSACS, FASE, ESOP, CC, TACAS), 14 satellite workshops (AVIS, CMCS, COCV, FAMAS, Feyerabend, FICS, LDTA, RSKD, SC, TACoS, UniGra, USE, WITS and WOOD), eight invited lectures (not including those that are specific to the satellite events), and several tutorials. We received a record number of submissions to the five conferences this year: over 500, making acceptance rates fall below 30% for every one of them. Congratulations to all the authors who made it to the final program! I hope that all the other authors still found a way of participating in this exciting event and I hope you will continue submitting.

A special event was held to honour the 65th birthday of Prof. Wlad Turski, one of the pioneers of our young science. The deaths of some of our "fathers" in the summer of 2002 — Dahl, Dijkstra and Nygaard — reminded us that Software Science and Technology is, perhaps, no longer that young. Against this sobering background, it is a treat to celebrate one of our most prominent scientists and his lifetime of achievements. It gives me particular personal pleasure that we are able to do this for Wlad during my term as chairman of ETAPS.

The events that comprise ETAPS address various aspects of the system development process, including specification, design, implementation, analysis and improvement. The languages, methodologies and tools which support these activities are all well within its scope. Different blends of theory and practice are represented, with an inclination towards theory with a practical motivation on the one hand and soundly based practice on the other. Many of the issues involved in software design apply to systems in general, including hardware systems, and the emphasis on software is not intended to be exclusive.

ETAPS is a loose confederation in which each event retains its own identity, with a separate program committee and independent proceedings. Its format is open-ended, allowing it to grow and evolve as time goes by. Contributed talks and system demonstrations are in synchronized parallel sessions, with invited lectures in plenary sessions. Two of the invited lectures are reserved for "unifying" talks on topics of interest to the whole range of ETAPS attendees. The aim of cramming all this activity into a single one-week meeting is to create a strong magnet for academic and industrial researchers working on topics within its scope, giving them the opportunity to learn about research in related areas, and thereby to foster new and existing links between work in areas that were formerly addressed in separate meetings.

ETAPS 2003 was organized by Warsaw University, Institute of Informatics, in cooperation with the Foundation for Information Technology Development, as well as:

- European Association for Theoretical Computer Science (EATCS);
- European Association for Programming Languages and Systems (EAPLS);
- European Association of Software Science and Technology (EASST); and

– ACM SIGACT, SIGSOFT and SIGPLAN.

The organizing team comprised:

Mikołaj Bojańczyk, Jacek Chrząaszcz, Piotr Chrząstowski-Wachtel, Grzegorz Grudziński, Kazimierz Grygiel, Piotr Hoffman, Janusz Jabłonowski, Mirosław Kowaluk, Marcin Kubica (publicity), Sławomir Leszczyński (www), Wojciech Moczydłowski, Damian Niwiński (satellite events), Aleksy Schubert, Hanna Sokołowska, Piotr Stańczyk, Krzysztof Szafran, Marcin Szczuka, Łukasz Sznuk, Andrzej Tarlecki (co-chair), Jerzy Tiuryn, Jerzy Tyszkiewicz (book exhibition), Paweł Urzyczyn (co-chair), Daria Walukiewicz-Chrząaszcz, Artur Zawłocki.

ETAPS 2003 received support from:[1]

– Warsaw University
– European Commission, High-Level Scientific Conferences and Information Society Technologies
– US Navy Office of Naval Research International Field Office,
– European Office of Aerospace Research and Development, US Air Force
– Microsoft Research

Overall planning for ETAPS conferences is the responsibility of its Steering Committee, whose current membership is:

Egidio Astesiano (Genoa), Pierpaolo Degano (Pisa), Hartmut Ehrig (Berlin), José Fiadeiro (Leicester), Marie-Claude Gaudel (Paris), Evelyn Duesterwald (IBM), Hubert Garavel (Grenoble), Andy Gordon (Microsoft Research, Cambridge), Roberto Gorrieri (Bologna), Susanne Graf (Grenoble), Görel Hedin (Lund), Nigel Horspool (Victoria), Kurt Jensen (Aarhus), Paul Klint (Amsterdam), Tiziana Margaria (Dortmund), Ugo Montanari (Pisa), Mogens Nielsen (Aarhus), Hanne Riis Nielson (Copenhagen), Fernando Orejas (Barcelona), Mauro Pezzè (Milano), Andreas Podelski (Saarbrücken), Don Sannella (Edinburgh), David Schmidt (Kansas), Bernhard Steffen (Dortmund), Andrzej Tarlecki (Warsaw), Igor Walukiewicz (Bordeaux), Herbert Weber (Berlin).

I would like to express my sincere gratitude to all of these people and organizations, the program committee chairs and PC members of the ETAPS conferences, the organizers of the satellite events, the speakers themselves, and Springer-Verlag for agreeing to publish the ETAPS proceedings. The final votes of thanks must go, however, to Andrzej Tarlecki and Paweł Urzyczyn. They accepted the risk of organizing what is the first edition of ETAPS in Eastern Europe, at a time of economic uncertainty, but with great courage and determination. They deserve our greatest applause.

Leicester, January 2003   José Luiz Fiadeiro
                                           ETAPS Steering Committee Chair

---

[1] The contents of this volume do not necessarily reflect the positions or the policies of these organizations and no official endorsement should be inferred.

Preface

The International Conference on Compiler Construction (CC) is concerned with recent developments in compiler construction, programming language implementation, and language design. It addresses work on all phases of compilation and for all language paradigms, emphasizing practical and efficient methods and tools. The broad area of compiler construction is reflected in these proceedings. The papers cover the full range of compiler topics including compiler tools, parsing, type analysis, static analysis, code optimization, register allocation, and run-time issues.

CC 2003 was held in Warsaw, Poland during 5–13 April 2003 and was the 12th conference in the series. This year, submissions reached a record number of 83 papers of which 77 were regular papers and 6 were short tool demonstration papers. Of these, 20 regular papers and one tool demonstration paper were selected for presentation and are included in these proceedings.

The proceedings also include two invited papers. The CC 2003 invited speaker was Barbara Ryder, whose talk was entitled *Dimensions of Precision in Reference Analysis of Object-Oriented Programming Languages*. In addition, we have the honor of including the paper by Tony Hoare who gave one of the two ETAPS "unifying" invited talks. The title of his talk was *The Verifying Compiler: a Grand Challenge for Computing Research*.

The selection of papers took place at an intense program committee meeting in Lund, Sweden, on December 6th, 2002. Eight of the PC members attended the meeting, and another seven joined in the discussion via a telephone conference call. I wish to thank all my colleagues on the program committee for their hard work, detailed reviews, and friendly cooperation. I am especially grateful to Nigel Horspool, Reinhard Wilhelm, and Evelyn Duesterwald, who, as members of the CC steering committee, gave me prompt advice whenever I needed it throughout the process of being the program chair. Many thanks also to the large number of additional reviewers who helped us read and evaluate the submitted papers.

Many people helped me in the administration of the PC work. In particular, I wish to thank Jonas Wisbrant for being very helpful in the organization of the program committee meeting and arranging a simple but very useful web facility for the PC members participating via telephone. Thanks also to Christian Andersson who helped me assemble these proceedings, and to Tiziana Margaria and Martin Karusseit at METAframe for their support of the electronic online conference system we used for submissions and reviewing. Finally, I wish to thank José Luiz Fiadeiro and the ETAPS team for their excellent organization and coordination of the whole ETAPS event.

Lund, January 2003   Görel Hedin

Program Committee

Uwe Aßmann (Linköpings Universitet, Sweden)
Isabelle Attali (INRIA Sophia Antipolis, France)
Judith Bishop (University of Pretoria, South Africa)
Mark van den Brand (CWI, The Netherlands)
Peter Dickman (Univeristy of Glasgow, UK)
Evelyn Duesterwald (IBM T.J. Watson Research Center, USA)
Tibor Gyimothy (University of Szeged, Hungary)
Görel Hedin – Chair (Lund University, Sweden)
Nigel Horspool (University of Victoria, Canada)
Uwe Kastens (Universität Paderborn, Germany)
Oege de Moor (Oxford University, UK)
Mooly Sagiv (Tel Aviv University, Israel)
Vivek Sarkar (IBM T.J. Watson Research Center, USA)
Pierluigi San Pietro (Politecnico di Milano, Italy)
Reinhard Wilhelm (Saarland University, Germany)
Jan Vitek (Purdue University, USA)
Jingling Xue (University of New South Wales, Australia)

Additional Reviewers

Giampaolo Agosta
John Aycock
Françoise Baude
Joerg Bauer
Nick Benton
David Bernstein
Rastislav Bodik
Qiong Cai
Calin Cascaval
Siddhartha Chatterjee
Alessandra Cherubini
Roberto Costa
Pascal Degenne
Stephan Diehl
Julian Dolby
Nurit Dor
Kemal Ebcioglu
Erik Eckstein
Torbjörn Ekman
Peter Faber
Hila Fatal
Rudolf Ferenc
Chap Flack

Guang Gao
Tamas Gergely
Christian Grothoff
David Grove
Flavius Gruian
Charles Hardnett
Ferenc Havasi
Roger Henriksson
Ludovic Henrio
Michael Hind
Qingguang Huang
Anders Ive
Barry Jay
Akos Kiss
Karsten Klohs
Jens Knoop
Jochen Kreimer
Uli Kremer
David Lacey
Ralf Laemmel
Marc Langenbach
Ken Friis Larsen
Dinh Khoi Le

Table of Contents

Pot Pourri

ETAPS Invited Talk

Optimization

Author Index

Combined Code Motion and Register Allocation Using the Value State Dependence Graph

Neil Johnson and Alan Mycroft

Computer Laboratory, University of Cambridge
William Gates Building, JJ Thompson Avenue,
Cambridge, CB3 0FD, UK
{Neil.Johnson,Alan.Mycroft}@cl.cam.ac.uk

Abstract. We define the Value State Dependence Graph (VSDG). The VSDG is a form of the Value Dependence Graph (VDG) extended by the addition of state dependence edges to model sequentialised computation. These express store dependencies and loop termination dependencies of the original program. We also exploit them to express the additional serialization inherent in producing final object code.

The central idea is that this latter serialization can be done incrementally so that we have a class of algorithms which effectively interleave register allocation and code motion, thereby avoiding a well-known phase-order problem in compilers. This class operates by first normalizing the VSDG during construction, to remove all duplicated computation, and then repeatedly choosing between: (*i*) allocating a value to a register, (*ii*) spilling a value to memory, (*iii*) moving a loop-invariant computation within a loop to avoid register spillage, and (*iv*) statically duplicating a computation to avoid register spillage.

We show that the classical two-phase approach (code motion then register allocation in both Chow and Chaitin forms) are examples of this class, and propose a new algorithm based on depth-first cuts of the VSDG.

1 Introduction

An important problem encountered by compiler designers is the *phase ordering* problem, which can be phrased as *"in which order does one schedule the register allocation and code motion phases to give the best target code?"*. These phases are antagonistic to each other—code motion may increase register pressure, while register allocation places additional dependencies between instructions, artificially constraining code motion. In this paper we show that a unified approach, in which both register allocation and code motion are considered together, sidesteps the problem of which phase to do first.

In support of this endeavour, we present a new program representation, the *Value State Dependence Graph* (VSDG), as an extension of the Value Dependence Graph (VDG) [21]. It is a simple unifying framework within which a wide range of code space optimizations can be implemented. We believe that the VSDG can be used in both intermediate code transformations, and all the way through to final target code generation.

G. Hedin (Ed.): CC 2003, LNCS 2622, pp. 1–16, 2003.

Traditional register allocation has been represented as a graph colouring problem, originally proposed by Chaitin [5], and based on the Control Flow Graph (CFG). Unfortunately the CFG imposes an artificial ordering of instructions, constraining the register allocator to the given order.

The VDG represents programs as value dependencies—there is an edge (p, n), drawn as an arrow $n \to p$, if node n requires the value of p to compute its own value. This representation removes any specific ordering of instructions (nodes), but does not elegantly handle loop and function termination dependencies.

The VSDG introduces state dependency edges to model sequentialised computing. These edges also have the surprising benefit of generalising the VSDG: by adding sufficient serializing edges we can select any one of a number of CFGs. Our thesis is that relaxing the exact serialization of the CFG into the more general VSDG supports a combined register allocation and code motion algorithm.

1.1   Paper Structure

This paper is structured as follows. Section 2 describes the forms of nodes and edges in the VSDG, while Section 3 explores additional serialization and liveness within the VSDG. In Section 4 we describe the general approach to joint register allocation and code motion ($RACM$) as applied to the VSDG, and show that classical Chaitin/Chow-style register colouring specialises it. Section 5 introduces our new greedy register allocation algorithm. Section 6 provides context for this paper with a review of related work, with Section 7 concluding.

2   Formalism

The Value State Dependence Graph is a directed graph consisting of operation nodes, loop and merge nodes together with value- and state-dependency edges. Cycles are permitted but must satisfy various restrictions. A VSDG represents a single procedure; this matches the classical CFG but differs from the VDG in which loops were converted to tail-recursive procedures called at the logical start of the loop. We justify this because of our interest in performing RACM at the same time; inter-procedural motion and allocation issues are considered a topic for future work.

An example VSDG is shown in Fig. 1. In (a) we have the original C source for a recursive factorial function. The corresponding VSDG (b) shows both value and state edges and a selection of nodes.

2.1   Definition of the VSDG

Definition 1. *A VSDG is a labelled directed graph $G = (N, E_V, E_S, \ell, N_0, N_\infty)$ consisting of nodes N (with unique entry node N_0 and exit node N_∞), value-dependency edges $E_V \subseteq N \times N$, state-dependency edges $E_S \subseteq N \times N$. The labelling function ℓ associates each node with an operator (§2.2 for details).*

```
int fac( int n ) {
    int result;

    if ( n == 1 )
        result = n;
    else
        result = n * fac( n - 1 );
    return result;
}
```

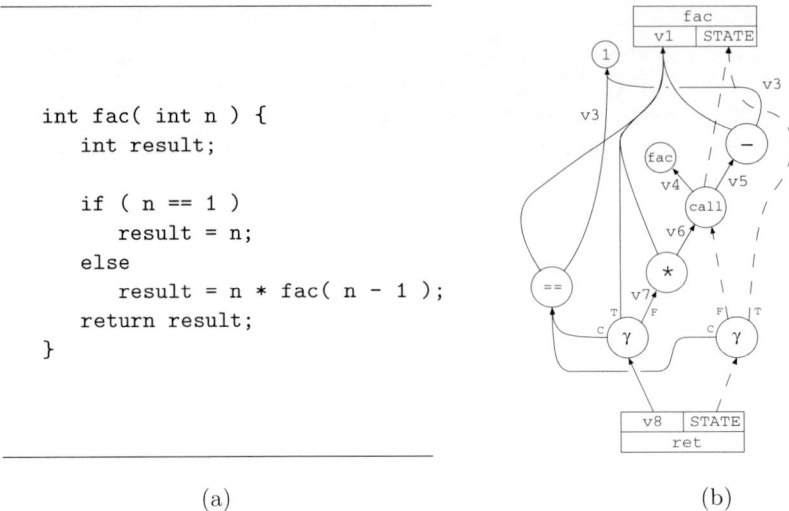

(a)   (b)

Fig. 1. A recursive factorial function, whose VSDG illustrates the key graph components—value dependency edges (solid lines), state dependency edges (dashed lines), a const node, a call node, two γ-nodes, a conditional node (==), and the function entry and exit nodes. The left-hand γ-node returns the original function argument if the condition is true, or that of the expression otherwise. The right-hand γ-node behaves similarly for the state edges, returning either the state on entry to the function, or that returned by the call node.

VSDGs have to satisfy two well-formedness conditions. Firstly ℓ and the (E_V) arity must be consistent, e.g. that a binary arithmetic operator must have two inputs; secondly (at least for the purposes of this paper) that the VSDG corresponds to a structured program, e.g. that there are no cycles in the VSDG except those mediated by θ (loop) nodes (see §3.2).

Value dependency (E_V) indicates the flow of values between nodes, and must be preserved during register allocation and code motion.

State dependency (E_S), for this paper, represents two things; the first is essential sequential dependency required by the original program, e.g. a given load instruction may be required to follow a given store instruction without being re-ordered, and a return node in general must wait for an earlier loop to terminate even though there might be no value-dependency between the loop and the return node. The second purpose, which in a sense is the centre of this work, is that state-dependency edges can be added incrementally until the VSDG corresponds to a unique CFG (§3.1). Such state dependency edges are called *serializing* edges.

An edge (n_1, n_2) represents the flow of data or control *from* n_1 to n_2, i.e. in the *forwards data flow direction*, so we will see n_1 as a predecessor of n_2. Similarly we will regard n_2 as a successor of n_1. If we wish to be specific we will write V-successors or S-successors for respectively E_V and E_S successors.

Similarly, we will write $succ_V(n)$, $pred_S(n)$ and the like for appropriate sets of successors or predecessors, and $dom(n)$ and $pdom(n)$ for sets of dominators and post-dominators respectively. We will draw pictures in the VDG form, with arrows following the *backwards data flow direction*, so that the edge (n_1, n_2) will be represented as an arrow *from n_2 to n_1*.

The VSDG inherits from the VDG the property that a program is implicitly represented in Static Single Assignment (SSA) form [8]: a given operator node, n, will have zero or more E_V-successors using its value. Note that, in implementation terms, a single register can hold the produced value for consumption at all successors; it is therefore useful to talk about the idea of an output *port* for n being allocated a specific register, r, to abbreviate the idea of r being used for each edge (n_1, n_2) where $n_2 \in succ(n_1)$. Similarly, we will talk about (say) the "right-hand input port" of a subtraction instruction, or of the R-input of a θ-node.

2.2   Node Labelling with Instructions

There are four main classes of VSDG nodes, based on those of the *tri*VM Intermediate Language [13]: value nodes (representing pure arithmetic), γ-nodes (conditionals), θ-nodes (loops), and state nodes (side-effects).

2.2.1   Value Nodes. The majority of nodes in a VSDG generate a value based on some computation (add, subtract, etc) applied to their dependent values (constant nodes, which have no dependent nodes, are a special case).

2.2.2 γ-Nodes. Our γ-node is similar to the γ-node of Gated Single Assignment form [2] in being dependent on a control predicate, rather than the control-independent nature of SSA ϕ-functions.

Definition 2. *A γ-node $\gamma(C, T, F)$ evaluates the condition dependency C, and returns the value of T if C is true, otherwise F.*

We generally treat γ-nodes as single-valued nodes (constrast θ-nodes, which are treated as tuples), with the effect that two separate γ-nodes with the same condition can be later combined (Section 4) into a tuple using a single test. Fig. 2 illustrates two γ-nodes that can be combined in this way.

2.2.3 θ-Nodes. The θ-node models the iterative behaviour of loops, modelling loop state with the notion of an *internal value* which may be updated on each iteration of the loop. It has five specific ports which represent dependencies at various stages of computation.

Definition 3. *A θ-node $\theta(C, I, R, L, X)$ sets its internal value to initial value I then, while condition value C holds true, sets L to the current internal value and updates the internal value with the repeat value R. When C evaluates to false computation ceases and the last internal value is returned through the X port.*

A loop which updates k variables will have: a single condition port C, initial-value ports $I_1, \ldots, I_k$, loop iteration ports $L_1, \ldots, L_k$, loop return ports $R_1, \ldots, R_k$, and loop exit ports $X_1, \ldots, X_k$. The example in Fig. 3 shows a pair (2-tuple) of values being used for I, R, L, X, one for each loop-variant value.

For some purposes the L and X ports could be fused, as both represent outputs within, or exiting, a loop (the values are identical, while the C input merely selects their routing). We avoid this for two reasons: (i) we have operational semantics for VSDGs G and these semantics require separation of these concerns; and (ii) our construction of G^{noloop} (§3.2) requires it.

The θ-node directly implements pre-test loops (`while`, `for`); post-test loops (`do...while`, `repeat...until`) are synthesised from a pre-test loop preceded by a duplicate of the loop body. At first this may seem to cause unnecessary duplication of code, but it has two important benefits: (i) it exposes the first loop body iteration to optimization in post-test loops (*cf.* loop-peeling), and (ii) it normalizes all loops to one loop structure, which both reduces the cost of optimization, and increases the likelihood of two schematically-dissimilar loops being isomorphic in the VSDG.

2.2.4   State Nodes. Loads, stores, and their volatile equivalents, compute a value and/or state (non-volatile loads return a value from memory without generating a new state). Accesses to volatile memory or hardware can change state independently of compiler-aware reads or writes (*cf.* IO-state [7]).

The `call` node takes both the name of the function to call and a list of arguments, and returns a list of results; it is treated as a state node as the function body may read or update state.

We maintain the simplicity of the VSDG by imposing the restriction that *all* functions have *one* return node (the exit node N_∞), which returns at least one result (which will be a state value in the case of `void` functions). To ensure that function calls and definitions are colourable, we suppose that the number of arguments to, and results from, a function is smaller than the number of physical registers—further arguments can be passed via a stack as usual.

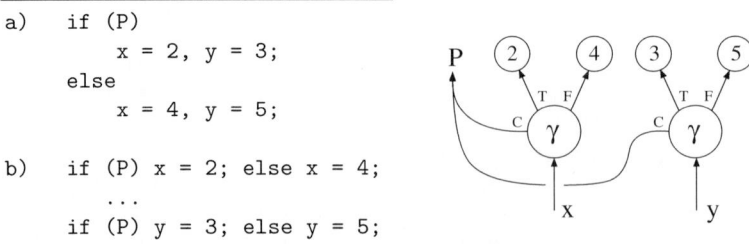

```
a)   if (P)
        x = 2, y = 3;
     else
        x = 4, y = 5;

b)   if (P) x = 2; else x = 4;
     ...
     if (P) y = 3; else y = 5;
```

Fig. 2. Two different code schemes (a) & (b) map to the same γ-node structure.

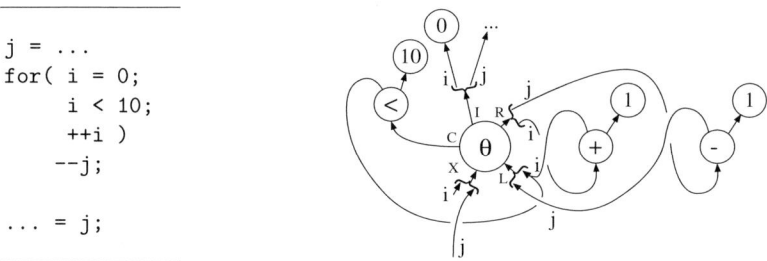

```
j = ...
for( i = 0;
     i < 10;
     ++i )
     --j;

... = j;
```

Fig. 3. A θ-node example showing a `for` loop. Evaluating the θ-node's **X** port triggers it to evaluate the **I** value (outputting the value on the **L** port). While **C** evaluates to true, it evaluates the **R** value (which in this case also uses the θ-node's **L** value). When **C** is false, it returns the final internal value through the **X** port. As i is not used after the θ-node loop then there is no dependency on the i port of **X**.

Note also that the VSDG neither forces loop invariant code into nor out-of loop bodies, but rather allows later phases to determine, by adding serializing edges, such placement of loop invariant nodes for later phases.

3   Applying the VSDG to RACM

3.1   Serialization

Weise *et al.* [21] observe that their mapping from CFGs to VDGs is many-one; that paper also suggests that *"Code motion optimizations are decided when the demand dependence graph is constructed from the VDG"*—*i.e.* that a VDG should be mapped back into a CFG for further processing—but does not give an algorithm or consider which of the many CFGs corresponding to a VSDG should be selected.

We identify VSDGs with 'enough' serializing edges with CFGs—such VSDGs can be simply transformed into CFGs if desired—the task of RACM then being to make the VSDG sufficiently sequential. The following informal definition captures this idea for the purposes of this paper.

Definition 4. *A* sequential *VSDG is one which has enough serializing edges to make it correspond to a single CFG.*

Here 'enough' means in essence that each node in the VSDG has a unique ($E_V \cup E_S$) immediate dominator which can be seen as its predecessor in the CFG. Exceptions arise for the start node (which has no predecessors in the VSDG or corresponding CFG), γ-nodes and θ-nodes. Given a γ-node, we interpret those nodes which the T port post-dominates as the *condition-true* sub-CFG and those which the F port post-dominates as the *condition-false* sub-CFG; a control-split node (corresponding to a CFG test node) is added to the VSDG as the immediate E_S-dominator of both sub-CFGs. For a θ-node, we recursively require this sequential property for its body, L, and interpret the "unique immediate dominator" property as a constraint on its I port.

3.2   VSDG Well-Formedness

As in the VDG we restrict attention to reducible graphs for the VSDG; recall that any CFG can be made reducible by duplicating code or by introducing additional boolean variables. For this paper we further restrict to programs whose only loops are `while`-loops and which exit them only by the condition becoming *false, i.e.* no `break` and the like (again this could be achieved with code duplication or with additional boolean variables).

In order to specify the "all cycles in a VSDG are mediated by θ-nodes" restriction, it is convenient to define a transformation on VSDGs.

Definition 5. *Given a VSDG, G, we define G^{noloop} to be identical to G except that each θ-node θ_i is replaced with two nodes, θ_i^{head} and θ_i^{tail}; edges to or from ports I or L of the original θ-node are redirected to θ_i^{head} whereas those to or from ports R, X, C are redirected to θ_i^{tail}.*

We then require G^{noloop} to be an acyclic graph.

When adding serializing edges we must maintain this acyclic property. To serialize nodes connected to a θ-node's X port we add serializing edges to θ^{tail}; all nodes within the body of the loop are on the sequential path from θ^{tail} to θ^{head}; all other nodes are serialized before θ^{head}. Definition 6 below sets out the conditions for a node to be within a loop.

Although this is merely a formal transformation, note that if we interpret θ^{tail} as a γ-node (or possibly a tuple thereof) and interpret θ^{head} as an identity operation then G^{noloop} represents a VSDG in which each loop is executed zero or one times according to the condition. Our θ^{head} and θ^{tail} nodes, while similar to GSA's μ- and η^F-functions [2], avoids the need for their "non-deterministic merge gate" to break cyclic dependencies.

The formal definition of a VSDG being well-formed is then:

Definition 6. *A VSDG, G, is well-formed if (i) G^{noloop} is acyclic and (ii) for each pair of $(\theta^{head},\theta^{tail})$ nodes in G^{noloop}, θ^{tail} post-dominates all nodes in $succ_{V\cup S}^+(\theta^{head}) \cap pred_{V\cup S}^+(\theta^{tail})$.*

The second condition says that no value computed during a loop can be used outside the loop, except via the X port of a θ-node.

3.3   VSDG Normalization

The RACM algorithms below will assume (for maximal optimization potential rather than correctness) that the VSDG has been normalized, roughly in the way of 'hash-CONSing': any two nodes which have identical input nodes, will be assumed to have been replaced with a single node *provided that this does not violate well-formedness by creating a cycle in the VSDG.* Consider

```
int f( int v[], int i ) {
    int a = v[i+1];
    v[7] = 0;
    return v[i+1] + a;
}
```

There will only be one node for the constant 1, and one for the addition of this node to the second formal parameter (i+1) but two nodes for the *loading* from v[i+1] because sharing this node would lead to a cycle in E_S by being both a predecessor and successor of the *store* to v[7].

Note that this is a safe form of CSE and loop invariant code lifting; this optimization is selectively undone (node cloning) during the joint RACM phase when required by register pressure.

3.4   Liveness in VSDGs

For the purposes of register allocation (*cf.* the register interference graph), we need to know which (output ports of) VSDG nodes may hold values simultaneously so we can forbid them being allocated the same register.

We define a *cut* to be a partition $N_1 \cup N_2$ of nodes in the VSDG with the property that there is no $E_V \cup E_S$ edge from N_2 to N_1 (excepting edges from L ports of θ-nodes—see the G^{noloop} construction).

We now define nodes n and n' to *interfere* if there is a cut $N_1 \cup N_2$ with $n, n' \in N_1$ and with both $succ(n)$ and $succ(n')$ having non-empty intersections with N_2.

This generalises the normal concept register of interference in a CFG; there a cut is just a program point and interference means "simultaneously live at any program point". Similarly "virtual register" corresponds to our "output port of a node". Note that we use the concept of "cut based on Depth From Root" in Section 5 for our new greedy algorithm.

4   Register Allocation and Code Motion

The goal of register allocation in the VSDG is to allocate one physical register (from a fairly small set) to each node's output ports. θ-nodes are a special case, as they require multiple registers on their tupled I, R, L and X ports.

Register requirements can be reduced by serializing computations (a register can be reused in two independent computations if we know that they do not interleave), or by reducing the range over which a value is live by duplicating a computation or by spilling a value to memory. In both cases the idea is that these operations reduce the register interference.

4.1   A Non-deterministic Approach

Given a VSDG we repeatedly apply the following non-deterministic algorithm until all the nodes are coloured and the VSDG is sequential:

1. Colour a port with a physical register—provided no port it interferes with is already coloured with the same register;
2. Add a serializing edge to force one node before another—this removes edges from the interference graph by forbidding interleaving of computations;

3. Clone a node, *i.e.* recalculate it to reduce register pressure.
4. Tunnel values through memory by introducing store/load spill nodes.
5. Merge two γ-nodes a and b into a tuple, provided their C ports reference the same node and there is no path from a to b or from b to a.

The first action assigns a physical register to a port of the given node. The second moves the node, with the effect of changing the register usage; the choice of *which* node to move is determinined by specific algorithms (see §4.2 and Section 5).

Node cloning replaces a single instance of a node that has multiple uses, with multiple copies (clones) of the node, each with a subset of the original dependency edges. For example, a node n with two dependent nodes p and q, can be cloned into n' and n'', with p dependent on n' and q dependent on n''.

Spilling follows the traditional Chaitin-style register spilling where we add store and load nodes, together with some temporary storage in memory.

Finally, because the initial VSDG was normalized to ensure that each γ-node represented the merge of a *single* variable, given a VSDG such as that in Fig. 2, we can either arrange to serialize the two γ-nodes (action 2) resulting in two separate tests (or conditional move instructions) or to merge them (action 5) so that a single test is used (as in Fig. 2(a)).

The cost of spilling loop-variant variables is rather higher than the store-and-reload for a normal spill. For θ-nodes where the tuple is wider than the available target registers, we must spill one or more of the θ-node variables over the loop test code, not merely within the loop itself. At most this requires two stores and three loads for each variable spilled. Fig. 4 shows the location of the five spill nodes (a), with table (b) describing the use of each of the spill nodes.

4.2   The Classical Algorithms

We can phrase the classical Chaitin/Chow-style register allocators as instances of the above algorithm:

1. Perform all code motion transforms through adding serializing edges and merging γ-nodes if not already sequentialised;

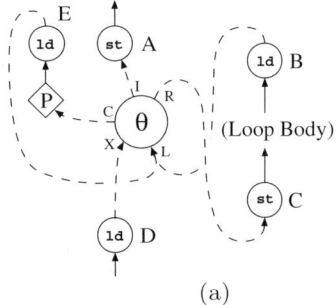

Spill Node	Needed if variable...
A	Is initialised
B	Is used in Loop Body
C	Is defined in Loop Body
D	Is used after the loop
E	Is used in the condition predicate **P**

(a)   (b)

Fig. 4. Illustrating the locations of the five spill nodes associated with a θ-node.

2. Map the VSDG onto a CFG by adding additional serializing edges;
3. If there are insufficient physical registers to colour a node port, then:
   a) Chaitin-style allocation [5]: spill nodes, with the restriction that the target register of the reload is the same as the source register of the store. Chaitin's cost estimates can be applied to determine which edge to spill;
   b) Chow-style allocation [6]: spill nodes, but without the register restriction of Chaitin-style, thus splitting the live-range of the virtual register; use Chow's heuristics to decide which edge to split.

In both Chaitin and Chow instances post-code-motion transformations during register allocation are limited to inserting store and load nodes into the program.

5   A New Register Allocation Algorithm

The Chaitin/Chow algorithms do not make full use of the dependence information within the VSDG; they assume that a previous phase has performed code motion to produce a sequential VSDG—corresponding to a single CFG—on which traditional register colouring algorithms are applied.

We now present the central point of this paper—a register allocation algorithm specifically designed to maximise the usage of information within the VSDG. The algorithm consists of two distinct phases:

1. Starting at the exit node N_∞, walk up the graph edges calculating the maximal Depth From Root (DFR) of each node (see Definition 7); for each set of nodes of equal depth calculate their liveness width (the number of distinct values on which they depend, taking into account control flow).
2. Apply a forward "snow-plough"[1]-like graph reshaping algorithm, starting from N_∞ and pushing up towards N_0, to ensure that the liveness width is never more than the number of physical resisters. This is achieved by splitting, spilling or adding serializing edges in greedy way so that the previously smoothed-out parts of the graph (nearer the exit) are not re-visited.

The result is a colourable VSDG; colouring it constitutes register assignment completing the algorithm.

5.1   Partitioning the VSDG

The first phase annotates the VSDG with the maximal Depth From Root. The second phase then processes each cut of the VSDG in turn.

Definition 7. *The maximal Depth From Root, $\mathcal{D}(n)$, of a node $n \in N$ is the length of the longest path $p \in (E_V \cup E_S)^*$ from the root to n. Loop bodies are traversed once, such that a θ-node has two DFRs—one each for the θ^{head} and θ^{tail} nodes.*

---

[1] Imagine a snow plough pushing forward, scooping up excess snow, and depositing it where there is little snow. The goal is to even out the peaks and troughs.

Definition 8. *A depth-first cut* $\mathcal{S}_{=d}$ *is the set of nodes with the same DFR d:*

$$\mathcal{S}_{=d} = \{n \in N \mid \mathcal{D}(n) = d\}$$

It is convenient also to write

$$\mathcal{S}_{\leq d} = \{n \in N \mid \mathcal{D}(n) \leq d\}$$
$$\mathcal{S}_{>d} = \{n \in N \mid \mathcal{D}(n) > d\}$$

Note that the partition $(\mathcal{S}_{\leq d}, \mathcal{S}_{>d})$ is a *cut* according to the definition of §3.4.

Computing the DFR of a given VSDG is equivalent to computing the depth-first search of the graph—we simply start at the root node N_∞ and recursively walk along all dependency edges, setting each node to the larger of the node's current DFR and the new DFR, terminating either at the entry node N_0 or nodes with DFRs greater than the current DFR. It has a complexity of $O(N+E_V+E_S)$.

5.2   Calculating Liveness Width

We wish to transform each cut so that the number of nodes having edges passing through it is no greater than $\mathcal{R}$, the number of registers available for colouring.

For a cut of depth d the set of such live nodes is given by

$$\mathcal{W}_{in}(d) = \mathcal{S}_{>d} \cap pred_V(\mathcal{S}_{\leq d})$$

i.e. those nodes which are further than d from the exit node but whose values may be used on the path to the exit node. Note that only E_V and not E_S edges count towards liveness.

One might expect that $|\mathcal{W}_{in}(d)|$ is the number of registers required to compute the nodes in $\mathcal{S}_{\leq d}$ but this overstates the number of registers required for conditional nodes. γ-nodes have the property that the edges of each of their selection dependencies are disjoint—on any given execution trace, exactly one path to the γ-node will be executed at a time, and so therefore we can reuse the same registers to colour its True- and False-dominated nodes.

We identify the γ-node dependency register sets using the dominance property thus:

Definition 9. *A node* $n \in N$ *is a* predicated node *iff it is post-dominated by either the* True *or the* False *port of a* γ*-node, but not by both.*

Note that replacing nodes in either of the *True* or *False* regions with no-ops each gives a lower-bound to the liveness width of the cut[2]. Moreover, the greater of the liveness widths for these modified VSDGs gives the corrected liveness width for the original VSDG.

We prefer to formulate this in constraint form.

---

[2] Such no-ops are nodes with no value dependencies on input or output, but with state-dependences where previously there was either a value or state edge so that the DFR is not affected.

Definition 10. *A VSDG is* colourable *with $\mathcal{R}$ registers if either:*

1. *Every cut of depth d has $|\mathcal{W}_{in}(d)| \leq \mathcal{R}$; or*
2. *Each VSDG resulting from replacing either* True *or* False *regions with no-ops satisfies 1.*

5.3   Pass through Edges

Some edges (*i.e.* of lifetime greater than one) pass *through* a cut. These pass-through (*PT*) edges may also interact with the cut. However, even the ordinary PT edges require a register, and so must be accommodated in any colouring scheme.

Definition 11. *The* lifetime *$\mathcal{L}$ of an edge (n, n') is the number of cuts over which it spans:*
$$\mathcal{L}(n, n') = \mathcal{D}(n) - \mathcal{D}(n')$$

Definition 12. *An edge $(n, n') \in E_V$ is a Pass Through (PT) edge over cut $\mathcal{S}$ of depth d when:*
$$\mathcal{D}(n) > d > \mathcal{D}(n')$$

A Used Pass Through (UPT) edge is a PT edge from a node which is also used by one or more nodes in $\mathcal{S}$, i.e. there is $n'' \in \mathcal{S}$ with $(n, n'') \in E_V$.

In particular, PT (and to a lesser extent UPT) edges are ideal candidates for spilling when transforming a cut. The next section discusses this further.

5.4   Register Allocation

In order to colour the graph successfully with $\mathcal{R}$ target machine registers no cut of the graph must be wider (*i.e.* the number of live registers) than the number of target registers available.

For every cut of depth d calculate $\mathcal{W}_{in}(d)$. Then, while $\mathcal{R} > |\mathcal{W}_{in}(d)|$ we apply three transformations to the VSDG in increasing order of cost: *(i)* node raising (code motion), *(ii)* node cloning (undoing CSE), or *(iii)* node spilling, where we first choose non-loop nodes followed by loop nodes.

The first—node raising—pushes a node up to the next cut by adding serializing edges from all other nodes in the cut. We repeat this until either the liveness width is less than the number of physical registers, or there is only one node left in the cut.

In node cloning, we take a node and generate copies (clones). Serializing edges are added to maintain the DFR of the the clones. A simple algorithm for this transformation is to produce as many clones as there are dependents of the node; a node recombining pass will recombine clones that end up in the same cut.

Node cloning is not always applicable as it may increase the liveness width of higher cuts (when the in-registers of the cloned node did not previously pass through the cut); placing a cloned node in a lower cut can increase the liveness width. But, used properly [18], node cloning can reduce the liveness width of lower cuts by splitting the live range of a node, which potentially has a lower cost than spilling.

Finally, when all other transformations are unable to satisfy the constraint, we must spill one or more edges to memory. PT edges are ideal candidates for spilling, as the lifetime of the edge affords good pipeline behaviour on superscalar RISC-like targets; likewise, UPT edges are similarly beneficial, but place some constraints on the location of the store node.

A related issue is the spilling of θ-nodes. As discussed previously the worst-case cost of spilling a loop-variant variable from a θ-node tuple is two stores and three loads, so these should always be done after spilling of PT nodes. By contrast, Chaitin/Chow colouring has to use approximate cost heuristics to decide to spill a variable in a loop or outside.

6   Related Work

6.1   Benefits over Other Program Graph Representations

The VSDG is based in part on the Value Dependence Graph (VDG) [21]. The VDG uses a λ-node to represent both functions and loop bodies, thereby combining loops and functions into one complex abstraction mechanism rather. In the VSDG we treat them separately with call and θ-nodes. One particular problem the VDG has is that of preserving the terminating properties of a program—*"Evaluation of the VDG may terminate even if the original program would not..."* [21].

Another significant issue with the VDG is the process of generating target code from the VDG. The authors describe converting the VDG into a demand-based Program Dependence Graph (dPDG)—a normal Program Dependence Graph [9] with additional edges representing demand dependence—then converting that into a traditional control flow graph (CFG) [1] before finally generating target code from the CFG with a standard back-end code generator; this is not as flexible (or as clearly specified) as the VSDG presented in this paper.

Many other program graphs (with many and varied edge forms) have been presented in the literature: the Program Dependence Graph [9], the Program Dependence Web [2], the System Dependence Graph [11] and the Dependence Flow Graph [15]. Our VSDG is both simpler—only two types of edge represent all of the above flow information—and more normalizing (§3.3).

6.2   Solving Phase Order Problems

The traditional view of register allocation as a graph colouring problem was proposed by Chaitin [5]. In §4.2 we generalise the both the Chaitin and Chow approaches.

Goodwin and Wilken [10] formulate global register allocation (including all possible spill placements) as a 0-1 integer programming problem. While they do achieve quite impressive results, the cost is very high: the complexity of their algorithm is $O(n^3)$ and for a given time period the allocator does not guarantee to allocate all functions.

Code motion as an optimization is not new (*e.g.* Partial Redundancy Elimination [14]). Perhaps the work closest in spirit to ours is that of Rüthing *et al.* [18] which presents algorithms for optimal placement of expressions and subexpressions, combining both raising and lowering of code within basic blocks.

Most work has concentrated on the instruction scheduling/register allocation phase order problem, which we now consider.

The CRAIG framework [4], implemented within the ROCKET compiler [19], takes a brute force approach:

1. attempt register allocation after instruction scheduling,
2. if the schedule cost is not acceptable (by some defined metric) attempt register allocation before scheduling,
3. then while the cost is acceptable (*i.e.* there is some better schedule) add back in information from the first pass until the schedule just becomes too costly.

Their experience with an instance of CRAIG (CRAIG$_0$) defines the metric as the existence of spill code. Their experimental results show improvements in execution time, but do not document the change in code size.

Rao [17] improves on CRAIG$_0$ with additional heuristics to allow *some* spilling, where it can be shown that spilling has a beneficial effect.

Touati's thesis [20] argues that register allocation is the primary determinant of performance, not scheduling. The goal of his thesis is again to minimize the insertion of spill-code, both through careful analysis of register pressure, and by adding serializing edges to each basic block data dependency DAG. It is basic-block-based.

An early attempt at combining register allocation with instruction scheduling was proposed by Pinter [16]. That work is based on an instruction level register-based intermediate code, and is preceded by a phase to determine data dependencies. This dependence information then drives the allocator, generating a *Parallelizable Interference Graph* to suggest possible register allocations. Further, the *Global Scheduling Graph* is then used to schedule instructions within a region.

Another region-based approach is that of Janssen and Corporaal [12], where regions correspond to the bodies of natural loops. They then use this hierarchy of nested regions to focus register allocation, with the inner-most regions being favoured by better register allocation (*i.e.* less spill code).

The Resource Spackling Framework of Berson *et al.* [3] applies a *Measure and Reduce* paradigm to combine both phases—their approach first measures the resource requirements of a program using a unified representation, and then moves instructions out of *excessive sets* into *resource holes*. This approach is basic-block-based: a local scheduler attempts to satisfy the target constraints without increasing the execution time of a block; the more complicated global scheduler moves instructions between blocks.

7   Conclusions and Further Work

In this paper we have defined the VSDG, an enhanced form of the VDG which includes state dependency edges to model sequentialized computation. By adding sufficient state-dependency edges we have shown that the VSDG is able to represent a single CFG; conversely fewer serializing edges relax the artificial constraints imposed by the CFG.

From this basis, we have shown that the VSDG framework supports a combined approach to register allocation and code motion, using an incremental algorithm which effectively interleaves the two phases, and thus avoiding the well-known phase-ordering problem. We have described an algorithm which, when given a well-formed, normalized VSDG then allocates registers, if necessary interleaving this with code motion, node splitting and register spilling.

The work presented here is the start of a larger project: an implementation of the algorithms in this paper is in progress.

Acknowledgements. The research reported here was supported with a grant from ARM Ltd. Thanks are due to Alistair Turnbull and Eben Upton for constructive debate on aspects of the VSDG, to Lee Smith for useful comments on an early draft of this paper, and to Mooly Sagiv and Tom Reps for helpful discussions at SAS'02.

References

1. AHO, A. V., SETHI, R., AND ULLMAN, J. D. *Compilers: Principles, Techniques and Tools.* Addison Wesley, 1986.
2. BALLANCE, R. A., MACCABE, A. B., AND OTTENSTEIN, K. J. The program dependence web: A representation supporting control-, data-, and demand-driven interpretation of imperative languages. In *Proc. Conf. Prog. Lang. Design and Implementation (PLDI'90)* (June 1990), ACM, pp. 257–271.
3. BERSON, D. A., GUPTA, R., AND SOFFA, M. L. Resource spackling: A framework for integrating register allocation in local and global schedulers. Tech. rep., Dept. Computer Science, University of Pittsburgh, February 1994.
4. BRASIER, T. S., SWEANY, P. H., BEATY, S. J., AND CARR, S. CRAIG: A practical framework for combining instruction scheduling and register assignment. In *Proc. Intl. Conf. Parallel Architectures and Compilation Techniques (PACT'95)* (Limassol, Cyprus, June 1995).
5. CHAITIN, G. Register allocation and spilling via graph coloring. *ACM SIGPLAN Notices 17*, 6 (June 1982), 98–105.
6. CHOW, F. C., AND HENNESSY, J. L. The priority-based coloring approach to register allocation. *ACM Trans. Prog. Lang. and Syst. 12*, 4 (October 1990), 501–536.
7. CLICK, C. From quads to graphs: an intermediate representation's journey. Tech. Rep. CRPC-TR93366-S, Center for Research on Parallel Computation, Rice University, October 1993.

8. CYTRON, R. K., FERRANTE, J., ROSEN, B. K., WEGMAN, M. N., AND ZADECK, F. K. Efficiently computing the static single assignment form and the control dependence graph. *ACM Trans. Programming Languages and Systems 12*, 4 (October 1991), 451–490.

9. FERRANTE, J., OTTENSTEIN, K. J., AND WARREN, J. D. The program dependence graph and its use in optimization. *ACM Trans. Prog. Lang. and Syst. 9*, 3 (July 1987), 319–349.

10. GOODWIN, D. W., AND WILKEN, K. D. Optimal and near-optimal global register allocation using 0-1 integer programming. *Software—Practice and Experience 26*, 8 (August 1996), 929–965.

11. HORWITZ, S., REPS, T., AND BINKLEY, D. Interprocedural slicing using dependence graphs. *ACM Trans. Prog. Langs and Systems 12*, 1 (January 1990), 26–60.

12. JANSSEN, J., AND CORPORAAL, H. Registers on demand: an integrated region scheduler and register allocator. In *Proc. Conf. on Compiler Construction* (April 1998).

13. JOHNSON, N. *tri*VM Intermediate Language Reference Manual. Tech. Rep. UCAM-CL-TR-529, University of Cambridge Computer Laboratory, 2002.

14. MOREL, E., AND RENVOISE, C. Global optimization by suppression of partial redundancies. *Comm. ACM 22*, 2 (February 1979), 96–103.

15. PINGALI, K., BECK, M., JOHNSON, R., MOUDGILL, M., AND STODGHILL, P. Dependence flow graphs: An algebraic approach to program dependencies. In *Proc. 18th ACM Symp. on Principles of Prog. Langs (POPL)* (January 1991), ACM, pp. 67–78.

16. PINTER, S. S. Register allocation with instruction scheduling: A new approach. In *Proc. ACM SIGPLAN Conference on Prog. Lang. Design and Implementation* (Albuquerque, NM, June 1993), pp. 248–257.

17. RAO, M. P. Combining register assignment and instruction scheduling. Master's thesis, Michigan Technological University, 1998.

18. RÜTHING, O., KNOOP, J., AND STEFFEN, B. Sparse code motion. In *Proc. 27th ACM SIGPLAN-SIGACT Symp. Principles of Prog. Langs (POPL)* (Boston, MA, 2000), ACM, pp. 170–183.

19. SWEANY, P., AND BEATY, S. Post-compaction register assignment in a retargetable compiler. In *Proc. 23rd Annual Workshop on Microprogramming and Microarchitecture* (November 1990), pp. 107–116.

20. TOUATI, S.-A.-A. *Register Pressure in Instruction Level Parallelism*. PhD thesis, Université de Versailles Saint-Quentin, June 2002.

21. WEISE, D., CREW, R. F., ERNST, M., AND STEENSGAARD, B. Value dependence graphs: Representation without taxation. In *ACM SIGPLAN-SIGACT Symp. on Principles of Prog. Langs (POPL)* (January 1994), ACM.

Early Control of Register Pressure for Software Pipelined Loops

Sid-Ahmed-Ali Touati and Christine Eisenbeis

INRIA Rocquencourt, 78153 Le Chesnay, France
{Sid-Ahmed-Ali.Touati,Christine.Eisenbeis}@inria.fr

Abstract. The register allocation in loops is generally performed after or during the software pipelining process. This is because doing a conventional register allocation at first step without assuming a schedule lacks the information of interferences between variable lifetime intervals. Thus, the register allocator may introduce an excessive amount of false dependences that reduce dramatically the ILP (Instruction Level Parallelism). We present a new framework for controlling the register pressure before software pipelining. This is based on inserting some anti-dependences edges (*register reuse* edges) labeled with *reuse distances*, directly on the data dependence graph. In this new graph, we are able to guarantee that the number of simultaneously alive variables in any schedule does not exceed a limit. The determination of register and distance reuse is parameterized by the desired critical circuit ratio (MII) as well as by the register pressure constraints - either can be minimized while the other one is fixed. After scheduling, register allocation is done cyclically on conventional register sets or on rotating register files. We give an optimal exact model, and another approximative one that generalizes the Ning-Gao [13] buffer optimization heuristics.

1 Introduction

This article addresses the problem of register pressure in simple loop data dependence graphs (DDGs), with multiple register types and non unit assumed latencies operations. Our aim is to decouple the registers constraints and allocation from the scheduling process and to analyze the trade-off between memory (register pressure) and parallelism constraints, measured as the critical ratio MII[1] of the DDG.

The principal reason is that we believe that register allocation is more important as an optimization issue than code scheduling. This is because the code performance is far more sensitive to memory accesses than to fine-grain scheduling (memory gap) : a cache miss may inhibit the processor from achieving a high dynamic ILP, even if the scheduler has extracted it at compile time. Even if someone would expect that spill codes exhibit high locality, and hence would likely produce cache hits, we cannot assert it at compile time. The authors in [6] related that about 66% of application execution times are spent to satisfying memory requests.

Another reason for handling register constraints prior to ILP scheduling is that register constraints are much more complex than resource constraints. Scheduling under resource

---

[1] We refer here to MII_{dep} since we will not consider any resource constraints.

G. Hedin (Ed.): CC 2003, LNCS 2622, pp. 17–32, 2003.
© Springer-Verlag Berlin Heidelberg 2003

constraints is a performance issue. Given a DDG, we are sure to find at least one valid schedule for any underlying hardware properties (a sequential schedule in extreme case, i.e., no ILP). However, scheduling a DDG with a limited number of registers is more complex. We cannot guarantee the existence of at least one schedule. In some cases, we must introduce spill code and hence we change the problem (the input DDG). Also, a combined pass of scheduling with register allocation presents an important drawback if not enough registers are available. During scheduling, we may need to insert load-store operations. We cannot guarantee the existence of a valid issue time for these introduced memory access in an already scheduled code; resource or data dependence constraints may prevent from finding a valid issue slot inside an already scheduled code. This forces to iteratively apply scheduling followed by spilling until reaching a solution.

All the above arguments make us re-think new ways of handling register pressure before starting the scheduling process, so that the scheduler would be free from register constraints and would not suffer from excessive serializations.

Existing techniques in this field usually apply register allocation after a step of software pipelining that is sensitive to register requirement. Indeed, if we succeed in building a software pipelined schedule that does not produce more than R values simultaneously alive, then we can build a cyclic register allocation with R available registers [3,14]. We can use either loop unrolling [3], inserting move operations [8], or a hardware rotating register file when available [14][2]. Therefore, a great amount of work tries to schedule a loop such that it does not use more than R values simultaneously alive [9,23,13,15,12,5,16,7,10]. In this paper we directly work on the loop DDG and modify it in order to satisfy the register constraints for any further subsequent software pipelining pass. This idea is already present in [1] for DAGs and use the concept of *reuse* edge or vector developed in [18,19].

Our article is organized as follows. Sect. 2 defines our loop model and a generic ILP processor. Sect. 3 starts the study with a simple example. The problem of cyclic register allocation is described in Sect. 4 and formulated with integer linear programming (intLP). The special case where a rotating register file (RRF) exists in the underlying processor is discussed in Sect. 5. In Sect.6, we present a polynomial subproblem. Finally, we synthesize our experiments in Sect. 7 before concluding.

2   Loop Model

We consider a simple innermost loop (without branches). It is represented by a graph $G = (V, E, \delta, \lambda)$, such that: V is the set of the statements in the loop body and E is the set of precedence constraints (flow dependences, or other serial constraints). We associate to each arc $e \in E$ a latency $\delta(e)$ in terms of processor clock cycles and a distance $\lambda(e)$ in terms of number of iterations. We denote by $u(i)$ the instance of the statement $u \in V$ of the iteration i. A valid schedule σ must satisfy:

$$\forall e = (u, v) \in E \ : \ \sigma\big(u(i)\big) + \delta(e) \leq \sigma\big(v(i + \lambda(e))\big)$$

---

[2] Insertion of *move* operations or using a rotating register file requires $R + 1$ registers at most [3].

We consider a target RISC-style architecture with multiple register types, where $\mathcal{T}$ denotes the set of register types (for instance, $\mathcal{T} = \{int, float\}$). We make a difference between statements and precedence constraints, depending if they refer to values to be stored in registers or not. $V_{R,t}$ is the set of values to be stored in registers of type $t \in \mathcal{T}$. We consider that each statement $u \in V$ writes into at most one register of a type $t \in \mathcal{T}$. The statements which define multiple values with different types are accepted in our model if they do not define more than one value of a certain type. $E_{R,t}$ is the set of flow dependence edges through a value of type $t \in \mathcal{T}$. The set of consumers (readers) of a value u^t is then the set :

$$Cons(u^t) = \{v \in V \mid (u, v) \in E_{R,t}\}$$

To consider static issue VLIW and EPIC/IA64 processors in which the hardware pipeline steps are visible to compilers (we consider dynamically scheduled superscalar processors too), we assume that reading from and writing into a register may be delayed from the beginning of the schedule time, and these delays are visible to the compiler (architectural visible). We define two delay (offset) functions $\delta_{r,t}$ and $\delta_{w,t}$ in which : the read cycle of u^t from a register of type t is $\sigma(u) + \delta_{r,t}(u)$, and the the write cycle of u^t into a register of type t is $\sigma(u) + \delta_{w,t}(u)$.

For superscalar and EPIC/IA64 processors, $\delta_{r,t}$ and $\delta_{w,t}$ are equal to zero.

A software pipelining is a function σ that assigns to each statement u a scheduling date (in terms of clock cycle) that satisfies at least the precedence constraints. It is defined by an initiation interval, noted II, and the scheduling date σ_u for the operations of the first iteration. The operation $u(i)$ of iteration i is scheduled at time $\sigma_u + (i - 1) \times II$. For all edge $e = (u, v) \in E$, this periodic schedule must satisfy:

$$\sigma_u + \delta(e) \leq \sigma_v + \lambda(e).II$$

Classically, by adding all such inequalities on any circuit C of G, we find that II must be greater than or equal to $\max_C \frac{\sum_{e \in C} \delta(e)}{\sum_{e \in C} \lambda(e)}$, that we commonly denote as MII (minimal initiation interval).

We consider now a number of available registers ρ and all the schedules that have no more than ρ simultaneously alive variables. Any actual following register allocation will induce new dependences in the DDG. Hence, register pressure has influence on the expected II, even if we assume unbounded resources. What we want to analyze here is the minimum II that can be expected for any schedule using less than ρ registers. We will denote this value as $MII(\rho)$ and we will try to understand the relationship between $MII(\rho)$ and ρ. Let us start by an example to fix the ideas.

3   Basic Ideas

We give now more intuitions to the new edges that we add between couples of operations. These edges represent possible reuse by the second operation of the register released by the first operation. This can be viewed as a variant of [1] or [18,19].

Let us consider a simple loop that consists of a unique flow dependence from u to v with distance $\lambda = 3$ (see Fig. 1.(a) where values to be stored in registers of the considered type are in bold circles, and flows are in bold edges). If we have an unbounded number of registers, all iterations of this loop can be run in parallel since there is no recurrence circuit in the DDG. At each iteration, operation u writes into a new register. Now, let

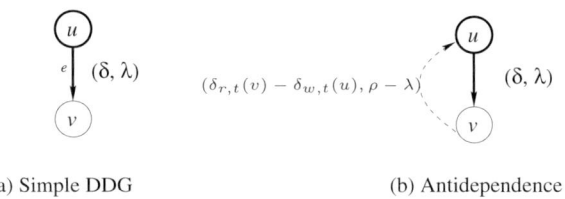

(a) Simple DDG   (b) Antidependence

Fig. 1. Simple Example

us assume that we only have $\rho = 5$ available registers. The different instances of u can use only $\rho = 5$ registers to cyclically carry their results. In this case, the operation $u(i + \rho)$ writes into the same register previously used by $u(i)$. This fact creates an anti-dependence from $v(i+\lambda)$, which reads the value defined by $u(i)$, to $u(i+\rho)$; this means an anti-dependence in the DDG from v to u with a distance $\rho - \lambda = 2$. Since u actually writes into its destination register $\delta_{w,t}(u)$ clock cycles after it is issued and v reads it $\delta_{r,t}(v)$ after it is issued, the latency of this anti-dependence is set to $\delta_{r,t}(v) - \delta_{w,t}(u)$ for VLIW or EPIC codes, and to 1 for superscalar (sequential) codes. Consequently, the DDG becomes cyclic because of storage limitations (see Fig. 1.(b), where the anti-dependence is dashed). The introduced anti-dependence, also called "Universal Occupancy Vector' '(UOV) in [18], must in turn be counted when computing the new minimum initiation interval since a new circuit is created.

When an operation defines a value that is read by more than one operation, we cannot know in advance which of these consumers actually kills the value (which is the last reader), and hence we cannot know in advance when a register is freed. We propose a trick which defines for each value u^t of type t a fictitious killing task k_{u^t}. We insert an edge from each consumer $v \in Cons(u^t)$ to k_{u^t} to reflect the fact that this killing task is scheduled after the last scheduled consumer (see Fig. 2). The latency of this serial edge is set to $\delta_{r,t}(v)$ because of the reading delay, and we set its distance to $-\lambda$ where λ is the distance of the flow dependence between u and its consumer v. This is done to model the fact that the operation $k_{u^t}(i + \lambda - \lambda)$, i.e., $k_{u^t}(i)$ is scheduled when the value $u^t(i)$ is killed. The iteration number i of the killer of $u(i)$ is only a convention and can be changed by retiming [11], without changing the nature of the problem.

Now, a register allocation scheme consists of defining the edges and the distances of reuse. That is, we define for each $u(i)$ the operation v and iteration $\mu_{u,v}$ such that $v(i + \mu_{u,v})$ reuses the same destination register as $u(i)$. This reuse creates a new anti-dependence from k_u to v with latency equal to $-\delta_{w,t}(v)$ for VLIW or EPIC codes, and to 1 for sequential superscalar codes. The distance $\mu_{u,v}$ of this edge has to be defined.

We will see in a further section that the register requirement can be expressed in terms of $\mu_{u,v}$.

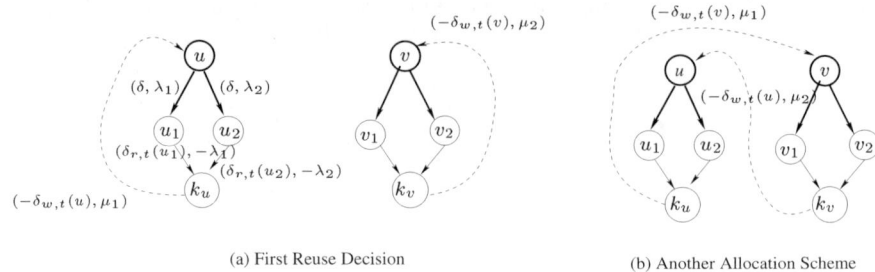

(a) First Reuse Decision   (b) Another Allocation Scheme

Fig. 2. Killing Tasks

Hence, controlling register requirement means, first, determining which operation should reuse the register killed by another operation (*where should anti-dependences be added?*). Secondly, we have to determine variable lifetimes, or equivalently register requirement (*how many iterations later (μ) should reuse occur*)? The lower is the μ, the lower is the register requirement, but also the larger is the MII.

Fig. 2.(a) presents a first reuse decision where each statement reuses the register freed by itself. This is illustrated by adding an anti-dependence from k_u (resp. k_v) to u (resp. v) with an appropriate distance μ, as we will see later. Another reuse decision (see Fig. 2.(b)) may be that the statement u (resp. v) reuses the register freed by v (resp. u). This is illustrated by adding an anti-dependence from k_u (resp. k_v) to v (resp. u). In both cases, the register requirement is $\mu_1 + \mu_2$, but it is easy to see that the two schemes do not have the same impact on MII: intuitively it is better that the operations share registers instead of using two different pools of registers. The next section gives a formal definition of the problem and provides an exact formulation.

4   Problem Description

4.1   Data Dependences and Reuse Edges

The reuse relation between the values (variables) is described by defining a new graph called *a reuse graph* that we note $G^r = (V_{R,t}, E_r, \mu)$. Fig. 3.(a) shows the first reuse decision where u (v resp.) reuses the register used by itself μ_1 (μ_2 resp.) iterations earlier. Fig. 3.(b) is the second reuse choice where u (v resp.) reuses the register used by v (u resp.) μ_1 (μ_2 resp.) iterations earlier. Each edge $e = (u, v) \in E_r$ with a distance $\mu(e)$ in the reuse graph means that there is an anti-dependence between k_u and v with a distance $\mu(e)$. The resulted DDG after adding the killing tasks and the anti-dependences to apply the register reuse decisions is called the *DDG associated with a reuse decision* : Fig. 2.(a) is the associated DDG with Fig. 3.(a), and Fig. 2.(b) is the one associated with Fig. 3.(b). We denote by $G_{\rightarrow r}$ the DDG associated to a reuse decision r.

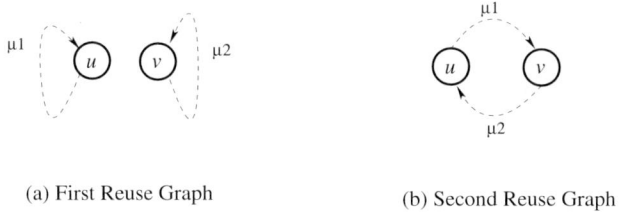

(a) First Reuse Graph   (b) Second Reuse Graph

Fig. 3. Reuse Graphs

A reuse graph must verify some constraints to be valid : first, the resulting DDG must be schedulable; second, each value reuses only one freed register, and each register is reused by only one value. The second constraint means that the reuse scheme is the same at each iteration. Generalizing this condition by allowing different (but periodic) reuse schemes is beyond the scope of this paper. This condition results in the following lemma.

Lemma 1. *[22] Let $G^r = (V_{R,t}, E_r, \mu)$ be a valid reuse graph of type t associated with a loop $G = (V, E, \delta, \lambda)$. Then :*

- *the reuse graph only consists of elementary and disjoined circuits ;*
- *any value $u^t \in V_{R,t}$ belongs to a unique circuit in the reuse graph.*

Any circuit C in a reuse graph is called a *reuse circuit*. We note $\mu(C)$ the sum of the μ distances in this circuit. Then, to each reuse circuit $C = (u_0, u_1, .., u_n, u_0)$, there exists an image $C' = (u_0 \rightsquigarrow k_{u_0}, u_1, ..., u_n \rightsquigarrow k_{u_n}, u_0)$ for it in the associated DDG. For instance in Fig. 2.(a), $C' = (v, v_1, k_v, v)$ is an image for the reuse circuit $C = (v, v)$ in Fig. 3.(a). Such image may not be unique.

If a reuse graph is valid, we can build a cyclic register allocation in the DDG associated with it, as explained in the following theorem. We require $\mu(G^r)$ registers, in which $\mu(G^r)$ is the sum of all μ distances in the reuse graph G^r.

Theorem 1. *[22] Let $G = (V, E, \delta, \lambda)$ be a loop and $G^r = (V_{R,t}, E_r, \mu)$ a valid reuse graph of a register type $t \in \mathcal{T}$. Then the reuse graph G^r defines a cyclic register allocation for G with exactly $\mu_t(G^r)$ registers of type t if we unroll the loop α times where :*

$$\alpha = lcm(\mu_t(C_1), \cdots, \mu_t(C_n))$$

with $\mathcal{C} = \{C_1, \cdots, C_n\}$ is the set of all reuse circuits, and lcm is the least common multiple.

For a complete and detailed proof, please refer to [22].

As a corollary, we can build a cyclic register allocation for all register types.

Corollary 1. *[22] Let $G = (V, E, \delta, \lambda)$ be a loop with a set of register types $\mathcal{T}$. To each type $t \in \mathcal{T}$ is associated a valid reuse graph G^r_t. The loop can be allocated with $\mu_t(G^r)$ registers for each type t if we unroll it α times, where*

$$\alpha = lcm(\alpha_{t_1}, \cdots, \alpha_{t_n})$$

where α_{t_i} is the unrolling degree of the reuse graph of type t_i.

It should be noted that the fact that the unrolling factor may be significantly high is not related to our method and would happen only if we actually want to allocate the variables on this minimal number of registers with the computed reuse scheme. However, there may be other reuse schemes for the same number of registers, or there may be other available registers in the architecture. In that case, the meeting graph framework [3] can help to control or reduce this unrolling factor.

From all above, we deduce a formal definition of the problem of optimal cyclic register allocation with minimal ILP loss. We call it Schedule Independent Register Allocation (SIRA).

Problem 1 (SIRA). Let $G = (V, E, \delta, \lambda)$ be a loop and $\mathcal{R}_t$ the number of available registers of type t. Find a valid reuse graph for each register type such that the corresponding

$$\mu_t(G^r) \leq \mathcal{R}_t$$

and the critical circuit in G is minimized.

This problem can be reduced to the classical NP-complete problem of minimal register allocation [22]. The following section gives an exact formulation of SIRA.

4.2   Exact Formulation

In this section, we give an intLP model for solving SIRA. It is built for a fixed execution rate II (the new constrained MII). Note that II is not the initiation interval of the final schedule, since the loop is not already scheduled. II denotes the value of the new desired critical circuit. Here, we assume VLIW or EPIC codes. For superscalar ones, we only have to set the anti-dependence latency to 1.

Our SIRA exact model uses the linear formulation of the logical implication ($\Longrightarrow$) and equivalence ($\Longleftrightarrow$) by introducing binary variables, as previously explained in [20, 21, 22]. The size of our system is bounded by $\mathcal{O}(|V|^2)$ variables and $\mathcal{O}(|E| + |V|^2)$ linear constraints.

Basic Variables

- a schedule variable $\sigma_u \geq 0$ for each operation $u \in V$, including one for each killing node k_{u^t}.
- a binary variables $\theta_{u,v}^t$ for each $(u, v) \in V_{R,t}^2$, and for each register type $t \in \mathcal{T}$. It is set to 1 iff (u, v) is a reuse edge of type t;
- $\mu_{u,v}^t$ for reuse distance for all $(u, v) \in V_{R,t}^2$, and for each register type.

Linear Constraints

- data dependences (the existence of at least one valid software pipelining schedule, including killing tasks constraints)

$$\forall e = (u, v) \in E : \sigma_u + \delta(e) \leq \sigma_v + II \times \lambda(e)$$

- there is an anti-dependence between k_{u^t} and v if (u, v) is a reuse edge :
$\forall t \in \mathcal{T}, \ \forall (u, v) \in V_{R,t}^2 :$

$$\theta_{u,v}^t = 1 \Longrightarrow \sigma_{k_{u^t}} - \delta_{w,t}(v) \leq \sigma_v + II \times \mu_{u,v}$$

- If there is no register reuse between two values $(reuse_t(u) \neq v)$, then $\theta_{u,v}^t = 0$. The anti-dependence distance $\mu_{u,v}^t$ must be set to 0 in order to not be cumulated in the objective function. $\forall t \in \mathcal{T}, \ \forall (u, v) \in V_{R,t}^2 :$

$$\theta_{u,v}^t = 0 \Longrightarrow \mu_{u,v}^t = 0$$

The reuse relation must be a bijection from $V_{R,t}$ to $V_{R,t}$:

- a register can be reused by only one operation :

$$\forall t \in \mathcal{T}, \ \forall u \in V_{R,t} : \sum_{v \in V_{R,t}} \theta_{u,v}^t = 1$$

- one value can reuse only one released register :

$$\forall t \in \mathcal{T}, \ \forall u \in V_{R,t} : \sum_{v \in V_{R,t}} \theta_{v,u}^t = 1$$

Objective Function. We want to minimize the number of registers required for the register allocation. So, we choose an arbitrary register type t which we use as objective function :

$$\text{Minimize} \sum_{(u,v) \in V_{R,t}^2} \mu_{u,v}^t$$

The other registers types are bounded in the model by their respective number of available registers :

$$\forall t' \in \mathcal{T} - \{t\} : \sum_{(u,v) \in V_{R,t'}^2} \mu_{u,v}^{t'} \leq \mathcal{R}_{t'}$$

As previously mentioned, our model includes writing and reading offsets. The non-positive latencies of the introduced anti-dependences generate a specific problem. Indeed, some circuits C in the constructed DDG may have non-positive distance $\lambda(C) \leq 0$. Even if such circuits do not prevent a DDG from being scheduled, it may be so in the presence of resource constraints. Thus, we prohibit such circuits (we will discuss it later). Note that this problem does not occur for superscalar (sequential) codes, because the introduced anti-dependences have positive latencies.

The unrolling degree is left free and over any control in SIRA formulation. This factor may theoretically grow exponentially. Minimizing the unrolling degree is to minimize $lcm(\mu_i)$, the least common multiple of the anti-dependence distances of reuse circuits. This non linear problem is very difficult an remains an open problem : as far as we know, there is not a satisfactory solution for it. Fortunately, there exists a hardware feature that allow to avoid loop unrolling. We study it in the next section.

5   Rotating Register Files

A rotating register file [4,14,17] is a hardware feature that moves (shift) implicitly architectural registers in a cyclic way. At every new kernel issue (special branch operation), each architectural register specified by program is mapped by hardware to a new physical register. The mapping function is (R denotes an architectural register and R' a physical register): $R_i \mapsto R'_{(i+RRB) \bmod s}$ where RRB is a rotating register base and s the total number of physical registers. The number of that physical register is decremented continuously at each new kernel. Consequently, the intrinsic reuse scheme between statements describes a hamiltonian reuse circuit necessarily. The hardware behavior of such register files does not allow other reuse patterns. SIRA in this case must be adapted in order to look only for hamiltonian reuse circuits.

Furthermore, even if no rotating register file exists, looking for only one hamiltonian reuse circuit makes the unrolling degree exactly equal to the number of allocated registers, and thus both are simultaneously minimized by the objective function.

Since a reuse circuit is always elementary (Lemma 1), it is sufficient to state that a hamiltonian reuse circuit with $n = |V_{R,t}|$ nodes is only a reuse circuit of size n. We proceed by forcing an ordering of statements from 1 to n according to the reuse relation. Thus, given a loop $G = (V, E, \delta, \lambda)$ and $G^r = (V_{R,t}, E_r, \mu)$ a valid reuse graph of type $t \in \mathcal{T}$, we define a hamiltonian ordering ho_t as a function:

$$ho_t : V_{R,t} \to \mathbb{N}$$
$$u^t \mapsto ho_t(u)$$

such that $\forall u, v \in V_{R,t}$:

$$(u, v) \in E_r \iff ho_t(v) = \Big(ho_t(u) + 1 \Big) \bmod |V_{R,t}|$$

The existence of a hamiltonian ordering is a sufficient and necessary condition to make the reuse graph hamiltonian, as stated in the following theorem.

Theorem 2. *[22] Let $G = (V, E, \delta, \lambda)$ be a loop and G^r a valid reuse graph. There exists a hamiltonian ordering iff the reuse graph is a hamiltonian graph.*

Hence, the problem of cyclic register allocation with minimal critical circuit on rotating register files can be stated as follows.

Problem 2 (SIRA_HAM). Let $G = (V, E, \delta, \lambda)$ be a loop and $\mathcal{R}_t$ the number of available registers of type t. Find a valid reuse graph with a hamiltonian ordering ho_t such that the

$$\mu_t(G^r) \leq \mathcal{R}_t$$

in which the critical circuit in G is minimized.

An exact formulation for it is deduced from the intLP model of SIRA. We have only to add some constraints to compute a hamiltonian ordering. We expand the exact SIRA intLP model by at most $\mathcal{O}(|V|^2)$ variables and $\mathcal{O}(|V|^2)$ linear constraints.

1. for each register type and for each value $u^t \in V_{R,t}$, we define an integer variable $ho_{u^t} \geq 0$ which corresponds to its hamiltonian ordering;
2. we add the linear constraints of the modulo hamiltonian ordering : $\forall u, v \in V_{R,t}^2$:

$$\theta_{u,v}^t = 1 \iff ho_{u^t} + 1 = |V_{R,t}| \times \beta_{u,v}^t + ho_{v^t}$$

where $\beta_{u,v}^t$ is a binary variable that holds to the integer division of $ho_{u^t} + 1$ on $|V_{R,t}|$.

When looking for a hamiltonian reuse circuit, we may need one extra register to construct such a circuit. In fact, this extra register virtually simulates moving values among registers if circular lifetimes intervals do not meet in a hamiltonian pattern.

Proposition 1. *[22] Hamiltonian SIRA needs at most one extra register than SIRA.*

Both SIRA and hamiltonian SIRA are NP-complete. Fortunately, we have some optimistic results. In the next section, we investigate the case in which SIRA can be solved in polynomial time complexity.

6 Fixing Reuse Edges

In [13], Ning and Gao analyzed the problem of minimizing the buffer sizes in software pipelining. In our framework, this problem actually amounts to deciding that each operation reuses the same register, possibly some iterations later. Therefore we consider now the complexity of our minimization problem when fixing reuse edges. This generalizes the Ning-Gao approach. Formally, the problem can be stated as follows.

Problem 3 (Fixed SIRA). Let $G = (V, E, \delta, \lambda)$ be a loop and $\mathcal{R}_t$ the number of available registers of type t. Let $E' \subseteq E$ be the set of already fixed anti-dependences (reuse) edges of a register type t. Find a distance $\mu_{u,v}$ for each anti-dependence $(k_{u^t}, v) \in E'$ such that

$$\mu_t(G^r) \leq \mathcal{R}_t$$

in which the critical circuit in G is minimized.

In following, we assume that $E' \subseteq E$ is the set of these already fixed anti-dependences (reuse) edges (their distances have to be computed). Deciding (at compile) time for fixed reuse decisions greatly simplifies the intLP system of SIRA. It can be solved by the following intLP, assuming a fixed desired critical circuit II. Here, we write a system for VLIW or EPIC codes. For superscalar, we have to set the anti-dependence latency to 1.

Minimize $\qquad\qquad \rho = \sum_{(k_{u^t},v)\in E'} \mu_{u,v}^t$

Subject to: $\qquad\qquad\qquad\qquad\qquad\qquad\qquad\qquad\qquad$ (1)

$II \times \mu_{u,v}^t + \sigma_v - \sigma_{k_{u^t}} \geq -\delta_w(v) \; \forall(k_{u^t}, v) \in E'$

$\sigma_v - \sigma_u \geq \delta(e) - II \times \lambda(e) \qquad \forall e = (u,v) \in E - E'$

Since II is a constant, we do the variable substitution $\mu'_u = II \times \mu^t_{u,v}$ and System 1 becomes:

Minimize $\qquad\qquad\qquad\qquad (II.\rho =) \sum_{u \in V_{R,t}} \mu'_u$

Subject to: $\qquad\qquad\qquad\qquad\qquad\qquad\qquad\qquad\qquad\qquad\qquad\qquad$ (2)
$$\mu'_u + \sigma_v - \sigma_{k_{u^t}} \geq -\delta_w(v) \quad \forall (k_{u^t}, v) \in E'$$
$$\sigma_v - \sigma_u \geq \delta(e) - II \times \lambda(e) \; \forall e = (u,v) \in E - E'$$

There are $\mathcal{O}(|V|)$ variables and $\mathcal{O}(|E|))$ linear constraints in this system.

Theorem 3. *[22] The constraint matrix of the integer programming model in System 2 is totally unimodular, i.e., the determinant of each square sub-matrix is equal to 0 or to ± 1.*

Consequently, we can use polynomial algorithms to solve this problem of finding the minimal value for the product $II.\rho$.

We must be aware that the back substitution in $\mu = \frac{\mu'}{II}$ may produce a non integral value for the distance μ. If we ceil it by setting $\mu = \lceil \frac{\mu'}{II} \rceil$, a sub-optimal solution may result[3]. It is easy to see that the loss in terms of number of registers is not greater than the number of loop statements that write into a register ($|V_{R,t}|$). This algorithm generalizes the heuristics proposed in [13]. We think that we can avoid ceiling μ by considering the already computed σ variables, as done in [13].

Furthermore, solving System 2 has two interesting follow-ups. First, it gives a polynomially computable lower bound for $MII_{rc}(\rho)$ as defined in the introduction, for this reuse configuration rc. Let us denote as m the minimal value of the objective function. Then

$$MII_{rc}(\rho) \geq \frac{m}{\rho}$$

This lower bound could be used in a heuristics such that the reuse scheme and the number of available registers ρ are fixed. Second, if II is fixed, then we obtain a lower bound on the number of registers ρ required in this reuse scheme rc.

$$\rho_{rc} \geq \frac{m}{II}$$

There are numerous choices for fixing reuse edges that can be used in practical compilers.

1. For each value $u \in V_{R,t}$, we can decide that $reuse_t(u) = u$. This means that each statement reuses the register freed by itself (no sharing of registers between different statements). This is similar to buffer minimization problem as described in [13].
2. We can fix reuse edges according to the anti-dependences present in the original code: if there is an anti-dependence between two statement u and v in the original code, then fix $reuse_t(u') = v$ with the property that u kills u'. This decision is a generalization to the problem of reducing the register requirement as studied in [23].

---

[3] Of course, if we have $MII = II = 1$ (case of parallel loops for instance), the solution remains optimal.

3. If a rotating register file is present, we can fix an arbitrary (or with a cleverer method) hamiltonian reuse circuit among statements.

As explained before, our model includes writing and reading offsets. The negative latencies of the introduced anti-dependences generate a specific problem for VLIW codes. The next section solves this problem.

Eliminating Non-positive Circuits. From the scheduling theory, circuits with non-positive distances do not prevent a DDG from being scheduled (if the latencies are non-positive too). But such circuits impose hard scheduling constraints that may not be satisfiable by resource constraints in the subsequent pass of instruction scheduling[4]. Therefore these circuits have to be forbidden.

Alain Darte provides us a solution deduced from [2]. We add a quadratic number of retiming constraints to avoid non-positive circuits. We define a retiming r_e for each edge $e \in E$. We have then a shift $r_e(u)$ for each node $u \in V$. We declare then an integer $r_{e,u}$ for all $(e, u) \in (E \times V)$. Any retiming r_e must satisfy the following constraints:

$$\begin{aligned} \forall e' = (u', v') \neq e, \quad & r_{e,v'} - r_{e,u'} + \lambda(e') \geq 0 \\ \text{for the edge } e = (u, v), \; & r_{e,v} - r_{e,u} + \lambda(e) \geq 1 \end{aligned} \tag{3}$$

Note that an edge $e = (k_{u^t}, v) \in E'$ is an anti-dependence, i.e., its distance is $\lambda(e) = \mu^t_{u,t}$, to be computed. Since we have $|E|$ distinct retiming functions, we add $|E| \times |V|$ variables and $|E| \times |E|$ constraints. The constraint matrix is totally unimodular, and it does not alter the total unimodularity of System 2. The following lemma proves that satisfying System 3 is a necessary and sufficient condition for building a DDG $G_{\rightarrow r}$ with positive circuits distances.

Lemma 2. *[22] Let $G_{\rightarrow r}$ the solution graph of System 1 or System 2. Then:*
System 3 is satisfied $\Longleftrightarrow$ any circuit in $G_{\rightarrow r}$ has a positive distance $\lambda(C) > 0$.

The next section summarizes our experimental results.

7 Experiments

All the techniques described in this paper have been implemented and tested on various numerical loops extracted from different benchmarks (Spec95, whetstone, livermore, lin-ddot). This section presents a summary.

Optimal and Hamiltonian SIRA. In almost all the cases, both of the two techniques need the same number of registers according to the same II. However, as proved by Prop.1, hamiltonian SIRA may need one extra register, but in very few cases (about 5% of experiments). Regarding the resulted unrolling degrees, even if it may grow exponentially with SIRA (from the theoretical perspective), experiments show that it is mostly lower than the number of allocated registers, i.e., better than hamiltonian SIRA. However, some few cases exhibit critical unrolling degrees which are not acceptable if code size expansion is a critical factor.

---
[4] This is because circuits with non-positive distances impose scheduling constraints of type "not later than".

Optimal SIRA versus Fixed SIRA. In a second step of experiments, we investigate the fixed SIRA strategies (Sect. 6) to compare their results versus the optimal ones (optimal SIRA). We checked the efficiency of two strategies : self reuse strategy (no register sharing), and fixing an arbitrary hamiltonian reuse circuit. Resolving the intLP systems of these strategies become very fast compared to optimal solutions, as can be seen the first part of Fig. 4. We couldn't explore optimal solutions for loops larger than 10 nodes because the computation time became intractable.

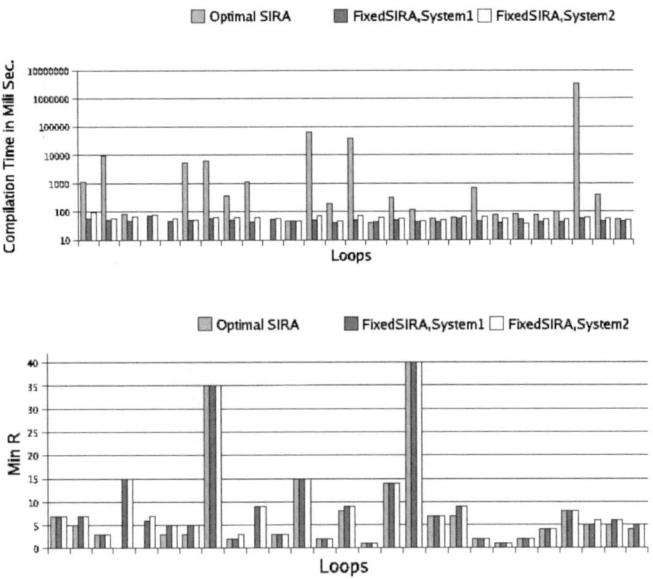

Fig. 4. Optimal versus Fixed SIRA with $II = MII$

For $II = MII$, some experiments do not exhibit a substantial difference. But if we vary II from MII to an upper-bound L, the difference is highlighted as follows.

- Regarding the register requirement, the self reuse strategy is, in most cases, far from the optimal. Disabling register sharing needs a high number of registers, since each statement needs at least one register. However, enabling sharing with an arbitrary hamiltonian reuse circuit is much more beneficial.
- Regarding the unrolling degree, the self reuse strategy exhibit the lowest ones, except in very few cases.

Fixed SIRA : System 1 versus System 2. The compilation time for optimal SIRA becomes intractable when the size of the loop exceeds 10 nodes. Hence, for larger loops, we advice to use our fixed SIRA strategies that are faster but allow sub-optimal results. We investigated the scalability (in terms of compilation time[5] versus the size of DDGs) for fixed SIRA when solving System 1 (non totally unimodular matrix) or System 2 (totally unimodular matrix). Fig. 5 plots the compilation times for larger loops (buffers and fixed hamiltonian). For loops larger than 300 nodes, the compilation time of System 1 becomes more considerable. The error ratio, induced by ceiling the μ variable as solved by System 2 compared to System 1, is depicted in Fig. 6. As can be seen, such error ratio asks us to improve the results of System 2 by re-optimizing the μ variables in a cleverer method as done in [13].

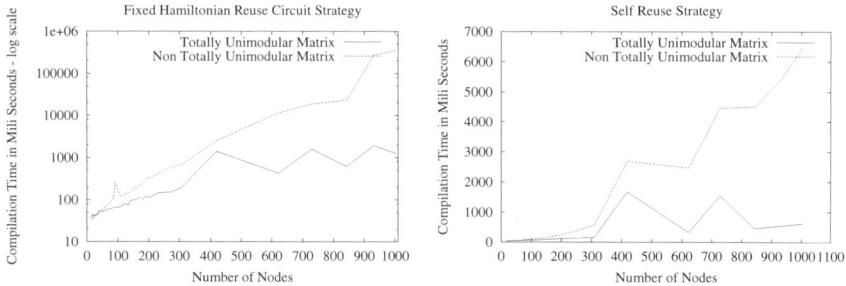

Fig. 5. Compilation Time versus the Size of the DDGs

8   Conclusion

This article presents a new approach consisting in virtually building an early cyclic register allocation before code scheduling, with multiple register types and delays in reading/writing. This allocation is expressed in terms of reuse edges and reuse distances to model the fact that two statements use the same register as storage location. An intLP model gives optimal solution with reduced constraint matrix size, and enables us to make a tradeoff between ILP loss (increase of MII) and number of required registers.

The spilling problem is left for future work. We believe that it is important to take it in consideration *before* instruction scheduling, and our framework should be very convenient for that.

When considering VLIW and EPIC/IA64 processors with reading/writing delays, we are faced to some difficulties because of the possible non-positive distance circuits that we prohibit. However, we allow anti-dependences to have non-positive latencies, because this amounts to consider that the destination register is not alive during the execution of the instruction and can be used for other variables. Since pipelined execution time is increasing, this feature becomes crucial in VLIW and EPIC codes to reduce the register requirement.

Each reuse decision implies loop unrolling with a factor depending on reuse circuits for each register type. The unrolling transformation can be applied before the software

---

[5] counted as the time for generating and solving the intLP systems, and building the allocated DDGs.

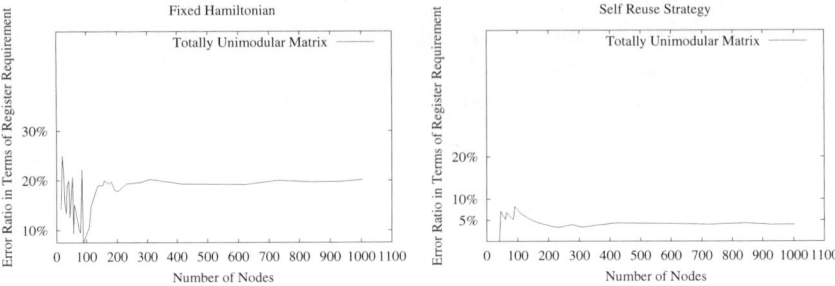

Fig. 6. Error Ratio in Terms of Register Requirement, Induced by System 2, versus the Size of the DDGs

pipelining pass (the inserted anti-dependences restrict the scheduler and satisfy register constraints) or after it during code generation step. It is better to unroll the loop after software pipelining in order to do not increase the scheduling complexity under resources constraints. Optimizing the unrolling factor is a hard problem and no satisfactory solution exists until now. However, we do not need loop unrolling in the presence of a rotating register file. We only need to seek a unique hamiltonian reuse circuit. The penalty for this constraint is at most one extra register than the optimal for the same II.

Since computing an optimal cyclic register allocation is intractable in real loops, we have identified one polynomial subproblem by fixing reuse edges. With this polynomial approach, we can compute $MII(\rho)$ for a given reuse configuration and a given register count ρ. We can also heuristically find a register usage for one given II.

Our experiments show that disabling sharing of registers with a self reuse strategy isn't a good reuse decision in terms of register requirement. We think that how registers are shared between different statements is one of the most important issues, and preventing this sharing by self reuse strategy consumes much more registers than needed by other reuse decisions.

References

1. D. Berson, R. Gupta, and M. Soffa. URSA: A Unified ReSource Allocator for Registers and Functional Units in VLIW Architectures. In *Conference on Architectures and Compilation Techniques for Fine and Medium Grain Parallelism*, pages 243–254, Orlando, Florida, Jan. 1993.
2. A. Darte, G.-A. Silber, and F. Vivien. Combining Retiming and Scheduling Techniques for Loop Parallelization and Loop Tiling. *Parallel Processing Letters*, 4(7):379–392, 1998.
3. D. de Werra, C. Eisenbeis, S. Lelait, and B. Marmol. On a Graph-Theoretical Model for Cyclic Register Allocation. *Discrete Applied Mathematics*, 93(2-3):191–203, July 1999.
4. J. C. Dehnert, P. Y.-T. Hsu, and J. P. Bratt. Overlapped Loop Support in the Cydra 5. In *Proceedings of Third International Conference on Architectural Support for Programming Languages and Operating Systems*, pages 26–38, New York, Apr. 1989. ACM Press.
5. A. E. Eichenberger, E. S. Davidson, and S. G. Abraham. Minimizing Register Requirements of a Modulo Schedule via Optimum Stage Scheduling. *International Journal of Parallel Programming*, 24(2):103–132, Apr. 1996.

6. W. fen Lin, S. K. Reinhardt, and D. Burger. Reducing DRAM Latencies with an Integrated Memory Hierarchy Design. In *Proceedings of the 7th International Symposium on High-Performance Computer Architecture*, Nuevo Leone, Mexico, Jan. 2001.

7. D. Fimmel and J. Muller. Optimal Software Pipelining Under Resource Constraints. *International Journal of Foundations of Computer Science (IJFCS)*, 12(6):697–718, 2001.

8. L. J. Hendren, G. R. Gao, E. R. Altman, and C. Mukerji. A Register Allocation Framework Based on Hierarchical Cyclic Interval Graphs. *Lecture Notes in Computer Science*, 641, 1992.

9. R. Huff. Lifetime-Sensitive Modulo Scheduling. In *PLDI 93*, pages 258–267, Albuquerque, New Mexico, June 1993.

10. J. Janssen. *Compilers Strategies for Transport Triggered Architectures*. PhD thesis, Delft University, Netherlands, 2001.

11. C. E. Leiserson and J. B. Saxe. Retiming Synchronous Circuitry. *Algorithmica*, 6:5–35, 1991.

12. J. Llosa. *Reducing the Impact of Register Pressure on Software Pipelined Loops*. PhD thesis, Universitat Politecnica de Catalunya (Spain), 1996.

13. Q. Ning and G. R. Gao. A Novel Framework of Register Allocation for Software Pipelining. In *Conference Record of the Twentieth ACM SIGPLAN-SIGACT Symposium on Principles of Programming Languages*, pages 29–42, Charleston, South Carolina, Jan. 1993. ACM Press.

14. B. R. Rau, M. Lee, P. P. Tirumalai, and M. S. Schlansker. Register Allocation for Software Pipelined Loops. *SIGPLAN Notices*, 27(7):283–299, July 1992. Proceedings of the ACM SIGPLAN '92 Conference on Programming Language Design and Implementation.

15. F. Sanchez and J. Cortadella. RESIS: A New Methodology for Register Optimization in Software Pipelining. In *Proceedings of Second International Euro-Par Conference, Euro-Par'96*, Lyon, France, August 1996.

16. A. Sawaya. *Pipeline Logiciel: Découplage et Contraintes de Registres*. PhD thesis, Université de Versailles Saint-Quentin-En-Yvelines, Apr. 1997.

17. Schlansker, B. Rau, and S. Mahlke. Achieving High Levels of instruction-Level Parallelism with Reduced Hardware Complexity. Technical Report HPL-96-120, Hewlet Packard, 1994.

18. M. M. Strout, L. Carter, J. Ferrante, and B. Simon. Schedule-Independent Storage Mapping for Loops. *ACM SIG-PLAN Notices*, 33(11):24–33, Nov. 1998.

19. W. Thies, F. Vivien, J. Sheldon, and S. Amarasinghe. A Unified Framework for Schedule and Storage Optimization. *ACM SIGPLAN Notices*, 36(5):232–242, May 2001.

20. S.-A.-A. Touati. EquiMax: A New Formulation of Acyclic Scheduling Problem for ILP Processors. In *Interaction between Compilers and Computer Architectures*. Kluwer Academic Publishers, 2001. ISBN 0-7923-7370-7.

21. S.-A.-A. Touati. Optimal Acyclic Fine-Grain Schedule with Cache Effects for Embedded and Real Time Systems. In *Proceedings of 9th nternational Symposium on Hardware/Software Codesign, CODES*, Copenhagen, Denmark, Apr. 2001. ACM.

22. S.-A.-A. Touati. *Register Pressure in Instruction Level Parallelisme*. PhD thesis, Université de Versailles, France, June 2002. ftp.inria.fr/INRIA/Projects/a3/touati/thesis.

23. J. Wang, A. Krall, and M. A. Ertl. Decomposed Software Pipelining with Reduced Register Requirement. In *Proceedings of the IFIP WG10.3 Working Conference on Parallel Architectures and Compilation Techniques, PACT95*, pages 277–280, Limassol, Cyprus, June 1995.

Register Allocation by Optimal Graph Coloring

Christian Andersson

Dept. of Computer Science, Lund University
Box 118, S-221 00 Lund, Sweden
chrisand@cs.lth.se

Abstract. We here present new insights of properties of real-life interference graphs emerging in register allocation. These new insights imply good hopes for a possibility of improving the coloring approach towards optimal solutions. The conclusions are based on measurements of nearly 28,000 real instances of such interference graphs. All the instances explored are determined to possess the so-called 1-perfectness property, a fact that seems to make them easy to color optimally. The exact algorithms presented not only produce better solutions than the traditional heuristic methods, but also, indeed, seem to perform surprisingly fast, according to the measurements on our implementations.

1 Introduction

For almost all architectures register allocation is among the most important of compiler optimizations. Computations involving only register operands are much faster than those involving memory operands. An effective utilization of the limited register file of the target machine may tremendously speed up program execution, compared to the same program compiled with a poor allocation.

Graph coloring is an elegant approach to the register allocation problem. Traditional algorithms used by compilers today [4,5,3,9,17] make use of approximate heuristics to accomplish the colorings.

Here we do not propose a new algorithm for register allocation. Our experiments, however, suggest that such an algorithm may well be designed, which guarantees optimal colorings for the purpose of a good allocation. Despite the fact that graph coloring is an NP-complete problem, the input graphs in the case of register allocation certainly seem to be efficiently colored, even when using an exact algorithm.

2 Background

Let $V = \{v_1, v_2, v_3, \ldots\}$ be the set of variables in a given intermediate representation (IR) of a program. Given a certain point p in the program flow, a variable $v_i \in V$ is said to be *live* if it is defined above p but not yet used for the last time. A *live range* (LR) for a variable $v_i \in V$ is a sequence of instructions beginning with the definition of v_i and ending with the last use of v_i. An *LR interference*

G. Hedin (Ed.): CC 2003, LNCS 2622, pp. 33–45, 2003.

is a pair $\langle \cdot, \cdot \rangle$ of variables whose live ranges intersect. Variables involved in such an interference can not be assigned to the same register. We denote by E the set of LR interference pairs. The *register allocation problem* is the problem of finding a mapping $c : V \mapsto \{r_1, r_2, \ldots, r_k\}$, where r_i are the registers of the target machine, such that $k \leq N$, where N is the total number of registers available and such that $\langle v_i, v_j \rangle \in E \Rightarrow c(v_i) \neq c(v_j)$. This corresponds closely to the well-known GRAPH-COLORING problem of finding a k-coloring of the graph $G = (V, E)$, which we call the *interference graph* (IG).

2.1   Graph Coloring

More exactly the GRAPH-COLORING problem is to determine for a given graph G and a positive integer k whether there exists a proper k-coloring. The smallest positive integer k for which a k-coloring exists is called the *chromatic number of G*, which is denoted by $\chi(G)$. GRAPH-COLORING is NP-complete [8].

The coloring problem seems not only practically impossible to solve exactly in the general case. Numerous works in this field from the past decades show that it is very hard to find algorithms that give good approximate solutions without restricting the types of input graphs. One well-known and obvious lower bound on the chromatic number $\chi(G)$ is the *clique number*, which is denoted by $\omega(G)$. A *clique Q* in a graph $G = (V, E)$ is a subset of V such that the subgraph G' induced by Q is *complete*, i.e., a graph in which all vertices are pairwise adjacent, and hence have to be colored using no less than $|Q|$ colors. The MAXIMUM-CLIQUE problem asks for the size of the largest clique of a given graph, the solution of which is the *clique number* $\omega(G)$. There are, however, two problems with this lower bound:

1. MAXIMUM-CLIQUE is (also) NP-complete [6].
2. According to, e.g., Kučera the gap between the clique number ω and the chromatic number χ is usually so large, that ω seems not to be usable as a lower bound on χ [14].

2.2   Traditional Approaches

Since GRAPH-COLORING is NP-complete [8], traditional register allocation implementations [4,5,3,9,17] rely on an approximate greedy algorithm for accomplishing the colorings. The technique used in all these implementations is based on a simple coloring heuristic [12]:

If $G = (V, E)$ contains a vertex v with a degree $\delta(v) < k$, i.e., with fewer than k neighbors, then let G' be the graph $G - \{v\}$, obtained by removing v, i.e., the subgraph of G induced by $V \setminus \{v\}$. If G' can be colored, then so can G, for when reinserting v into the colored graph G', the neighbors of v have at most $k - 1$ colors among them. Hence a free color can always be found for v.

The reduction above is called the *simplify* pass. The vertices reduced from the graph are temporarily pushed onto a stack. If, at some point during simplification, the graph G has vertices only of *significant degree*, i.e., vertices v of degree $\delta(v) \geq k$, then the heuristic fails and one vertex is marked for *spilling*. That is, we choose one vertex in the graph and decide to represent it in memory, not registers, during program execution. If, during a simplify pass, one or more vertices are marked for spilling, the program must be rewritten with explicit loads and stores, and new live ranges must be computed. Then the simplify pass is repeated. This process iterates until *simplify* succeeds with no spills. Finally, the graph is rebuilt, popping vertices from the stack and assigning colors to them. This pass is called *select*.

3   Interference Graph Characterization

The traditional methods described above, which are used in register allocation algorithms today, are approximate. Our experiments show, however, that making optimal colorings using exponential algorithms, may actually be a possible way of coloring graphs in the register allocation case. The key to this conjecture is the claimed so-called 1-perfectness of interference graphs.

3.1   Graph Perfectness

In the study of the so-called Shannon capacity of graphs, László Lovász in the 1970's introduced the ϑ-function, which has enjoyed a great interest in the last decades. For instance, its properties constitute the basis of a later on proven fact, that there are important instances of graphs (the so-called *perfect* graphs), whose possible k-colorability can indeed be determined in polynomial time.

The $\vartheta(G)$ function has two important and quite remarkable properties [11]:

1. $\omega(G) \leq \vartheta(\overline{G}) \leq \chi(G)$ [1] (The Sandwich Theorem)
2. For all graphs G, $\vartheta(G)$ is computable in polynomial time.

Those special instances of graphs G for which $\omega(G') = \chi(G')$ holds for each induced subgraph G' are said to be *perfect*, and they are indeed perfect in that particular sense that their possible k-colorability can be determined in polynomial time, as a direct consequence of the above properties. There are, however, no (or at least very few) proposals of algorithms which use this fact, and which run efficiently in practice. Moreover, the status of the recognition problem of the class of all perfect graphs is unknown.

Despite the fact that nobody has succeeded in designing an algorithm that efficiently solves the polynomial problem of perfect graphs, the elegance of the theory of these special instances makes it interesting to explore the possible perfectness of the interference graphs occurring in register allocation.

---

[1] The *complement graph of* $G = (V, E)$ is the graph $\overline{G} = (V, \overline{E})$, where

$$\overline{E} = \left\{ e = \langle u, v \rangle \mid u, v \in V, \ u \neq v, \text{and } \langle u, v \rangle \notin E \right\}.$$

Furthermore, Olivier Coudert, who works in the field of logic synthesis and verification, wrote in 1997 a very interesting paper [7], on the claimed simplicity of coloring "real-life" graphs, i.e., graphs which occur in problem domains such as VLSI CAD, scheduling, and resource binding and sharing. This simplicity is, according to Coudert, basically a consequence of the fact that most of the graphs investigated are *1-perfect*, i.e., they are graphs such that $\omega(G) = \chi(G)$, however, not necessarily for all subgraphs as in the case of perfect graphs.

4   Interference Graph Experiments

The input graphs we have used for our metrics come from two sources:

- Andrew W. Appel and Lal George have published a large set of interference graphs [1] generated by their compiler for Standard ML of New Jersey, compiling itself. The 27,921 actual LR interference graphs differ in size from around 25 vertices and 200 edges up to graphs with 7,500 vertices and 70,000 edges. These graphs do not, however, constitute the data used in empirical measurements reported by the authors in their articles on Iterated Register Coalescing [9,10].
- In a project task in the Lund University course on optimizing compilers[2], an SSA based experimental lab compiler for a subset of the C programming language is provided, in which students are to implement optimization algorithms. The best contribution in the fall 2000 course was provided by Per Cederberg, PhD candidate at the Division of Robotics, Department of Mechanical Engineering, Lund University[3]. His implementation included, for instance, algorithms for constant and copy propagation, dead code elimination, global value numbering, loop-invariant code motion and the register allocation algorithm proposed by George and Appel. Cederberg kindly let us use his implementation for our experiments.

When looking at the interference graphs we have had access to, they indeed seem to demonstrate some characteristics that point towards their potential 1-perfectness. For example, interference graphs tend not to be very dense, although they have large cliques. In other words, the density of these graphs seems not to be uniformly spread out over the whole graph, but rather localized to one or a few "clique-like" parts. Such characteristics certainly suggest a possibility of 1-perfectness, and make it interesting to investigate whether Coudert's conjecture can or cannot be confirmed for interference graphs.

In order to decide whether a graph G is 1-perfect, we need to solve two NP-hard problems (as far as we know today), the GRAPH-COLORING problem and the MAXIMUM-CLIQUE problem. Our only possibility is to implement exact algorithms, i.e., an approximate solution to either of these problems is not adequate.

---

[2] http://www.cs.lth.se/Education/Courses/EDA230/
[3] http://www.robotics.lu.se/

The algorithms for exactly solving both of these problems are fairly simple and well-known. The simplicity of the algorithm does, however, not imply that they are fast — both of them obviously have exponential worst case execution time, since we may need to perform an exhaustive search to find the optimal solution.

4.1 Sequential Coloring

Algorithm 1 shows a backtracking search for an optimal coloring of an input graph G. By initially searching for the maximum clique Q we get not only a lower bound ω on the chromatic number χ, but also a partial coloring of the graph. (The vertices of Q are colored using ω colors, which is optimal since all those vertices are pairwise adjacent in G.) If we are lucky, the graph is 1-perfect, and when the recursive part of the algorithm finds a coloring using ω colors, the search can be interrupted.

Algorithm 1 Create an optimal proper coloring of a graph G using a standard backtracking search algorithm. Return the chromatic number $\chi(G)$, and leave the coloring in a map *color*, indexed by vertices.

SEQUENTIAL-COLOR(G)
1   $Q \leftarrow$ MAXIMUM-CLIQUE(G)
2   $k \leftarrow 0$
3   **foreach** $v \in Q$ **do**
4        $k \leftarrow k + 1$
5        $color[v] \leftarrow k$
6   **return** SEQUENTIAL-COLOR-RECURSIVE(G, k, $|V(G)| + 1$, $|Q|$)

Input: G is a graph, partially colored using k colors. χ is the current value on the chromatic number and ω is the lower bound given by MAXIMUM-CLIQUE.
SEQUENTIAL-COLOR-RECURSIVE(G, k, χ, ω)
1   **if** G is entirely colored **then**
2   **return** k
3   $v \leftarrow$ an uncolored vertex of G
4   **foreach** $c \in [1, \text{MIN}(k + 1, \chi - 1)]$ **do**
5   **if** $\forall n \in N[v]$, $color[n] \neq c$ **then** $\triangleright$ $N[v]$ is the neighborhood of v
6             $color[v] \leftarrow c$
7             $\chi \leftarrow$ SEQUENTIAL-COLOR-RECURSIVE(G, MAX(c, k), χ, ω)
8   **if** $\chi = \omega$ **then** $\triangleright$ 1-perfect graph
9   **return** χ
10 **return** χ $\triangleright$ result after an exhaustive search

---

If, on the other hand, the graph is not 1-perfect, the maximum clique calculation will not be of any help at all. The algorithm then has to exhaustively enumerate all potential colorings that would improve on the chromatic number, which can take exponential time. The problem is that the lower bound is static in the sense that it is not reevaluated at each recursion. Moreover, the algorithm simultaneously uses several *unsaturated* colors. (A color c is said to be *saturated* if it can not be used anymore to extend a partial coloring.) Efficiently estimating a lower bound on the number of colors necessary to complete an unsaturated coloring is an open problem.

In [7] it is concluded that the maximum clique is tremendously important when coloring 1-perfect graphs. If the clique found is not maximal, we are left with the same problem as when trying to color graphs which are not 1-perfect.

One important part of the algorithm is left unspecified: In what order should the uncolored vertices be picked? Kučera showed in 1991, that it is practically impossible to find an ordering which performs well in the general case when using a greedy approach to the coloring problem [15].

The ordering of the vertices in the exact sequential algorithm may, however, have a strong impact on the efficiency of the search. Brélaz in 1979 proposed an efficient method called the DSATUR heuristic [2]. It consists of picking the vertex that has the largest saturation number, i.e., the number of colors used by its neighbors. If implementing the algorithm carefully, the information on vertex saturation can in fact be efficiently maintained, using so-called *shrinking* sets, as shown by, for example, Turner [16].

4.2   Obtaining the Maximum Clique

Algorithm 2 shows a simplified branch-and-bound approach to the MAXIMUM-CLIQUE problem. The algorithm relies partially on the calculation of an approximate coloring of the graph, which is used as an upper bound.

Algorithm 2 can be improved in a number of ways without jeopardizing optimality of the computed clique [7]. Let G be the graph at some point of the recursion, Q the clique under construction, $\widehat{Q}$ the current best solution, and $\{I_1, \ldots, I_k\}$ a k-coloring obtained on G. Then the following improvements apply:

- When we reach a state where $|Q| + |V(G)| \leq |\widehat{Q}|$, we can immediately prune the search space, since it is impossible to find a larger clique.
- Every vertex v such that $\delta(v) < |\widehat{Q}| - |Q|$ must be removed from the graph, because it can not be a member of a larger clique.
- Every vertex v such that $\delta(v) > |V(G)| - 2$, must be put into Q, since excluding it can not produce a larger clique.
- Every vertex v that can be colored with q colors, where $q > |Q| - |\widehat{Q}| + k$, yield unsuccessful branches, and can be left without further consideration.

The approximate coloring part of MAXIMUM-CLIQUE is a very simple greedy algorithm, using no particular heuristic for the ordering of vertices. The graphs have been represented simply as two-dimensional bit matrices. For the sake of efficiency, the graphs ought to have been redundantly represented as adjacency lists as well as matrices, a representation that has been chosen in register allocators ever since Chaitin's original algorithm. Our data structures are of course easy to extend to this double representation.

Algorithm 2 Find the maximum clique of a graph G using a simplified branch-and-bound technique. Return the set of vertices contained in the maximum clique found.

MAXIMUM-CLIQUE(G)
   1   **return** MAXIMUM-CLIQUE-RECURSIVE(G, $\emptyset$, $\emptyset$, ∞)

Input: G is the remaining part of the graph, Q is the clique under construction, $\widehat{Q}$ is the largest clique found so far, and u is an upper bound on ω (size of the maximum clique)

MAXIMUM-CLIQUE-RECURSIVE(G, Q, $\widehat{Q}$, u)
   1   **if** G is empty **then**
   2   **return** Q
   3   $\{I_1, \ldots, I_k\} \leftarrow$ APPROXIMATE-COLOR(G)
   4   $u \leftarrow$ MIN(u, $|Q| + k$) $\triangleright$ compute a new upper bound
   5   **if** $u \leq |\widehat{Q}|$ **then**
   6   **return** $\widehat{Q}$
   7   $v \leftarrow$ a maximum degree vertex of G
   8   $G' \leftarrow$ subgraph induced by $N[v]$
   9   $\widehat{Q} \leftarrow$ MAXIMUM-CLIQUE-RECURSIVE(G', $Q \cup \{v\}$, $\widehat{Q}$, u)
  10   **if** $u = \widehat{Q}$ **then**
  11   **return** $\widehat{Q}$
  12   $G'' \leftarrow$ graph induced by $V[G] - \{v\}$
  13   **return** MAXIMUM-CLIQUE-RECURSIVE(G'', Q, $\widehat{Q}$, u)

---

5   Experimental Results and Issues for Future Research

In the experiments with the graphs, using algorithms shown in Section 4, several interesting observations have been made. First and very importantly, *every single graph investigated turned out to be 1-perfect*, that is, for every single instance of the almost 28,000 graphs investigated, the chromatic number was determined to be exactly equal to the clique number.

The chromatic numbers of the Appel-George graphs range between 21 and 89. Most of them (27,590 graphs) have $\chi = 21$; 238 graphs have $\chi = 29$. Other test programs written, and compiled with the Cederberg compiler, get chromatic numbers on the interference graphs with a size of up to 15. All of them are 1-perfect. Despite numerous persistent tries, we have not managed to create one single program that results in a non-1-perfect interference graph using our compilers.

This experimental result raises two important questions to be further explored:

1. Are interference graphs always 1-perfect? Our experiments give strong empirical evidence for this. If it is the case, we need to determine why. That is, what in the earlier structural optimizations makes the graphs 1-perfect? Further graph sets from different (kinds of) compilers need to be examined in the future.

2. If all, or almost all, interference graphs are 1-perfect, how can we use this fact, in order to improve on the efficiency of the existing register allocation algorithms? Or should we rather incorporate qualities, such as simplification and/or copy propagation by live range coalescing, from the approximate algorithms into the exact algorithm?

The second question partially gets an answer through the second of our experimental results. We noted when running the exact algorithms on the graphs, that they seemed to be surprisingly fast. Hence, the George-Appel allocator was also implemented, using the pseudo-code given in [10], and the same data structures for graph representation as in the exact algorithms. Repeatedly running this algorithm for all the graphs, using an N-value equal to the chromatic number determined by the exact algorithm, and comparing execution times to those of the exact algorithm, gave the following result:

The exact algorithm for computing an optimal coloring is faster than George-Appel's approximate iteration algorithm.

Of course, the George-Appel allocator suffers a penalty through our choice of a data structure — the authors recommend a combination of bit matrices and adjacency lists.

But a change of the data structure would improve on the execution time of the exact algorithm as well. The operation for determining the neighborhood of a given vertex is expensive when using bit matrices, and it is very frequently used in both algorithms.

The execution times for the two algorithms have been plotted as functions of the sizes of the graphs in Fig. 1. One large and, for some reason, very tough, however, still 1-perfect graph instance containing 6,827 vertices, 45,914 edges, and 4,804 move related instructions has been removed from the data. (The time needed by the George-Appel algorithm to create the coloring was 3,290 seconds. The exact algorithm needed 120 seconds.)

In order to show the difference trend in the execution times of the two algorithms, a second degree polynomial has been fitted to the samples using the least-squares method. We do not, however, assert that the execution times are quadratic in the sizes of the graphs; the exact algorithm is obviously exponential in the worst case.

In Fig. 2 the same execution times are plotted for the 23,000 smallest graphs only, excluding the few very large and extremely tough instances.

There is one more thing which is important to note in the comparison of the two algorithm approaches. In 46 of the 28,000 graphs, the George-Appel algorithm fails to find optimum, and spills one or two variables to memory. This number of failures is actually impressively low, as the algorithm uses an approximate, heuristic method for the NP-complete problem of coloring. Perhaps the reason for the good performance of the approximate algorithm is the 1-perfectness of the graphs? Nevertheless, in comparison to the exact algorithm, these spills are of course unfortunate, especially since it does not seem to take longer time to find optimal colorings of the graphs using the exact algorithm.

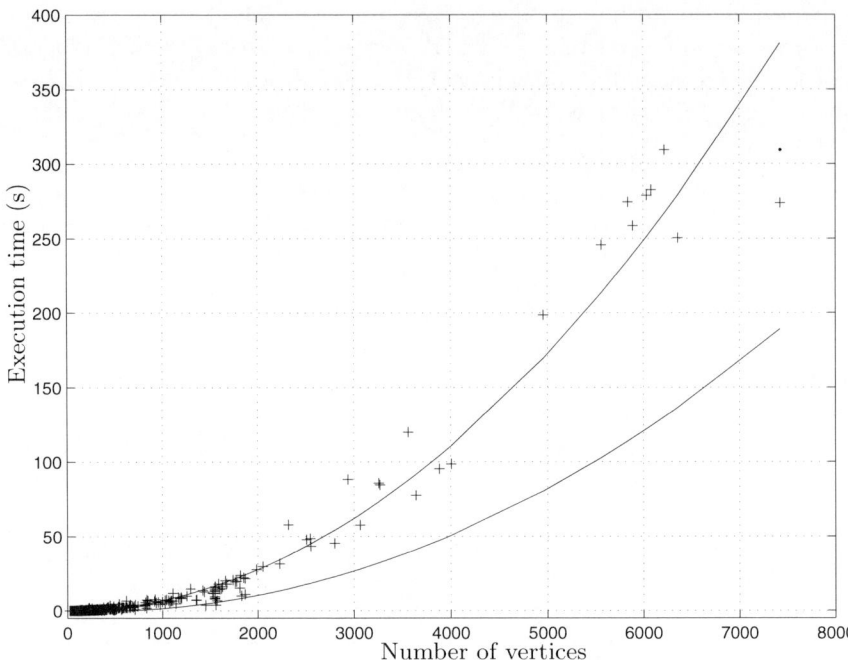

Fig. 1. Execution times for the two algorithms, coloring all graph instances. The dots correspond to the exact algorithm; the pluses correspond to the George-Appel allocator. The continuous functions are the best approximate second degree polynomials in the least-squares sense. We do *not*, however, assert that the execution times are quadratic in the sizes of the graphs. The intention is simply to compare the average execution times of the algorithms for the graphs in question.

6   Conclusions

Graph coloring is an elegant approach to the register allocation problem. The algorithms used by compilers today make use of approximate heuristics to accomplish the colorings.

In this paper, we do not propose a new algorithm for register allocation. The experiments, however, suggest that such an algorithm may well be designed, which guarantees optimal colorings for the purpose of a good allocation. Despite the fact that graph coloring is an NP-complete problem, the input graphs in the case of register allocation certainly seem to be efficiently colored, even when using an exact algorithm.

In the implementation of the sequential coloring algorithm, none of the typical improvements designed for register allocation, such as copy propagation by coalescing, graph simplification by vertex removal/merging, or interference reduction by live range splitting, have been accounted for. Our original purpose

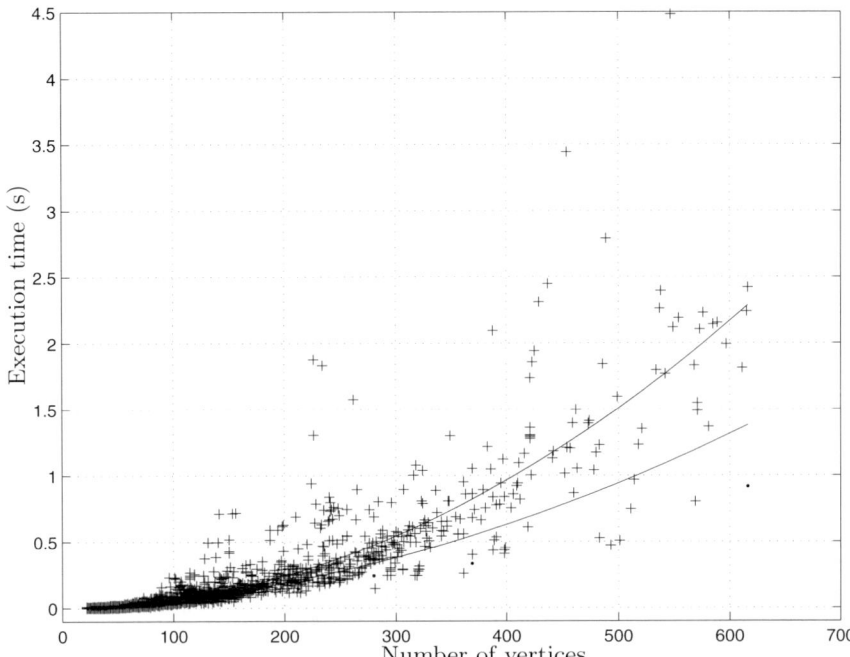

Fig. 2. Execution times for the two algorithms, coloring the 23,000 smallest graphs. The dots and the lower function estimate correspond to the exact algorithm; the pluses and the upper estimate correspond to the George-Appel allocator. The functions are second degree polynomials estimated from all the measured points using the least-squares method.

was simply to determine whether the graphs were 1-perfect, since this could have the effect of making optimal colorings efficiently computable.

In order to become applicable for register allocation, the algorithms need to implement such functionality. After all, most of the graphs investigated have much too large chromatic numbers, when not simplified, to fit into the register file of most processors. Even if the processor has a large register file, it is still desirable that programs do not use more registers than necessary, since loads and stores, made for instance at procedure calls, suffer most considerably when having to switch large numbers of registers into and out of memory.

In order to complete the goal of improving the register allocation algorithms, some questions remain to be answered:

- Do coalescing, merging, or splitting, the way we use these improvements in register allocators, jeopardize the 1-perfectness of the graphs?
- Is the 1-perfectness of interference graphs provable?
- Can we perhaps further strengthen the constraints in order to restrict the graph classes towards perfectness?

- How expensive does the exact coloring algorithm become if the graphs are not 1-perfect?
- Is it at all possible to implement an efficient register allocator that contains the different graph simplifications, and still guarantees the optimality of the produced colorings?

We believe that the answer to the last of these questions may well be positive, and our work will be continued with the goal of achieving such an implementation.

Acknowledgments. The author would like to thank

- *Dr. Jonas Skeppstedt* for his enthusiastic support in all parts of this work,
- *Per Cederberg* for lending us his experimental compiler implementation.

References

[1] Andrew W. Appel and Lal George. Sample graph coloring problems. Available online at `http://www.cs.princeton.edu/~appel/graphdata/`, 1996. 27,921 actual register-interference graphs generated by Standard ML of New Jersey version 1.09, compiling itself.

[2] Daniel Brélaz. New methods to color the vertices of a graph. *Communications of the ACM*, 22(4):251–256, April 1979.

[3] Preston Briggs, Keith D. Cooper, and Linda Torczon. Improvements to graph coloring register allocation. *ACM Transactions on Programming Languages and Systems*, 16(3):428–455, May 1994.

[4] G. J. Chaitin. Register allocation and spilling via graph coloring. In *Proceedings of the ACM SIGPLAN '82 Symposium on Compiler Construction*, pages 98–105, Boston, Massachusetts, June 1982. The Association for Computing Machinery.

[5] Fred C. Chow and John L. Hennessy. Register allocation by priority-based coloring. In *Proceedings of the ACM SIGPLAN '84 Symposium on Compiler Construction*, pages 222–232, Montreal, June 1984. The Association for Computing Machinery.

[6] Thomas H. Cormen, Charles E. Leiserson, Ronald L. Rivest, and Clifford Stein. *Introduction to Algorithms*. The MIT Press, Massachusetts Institute of Technology, Cambridge, Massachusetts 02142, second edition, 2001.

[7] Olivier Coudert. Exact coloring of real-life graphs is easy. In *Proceedings of the 34th annual conference on Design automation conference*, pages 121–126, Anaheim, CA USA, June 1997. The Association for Computing Machinery.

[8] Michael R. Garey and David S. Johnson. *Computers and Intractability: A Guide to the Theory of NP-Completeness*. W. H. Freeman and Company, New York, 1979.

[9] Lal George and Andrew W. Appel. Iterated register coalescing. In *Proceedings of the 23rd ACM SIGPLAN-SIGACT symposium on Principles of programming languages*, pages 208–218, St. Petersburg Beach, FL USA, January 1996. The Association for Computing Machinery.

[10] Lal George and Andrew W. Appel. Iterated register coalescing. *ACM Transactions on Programming Languages and Systems*, 18(3):300–324, May 1996.

[11] Martin Grötschel, László Lovász, and Alexander Schrijver. *Geometric Algorithms and Combinatorial Optimization*. Springer–Verlag, Berlin Heidelberg, Germany, 1988.

[12] Alfred Bray Kempe. On the geographical problem of the four colours. *American Journal of Mathematics*, 2:193–201, 1879.

[13] Robert Kennedy, Sun Chan, Shin-Ming Liu, Raymond Lo, Peng Tu, and Fred Chow. Partial redundancy elimination in SSA form. *ACM Transactions on Programming Languages and Systems*, 21(3):627–676, May 1999.

[14] Luděk Kučera. *Combinatorial Algorithms*. Adam Hilger, Redcliff Way, Bristol BS1 6NX, England, 1990.

[15] Luděk Kučera. The greedy coloring is a bad probabilistic algorithm. *Journal of Algorithms*, 12(4):674–684, December 1991.

[16] Jonathan S. Turner. Almost all k-colorable graphs are easy to color. *Journal of Algorithms*, 9(1):63–82, March 1988.

[17] Steven R. Vegdahl. Using node merging to enhance graph coloring. In *Proceedings of the ACM SIGPLAN '99 conference on Programming language design and implementation*, pages 150–154, Atlanta, GA USA, May 1999. The Association for Computing Machinery.

[18] Mark N. Wegman and F. Kenneth Zadeck. Constant propagation with conditional branches. *ACM Transactions on Programming Languages and Systems*, 13(2):181–210, 1991.

A   A Simple Example

Fig. 3 presents parts of a sample compiling session using the Cederberg compiler. First a high-level source code is input to the front-end. The intermediate representation produced by the front-end is presented to the right. For the purpose of simplicity, the user I/O functions, `get` and `put`, are assumed to be implemented as processor instructions.

Temporary variables in the program are named `t1, t2, t3,...`; basic blocks are labeled `x1, x2, x3,....`

The IR from the front-end is transformed into SSA form and is subject to two optimizations, *constant propagation with conditional branches* [18] and *partial redundancy elimination* [13], the result of which is shown down to the left on normal form, i.e., transformed back from SSA.

Analyzing the live ranges of the variables, inserting an edge between ranges that interfere, gives the interference graph presented down to the right. The graph has the maximum clique

$$Q = \{\mathtt{t11}, \mathtt{t16}, \mathtt{t17}, \mathtt{t21}, \mathtt{t22}\}, \quad \omega = 5,$$

and we conclude, directly from the figure, that the chromatic number χ is no larger than ω. Hence the graph is 1-perfect.

```
int f()
{
    int a;
    int b;
    int c;

    a = get(); /* from user */
    if (a < 0)
        return -a;
    b = 1024;
    c = b / 1024;

    while (b < a)
    {
        c = c + a * a + b + a;
        b = b - 1;
    }

    put(c); /* to user */
    return 0;
}
```

```
x1:  get                 t1
     mov    t1           a
     slt    a      0      t2
     bf     t2            x3
x2:  neg    a            t3
     ret    t3
x3:  mov    1024          b
     div    b      1024   t4
     mov    t4           c
     ba                  x5
x4:  mul    a      a      t5
     add    c      t5     t6
     add    t6     b      t7
     add    t7     a      t8
     mov    t8           c
     sub    b      1      t9
     mov    t9           b
x5:  sgt    b      a      t10
     bt     t10          x4
x6:  put    c
     ret    0
```

```
x1:  get                 t11
     slt    t11    0      t12
     bf     t12          x3
x2:  neg    t11          t13
     ret    t13
x3:  mul    t11    t11    t19
     mov    1            t16
     mov    1024         t17
     ba                  x5
x4:  add    t16    t19    t20
     add    t20    t17    t21
     add    t21    t11    t22
     sub    t17    1      t23
     mov    t22          t16
     mov    t23          t17
x5:  sgt    t17    t11    t18
     bt     t18          x4
x6:  put    t16
     ret    0
```

Fig. 3. *Top-left*: A high-level source code which is input to the compiler front-end. *Top-right*: IR output from the front-end. *Bottom-left*: The final improved IR from the optimizer. *Bottom-right:* IG with the maximum clique Q of size $\omega = 5$ shown with shaded vertices. Since, apparently, $\chi = \omega$ the graph is 1-perfect.

A Compilation and Optimization Model for Aspect-Oriented Programs*

H. Masuhara, G. Kiczales, and C. Dutchyn

[1] Graduate School of Arts and Sciences, University of Tokyo
[2] Intentional Software Corporation
[3] Department of Computer Science, University of British Columbia

Abstract. This paper presents a semantics-based compilation model for an aspect-oriented programming language based on its operational semantics. Using partial evaluation, the model can explain several issues in compilation processes, including how to find places in program text to insert aspect code and how to remove unnecessary run-time checks. It also illustrates optimization of calling-context sensitive pointcuts (`cflow`), implemented in real compilers.

1 Introduction

This work is part of a larger project, the Aspect SandBox (ASB), that aims to provide concise models of aspect-oriented programming (AOP) for theoretical studies and to provide a tool for prototyping alternative AOP semantics and implementation techniques[1].

In this paper we report one result from the ASB project—an operational-semantics based explanation of the compilation and optimization strategy for AspectJ-like languages[5,9]. To avoid difficulties to develop formal semantics directly from artifacts as complex as AspectJ, we used a simplified language. It yet has sufficient features to discuss compilation and optimization of real languages.

The idea is to use partial evaluation to perform as many tests as possible at compile-time, and to insert applicable advice bodies directly into the program. Our model also explains the optimization used by the AspectJ compiler for calling-context sensitive pointcuts (`cflow` and `cflowbelow`).

Some of the issues our semantic model clarifies include:

- The mapping between dynamic join points and the points in the program text, or *join point shadows*, where the compiler actually operates.
- What dispatch can be 'compiled-out' and what must be done at runtime.
- The performance impact different kinds of advice and pointcuts can have on a program.
- How the compiler must handle recursive application of advice.

---

* An early version of the paper was presented at FOAL 2002, Workshop on Foundations of Aspect-Oriented Languages at AOSD 2002.

[1] http://www.cs.ubc.ca/labs/spl/projects/asb.html

G. Hedin (Ed.): CC 2003, LNCS 2622, pp. 46–60, 2003.

1.1   Join Point Models

Aspect-oriented programming (AOP) is a paradigm to modularize crosscutting concerns[10]. An AO program is effectively written in multiple modularities— concerns that are local in one are diffuse in another and vice-versa. Thus far, several AOP languages are proposed[3,9,13,14].

The ability of an AOP language to support crosscutting lies in its *join point model* (JPM). A JPM consists of three elements:

- The *join points* are the points of reference that programs including aspects can affect. *Lexical* join points are locations in the program text (*e.g.,* "the body of a method"). *Dynamic* join points are run-time actions, such as events that take place during execution of the program (*e.g.,* "an invocation of a method").
- A *means of identifying* join points. (*e.g.,* "the bodies of methods in a particular class," or "all invocations of a particular method")
- A *means of effecting* at join points. (*e.g.,* "run this code beforehand")

In this paper, we will be working with a simplified JPM similar to the one from AspectJ. (See Section 2.1 for details.)

The rest of the paper is organized as follows. Section 2 introduces our simplified JPM, namely Pointcut and Advice (PA), and shows its interpreter. Section 3 presents a compilation scheme for PA excluding context-sensitive pointcuts, which are deferred to Section 4. Section 5 relates our study to other formal studies in AOP and other compilation schemes. Section 6 concludes the paper with future directions.

2   PA: Dynamic Join Point Model AOP Language

This section introduces our small join point model, namely Pointcut and Advice (PA), which implements core features of the AspectJ's dynamic join point model. PA is modeled as an AOP extension to a simple object-oriented language. Its operational semantics is given as an interpreter written in Scheme. A formalization of a procedural subset of PA is presented by Wand, Kiczales and Dutchyn[19].

2.1   Informal Semantics

We first informally present the semantics of PA. In short, PA is a dynamic join point model that covers core features of AspectJ on top of a simple object-oriented language with classes, objects, instance variables, and methods.

Object Semantics. Figure 1 is an example program[2]. For readability, we use a Java-like syntax in the paper[3]. It defines a `Point` class with one integer instance variable x, a unary constructor, and three methods `set`, `move` and `main`.

---

[2] For simplicity later in the paper, we are using one-dimensional points as an example.
[3] Our implementation actually uses an S-expression based syntax.

```
class Point {
  int x;
  Point(int ix)       { this.set(ix); }
  void set(int newx) { this.x = newx; }
  void move(int dx)  { this.set(this.x + dx); }
  void main()         { Point p = new Point(1);
                        p.move(5); write(p.x); newline(); } }
```

Fig. 1. An Example Program. (`write` and `newline` are primitive operators.)

When method `main` of a `Point` object is executed, it creates another `Point` object, and runs the constructor body. The `main` method then invokes method `move` on the created object, reads the value of variable `x` of the object and displays it.

Aspect Semantics. To explain the semantics of AOP features, we first define the PA join point model.

Join Point. The *join point* is an action during program execution, including method calls, method executions, object creations, and advice executions. (Note that a method invocation is treated as a call join point at the caller's side and an execution join point at the receiver's side.) The *kind* of the join point is the kind of action (*e.g.,* call and execution).

Means of Identifying Join Points. The means of identifying join points is the pointcut mechanism. A *pointcut* is a predicate on join points, which is used to specify the join points that a piece of advice applies to. There are five kinds of primitive pointcuts, namely `call`(m), `execution`(m), `new`(m), `target`(t v), and `args`(t v,...), three operators (`&&`, `||` and `!`), and two higher-order pointcuts, namely `cflow`(p) and `cflowbelow`(p).

The first three primitive pointcuts (`call`, `execution`, and `new`) match join points that have the same kind and signature as the pointcut. The next two primitive pointcuts (`target` and `args`) match any join point that has values of specified types. The three operators logically combine or negate pointcuts. The last two higher-order pointcuts match join points that have a join point matching their sub-pointcuts in the call-stack. These are discussed in Section 4 in more detail. Interpretation of pointcuts is formally presented in other literature[19].

Means of Effecting at Join Points. The means of effecting at join points is the advice mechanism. A piece of *advice* contains a pointcut and a body expression. When a join point is created, and it matches the pointcut of the advice, the advice body is executed. There are two types of advice, namely `before` and `after`[4]. A

---

[4] For simplicity we omit `around` advice and `after returning` advice which can inspect return values. However, our experimental implementation actually supports those types of advice.

```
(define eval
 (lambda (exp env jp)
  (cond ((const-exp? exp) (const-value exp))
        ((var-exp? exp)   (lookup env (var-name exp)))
        ((call-exp? exp)  (call (call-signature exp)
                                (eval (call-target exp) env jp)
                                (eval-rands (call-rands exp) env jp) jp))
        ...)))
(define call
  (lambda (sig obj args jp)
    (execute (lookup-method (object-class obj) sig) obj args jp)))
(define execute
  (lambda (method this args jp)
    (eval (method-body method)
          (new-env (append '(this %host) (method-params method))
                   (append (list this (method-class method)) args))
          jp)))
```

Fig. 2. Expression Interpreter.

before advice runs before the original action is taken place. Similarly, the **after** runs after the completion of the original action.

The following example advice definition lets the example program to print a message before every call to method **set**:

```
before : call(void Point.set(int)) && args(int z)
{ write("set:"); write(z); newline(); }
```

It consists of a keyword for the kind of the advice (**before**), a pointcut, and a body in braces. The pointcut matches join points that call method **set** of class **Point**, and the **args** sub-pointcut binds variable z to the argument to method **set**. The body of the advice prints messages and the value of the argument.

When the **Point** program is executed together with the above advice, the advice matches to the call to **set** twice (in the constructor and in method **set**), it thus will print "set:1", "set:6" and "6".

2.2   Interpreter

The interpreter consists of an expression interpreter and several definitions for AOP features including the data structure for a join point, wrappers for creating join points, a weaver, and a pointcut interpreter.

Expression Interpreter. Figure 2 shows the core of the expression interpreter excluding support for AOP features. The main function **eval** takes an expression, an environment, and a join point as its parameters. The join point is an execution join point at the enclosing method or constructor.

An expression is a parsed abstract syntax tree, which can be tested with **const-exp?**, etc., and can be accessed with **const-value**, etc. An environment

```
(define call
  (lambda (sig obj args jp)
    (weave (make-jp 'call  sig obj args jp)
           (lambda (args jp) ...body of the original call...)
           args)))
```

Fig. 3. A Wrapped Interpreter Function.

binds variables to mutable cells. An object is a Scheme data structure that has a class information and mutable fields for instance variables.

The body of `eval` is a simple case-based test on expression types. Some operations are defined as separated functions for the later extension of AOP features.

Join Point. A join point is a data structure that is created upon an action in the expression interpreter:[5]

```
(define-struct jp (kind name target args stack))
```

The `kind` field specifies the kind of the join point as a symbol (*e.g.,* `'call`). The `name` field has the name of the method being called. The `target` and `args` fields have the target object and the arguments of the method invocation, respectively. The `stack` field will be explained in Section 4.

Wrapper. In order to advice actions performed in the expression interpreter, we wrap the interpreter functions so that they create dynamic join points. Figure 3 shows how `call`—one of such a function—is wrapped. When a method is to be called, the function first creates a join point that represents the call action and applies it to `weave`, which executes advice applicable to the join point (explained below). The lambda-closure passed to `weave` defines the action of the original `call`, which is executed during the weaving process.

Likewise, the other functions including method execution, object creation, and advice execution (defined later) are wrapped.

Weaver. Figure 4 shows the definition of the weaver. Function `weave` takes a join point, a lambda-closure for continuing the original action, and a list of arguments to the closure. It also uses advice definitions in global variables (`*befores*` and `*afters*`). It defines the order of advice execution; it executes `befores` first, then the original action, followed by `afters` last.

Function `call-befores/afters` processes a list of advice. It matches the pointcut of each piece of advice against the current join point, and executes the body of the advice if they match. In order to advise execution of advice, the

---

[5] This non-standard Scheme construct defines a structure named `jp` with five fields named `kind`, `name`, `target`, `args`, and `stack`.

```
(define weave
  (lambda (jp action args)
    (call-befores/afters *befores* args jp)
    (let ((result (action args jp)))
      (call-befores/afters *afters* args jp)
      result)))
(define call-befores/afters
  (lambda (advs args jp)
    (for-each (call-before/after args jp) advs)))
(define call-before/after
  (lambda (args jp)
    (lambda (adv)
      (let ((env (pointcut-match? (advice-pointcut adv) jp)))
        (if env (execute-before/after adv env jp))))))
(define execute-before/after
  (lambda (adv env jp)
    (weave (make-jp 'aexecution adv #f #f '() jp)
           (lambda (args jp) (eval (advice-body adv) env jp))
           '())))
```

Fig. 4. Weaver.

```
(define pointcut-match?
  (lambda (pc jp)
    (cond ((and (call-pointcut? pc) (call-jp? jp)
               (sig-match? (pointcut-sig pc) (jp-name jp)))
           (make-env '() '()))
          ((and (args-pointcut? pc)
               (types-match? (jp-args jp) (pointcut-arg-types pc)))
           (make-env (pointcut-arg-names pc) (jp-args jp)))
          ...
          (else #f))))
```

Fig. 5. Pointcut Interpreter.

function `execute-before/after` is also wrapped. The lambda-closure in the function actually executes the advice body.

Calling **around** advice has basically the same structure for the **before** and **after**. It is, however, more complicated due to its interleaved execution for the **proceed** mechanism.

Pointcut interpreter. The function `pointcut-match?` in Figure 5 matches a pointcut to a join point. Due to space limitations, we only show rules for two types of pointcuts. The first clause of the **cond** matches a **call**(m) pointcut to a **call** join point that has a matching **name** field matches to m. It returns an empty environment that represent 'true'. The second clause matches an **args**(t x,...) pointcut to any join point when **args** filed has values of types t, ... The result in this case is an environment that binds variables x,... to the values in the **args** field. The last clause returns false for unmatched cases.

3   Compiling Programs by Partial Evaluation

Our compilation scheme is to partially evaluate an interpreter, which is known as *the first Futamura projection*[7]. Given an interpreter of a language and a program to be interpreted, partial evaluation of the interpreter with respect to the subject program generates a compiled program (called a *residual* program). By following this scheme, partial evaluation of an AOP interpreter with respect to a subject program *and* advice definitions would generate a compiled, or *statically woven* program.

The effect of partial evaluation is removal of unnecessary pointcut tests. While the interpreter tests-and-executes *all* pieces of advice at each *dynamic* join point, our compilation scheme successfully inserts *only* applicable advice to each shadow of join points. This is achieved in the following way:

1. Our compilation scheme partially evaluates the interpreter with respect to each method definition.
2. The partial evaluator (PE) processes the expression interpreter, which virtually walks over the expressions in the method. All shadows of join points are thus instantiated.
3. At each shadow of join points, the PE further processes the weaver. Using statically given advice definitions, it (conceptually) inserts test-and-execute sequence of all advice.
4. For each piece of advice, the PE reduces the test-and-execute code into a conditional branch that has either a constant or dynamic value as its condition, and the advice body as its then-clause. Depending on the condition, the entire code or the test code may be removed.
5. The PE processes the code that executes the advice body. It thus instantiates shadows of join points in the advice body. The steps from 3 recursively compiles 'advised advice execution.'

We used PGG, an offline partial evaluator for Scheme[17], for partial evaluation.

3.1   How the Interpreter Is Partially Evaluated

An offline partial evaluator processes a program in the following way. It first annotates expressions in the program as either *static* or *dynamic*, based on their dependency on the statically known parameters. Those annotations are often called *binding-times*. It then processes the program by actually evaluating static expressions and by returning symbolic expressions for dynamic expressions. The resulted program, which is called *residual program*, consists of dynamic expressions in which statically computed values are embedded.

This subsection explains how the interpreter is partially evaluated with respect to a subject program, by emphasizing what operations can be performed at partial evaluation time. Although the partial evaluation is an automatic process, we believe understanding this process is crucially important for identifying compile-time information and also for developing better insights into design of hand-written compilers.

Compilation of Expressions. The essence of the first Futamura projection is to evaluate computation involving `exp` away. In fact, occurrences of `exp` in the interpreter are annotated as static except for the first argument to `execute` in function `call`. The argument is dynamic due to the nature of dynamic dispatching in object-oriented languages. We therefore invoke the partial evaluator for each method definition, and replaced the function `execute` with the one that dynamically dispatches on a receiver's type. This standard partial evaluation technique is known as 'The Trick.'

The environment (`env`) is regarded as a partially-static data structure; *i.e.*, the variable names are static and the values are dynamic. As a result, the partial evaluator compiles variable accesses in the subject program into accesses to elements of the argument list in the residual code.

Compilation of Advice. As is mentioned at the beginning of the section, our compilation scheme inserts advice bodies into their applicable shadows of join points with appropriate guards. Below, we explain how this is done by the partial evaluator.

1. A wrapper (*e.g.*, Figure 3) creates a join point upon calling `weave`. The first two fields of the join point, namely `kind` and `name`, are static because they only depend on the program text. The rest fields have values computed at run-time. We actually split the join point into two data structures so that static and dynamic fields are stored separately. With partial evaluators that support partially static data structures[4], we would get the same result without splitting the join point structure.
2. Function `weave` (Figure 4) is executed with the static join point, an action, and dynamic arguments. Since the advice definitions are statically available, the partial evaluator unrolls the `for-each` in in function `eval-befores/afters`.
3. The result of `pointcut-match?` can be either static or dynamic depending on the type of a pointcut. Therefore, the test-and-execute sequence (in `eval-before/after`) becomes one of the following three:
   Statically false: No code is inserted into compiled code.
   Statically true: The body of the advice is partially evaluated; *i.e.*, the body is inserted in compiled code.
   Dynamic: Partial evaluation of `pointcut-match?` generates an if expression with the body of advice in the then-clause and an empty else-clause. Essentially, the advice body is inserted with a guard.
4. In the statically true or dynamic cases at the above step, the partial evaluator processes the evaluation of the advice body. If the advice is applicable to more than one join point shadows in a method, the compiled body is shared as a Scheme function thanks to a mechanism in the partial evaluator. Since the wrapper of the `execute-before/after` calls `weave`, application of advice to the advice body is also compiled.
5. When the original action is evaluated, the residual code of the original action is inserted. This residual code from `weave` will thus have the original computation surrounded by applicable advice bodies.

```
(define point-move
  (lambda (this1 args2 jp3)
    (let* ((jp4   (make-jp 'execution 'move this1 args2 jp3))
           (args5 (list (+ (get-field this1 'x) (car args2))))
           (jp6   (make-jp 'call 'set this1 args5 jp4)))
      (if (type-match? args5 '(int))
          (begin (write "set:") (write (car args5)) (newline)))
      (execute* (lookup-method (object-class this1) 'set)
                this1 args5 jp6)))))
```

Fig. 6. Compiled code of `move` method of `Point` class.

Compilation of Pointcut. In step 3 above, `pointcut-match?` is partially evaluated with a static pointcut and static fields in a join point. The partial evaluation process depends on the type of the pointcut. For pointcuts that depend on only static fields of a join point (*e.g.*, `call`), the condition is statically computed to either an environment or false. For pointcuts that test values in the join point (*e.g.*, `target`), the partial evaluator returns residual code that dynamically tests the types of the values in the join point. For example, when `pointcut-match?` is partially evaluated with respect to `args(int x)`, the following expression is returned as the residual code:

```
(if (types-match? (jp-args jp) '(int))
    (make-env '(x) (jp-args jp))
    #f)
```

Logical operators (namely `&&`, `||` and `!`) are partially evaluated into an expression that combines the residual expressions of its sub-pointcuts. The remaining two pointcuts (`cflow` and `cflowbelow`) are discussed in the next section.

The actual `pointcut-match?` is written in a continuation-passing style so that partially evaluator can reduce a conditional branch in `call-before/after` for the static cases. This is a standard technique in partial evaluation, but is crucially important to get right results.

3.2   Compiled Code

Figure 6 shows the compiled code for `Point.move` combined with the advice given in Section 2.1. For readability, we post-processed the residual code by eliminating dead code, propagating constants, renaming variable names, combining split join point structures, and so forth. The post-process was done automatically except for renaming and combining.

The compiled function first creates a join point `jp4` for the method execution, a parameter list and a join point `jp6` for the method call. The `if` expression is the advice body with a guard. The guard checks the residual condition for `args` pointcut. (Note that no run-time checks are performed for `call` pointcut.) If matched, the body of the advice is executed. Finally, the original action is performed.

As we see, advice execution is successfully compiled. Even though there is a shadow of `execution` join points at the beginning of the method, no advice bodies are inserted in the compiled function as it does not match any advice.

4   Compiling Calling-Context Sensitive Pointcuts

As briefly mentioned before, `cflow` and `cflowbelow` pointcuts can investigate join points in the call-stack; *i.e.,* their truth value is sensitive to calling context. Here, we first show a straightforward implementation that is based on a stack of join points. It is inefficient, however, and can not be compiled properly.

We then show an optimized implementation that can be found in AspectJ compiler. The implementation exploits incremental natures of those pointcuts, and is presented as a modified version of PA interpreter. We can also see those pointcuts can be properly compiled by using our compilation scheme.

To keep discussion simple, we only explain `cflow` in this section. Extending our idea to `cflowbelow` is easy and actually done in our experimental system.

4.1   Calling-Context Sensitive Pointcut: cflow

A pointcut `cflow(p)` matches to any join points if there is a join point that matches to p in its call-stack. The following definition is an example advice that uses a `cflow` pointcut. The `cflow` pointcut matches join points that are created during method calls to `move`. When this pointcut matches a join point, the `args(int w)` sub-pointcut gets the parameter to `move` from the stack.

```
after : call(void Point.set(int))
           && cflow(call(void Point.move(int)) && args(int w))
{ write("under move:"); write(w); newline(); }
```

As a result, execution of the `Point` program with two pieces of advice presented in Section 2.1 and above prints "`set:1`" first, "`set:6`" next, and then "`under move:5`" followed by "`6`" last. The call to `set` from the constructor is not advised by the advice using `cflow`.

4.2   Stack-Based Implementation

A straightforward implementation is to keep a stack of join points and to examine each join point in the stack from the top when `cflow` is evaluated.

We use the `stack` field in a join point to maintain the stack. Whenever a new join point is created, we record previous join point in the `stack` field (as is done as the last argument to `make-jp` in Figure 3). Since join points are passed along method calls, the join points chained by the `stack` field from the current one form a stack of join points. Restoring old join points is implicitly achieved by merely using the original join point in the caller's continuation.

The following definition shows the algorithm to interpret `cflow(p)` that simply runs down the stack until it finds a join point that matches to p. If it reaches the bottom of the stack, the result is false.

```
(define pointcut-match?
  (lambda (pc jp)
    (cond ((cflow-pointcut? pc)
           (let loop ((jp jp))
             (and (not (bottom? jp))
                  (or (pointcut-match? (pointcut-body pc) jp)
                      (loop (jp-stack jp))))))
          ...)))
```

The problem with this implementation is run-time overhead. In order to manage the stack, we have to push[6] a join point each time a new join point is created. Evaluation of cflow takes linear time in the stack depth at worst. When cflow pointcuts in a program match only specific join points, keeping the other join points in the stack and testing them is waste of time and space.

4.3   State-Based Implementation

A more optimized implementation of cflow in AspectJ compiler is to exploit its incremental nature. This idea can be explained by an example. Assume (as shown previously) that there is pointcut "cflow(call(void Point.move(int)))" in a program. The pointcut becomes true once move is called. Then, until the control returns from move (or another call to move is taken place), the truth value of the pointcut is unchanged. This means that the system only needs managing the state of each cflow(p) and updating that state at the beginning and the end of join points that make p true. Note that the state should be managed by a stack because it has to be rewound to its previous state upon returning from actions.

This state-based optimization can be explained in the following regards:

- It avoids repeatedly matching cflow bodies to the same join point in the stack by evaluating bodies of cflow upon creation of each join point, and recording the result.
- It makes static evaluation (*i.e.*, compilation) of cflow bodies possible because they are evaluated at each shadow of join points. As a result, management of a cflow state is only taken place at shadows of join points matching to the body of cflow.
- It evaluates cflow pointcut in constant time by merely peeking the top of a stack of states for each cflow pointcut.

It is straightforward to implement this idea in the PA interpreter. Figure 7 outlines the algorithm. Before running a subject program, the system collects all cflow pointcuts in the program, including those appear inside of other cflow pointcuts, and stores in a global variable *cflow-pointcuts*. The system also gives unique identifiers to them, which are accessible via pointcut-id. We rename the last field of a join point from stack to state, so that it stores the current states of all cflow pointcuts.

---

[6] By having a pointer to 'current' join point in parameters to each function, pop can be automatically done by returning from the function.

```
(define weave
  (lambda (jp action args)
    (let ((new-jp (update-states *cflow-pointcuts* jp)))
      ...the body of original weave...)))
(define update-states
  (lambda (pcs jp)
    (fold (lambda (pc njp) ;; fold: ('a*'b->'a)*'a*'b list->'a
            (let ((env (pointcut-match? (pointcut-body pc jp))))
              (if env (update-state njp (pointcut-id pc) env)
                      njp)))
          jp pcs)))
(define pointcut-match?
  (lambda (pc jp)
    (cond ((cflow-pointcut? pc) (lookup-state jp (pointcut-id pc)))
          ...)))
```

Fig. 7. State-based Implementation of cflow. (update-state *jp id new-state*) returns a copy of *jp* in which *id*'s state is changed to *new-state*. (lookup-state *jp id*) returns the state of *id* in *jp*.

When evaluation of an expression creates a join point, it first updates the states of all cflow pointcuts by wrapping weave by calling function update-states. The function update-states evaluates the body of each cflow pointcut, and updates the state only if the result is true. Otherwise, the state is unchanged. Therefore, after partial evaluation, the code for updating state is also eliminated when the body of the cflow is statically determined as false. The conditional case for cflow pointcuts in pointcut-match? merely looks up the state in the current join point.

Support for cflowbelow pointcuts is to extend the state to a pair of states. We omit details due to space limitation.

Those two stack- and state-based implementations can also be understood as initial- and final-algebra representations[18, etc.] of join points. The stack-based implementation defines a join point as the following data structure:

```
(define-struct jp (kind name target args stack))
```

By noticing that the stack field of join points is accessed only for matching the join points to the cflow pointcuts in the program, the structure can take a final-algebra representation:

```
(define-struct jp (kind name target args r1 r2 ... rn))
```

where *ri* is the result of pointcut-match? on the *i*'th cflow pointcut in the program. This is exactly what we have done for the state-based implementation.

4.4   Compilation Result

Figures 8 shows excerpts of compiled code for the Point program with the two advice definitions shown before. The compiler gave _g1 to the cflow pointcut as its identifier.

```
(let* ((val7 ...create a point object ...);----compiled code of p.move(5)
       (args9 '(5))
       (jp8 (make-jp this1 args9 (jp-state jp3))))
  (if (types-match? args9 '(int))
      (begin (execute* (lookup-method (object-class val7) 'move)
                       val7 args9
                       (state-update jp8 '_g1 (new-env '(w) args9)))
             ... write and newline ...)
      ... omitted ...))
(define point-move ;-----------------------compiled code of Point.move
  (lambda (this1 args2 jp3)
    (let* ((args5 (list (+ (get-field this1 'x) (car args2))))
           (jp6 (make-jp this1 args5 (jp-state jp3))))
      (if (types-match? args5 '(int))
          (begin (write "set:") (write (car args5)) (newline)
                 (let* ((val7 (execute* (lookup-method (object-class this1)
                                                       'set)
                                        this1 args5 jp6))
                        (env8 (state-lookup jp6 '_g1)))
                   (if env8 (begin (write "under move:")
                                   (write (lookup env8 'w)) (newline)))
                   val7))
          ...omitted...)))))
```

Fig. 8. Compiled code of p.move(5) and Point.main with cflow advice.

The first expression corresponds to p.move(5); in Point.main. Since the method call to move makes the state of the cflow to true, the compiled code updates the state of _g1 to an environment created by args pointcut in the join point, and passes the updated join point to the method.

The next function shows the compiled move method. The second if expression and the preceding state-lookup are for the advice using cflow. It evaluates the cflow pointcut by merely looking its state up, and runs the body of advice if the pointcut is true. The value of variable w, which is bound by args pointcut in cflow, is taken from the recorded state of cflow pointcut. Since the state is updated when move is to be called, it gives the argument value to move method.

To summarize, our scheme compiles a program with cflow pointcuts into one with state update operations at each join point that matches the sub-pointcut of each cflow pointcut, and state look-ups in the guard of advice bodies. By comparing the compiled code with the one generated by AspectJ compiler, we observe that those two compilation frameworks insert update operations for the cflow states into the same places.

5   Related Work

In reflective languages, some crosscutting concerns can be controlled through meta-programming[8,16]. Several studies successfully compiled reflective programs by using partial evaluation[2,11,12]. It is more difficult to ensure successful compilation in reflective languages because the programmer can write arbitrary meta-programs.

Wand, Kiczales and Dutchyn presented a formal model of the procedural version of PA[19]. Our model is based on this, and used it for compilation and optimizing `cflow` pointcuts.

Douence et al. showed an operational semantics of an AOP system[6]. In their system, a 'monitor' pattern matches a stream of events from a program execution, and invokes advice code when matches. A program transformation system inserts code into the monitored program so that it triggers the monitor. In our scheme, partial evaluator automatically performs this insertion.

Andrews proposed process algebras as a formal basis of AOP languages[1], in which advice execution is represented as synchronized processes. 'Compilation' can be understood as removal of the synchronization. However, our experience suggests that transformation techniques as powerful as partial evaluation would be necessary to properly remove run-time checks.

6   Conclusion and Future Work

In this paper, we presented a compilation model to an aspect-oriented programming (AOP) language based on operational semantics and partial evaluation techniques. The model explains issues in AOP compilers including identifying join point shadows, compiling-out pointcuts and recursively applying advice. It also explains the optimized `cflow` implementation in AspectJ compiler.

The use of partial evaluation allows us to keep simple operational semantics and to relate the semantics to compilation. It also helped us to understand the data dependency in our interpreter by means of its binding-time analysis. We believe this approach would be also useful to prototyping new AOP features with effective compilation in mind.

Although our language supports only core features of practical AOP languages, we believe that this work could bridge between formal studies and practical design and implementation of AOP languages.

Future directions of this study could include the following topics. Optimization algorithms could be studied for AOP programs based on our model, for example, elimination of more run-time checks with the aid of static analysis[15]. Our model could be refined into more formal systems so that we could relate between semantics and compilation with correctness proofs. Our system could also be applied to design and test new AOP features.

Acknowledgments. The authors are grateful to Kenichi Asai, Oege de Moor, Kris de Volder, Mitchell Wand and participants of FOAL2002 workshop for their comments on the previous version the paper. The discussion on the initial- and final-algebra representations was first pointed out by Mitchell Wand. We would also like to thank the anonymous reviewers for their comments. Most of the work is carried out during the first author's visit to University of British Columbia.

References

1. James H. Andrews. Process-algebraic foundations of aspect-oriented programming. In Yonezawa and Matsuoka [20], pages 187–209.
2. Kenichi Asai, Satoshi Matsuoka, and Akinori Yonezawa. Duplication and partial evaluation – for a better understanding of reflective languages –. *Lisp and Symbolic Computation*, 9:203–241, 1996.
3. Lodewijk Bergmans and Mehmet Aksit. Composing crosscutting concerns using composition filters. *Communications of the ACM*, 44(10):51–57, October 2001.
4. Anders Bondorf. Improving binding times without explicit CPS-conversion. In *ACM Conferenceon Lisp and Functional Programming*, pages 1–10, 1992.
5. Yvonne Coady, Gregor Kiczales, Mike Feeley, and Greg Smolyn. Using AspectC to improve the modularity of path-specific customization in operating system code. In *FSE-9*, pages 88–98, 2001.
6. Rémi Douence, Olivier Motelet, and Mario Südholt. A formal definition of cross-cuts. In Yonezawa and Matsuoka [20], pages 170–186.
7. Yoshihiko Futamura. Partial evaluation of computation process—an approach to a compiler-compiler. *Higher-Order and Symbolic Computation*, 12(4):381–391, 1999. Reprinted from *Systems, Computers, Controls*, 2(5):45–50, 1971.
8. Gregor Kiczales, Jim des Rivières, and Daniel G. Bobrow. *The Art of the Metaobject Protocol*. MIT Press, 1991.
9. Gregor Kiczales, Erik Hilsdale, Jim Hugunin, Mik Kersten, Jeffrey Palm, and William G. Griswold. An overview of AspectJ. In *ECOOP 2001*, pages 327–353, 2001.
10. Gregor Kiczales, John Lamping, Anurag Menhdhekar, Chris Maeda, Cristina Lopes, Jean-Marc Loingtier, and John Irwin. Aspect-oriented programming. In *ECOOP '97*, pages 220–242, 1997.
11. Hidehiko Masuhara, Satoshi Matsuoka, Kenichi Asai, and Akinori Yonezawa. Compiling away the meta-level in object-oriented concurrent reflective languages using partial evaluation. In *OOPSLA'95*, pages 300–315, 1995.
12. Hidehiko Masuhara and Akinori Yonezawa. Design and partial evaluation of meta-objects for a concurrent reflective language. In *ECOOP'98*, pages 418–439, 1998.
13. Doug Orleans and Karl Lieberherr. DJ: Dynamic adaptive programming in Java. In Yonezawa and Matsuoka [20], pages 73–80.
14. Harold Ossher and Peri Tarr. Multi-dimensional separation of concerns using hyperspaces. Research Report 21452, IBM, April 1999.
15. Damien Sereni and Oege de Moor. Static analysis of aspects. In *AOSD2003*, 2003.
16. Brian Cantwell Smith. Reflection and semantics in Lisp. In *Conference record of Symposium on Principles of Programming Languages*, pages 23–35, 1984.
17. Peter J. Thiemann. Cogen in six lines. In *ICFP'96*, 1996.
18. Mitchell Wand. Final algebra semantics and data type extension. *Journal of Computer and System Sciences*, 19:27–44, 1979.
19. Mitchell Wand, Gregor Kiczales, and Chris Dutchyn. A semantics for advice and dynamic join points in aspect-oriented programming. In *Proceedings of FOAL2002*, pages 1–8, 2002.
20. Akinori Yonezawa and Satoshi Matsuoka, editors. *Third International Conference Reflection 2001*, volume 2192 of *Lecture Notes in Computer Science*, 2001.

A Pattern Matching Compiler for Multiple Target Languages

Pierre-Etienne Moreau[1], Christophe Ringeissen[1], and Marian Vittek[2]

[1] LORIA-INRIA, 615, rue du Jardin Botanique,
BP 101, 54602 Villers-lès-Nancy Cedex France
{moreau,ringeiss}@loria.fr, elan.loria.fr/tom
[2] Institut of Informatica Mlynska dolina,
842 15 Bratislava, Slovakia
vittek@fmph.uniba.sk

Abstract. Many processes can be seen as transformations of tree-like data structures. In compiler construction, for example, we continuously manipulate trees and perform tree transformations. This paper introduces a pattern matching compiler (TOM): a set of primitives which add pattern matching facilities to imperative languages such as C, Java, or Eiffel. We show that this tool is extremely non-intrusive, lightweight and useful to implement tree transformations. It is also flexible enough to allow the reuse of existing data structures.

1   Introduction

For the compiler construction, there is an obvious need for programming transformation of structured documents like trees or terms: parse trees, abstract syntax trees (ASTs for short). In this paper, our aim is to present a tool which is particularly well-suited for programming various transformations on trees/terms. In the paper we will often talk about "term" instead of "tree" due to the one-to-one correspondence between these two notions. Our tool results from our experience on using existing programming languages and programming paradigms to implement transformations of terms.

In declarative (logic/functional) programming languages, we may find some built-in support to manipulate structured expressions or terms. For instance, in functional programming, a transformation can be conveniently implemented as a function declared by pattern matching [2,6,12],where a set of patterns represents the different forms of terms we are interested in. A pattern may contain variables (or holes) to schematize arbitrary terms. Given a term to transform, the execution mechanism consists in finding a pattern that *matches* the term. When a match is found, variables are initialized and the code related to the pattern is executed. Thanks to the mechanism of pattern matching, one can implement a transformation in a declarative way, thus reducing the risk to implement it in the wrong way.

For efficiency reasons, it may be interesting to implement similar tree-like transformations using (low-level) imperative programming languages for which

G. Hedin (Ed.): CC 2003, LNCS 2622, pp. 61–76, 2003.

efficient compilers exist. Unfortunately, in such languages, there are no built-in facilities to manipulate term structures and to perform pattern matching. There are two common solutions to this problem.

One possibility would be to enrich an existing imperative programming language with pattern matching facilities [5,7,8,13]. This hard-wired approach ties users to a specific programming language. The situation is thus little better than that in declarative languages. Furthermore, because terms are built-in, user-defined data structures must be converted to the term structure. Such marshalling complicates the user's program, and it incurs a significant performance penalty.

A simpler solution would be to develop a special library implementing pattern matching functionality. This approach is followed for example in the ASF+SDF group [10] where a C library called ATERMS [9] has been developed. In this library, pattern matching is implemented via a function called `ATmatch`, which consists in matching a term against a single pattern represented by a string or a term. Therefore, it is possible to define a transformation by pattern matching, thanks to a sequence of `if-then-else` instructions, where each condition is a call to the `ATmatch` function. But this approach has three drawbacks. First, matching is performed sequentially: patterns are tried one by one. This can be rather inefficient for a large number of patterns. Second, terms and patterns are untyped, and thus may be error prone. Third, the programming language and the data structure are imposed by the library, and so the programmer cannot use his favorite language as well as his own data structure to represent terms.

To solve the deficiencies of the above two solutions, and in particular for the sake of efficiency, we are interested in the *compilation* of pattern matching. By compilation we mean an approach where all patterns are compiled together producing a *matching automaton*. This automaton then performs matching against all patterns simultaneously. Our research on this topic is guided by the following concerns:

- How to efficiently compile different forms of pattern matching? We are concerned by simple syntactic matching but also by matching modulo an equational theory. In such a case, for example a pattern x+3 can match expression 3+7 thanks to commutativity of plus.
- How to implement compilation of pattern matching in a uniform way for a large class of programming languages and for any representation of terms?

To tackle the above mentioned problems, we develop a non-intrusive pattern matching compiler called TOM. Its design follows our experiences on the efficient compilation of rule-based systems [3,11]. Our tool can be viewed as a YACC-like compiler translating patterns into executable pattern matching automata. Similarly to YACC, when a match is found, the corresponding "semantic action" (a sequence of instructions written in an imperative language) is triggered and executed. In a way, we can say that TOM translates a *declarative-imperative* function – defined by pattern matching and imperative instructions – into a *fully imperative* function. The resulting function can be integrated to an application written in a classical language such as C, Java, or Eiffel, called the *target language* in the rest of the document. In this paper, we illustrate the different advantages of the approach implemented by TOM, namely:

Efficiency. The gain of efficiency follows from the compilation of matching as implemented in TOM.

Flexibility. When trying to integrate a black-box tool in an existing system, one of the main bottlenecks comes from data conversion and the flexibility offered to the user. One of the main originalities of our system is its independence of term representation. The programmer can use (or re-use) his own data structures for terms/trees and then execute matching upon those data structures. We propose to access terms using only a simple *Application Programming Interface* (API) defined by the user.

Generality. TOM is able to consider multiple target languages (C, Java, and Eiffel). TOM is implemented in TOM itself as a series of AST transformations. The code generation is performed at the very end, depending on the target language we are interested in. Hence, the target language is really a parameter of TOM.

Expressivity. TOM supports non-linear patterns and equational matching like modern rule-based programming languages. Currently, we have implemented pattern matching with list operators. This form of associative matching with neutral element is very useful for practical applications. The main difference with standard (syntactic) matching is that a single variable may have multiple assignments.

The paper is organized as follows: Section 2 motivates the main features of TOM on a very simple example. In Section 3, we present the main language constructs and their precise meanings. Further applications are described in Section 4. Since TOM is non-intrusive, it can be used in the context of existing applications to implement in a declarative way some functionalities which can be naturally expressed as transformations of terms (Section 4.1). Furthermore, we show how TOM is used in designing a compiler, via some transformations of ASTs performed by pattern matching: in fact, this example is the current implementation of TOM itself (Section 4.2). Section 5 presents some related work and Section 6 concludes with final remarks and future work.

2   What Is Tom?

In this section, we outline the main characteristics of TOM and we illustrate its usage on a very simple example specifying a well-known algebraic data type, namely the Naturals.

TOM does not really define a new language: it is rather a language extension which adds new matching primitives to an existing imperative language. From an implementation point of view, it is a compiler which accepts different *native languages*: C, Java, and Eiffel. The compilation process consists of translating new matching constructs into the underlying native language. Since the native language and the *target language* are identical and only introduced constructs are expanded, the presented tool can also be seen as a kind of preprocessor. On the other hand, the support of multiple target languages, and the fact that the input program has to be completely parsed before the transformation process can begin, make us consider TOM as a compiler.

For expository reasons, we assume that TOM only adds one new construct: %match. This construct is similar to the match primitive found in ML and related languages: given a term (called subject) and a list of pairs: pattern-action, the match primitive selects a pattern that matches the subject and performs the associated action. This construct may thus be seen as an extension of the classical switch/case construct. The main difference is that the discrimination occurs on a *term* and not on atomic values like characters or integers: the patterns are used to discriminate and retrieve information from an algebraic data structure.

To give a better understanding of TOM's features, let us consider a simple symbolic computation (addition) defined on Peano integers represented by *zero* and *successor*. When using Java as the native language, the sum of two integers can be described in the following way:

```
Term plus(Term t1, Term t2) {
  %match(Nat t1, Nat t2) {
    x,zero    -> { return x; }
    x,suc(y) -> { return suc(plus(x,y)); }
  }
}
```

This example should be read as follows: given two terms t_1 and t_2 (that represent Peano integers), the evaluation of plus returns the sum of t_1 and t_2. This is implemented by pattern matching: t_1 is matched by x, t_2 is possibly matched by the two patterns *zero* and *suc(y)*. When *zero* matches t_2, the result of the addition is x (with $x = t_1$, instantiated by matching). When *suc(y)* matches t_2, this means that t_2 is rooted by a *suc* symbol: the subterm y is added to x and the successor of this number is returned. The definition of plus is given in a functional programming style, but the plus function can be used in Java to perform computations. This first example illustrates how the %match construct can be used in conjunction with the considered native language.

In order to understand the choices we have made when designing TOM, it is important to consider TOM as a *restricted* compiler: it is not necessary to parse the native language in detail in order to be able to replace the %match constructs by a sequence of native language instructions (Java in this example). This could be considered as a kind of island parsing, where only the TOM constructs are parsed in detail. The first phase of the transformation process consists of *reading* the program: during this phase, the text is read and TOM constructs are recognized, whereas remaining parts are considered as target language constructs. The output of this first phase is a tree which contains two kinds of nodes: *target language nodes* and TOM *construct nodes*. When applied to the previous example, we get the following program with a unique TOM node, represented by a box as follows:

```
Term plus(Term t1, Term t2) {
  %match(Nat t1, Nat t2) {
    x,zero   ->           { return x; }
    x,suc(y) ->           { return suc(plus(x,y)); }
  }
}
```

TOM never uses any semantic information of the *target language nodes* during the compilation process, it does not inspect nor modify the source language part. It only replaces the TOM constructs by instructions of the native language. In particular, the previous `%match` construct will be replaced by two nested `if-then-else` constructs.

At this point, it is interesting to note that `plus` is a function which takes two `Term` data structures as arguments, whereas the matching construct is defined on the algebraic data type `Nat`. This remark introduces the second generic aspect of TOM: the matching can be performed on any data structure. For this purpose, the user has to define its term representation and the mapping between the concrete representation and the algebraic data type used in matching constructs.

To make our example complete, we have to define the term representation `Term` and the algebraic data type which defines the sort Nat and three operators: $\{zero :\mapsto Nat, \quad suc : Nat \mapsto Nat, \quad plus : Nat \times Nat \mapsto Nat\}$

For simplicity, we consider in this example that the ATERM library [9] is used for term representation. This library is a concrete implementation of the Annotated Terms data type (ATERMS). In particular it defines an interface to create and manipulate term data structures. Furthermore, it offers the possibility to represent function symbols, to get the arity of such a symbol, to get the root symbol of a term, to get a given subterm, *etc.* The main characteristic of this library is to provide a garbage collector and to ensure maximal sharing of terms. Using this library, it becomes easy to give a concrete implementation of function symbols $zero$ and suc (the second argument of `makeAFun` defines the arity of the operator): `AFun f_zero = makeAFun("zero",0)` and `AFun f_suc = makeAFun("suc",1)`. The representation of the constant $zero$, for example, is given by `makeAppl(f_zero)`. Similarly, given a Peano integer `t`, its successor can be built by `makeAppl(f_suc,t)`. So far we have shown how to represent data using the ATERM library, and how defining matching with TOM, but, we have yet to reveal how these two notions are related. Given a Peano integer `t` of sort `Term`, we have to define how to get its root symbol (using `getAFun` for example) and how to know if this symbol corresponds to the algebraic function symbol suc, intuitively `getAFun(t).isEqual(f_suc)`.

This mapping from the algebraic data type to the concrete implementation is done via the introduction of new primitives, `%op` and `%typeterm`, which are described in the next section.

3   The Tom Language: Main Constructs

In the previous section we introduced the `match` construct of TOM via an example. In this section, we give an in-depth presentation of TOM by explaining all existing constructs and their behavior. As mentioned previously, TOM introduces a new construct (%match) which can be used by the programmer to decompose by pattern matching a tree-like data structure (an ATERM for example). TOM also introduces a second family of constructs which is used to define the mapping between the algebraic abstract data type and the concrete implementation. We distinguish two main constructs: %typeterm and %op are used to define respectively algebraic sorts and many-sorted signature of the algebraic constructors.

3.1   Sort Definition

In TOM, terms, variables, and patterns are many-sorted. Their algebraic sorts have to be introduced by the %typeterm primitive. In addition to this primitive, the mapping from algebraic sorts to concrete sorts (the target language type, such as Term) has to be defined. Several sub-functions are used for this purpose. To support the intuition, let us consider again the Naturals example where the *Nat* algebraic sort is implemented by ATERMS. One possible mapping is the following:

```
%typeterm Nat {
   implement { Term }
   get_fun_sym(t)     { t.getAFun()      }
   cmp_fun_sym(s1,s2) { s1.isEqual(s2)   }
   get_subterm(t,n)   { t.getArgument(n) }
   equals(t1,t2)      { t1.isEqual(t2)   }
}
```

- The implement construct describes how the algebraic type is implemented. The target language part (written between braces: '{' and '}') is never parsed, it is only used by the compiler to declare some functions and variables. This is analogous to the treatment of semantic actions in YACC.
  Since in this example we focus our attention on the ATERM library, we implement the algebraic data type using the "implement { Term }" construct. But, if we suppose that another data structure is used, "struct myTerm*" for example, the "implement { struct myTerm* }" construct should be used to define the mapping.
- get_fun_sym(t) denotes a function (parameterized by a term variable t) that should return the root symbol of the term referenced by t.
  As in the C preprocessor, the body of this definition is not parsed, but the formal parameter (t) can be used in the body (t.getAfun() in our example).
- cmp_fun_sym(s1,s2) denotes a predicate (parameterized by two symbol variables s_1 and s_2). This predicate should return true if the symbols s_1 and s_2 are "equal". The true value should correspond to the built-in true value of the considered target language. (true in Java, and something different from 0 in C for example).
- get_subterm(t,n) denotes a function (parameterized by a term variable t and an integer n). This function should return the n-th subterm of t. This

function is only called with a value of n between 0 and the arity of the root symbol of t minus 1.

– `equals(t1,t2)` denotes a predicate (parameterized by two term variables t_1 and t_2). Similarly to `cmp_fun_sym(s1,s2)`, this predicate should return `true` if terms t_1 and t_2 are "equal". This last optional definition is only used to compile non-linear patterns. It is not required when the specification does not contain such patterns.

When using the ATERM library, it is defined by "`{ t1.isEqual(t2) }`"

To clarify the presentation we only used the ATERMS data structure, but it should be noticed that any other data structure could be used as well. TOM is a multi target language compiler that supports C, Java, and Eiffel.

3.2   Constructor Definition

In TOM, the definition of a new operator is done via the `%op` construct. The many-sorted signature of the operator is given in a prefix notation. Let us consider the $suc : Nat \mapsto Nat$ operator for instance, its definition is: "`%op Nat suc(Nat)`". We stress once again that because TOM has no knowledge, the user has to describe how to represent the newly introduced operator:

– `fsym` defines the concrete representation of the constructor. The expression that parameterizes `fsym` should correspond to the expression returned by the function `get_fun_sym` applied to a term rooted by the considered symbol.
– `make(t1,...,tn)` denotes a function parameterized by n variables, where n is the arity of the considered symbol. This function should define how a term rooted by the considered symbol can be built. The definition of this function is optional since it is not used by TOM during the matching phase. However, when defined, it can be used by the programmer to simplify the construction of terms (see Section 3.4).

In our setting the definition of suc and $zero$ can be done as follows:

```
%op Nat zero {
   fsym { f_zero }
   make { makeAppl(f_zero) }
}
```

```
%op Nat suc(Nat) {
   fsym    { f_suc }
   make(t) { makeAppl(f_suc,t) }
}
```

When all needed operators are defined, it becomes possible to use them to define terms and patterns. Terms are written using standard prefix notation. By convention, all identifiers not defined as constants are seen as variables. Thus, the pattern `suc(y)` corresponds to the term $suc(y)$ where y is a variable, and the pattern `suc(zero)` corresponds to the Peano integer *one*.

3.3   The `%match` Construct

The `%match` construct is parameterized by a subject (a list of terms) on which the discrimination should be performed, and a body. As for the `switch/case` construct of C and Java, the body is a list of pairs: *pattern-action*. The pattern is a list of terms (with free variables) which are matched against a list of terms that compose the subject. When the *pattern* matches the subject, the free variables are instantiated and the corresponding *action* is executed. Note that this is a hybrid language construct, mixing two formalisms: the patterns are written in a pure algebraic specification style using constructors and variables, whereas the action parts are directly written in the native language, using the variables introduced by the patterns. Since TOM has no knowledge of what is done inside an action, the action part should be written in such way that the function has the desired behavior. In our Peano example, the suc(plus(x,y)) expression corresponds to a recursive call of the plus function while the suc function is supposed to build a successor. Note that this part has nothing to do with TOM: it only depends on the considered target language. The semantic of the %match construct is as follows:

Matching: given a subject, the execution control is transferred to the first pattern that matches the subject. If no such pattern exists, the evaluation of the %match construct is finished.

Selected pattern: given a pattern which matches the subject, the associated action is executed, using the free variables instantiated during the matching phase. If the execution control is transferred outside the %match construct (by a goto, break, or return statement for example), the matching process ends. Otherwise, the execution control is transferred to the next *pattern-action* whose pattern matches the subject.

End: when no more pattern matches the subject, the %match construct ends, and the execution control is transferred to the next target language instruction.

3.4   Making Terms

In addition to sort definition, construction definition and matching constructs, TOM provides a mechanism to easily build ground terms over the defined signature. This mechanism, called *back-quote* (and written ''), can be used in any target language block as a kind of escape mechanism. The syntax is simple: the *back-quote* is followed by a well-formed term written in prefix notation. The last closing parenthesis denotes the end of the escape mechanism.

Considering the previously defined addition function on Peano integers, the right-hand side could have been written 'suc(plus(x,y)) and the construction of the suc node would have been done by TOM, using the make attribute introduced in Section 3.2.

3.5   Equational Matching

An important feature of TOM is to support equational matching. In particular, list matching, also known as associative matching with neutral element.

Since a list can be efficiently and naturally represented by a (head,tail) tuple, TOM provides an extra construct for defining associative data structures: the %typelist primitive. When defining such a structure, three extra access functions have to be introduced: get_head, get_tail and is_empty:

- get_head(l) denotes a function parameterized by a list variable l that should return the first element of the list l. When using the TermList data type, the definition is "get_head(l) { l.getHead() }".
- get_tail(l) denotes a function parameterized by a list variable l that should return the tail of the list l. Using ATERMS, it can be defined by "get_tail(l) { l.getTail() }".
- is_empty(l) denotes a predicate parameterized by a list variable l. This predicate should return true if the list l contains no element. One more time, the mapping to ATERMS is obvious: "is_empty(l) { l.isEmtpy() }".

Similarly to the %op construct, TOM provides the %oplist construct to define list operators. When using such a construct, the user has to specify how a list can be built. This is done via the two following functions:

- make_empty() should return an empty list. This object corresponds to the neutral element of the considered data structure.
- make_insert(e,l) should return a new list l' where the element e is inserted at the head of the list l (i.e. expressions equals(get_head(l'),e) and equals(get_tail(l'),l) should be true).

One characteristic of list-matching is the possibility to return several matches. Thus, the semantic of the %match construct has to be extended as follows:

Selected pattern: given a pattern which matches the subject, for each computed match, the list of free variables is instantiated and the action part is executed. If the execution control is transferred outside the %match construct the matching process ends. Otherwise, *another match is computed*. When no more match is available, the execution control is transferred to the next *pattern-action* whose pattern matches the subject.

This principle can be used to implement a sorting algorithm using a conditional pattern matching definition. In the following, we consider an associative data structure List and an associative operator conc:

```
%typeterm List {
  implement { TermList }
  get_fun_sym(t)      { f_conc     }
  cmp_fun_sym(t1,t2) { t1 == t2    }
  equals(l1,l2)       { l1 == l2   }
  get_head(l)         { l.getFirst() }
  get_tail(l)         { l.getNext()  }
  is_empty(l)         { l.isEmpty()  }
}
```

```
%oplist List conc( Term* ) {
  fsym                { f_conc }
  make_empty()        { makeList() }
  make_insert(e,l)    { l.insert(e) }
}
```

Considering that two `Term` elements can be compared by a function `greaterThan`, a sorting algorithm can be implemented as follows:

```
public TermList sort(TermList l) {
  %match(List l) {
    conc(X1*,x,X2*,y,X3*) -> {
      if(greaterThan(x,y)) { return 'sort(conc(X1*,y,X2*,x,X3*)); }
    }
    _ -> { return l; }
  }
}
```

In this example, one can remark the use of *list variables*, annotated by a '*': such a variable should be instantiated by a (possibly empty) list. Given a partially sorted list, the `sort` function tries to find two elements x and y such that x is greater than y. If two such elements exist, they are swapped and the `sort` function is recursively applied. Otherwise, all other possible matches are tried (unsuccessfully). As a consequence, the first pattern-action is not exited by a `return` statement. Thus, as mentioned previously, the execution control is transferred to the next pattern-action whose pattern matches the subject (the second one in this example), and the sorted list l is returned.

4   Applications

4.1   Implementing Matching Operations Using Tom

As an example of using list matching, we consider the problem of retrieving information in a queue of messages containing two fields: destination and data. In our example, we define a function which looks for a particular kind of message: a message addressed to `b` and whose data has a given `subject`. To illustrate the flexibility of TOM, we no longer use the ATERM library, and all data structures are internally defined. Thus we use the language C, and we respectively consider `term` and `list` data structures to represent messages and queues.

```
struct term { int symbol;
              int arity;
        struct term **subterm;
};
%typeterm Term {
  implement { struct term* }
  get_fun_sym(t)      { t->symbol }
  cmp_fun_sym(t1,t2) { t1 == t2  }
  get_subterm(t,n) { t->subterm[n] }
}
%op Term a { fsym { A } }
%op Term b { fsym { B } }
%op Term subject(Term)
           { fsym { SUBJECT } }
%op Term msg(Term,Term)
           { fsym { MSG } }
```

```
struct list { struct term *head;
              struct list *tail; };
%typelist List {
  implement { struct list* }
  get_fun_sym(t)      { CONC       }
  cmp_fun_sym(t1,t2) { t1 == t2 }
  equals(l1,l2) { list_equal(l1,l2) }
  get_head(l)          { l->head   }
  get_tail(l)          { l->tail   }
  is_empty(l)        { (l == NULL) }
}
%oplist List conc( Term* ) {
  fsym                 { CONC      }
  make_empty()         { NULL      }
  make_insert(e,l) { cons(e,l)  }
}
```

In the following function, we use a list-matching pattern to search for a particular message in a given queue:

```
struct list *read_msg_for_b(struct list *queue,struct term *search_data) {
  %match(List queue) {
    conc(X1*,msg(b,subject(x)),X2*) -> {
      if(term_equal(x,search_data)) {
        print_term("read_msg: ",x);
        return `conc(X1*,X2*);
      }
    }
    _ -> { /* msg not found */ return queue; }
  }
}
```

In this function, when a message addressed to b is found but does not correspond to search_data, another match is computed (all possible instances of
X1, x and X2 are tried). If no match satisfies this condition, the default case is
executed.

4.2 Implementing Compilers and Transformation Tools

The presented language extension has an implementation: jtom[1]. One characteristic of this implementation is that it is written in TOM itself (Java+TOM to
be more precise).

Compiling a program consists in transforming this program (written in some
source language) into another equivalent program written in some *target language*. This transformation can be seen as a textual or syntactic transformation,
but in general, this transformation should be done at a more abstract level to
ensure the equivalence of the two programs. A good and well-known approach
consists in performing the transformation of the AST that represents the program.

Representing an AST can be done in a "traditional way" by defining a data
structure or a class (in an object oriented framework) for each kind of node.
Another interesting approach consists in representing this tree by a term. Such
an approach has several advantages. First, it is a universal representation for
every manipulated information. Second, compared to a collection of spreaded
objects in memory, a term can be more easily printed and exchanged with other
tools at any stage of the transformation. Last, all the information is always
available in the term itself.

Thus, given a program, its compilation can be seen as the transformation of
a term (the AST of the source language program) into another term (the AST
of the target language program). Transformation rules are usually expressed by
pattern matching, which is exactly what TOM is suited for.

The implementation of the TOM compiler is an application of this principle:
it is composed of several phases that respectively transform a term into another
one. The general layout of the compiler is shown in Figure 1.

As illustrated, four main compilation phases can be distinguished. Each phase
corresponds to an abstract syntax whose signature is defined in TOM, using the
signature definition formalism presented in Sections 3.1 and 3.2.

---

[1] available at http://elan.loria.fr/tom

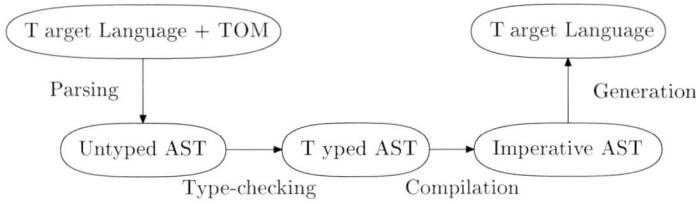

Fig. 1. General layout of the Tom compiler

Parsing. The Tom parser reads a program enriched by Tom constructs and generates an Abstract Syntax Tree. As mentioned previously, the source language is a superset of the target language, and we have the following particular equation: `source language = target language + TOM constructs.`

In order to be as general as possible, the current Tom parser is only slightly dependent on the supported target languages. In particular, it does not include a full native language parser: it should only be able to parse comments, strings, and should recognize the beginning and the end of a block ('{' and '}' in C or Java). Using this knowledge, the parser can detect and parse all Tom constructs. The resulting AST is a list of nodes of two kinds: (1) A *Target Language Node* is a string that contains a piece of code written in the target language. This node does not contain any Tom construct; (2) A Tom *Construct Node* is an AST that represents a Tom construct. The role of the Tom compiler consists in replacing all Tom *Construct Nodes* by new *Target Language Nodes*, without modifying, and even parsing, the remaining *Target Language Nodes*. When considering the Naturals example, after parsing, the pattern $suc(y)$ is represented by the following AST:

```
Term(Appl(Name("suc"),[Appl(Name("y"),[])]))
```

Informally, this means that an operator called `suc` is applied to a list of subterms. This list is made of a unique term corresponding to the application of `y` to the empty list. At this current stage, it is not yet possible to know whether `y` is a variable or a constant. We can also remark that there is no type information.

Type-checking. For sake of simplicity, no type information is needed when writing a matching construct. In particular, Tom variables do not need to be declared, and the definition of the signature can appear anywhere. Consequently, any constant not declared in the signature naturally becomes a variable. Unfortunately, it makes the compilation process harder. During this phase, the Tom type-checker determines the type of each Tom construct and modifies the AST accordingly. The output formalism of this phase is a typed Tom AST as exemplified below:

```
Term(Appl(Symbol(Name("suc"),
       TypesToType([Type(TomType("Nat"),TLType("Term"))],
                Type(TomType("Nat"),TLType("Term"))), TLCode("f_suc")),
       [Variable(Name("y"),Type(TomType("Nat"),TLType("Term")))]))
```

We can notice that the AST syntax (`Term`, `Appl`, `Name`, *etc.*) has been extended by several new constructors, such as `Symbol`, `TypesToType`, `Variable`, *etc.* A term corresponds now to the application of a *symbol* (and no longer a *name*) to a list of subterms. A symbol is defined by its name, its profile and its implementation in the target language (`f_suc` in this example). We can also notice that the profile contains two kinds of type information: the algebraic specification type (`Nat`) and the implementation of this type in the target language (`Term`).

Compilation. This phase is the kernel of the TOM compiler: it replaces all TOM constructs by a sequence of imperative programming language instructions. To remain independent of the target language, this transformation is performed at the abstract level: instead of generating concrete target language instructions, the compilation phase generates abstract instructions such as `DeclareVariable`, `AssignVariable`, `IfThenElse`. The output formalism also contains some abstract instructions to access the term data structure, such as `GetFunctionSymbol`, `GetSubterm`, *etc.* After compiling the previous term, we get the following AST (for a better readability, some parts have been removed and replaced by `"..."`):

```
CompiledMatch([
  Declaration(Variable(Position([match1,1]),
              Type(TomType("Nat"),TLType("Term})))),
  Assign(Variable(Position([match1,1]),...),
         Variable(Name("t2"),Type(TomType("Nat"),TLType("Term"))))
  ...
  IfThenElse(
    EqualFunctionSymbol(Variable(Position([match1,1]),...),
                        Appl(Symbol(Name("suc"),...))),
    Assign(Variable(Position([match1,1,1]),...),
           GetSubterm(Variable(Position([match1,1]),...),0))
    ...
    Action([TL("return suc(plus(x,y));")]),
    ...
    // else part
  ) ...
)
```

The main advantage of this approach is that the algorithm for compiling pattern matching does not depend on neither the target language nor the term data structure. During this phase, a `match` construct is analyzed, and depending on its structure, abstract instructions are generated (a `Declaration` and an `Assignment` when a variable is encountered for example, or a `IfThenElse` when a constructor is found for example).

```
TermList genTermMatchAuto(Term term, TermList path, TermList actionList){
  %match(Term term) {
    Variable(_, termType) -> {
      assign = `Assign(term,Variable(Position(path),termType));
```

```
      action = 'Action(actionList);
      return assign.append(action);
    }
    UnamedVariable(termType) -> {
      action = 'Action(actionList);
      return action;
    }
    Appl(Symbol(...),termArgs) -> {
      // generate Declarations, Assignments and an IfThenElse
      failureList = makeList();
      ...
      succesList   = declList.append(assignList.append(automataList));
      cond = 'EqualFunctionSymbol(subjectVariableAST,term);
      return result.append('IfThenElse(cond,succesList,failureList));
    }
  }
}
```

Generation. This phase corresponds to the back-end generator: it produces a program written in the target language. The mapping between the abstract imperative language and the concrete target language is implemented by pattern matching. To each abstract instruction corresponds a pattern, and an associated action which generates the correct sequence of target language instructions. In Java and C for example, the pattern-action associated to the IfThenElse abstract instruction is:

```
  IfThenElse(cond,succes,failure) -> {
    prettyPrint("if(" + generate(cond) + ") {");
    generate(succes);
    prettyPrint("} else {");
    generate(failure);
    prettyPrint("}");
  }
```

Due to lack of space, we cannot give much more detail about the compilation of TOM. But, our experience clearly shows that the main interests of TOM can be characterized by the expressiveness and the efficiency introduced by the powerful matching constructs. In practice, the use of pattern matching and list-matching helps the programmer to clearly express the algorithms and, as illustrated in the following table, it reduces the size of the programs by a factor 2 or 3 in average. We presents statistics for three typical TOM applications, corresponding to the three main components of the system: the type-checker, the compiler, and the generator. For each component, we report the self-compilation time in the last column (measured on a Pentium III, 1200 MHz). The first two columns give some size information. For instance, the type-checker consists of 555 lines including 40 pattern matching constructs. After being compiled, the generated Java code consists of 1484 lines. As illustrated by the compilation speed, the efficiency of the generated code is sufficient in practice for this kind of application.

Specification	Tom (patterns/lines)	Generated Java code (lines)	Tom to Java compilation time (s)
Tom checker	40/555	1484	0.331
Tom compiler	81/1490	2833	0.600
Tom generator	87/1124	3804	0.812

5   Related Work

Several systems have been developed in order to integrate pattern matching and transformation facilities into imperative languages. For instance, R++ [1] and App [7] are preprocessors for C++: the first one adds production rule constructs to C++, whereas the second one extends C++ with a match construct. Prop [4] is a multi-paradigm extension of C++, including pattern matching constructs. Pizza [8] is a Java extension that supports parametric polymorphism, first-class functions, class cases and pattern matching. Finally, JaCo [13] is an extensible Java compiler written in an extension of itself: Java + extensible algebraic types.

All these approaches propose some very powerful constructs, but from our point of view, they are too powerful and less generic than Tom. In spirit, Prop, Pizza and JaCo are very close to Tom: they add pattern matching facilities to a classical imperative language, but the method of achieving this is completely different. Indeed, Prop, Pizza and JaCo are more intrusive than Tom: they really extend C++ and Java with several new pattern matching constructions. On the one hand, the integration is better and more transparent. But on the other hand, the term data structure cannot be user-defined: the pattern matching process can only act on internal data structures. This may be a drawback when one wants to extend an existing project, since it is hard to convince a user to program in a declarative way if the first thing to do is to translate the existing main data structures.

6   Conclusion and Further Work

In this paper we have presented a non-intrusive tool for extending existing programming languages with pattern matching. In our opinion, Tom is a key component for the implementation of rule-based language compilers, as well as for the design of program transformation tools, provided that programs are represented by terms (using for instance ATerms or XML representations). In this context, a prototype of ELAN compiler using Tom as back-end has already been successfully implemented for a subset of the language, and the Asf+Sdf group[2] and the ELAN group[3] are currently designing a common extensible compiler based on Tom.

For the sake of expressiveness, it is important to continue the integration of equational matching into Tom. For now, we have successfully considered the

---

[2] http://www.cwi.nl/projects/MetaEnv
[3] http://elan.loria.fr

case of list-matching, which was already supported by ASF+SDF. In the future, we still have to go beyond this first case-study by considering other more complicated and useful equational theories like Associativity-Commutativity and its extensions.

Acknowledgments. We would like to thank Mark van den Brand, Jurgen Vinju and Eelco Visser for fruitful discussions and comments on the design of TOM. We also thank the anonymous referees for valuable comments and suggestions that led to a substantial improvement of the paper.

References

1. J. M. Crawford, D. Dvorak, D. Litman, A. Mishra, and P. F. Patel-Schneider. Path-based rules in object-oriented programming. In *Proceedings of the Eighth Innovative Applications of Artificial Intelligence Conference*, pages 490–497, Menlo Park, 1996. AAAI Press / MIT Press.
2. P. Hudak, S. L. Peyton Jones, and P. Wadler (editors). Report on the Programming Language Haskell, A Non-strict Purely Functional Language (Version 1.2). *SIGPLAN Notices*, Mar, 1992.
3. H. Kirchner and P.-E. Moreau. Promoting rewriting to a programming language: A compiler for non-deterministic rewrite programs in associative-commutative theories. *Journal of Functional Programming*, 11(2):207–251, 2001.
4. L. Leung. Prop homepage: `cs1.cs.nyu.edu/phd_students/leunga/prop.html`.
5. J. Liu and A. C. Myers. Jmatch: Iterable abstract pattern matching for java. In V. Dahl and P. Wadler, editors, *Proceedings of PADL'03*, volume 2562 of *LNCS*, pages 110–127. Springer-Verlag, 2003.
6. R. Milner, M. Tofte, and R. Harper. *The definition of Standard ML*. MIT Press, 1990.
7. G. Nelan. App homepage: `www.primenet.com/~georgen/app.html`.
8. M. Odersky and P. Wadler. Pizza into Java: Translating theory into practice. In *Proceedings of the 24th ACM Symposium on Principles of Programming Languages (POPL'97)*, Paris, France, pages 146–159. ACM Press, USA, 1997.
9. M. G. J. van den Brand, H. A. de Jong, P. Klint, and P. Olivier. Efficient annotated terms. *Software-Practice and Experience*, 30:259–291, 2000.
10. M. G. J. van den Brand, P. Klint, and P. Olivier. Compilation and Memory Management for ASF+SDF. In *Proceedings of Compiler Construction, 8th International Conference*, volume 1575 of *LNCS*, pages 198–213. Springer, 1999.
11. M. Vittek. A compiler for nondeterministic term rewriting systems. In H. Ganzinger, editor, *Proceedings of RTA'96*, volume 1103 of *LNCS*, pages 154–168, New Brunswick (New Jersey), 1996. Springer-Verlag.
12. P. Weis, M. Aponte, A. Laville, M. Mauny, and A. Suárez. *The CAML Reference Manual*. INRIA-ENS, 1987.
13. M. Zenger and M. Odersky. Extensible algebraic datatypes with defaults. In *Proceedings of the 6th ACM SIGPLAN International Conference on functional Programming (ICFP'2001)*, Florence, Italy, pages 241–252. ACM Press, 2001.

A New One-Pass Transformation into Monadic Normal Form

Olivier Danvy

BRICS* Department of Computer Science, University of Aarhus
Ny Munkegade, Building 540, DK-8000 Aarhus C, Denmark
(danvy@brics.dk)

Abstract. We present a translation from the call-by-value λ-calculus to monadic normal forms that includes short-cut boolean evaluation. The translation is higher-order, operates in one pass, duplicates no code, generates no chains of thunks, and is properly tail recursive. It makes a crucial use of symbolic computation at translation time.

1 Introduction

Program transformation and code generators offer typical situations where symbolic computation makes it possible to merge several passes into one. The CPS transformation is a canonical example: it transforms a term in direct style into one in continuation-passing style (CPS) [39, 43]. It appears in several Scheme compilers, including the first one [30, 33, 42], where it is used in two passes: one for the transformation proper and one for the simplifications entailed by the transformation (the so-called "administrative redexes"). One-pass versions have been developed that perform administrative reductions at transformation time [2,15,48]. They form one of the first, if not the first, instances of higher-order and natively executable two-level specifications.

The notion of binding times was discovered early by Jones and Muchnick [27] in the context of programming languages. Later it proved instrumental for partial evaluation [28], for program analysis [37], and for code generation [50]. It was then soon noticed that two-level specifications (i.e., 'staged' [29], or 'binding-time separated' [35], or again 'binding-time analyzed' [25] specifications) were directly expressible in languages such as Lisp and Scheme that offer quasiquote and unquote—a metalinguistic capability that has since been rediscovered in 'C [19], cast in a typed setting in MetaML [45], and connected both to modal logic [18] and to temporal logic [17]. In Lisp, quasiquote and unquote are used chiefly to write macros [5], an early example of symbolic computation during code generation [32]. In partial evaluation [10, 26], two-level specifications are called 'generating extensions'. Nesting quasiquote and unquote yields macros that generate macros and multi-level generating extensions.

---

* Basic Research in Computer Science (www.brics.dk), funded by the Danish National Research Foundation.

G. Hedin (Ed.): CC 2003, LNCS 2622, pp. 77–89, 2003.

The goal of this article is to present a one-pass transformer into monadic normal forms [23, 36] that performs short-cut boolean evaluation, duplicates no code, generates no chains of thunks, and is properly tail recursive. We consider the following source language:

$$\Lambda^E \ni e ::= \ell \mid x \mid \lambda x.e \mid e\,e \mid \text{if } b \text{ then } e \text{ else } e$$
$$\Lambda^B \ni b ::= e \mid b \wedge b \mid b \vee b \mid \neg b \mid \text{if } b \text{ then } b \text{ else } b$$

We translate programs in this source language into programs in the following target language:

$$\Lambda^C_{ml} \ni c ::= \text{return } v \mid$$
$$\text{let } x = v\,v \text{ in } c \mid v\,v \mid$$
$$\text{if } v \text{ then } c \text{ else } c \mid$$
$$\text{let } x = \lambda().c \text{ in } c \mid x\,()$$
$$\Lambda^V_{ml} \ni v ::= \ell \mid x \mid \lambda x.c$$

The source language is that of the call-by-value λ-calculus with literals, conditional expressions, and computational effects. The target language is that of monadic normal forms (sometimes called A-normal forms [21]), with a syntactic separation between computations (c, the serious expressions) and values (v, the trivial expressions), as traditional since Reynolds and Moggi [36, 41]. The return production is the unit and the first let production is the bind of monadic style [47]. Computations are carried out by applications, which can either be named with a let expression or occur in tail position. Conditional expressions exclusively occur in tail position. The last two productions specify the declaration and activation of thunks, which are used to ensure that no code is duplicated.

For example, a source term such as

$$\lambda x.g_0\,(h_0\,(\text{if } (g_1\,(h_1\,x)) \vee x \text{ then } g_2\,(h_2\,x) \text{ else } x))$$

is translated into the following target term (automatically pretty printed in Standard ML for clarity), in one pass.

```
return (fn x => let val k0 = fn w1 => let val w2 = h0 w1
                                       in g0 w2
                                       end
                    val t5 = fn () => let val w3 = h2 x
                                          val w4 = g2 w3
                                      in k0 w4
                                      end
                    val w6 = h1 x
                    val w7 = g1 w6
                in if w7
                   then t5 ()
                   else if x
                        then t5 ()
                        else k0 x
                end)
```

In this target term, the source context $g_0 \ (h_0 \ [\cdot])$ is translated into the function
k0, where the outside call occurs tail recursively. Because of the disjunction in
the test, a thunk t5 is created for the then branch. In this thunk, the outside
call occurs tail recursively. The composition of g_1 and h_1 is sequentialized and
its result is tested. If it holds true, t5 is activated; otherwise, the second half
of the disjunction is tested. If it holds true, t5 is activated (the code for t5 is
shared). Otherwise, the value of x is passed to the (sequentialized) composition
of g_0 and h_0. Free variables (i.e., g_0, h_0, g_1, h_1, g_2, and h_2) have been translated
to themselves (i.e., g0, h0, g1, h1, g2, and h2, respectively).

Monadic normal forms offer the main advantages of CPS (i.e., all intermediate
results are named and their computation is sequentialized),[1] and they have been
used in compilers for functional languages [7, 6, 21, 22, 23, 38, 40, 46]. Therefore,
a one-pass transformation into monadic normal form with short-cut boolean
evaluation could well be of practical use (i.e., outside academia).

The rest of this article is organized as follows. We present a standard, two-
pass translation from the source language to the target language (Section 2),
and then its one-pass counterpart (Section 3). We then illustrate it (Section 4),
assess it (Section 5), and then review related work and conclude (Section 6).

2 A Standard, Two-Pass Translation

The first part of the translation is simple enough: it is the standard encoding of
the call-by-value λ-calculus into the computational metalanguage, straightfor-
wardly extended to handle conditional expressions.

$$\mathcal{E}_v[\![\ell]\!] = \text{return } \ell$$
$$\mathcal{E}_v[\![x]\!] = \text{return } x$$
$$\mathcal{E}_v[\![\lambda x.e]\!] = \text{return } \lambda x.\mathcal{E}_v[\![e]\!]$$
$$\mathcal{E}_v[\![e_0 \ e_1]\!] = \text{let } w_0 = \mathcal{E}_v[\![e_0]\!] \text{ in let } w_1 = \mathcal{E}_v[\![e_1]\!] \text{ in } w_0 \ w_1$$
$$\mathcal{E}_v[\![\text{if } b \text{ then } e_1 \text{ else } e_0]\!] = \text{if } \mathcal{B}_v[\![b]\!] \text{ then } \mathcal{E}_v[\![e_1]\!] \text{ else } \mathcal{E}_v[\![e_0]\!]$$

$$\mathcal{B}_v[\![e]\!] = \mathcal{E}_v[\![e]\!]$$
$$\mathcal{B}_v[\![b_1 \wedge b_2]\!] = \text{if } \mathcal{B}_v[\![b_1]\!] \text{ then } \mathcal{B}_v[\![b_2]\!] \text{ else } \textit{false}$$
$$\mathcal{B}_v[\![b_1 \vee b_2]\!] = \text{if } \mathcal{B}_v[\![b_1]\!] \text{ then } \textit{true} \text{ else } \mathcal{B}_v[\![b_2]\!]$$
$$\mathcal{B}_v[\![\neg b]\!] = \text{if } \mathcal{B}_v[\![b]\!] \text{ then } \textit{false} \text{ else } \textit{true}$$
$$\mathcal{B}_v[\![\text{if } b_2 \text{ then } b_1 \text{ else } b_0]\!] = \text{if } \mathcal{B}_v[\![b_2]\!] \text{ then } \mathcal{B}_v[\![b_1]\!] \text{ else } \mathcal{B}_v[\![b_0]\!]$$

The second pass of the translation consists in performing monadic simplifications [24] and in unnesting conditional expressions until the simplified term
belongs to Λ_{ml}^C.

---

[1]   The jury is still out about the other advantages of CPS [40].

3   A One-Pass Translation

In this section, we build on the full one-pass transformation into monadic normal form for the call-by-value λ-calculus:

$$
\begin{aligned}
\mathcal{E} \; &: \; \Lambda^E \to \Lambda^C_{ml} \\
\mathcal{E}[\![\ell]\!] \; &= \; \underline{\text{return}} \; \ell \\
\mathcal{E}[\![x]\!] \; &= \; \underline{\text{return}} \; x \\
\mathcal{E}[\![\lambda x.e]\!] \; &= \; \underline{\text{return}} \; \underline{\lambda} x.\mathcal{E}[\![e]\!] \\
\mathcal{E}[\![e_0 \; e_1]\!] \; &= \; \mathcal{E}_c[\![e_0]\!] \; \overline{\lambda} v_0.\mathcal{E}_c[\![e_1]\!] \; \overline{\lambda} v_1.v_0 \; \overline{@} \; v_1 \\[1em]
\mathcal{E}_c \; &: \; \Lambda^E \to (\Lambda^V_{ml} \to \Lambda^C_{ml}) \to \Lambda^C_{ml} \\
\mathcal{E}_c[\![\ell]\!] \; \kappa \; &= \; \kappa \; \overline{@} \; \ell \\
\mathcal{E}_c[\![x]\!] \; \kappa \; &= \; \kappa \; \overline{@} \; x \\
\mathcal{E}_c[\![\lambda x.e]\!] \; \kappa \; &= \; \kappa \; \overline{@} \; \underline{\lambda} x.\mathcal{E}[\![e]\!] \\
\mathcal{E}_c[\![e_0 \; e_1]\!] \; \kappa \; &= \; \mathcal{E}_c[\![e_0]\!] \; \overline{\lambda} v_0.\mathcal{E}_c[\![e_1]\!] \; \overline{\lambda} v_1.\underline{\text{let}} \; w = v_0 \; \overline{@} \; v_1 \; \underline{\text{in}} \; \kappa \; \overline{@} \; w
\end{aligned}
$$

The function $\mathcal{E}$ is applied to subterms occurring in tail position, and the function $\mathcal{E}_c$ to the other subterms; it is indexed with a functional accumulator κ.[2] This transformation is higher-order (witness the type of $\mathcal{E}_c$) and it is also two level: the underlined terms are hygienic syntax constructors and the overlined terms are reduced at transformation time (@ denotes infix application). We show in appendix how to program it in ML. This transformation is similar to a higher-order one-pass CPS transformation, which can be transformationally derived from a two-pass specification [16].

The question now is to generalize this one-pass transformation to the full Λ^E and Λ^B from Section 1. Our insight is to index the translation of each boolean expression with the translation of the corresponding consequent and alternative. Each of them can be the name of a thunk, which we can use non-linearly, or a thunk, which we should only use linearly since we want to avoid code duplication. Enumerating, we define four translation functions for boolean expressions:

$$
\begin{aligned}
\mathcal{B}_{cc} &: \Lambda^B \to (1 \to \Lambda^C_{ml}) \times (1 \to \Lambda^C_{ml}) \to \Lambda^C_{ml} \\
\mathcal{B}_{vv} &: \Lambda^B \to \Lambda^V_{ml} \times \Lambda^V_{ml} \to \Lambda^C_{ml} \\
\mathcal{B}_{cv} &: \Lambda^B \to (1 \to \Lambda^C_{ml}) \times \Lambda^V_{ml} \to \Lambda^C_{ml} \\
\mathcal{B}_{vc} &: \Lambda^B \to \Lambda^V_{ml} \times (1 \to \Lambda^C_{ml}) \to \Lambda^C_{ml}
\end{aligned}
$$

The problem then reduces to following the structure of the boolean expressions and introducing residual let expressions to name computations if their result needs to be used more than once.

---

[2] We refrain from referring to κ as a continuation since it is not applied tail recursively.

$$\mathcal{B}_{cc} \ : \ \Lambda^B \to (1 \to \Lambda^C_{ml}) \times (1 \to \Lambda^C_{ml}) \to \Lambda^C_{ml}$$

$$\mathcal{B}_{cc}[\![b_1 \wedge b_2]\!] \langle \kappa_1, \kappa_0 \rangle = \underline{\mathsf{let}}\ t_0 = \underline{\lambda}().\kappa_0\ \overline{@}\ ()$$
$$\underline{\mathsf{in}}\ \mathcal{B}_{cv}[\![b_1]\!] \langle \overline{\lambda}().\mathcal{B}_{cv}[\![b_2]\!] \langle \kappa_1, t_0 \rangle, t_0 \rangle$$

$$\mathcal{B}_{cc}[\![b_1 \vee b_2]\!] \langle \kappa_1, \kappa_0 \rangle = \underline{\mathsf{let}}\ t_1 = \underline{\lambda}().\kappa_1\ \overline{@}\ ()$$
$$\underline{\mathsf{in}}\ \mathcal{B}_{vc}[\![b_1]\!] \langle t_1, \overline{\lambda}().\mathcal{B}_{vc}[\![b_2]\!] \langle t_1, \kappa_0 \rangle \rangle$$

$$\mathcal{B}_{cc}[\![\neg b]\!] \langle \kappa_1, \kappa_0 \rangle = \mathcal{B}_{cc}[\![b]\!] \langle \kappa_0, \kappa_1 \rangle$$

$$\mathcal{B}_{cc}[\![\mathsf{if}\ b_2\ \mathsf{then}\ b_1\ \mathsf{else}\ b_0]\!] \langle \kappa_1, \kappa_0 \rangle = \underline{\mathsf{let}}\ t_1 = \underline{\lambda}().\kappa_1\ \overline{@}\ ()$$
$$\underline{\mathsf{in}}\ \underline{\mathsf{let}}\ t_0 = \underline{\lambda}().\kappa_0\ \overline{@}\ ()$$
$$\underline{\mathsf{in}}\ \mathcal{B}_{cc}[\![b_2]\!] \langle \overline{\lambda}().\mathcal{B}_{vv}[\![b_1]\!] \langle t_1, t_0 \rangle,$$
$$\overline{\lambda}().\mathcal{B}_{vv}[\![b_0]\!] \langle t_1, t_0 \rangle \rangle$$

For example, let us consider $\mathcal{B}_{cc}[\![b_1 \wedge b_2]\!] \langle \kappa_1, \kappa_0 \rangle$, i.e., the translation of a conjunction in the presence of two thunks κ_1 and κ_0. The activation of κ_1 and κ_0 will yield the translation of the consequent and of the alternative of this conjunction. Naively, we could want to define the translation as follows:

$$\mathcal{B}_{cc}[\![b_1]\!] \langle \overline{\lambda}().\mathcal{B}_{cc}[\![b_2]\!] \langle \kappa_1, \kappa_0 \rangle, \kappa_0 \rangle$$

Doing so, however, would duplicate κ_0, i.e., the translation of the alternative of the conjunction. Therefore we name its result with a let. The rest of the translation follows the same spirit.

$$\mathcal{B}_{vv} \ : \ \Lambda^B \to \Lambda^V_{ml} \times \Lambda^V_{ml} \to \Lambda^C_{ml}$$

$$\mathcal{B}_{vv}[\![b_1 \wedge b_2]\!] \langle v_1, v_0 \rangle = \mathcal{B}_{cv}[\![b_1]\!] \langle \overline{\lambda}().\mathcal{B}_{vv}[\![b_2]\!] \langle v_1, v_0 \rangle, v_0 \rangle$$

$$\mathcal{B}_{vv}[\![b_1 \vee b_2]\!] \langle v_1, v_0 \rangle = \mathcal{B}_{vc}[\![b_1]\!] \langle v_1, \overline{\lambda}().\mathcal{B}_{vv}[\![b_2]\!] \langle v_1, v_0 \rangle \rangle$$

$$\mathcal{B}_{vv}[\![\neg b]\!] \langle v_1, v_0 \rangle = \mathcal{B}_{vv}[\![b]\!] \langle v_0, v_1 \rangle$$

$$\mathcal{B}_{vv}[\![\mathsf{if}\ b_2\ \mathsf{then}\ b_1\ \mathsf{else}\ b_0]\!] \langle v_1, v_0 \rangle = \mathcal{B}_{cc}[\![b_2]\!] \langle \overline{\lambda}().\mathcal{B}_{vv}[\![b_1]\!] \langle v_1, v_0 \rangle,$$
$$\overline{\lambda}().\mathcal{B}_{vv}[\![b_0]\!] \langle v_1, v_0 \rangle \rangle$$

$$\mathcal{B}_{cv} \ : \ \Lambda^B \to (1 \to \Lambda^C_{ml}) \times \Lambda^V_{ml} \to \Lambda^C_{ml}$$

$$\mathcal{B}_{cv}[\![b_1 \wedge b_2]\!] \langle \kappa_1, v_0 \rangle = \mathcal{B}_{cv}[\![b_1]\!] \langle \overline{\lambda}().\mathcal{B}_{cv}[\![b_2]\!] \langle \kappa_1, v_0 \rangle, v_0 \rangle$$

$$\mathcal{B}_{cv}[\![b_1 \vee b_2]\!] \langle \kappa_1, v_0 \rangle = \underline{\mathsf{let}}\ t_1 = \underline{\lambda}().\kappa_1\ \overline{@}\ ()$$
$$\underline{\mathsf{in}}\ \mathcal{B}_{vc}[\![b_1]\!] \langle t_1, \overline{\lambda}().\mathcal{B}_{vv}[\![b_2]\!] \langle t_1, v_0 \rangle \rangle$$

$$\mathcal{B}_{cv}[\![\neg b]\!] \langle \kappa_1, v_0 \rangle = \mathcal{B}_{vc}[\![b]\!] \langle v_0, \kappa_1 \rangle$$

$$\mathcal{B}_{cv}[\![\mathsf{if}\ b_2\ \mathsf{then}\ b_1\ \mathsf{else}\ b_0]\!] \langle \kappa_1, v_0 \rangle = \underline{\mathsf{let}}\ t_1 = \underline{\lambda}().\kappa_1\ \overline{@}\ ()$$
$$\underline{\mathsf{in}}\ \mathcal{B}_{cc}[\![b_2]\!] \langle \overline{\lambda}().\mathcal{B}_{vv}[\![b_1]\!] \langle t_1, v_0 \rangle,$$
$$\overline{\lambda}().\mathcal{B}_{vv}[\![b_0]\!] \langle t_1, v_0 \rangle \rangle$$

$$\mathcal{B}_{vc} \;:\; \Lambda^B \to \Lambda_{ml}^V \times (1 \to \Lambda_{ml}^C) \to \Lambda_{ml}^C$$

$$\mathcal{B}_{vc}[\![b_1 \wedge b_2]\!]\,\langle v_1, \kappa_0 \rangle = \underline{\mathsf{let}}\; t_0 = \underline{\lambda}().\kappa_0 \;\overline{@}\; ()$$
$$\underline{\mathsf{in}}\; \mathcal{B}_{cv}[\![b_1]\!]\,\langle \overline{\lambda}().\mathcal{B}_{vv}[\![b_2]\!]\,\langle v_1, t_0 \rangle, t_0 \rangle$$

$$\mathcal{B}_{vc}[\![b_1 \vee b_2]\!]\,\langle v_1, \kappa_0 \rangle = \mathcal{B}_{vc}[\![b_1]\!]\,\langle v_1, \overline{\lambda}().\mathcal{B}_{vc}[\![b_2]\!]\,\langle v_1, \kappa_0 \rangle \rangle$$

$$\mathcal{B}_{vc}[\![\neg b]\!]\,\langle v_1, \kappa_0 \rangle = \mathcal{B}_{cv}[\![b]\!]\,\langle \kappa_0, v_1 \rangle$$

$$\mathcal{B}_{vc}[\![\mathsf{if}\; b_2 \;\mathsf{then}\; b_1 \;\mathsf{else}\; b_0]\!]\,\langle v_1, \kappa_0 \rangle = \underline{\mathsf{let}}\; t_0 = \underline{\lambda}().\kappa_0 \;\overline{@}\; ()$$
$$\underline{\mathsf{in}}\; \mathcal{B}_{cc}[\![b_2]\!]\,\langle \overline{\lambda}().\mathcal{B}_{vv}[\![b_1]\!]\,\langle v_1, t_0 \rangle,$$
$$\overline{\lambda}().\mathcal{B}_{vv}[\![b_0]\!]\,\langle v_1, t_0 \rangle \rangle$$

As for the connection between translating a boolean expression and translating an expression, we make it using a functional accumulator that will generate a conditional expression when it is applied.

$$\mathcal{B}_{cc}[\![e]\!]\,\langle \kappa_1, \kappa_0 \rangle = \mathcal{E}_c[\![e]\!]\,\overline{\lambda}v.\underline{\mathsf{if}}\; v \;\underline{\mathsf{then}}\; \kappa_1 \;\overline{@}\; () \;\underline{\mathsf{else}}\; \kappa_0 \;\overline{@}\; ()$$

$$\mathcal{B}_{vv}[\![e]\!]\,\langle v_1, v_0 \rangle = \mathcal{E}_c[\![e]\!]\,\overline{\lambda}v.\underline{\mathsf{if}}\; v \;\underline{\mathsf{then}}\; v_1 \;\overline{@}\; () \;\underline{\mathsf{else}}\; v_0 \;\overline{@}\; ()$$

$$\mathcal{B}_{cv}[\![e]\!]\,\langle \kappa_1, v_0 \rangle = \mathcal{E}_c[\![e]\!]\,\overline{\lambda}v.\underline{\mathsf{if}}\; v \;\underline{\mathsf{then}}\; \kappa_1 \;\overline{@}\; () \;\underline{\mathsf{else}}\; v_0 \;\overline{@}\; ()$$

$$\mathcal{B}_{vc}[\![e]\!]\,\langle v_1, \kappa_0 \rangle = \mathcal{E}_c[\![e]\!]\,\overline{\lambda}v.\underline{\mathsf{if}}\; v \;\underline{\mathsf{then}}\; v_1 \;\overline{@}\; () \;\underline{\mathsf{else}}\; \kappa_0 \;\overline{@}\; ()$$

Finally we connect translating an expression and translating a boolean expression as follows.

$$\mathcal{E}[\![\mathsf{if}\; b \;\mathsf{then}\; e_1 \;\mathsf{else}\; e_0]\!] = \mathcal{B}_{cc}[\![b]\!]\,\langle \overline{\lambda}().\mathcal{E}[\![e_1]\!], \overline{\lambda}().\mathcal{E}[\![e_0]\!] \rangle$$

$$\mathcal{E}_c[\![\mathsf{if}\; b \;\mathsf{then}\; e_1 \;\mathsf{else}\; e_0]\!]\,\kappa = \underline{\mathsf{let}}\; k = \underline{\lambda}w.\kappa \;\overline{@}\; w$$
$$\underline{\mathsf{in}}\; \mathcal{B}_{cc}[\![b]\!]\,\langle \overline{\lambda}().\mathcal{E}_v[\![e_1]\!]\,k, \overline{\lambda}().\mathcal{E}_v[\![e_0]\!]\,k \rangle$$

$$\mathcal{E}_v \;:\; \Lambda^E \to \Lambda_{ml}^V \to \Lambda_{ml}^C$$

$$\mathcal{E}_v[\![\ell]\!]\,k = k \;\overline{@}\; \ell$$

$$\mathcal{E}_v[\![x]\!]\,k = k \;\overline{@}\; x$$

$$\mathcal{E}_v[\![\lambda x.e]\!]\,k = k \;\overline{@}\; \lambda x.\mathcal{E}[\![e]\!]$$

$$\mathcal{E}_v[\![e_0\, e_1]\!]\,k = \mathcal{E}_c[\![e_0]\!]\,\overline{\lambda}v_0.\mathcal{E}_c[\![e_1]\!]\,\overline{\lambda}v_1.\underline{\mathsf{let}}\; w = v_0 \;\overline{@}\; v_1 \;\underline{\mathsf{in}}\; k \;\overline{@}\; w$$

$$\mathcal{E}_v[\![\mathsf{if}\; b \;\mathsf{then}\; e_1 \;\mathsf{else}\; e_0]\!]\,k = \mathcal{B}_{cc}[\![b]\!]\,\langle \overline{\lambda}().\mathcal{E}_v[\![e_1]\!]\,k, \overline{\lambda}().\mathcal{E}_v[\![e_0]\!]\,k \rangle$$

In the second equation, a let expression is inserted to name the context (and to avoid its duplication). $\mathcal{E}_v$ is there to avoid generating chains of thunks when translating nested conditional expressions.

The result can be directly coded in ML (see appendix): the source and target languages are implemented as data types and the translation as a function. A side benefit of using ML is that its type inferencer acts as a theorem prover to tell us that the translation maps terms from the source language into terms in the target language (a bit more reasoning, however, is necessary to show that the translation generates no chains of thunks). Finally, since the translation is specified compositionally, it does operate in one pass.

4   Two Examples

4.1   No Chains of Thunks

The term $\lambda x.g\ (h\ (\text{if } a \text{ then if } b_2 \text{ then } b_1 \text{ else } b_0 \text{ else } x))$ is translated into the following target term in one pass.

```
return (fn x => let val k0 = fn v1 => let val v2 = h v1
                                      in g v2
                                      end

               in if a
                  then if b2
                       then k0 b1
                       else k0 b0
                  else k0 x
               end)
```

Each conditional branch directly calls k0.

4.2   Short-Cut Boolean Evaluation

The term $\lambda x.\text{if } a_1 \wedge a_2 \wedge a_3 \wedge a_4 \text{ then } x \text{ else } g\ (h\ x)$ is translated into the following target term in one pass.

```
return (fn x => let val f1 = fn () => let val v0 = h x
                                      in g v0
                                      end

               in if a1
                  then if a2
                       then if a3
                            then if a4
                                 then return x
                                 else f1 ()
                            else f1 ()
                       else f1 ()
                  else f1 ()
               end)
```

All the else branches directly call f1.

5   Assessment

A similar development yields, mutatis mutandis, a CPS transformation that is higher-order, operates in one pass, duplicates no code, generates no chain of thunks, and is properly tail recursive.

The author has implemented both transformations in his academic Scheme compiler. Their net effect is to fuse two compiler passes into one and to avoid, in effect, an entire copy of the source program. In particular, an escape analysis of the transformations themselves shows that all of their higher-order functions are stack-allocatable [4]. The transformations therefore have a minimal footprint in that they only allocate heap space to construct their result, making them well suited in a JIT situation.

6   Related Work, Conclusion, and Future Work

We have presented a two-level program transformation that encodes call-by-value λ-terms into monadic normal form and achieves short-cut boolean evaluation. The transformation operates in one pass in that it directly constructs the normal form without intermediate representations that need further processing. As usual with two-level specifications, erasing all overlines and underlines yields something meaningful—here an interpreter for the call-by-value λ-calculus in the monadic metalanguage.

The program transformation can be easily adapted to other evaluation orders.

Short-cut evaluation is a standard topic in compiling [1,9,34]. The author is not aware of any treatment of it in one-pass CPS transformations or in one-pass transformations into monadic normal form.

Our use of higher-order functions and of an underlying evaluator to fuse a transformation and a form of normalization is strongly reminiscent of the notion of *normalization by evaluation* [8,11,13,20]. And indeed the author is convinced that the present one-pass transformation could be specified as a formal instance of normalization by evaluation—a future work.

Monadic normal forms and CPS terms are in one-to-one correspondence [12], and Kelsey and Appel have noticed the correspondence between continuation-passing style and static single assignment form (SSA) [3, 31]. Therefore, the one-pass transformation with short-cut boolean evaluation should apply directly to the SSA transformation [49]—another future work.

Acknowledgments. Thanks are due to Mads Sig Ager, Jacques Carette, Samuel Lindley, and the anonymous reviewers for comments.

A   Two-Level Programming in ML

We briefly outline how to program the one-pass translation of Section 2 [14].

First, we assume a type for identifiers as well as a module generating fresh identifiers in the target abstract syntax:

```
type ide = string

signature GENSYM = sig
                    val init : unit -> unit
                    val new : string -> ide
                 end
```

Given this type, the source and the target abstract syntax (without conditional expressions) are defined with two data types:

```
structure Source = struct
                    datatype e = VAR of ide
                               | LAM of ide * e
                               | APP of e * e
                 end

structure Target = struct
                    datatype e = RETURN of t
                               | TAIL_APP of t * t
                               | LET_APP of ide * (t * t) * e
                         and t = VAR of ide
                               | LAM of ide * e
                 end
```

Given a structure `Gensym` : `GENSYM`, the two translation functions $\mathcal{E}$ and $\mathcal{E}_c$ are
recursively defined as two ML functions `trans0` and `trans1`. In particular, `trans1`
is uncurried and higher order. For readability of the output, the main translation
function `trans` initializes the generator of fresh identifiers before calling `trans0`:

```
(*  trans0 : Source.e -> Target.e                          *)
(*  trans1 : Source.e * (Target.t -> Target.e) -> Target.e  *)
fun trans0 (Source.VAR x)
    = Target.RETURN (Target.VAR x)
  | trans0 (Source.LAM (x, e))
    = Target.RETURN (Target.LAM (x, trans0 e))
  | trans0 (Source.APP (e0, e1))
    = trans1 (e0,
              fn v0 => trans1 (e1,
                               fn v1 => Target.TAIL_APP (v0, v1)))
and trans1 (Source.VAR x, k)
    = k (Target.VAR x)
  | trans1 (Source.LAM (x, e), k)
    = k (Target.LAM (x, trans0 e))
  | trans1 (Source.APP (e0, e1), k)
    = trans1 (e0,
              fn v0 => trans1 (e1,
                               fn v1 => let val v = Gensym.new "v"
                                        in Target.LET_APP
                                             (v, (v0, v1),
                                              k (Target.VAR v))
                                        end))
```

```
(*  trans : Source.e -> Target.e  *)
fun trans e
    = (Gensym.init (); trans0 e)
```

References

1. Alfred V. Aho, Ravi Sethi, and Jeffrey D. Ullman. *Compilers: Principles, Techniques and Tools*. World Student Series. Addison-Wesley, Reading, Massachusetts, 1986.
2. Andrew W. Appel. *Compiling with Continuations*. Cambridge University Press, New York, 1992.
3. Andrew W. Appel. SSA is functional programming. *ACM SIGPLAN Notices*, 33(4):17–20, April 1998.
4. Anindya Banerjee and David A. Schmidt. Stackability in the typed call-by-value lambda calculus. *Science of Computer Programming*, 31(1):47–73, 1998.
5. Alan Bawden. Quasiquotation in Lisp. In Olivier Danvy, editor, *Proceedings of the ACM SIGPLAN Workshop on Partial Evaluation and Semantics-Based Program Manipulation*, Technical report BRICS-NS-99-1, University of Aarhus, pages 4–12, San Antonio, Texas, January 1999. Available online at http://www.brics.dk/~pepm99/programme.html.
6. Nick Benton and Andrew Kennedy. Monads, effects, and transformations. In *Third International Workshop on Higher-Order Operational Techniques in Semantics*, volume 26 of *Electronic Notes in Theoretical Computer Science*, pages 19–31, Paris, France, September 1999.
7. Nick Benton, Andrew Kennedy, and George Russell. Compiling Standard ML to Java byte-codes. In Paul Hudak and Christian Queinnec, editors, *Proceedings of the 1998 ACM SIGPLAN International Conference on Functional Programming*, pages 129–140, Baltimore, Maryland, September 1998. ACM Press.
8. Ulrich Berger, Matthias Eberl, and Helmut Schwichtenberg. Normalization by evaluation. In Bernhard Möller and John V. Tucker, editors, *Prospects for hardware foundations (NADA)*, number 1546 in Lecture Notes in Computer Science, pages 117–137. Springer-Verlag, 1998.
9. Keith Clarke. One-pass code generation using continuations. *Software—Practice and Experience*, 19(12):1175–1192, 1989.
10. Charles Consel and Olivier Danvy. Tutorial notes on partial evaluation. In Susan L. Graham, editor, *Proceedings of the Twentieth Annual ACM Symposium on Principles of Programming Languages*, pages 493–501, Charleston, South Carolina, January 1993. ACM Press.
11. Thierry Coquand and Peter Dybjer. Intuitionistic model constructions and normalization proofs. *Mathematical Structures in Computer Science*, 7:75–94, 1997.
12. Olivier Danvy. Back to direct style. *Science of Computer Programming*, 22(3):183–195, 1994.
13. Olivier Danvy. Type-directed partial evaluation. In John Hatcliff, Torben Æ. Mogensen, and Peter Thiemann, editors, *Partial Evaluation – Practice and Theory; Proceedings of the 1998 DIKU Summer School*, number 1706 in Lecture Notes in Computer Science, pages 367–411, Copenhagen, Denmark, July 1998. Springer-Verlag.
14. Olivier Danvy. Programming techniques for partial evaluation. In Friedrich L. Bauer and Ralf Steinbrüggen, editors, *Foundations of Secure Computation*, NATO Science series, pages 287–318. IOS Press Ohmsha, 2000.

15. Olivier Danvy and Andrzej Filinski. Abstracting control. In Mitchell Wand, editor, *Proceedings of the 1990 ACM Conference on Lisp and Functional Programming*, pages 151–160, Nice, France, June 1990. ACM Press.

16. Olivier Danvy and Lasse R. Nielsen. A first-order one-pass CPS transformation. In Mogens Nielsen and Uffe Engberg, editors, *Foundations of Software Science and Computation Structures, 5th International Conference, FOSSACS 2002*, number 2303 in Lecture Notes in Computer Science, pages 98–113, Grenoble, France, April 2002. Springer-Verlag. Extended version available as the technical report BRICS RS-01-49. To appear in TCS.

17. Rowan Davies. A temporal-logic approach to binding-time analysis. In Edmund M. Clarke, editor, *Proceedings of the Eleventh Annual IEEE Symposium on Logic in Computer Science*, pages 184–195, New Brunswick, New Jersey, July 1996. IEEE Computer Society Press.

18. Rowan Davies and Frank Pfenning. A modal analysis of staged computation. In Steele Jr. [44], pages 258–283.

19. Dawson R. Engler, Wilson C. Hsieh, and M. Frans Kaashoe. 'C: A language for high-level, efficient, and machine-independent dynamic code generation. In Steele Jr. [44], pages 131–144.

20. Andrzej Filinski. Normalization by evaluation for the computational lambda-calculus. In Samson Abramsky, editor, *Typed Lambda Calculi and Applications, 5th International Conference, TLCA 2001*, number 2044 in Lecture Notes in Computer Science, pages 151–165, Kraków, Poland, May 2001. Springer-Verlag.

21. Cormac Flanagan, Amr Sabry, Bruce F. Duba, and Matthias Felleisen. The essence of compiling with continuations. In David W. Wall, editor, *Proceedings of the ACM SIGPLAN'93 Conference on Programming Languages Design and Implementation*, SIGPLAN Notices, Vol. 28, No 6, pages 237–247, Albuquerque, New Mexico, June 1993. ACM Press.

22. Matthew Fluet and Stephen Weeks. Contification using dominators. In Xavier Leroy, editor, *Proceedings of the 2001 ACM SIGPLAN International Conference on Functional Programming*, SIGPLAN Notices, Vol. 36, No. 10, pages 2–13, Firenze, Italy, September 2001. ACM Press.

23. John Hatcliff and Olivier Danvy. A generic account of continuation-passing styles. In Hans-J. Boehm, editor, *Proceedings of the Twenty-First Annual ACM Symposium on Principles of Programming Languages*, pages 458–471, Portland, Oregon, January 1994. ACM Press.

24. John Hatcliff and Olivier Danvy. A computational formalization for partial evaluation. *Mathematical Structures in Computer Science*, pages 507–541, 1997. Extended version available as the technical report BRICS RS-96-34.

25. Neil D. Jones. Tutorial on binding time analysis. In Paul Hudak and Neil D. Jones, editors, *Proceedings of the ACM SIGPLAN Symposium on Partial Evaluation and Semantics-Based Program Manipulation*, SIGPLAN Notices, Vol. 26, No 9, New Haven, Connecticut, June 1991. ACM Press.

26. Neil D. Jones, Carsten K. Gomard, and Peter Sestoft. *Partial Evaluation and Automatic Program Generation*. Prentice-Hall International, London, UK, 1993. Available online at http://www.dina.kvl.dk/~sestoft/pebook/.

27. Neil D. Jones and Steven S. Muchnick. Some thoughts towards the design of an ideal language. In Susan L. Graham, editor, *Proceedings of the Third Annual ACM Symposium on Principles of Programming Languages*, pages 77–94. ACM Press, January 1976.

28. Neil D. Jones, Peter Sestoft, and Harald Søndergaard. MIX: A self-applicable partial evaluator for experiments in compiler generation. *Lisp and Symbolic Computation*, 2(1):9–50, 1989.

29. Ulrik Jørring and William L. Scherlis. Compilers and staging transformations. In Mark Scott Johnson and Ravi Sethi, editors, *Proceedings of the Thirteenth Annual ACM Symposium on Principles of Programming Languages*, pages 86–96, St. Petersburg, Florida, January 1986. ACM Press.

30. Richard A. Kelsey. *Compilation by Program Transformation*. PhD thesis, Computer Science Department, Yale University, New Haven, Connecticut, May 1989. Research Report 702.

31. Richard A. Kelsey. A correspondence between continuation passing style and static single assignment form. In Michael Ernst, editor, *ACM SIGPLAN Workshop on Intermediate Representations*, SIGPLAN Notices, Vol. 30, No 3, pages 13–22, San Francisco, California, January 1995. ACM Press.

32. Oleg Kiselyov. Macros that compose: Systematic macro programming. In Don Batory, Charles Consel, and Walid Taha, editors, *Proceedings of the 2002 ACM SIGPLAN/SIGSOFT Conference on Generative Programming and Component Engineering*, number 2487 in Lecture Notes in Computer Science, pages 202–217, Pittsburgh, Pennsylvania, October 2002. Springer-Verlag.

33. David A. Kranz. *ORBIT: An Optimizing Compiler for Scheme*. PhD thesis, Computer Science Department, Yale University, New Haven, Connecticut, February 1988. Research Report 632.

34. George Logothetis and Prateek Mishra. Compiling short-circuit boolean expressions in one pass. *Software—Practice and Experience*, 11:1197–1214, 1981.

35. Torben Æ. Mogensen. Separating binding times in language specifications. In Joseph E. Stoy, editor, *Proceedings of the Fourth International Conference on Functional Programming and Computer Architecture*, pages 14–25, London, England, September 1989. ACM Press.

36. Eugenio Moggi. Notions of computation and monads. *Information and Computation*, 93:55–92, 1991.

37. Flemming Nielson and Hanne Riis Nielson. *Two-Level Functional Languages*, volume 34 of *Cambridge Tracts in Theoretical Computer Science*. Cambridge University Press, 1992.

38. Dino P. Oliva and Andrew P. Tolmach. From ML to Ada: strongly-typed language interoperability via source translation. *Journal of Functional Programming*, 8(4):367–412, 1998.

39. Gordon D. Plotkin. Call-by-name, call-by-value and the λ-calculus. *Theoretical Computer Science*, 1:125–159, 1975.

40. John Reppy. Optimizing nested loops using local CPS conversion. *Higher-Order and Symbolic Computation*, 15(2/3), 2002. To appear.

41. John C. Reynolds. Definitional interpreters for higher-order programming languages. *Higher-Order and Symbolic Computation*, 11(4):363–397, 1998. Reprinted from the proceedings of the 25th ACM National Conference (1972).

42. Guy L. Steele Jr. Lambda, the ultimate declarative. AI Memo 379, Artificial Intelligence Laboratory, Massachusetts Institute of Technology, Cambridge, Massachusetts, November 1976.

43. Guy L. Steele Jr. Rabbit: A compiler for Scheme. Master's thesis, Artificial Intelligence Laboratory, Massachusetts Institute of Technology, Cambridge, Massachusetts, May 1978. Technical report AI-TR-474.

44. Guy L. Steele Jr., editor. *Proceedings of the Twenty-Third Annual ACM Symposium on Principles of Programming Languages*, St. Petersburg Beach, Florida, January 1996. ACM Press.

45. Walid Taha. *Multi-Stage Programming: Its Theory and Applications*. PhD thesis, Oregon Graduate Institute of Science and Technology, Portland, Oregon, 1999. CSE-99-TH-002.

46. David Tarditi, Greg Morrisett, Perry Cheng, and Chris Stone. TIL: a type-directed optimizing compiler for ML. In *Proceedings of the ACM SIGPLAN'96 Conference on Programming Languages Design and Implementation*, SIGPLAN Notices, Vol. 31, No 5, pages 181–192. ACM Press, June 1996.

47. Philip Wadler. The essence of functional programming (invited talk). In Andrew W. Appel, editor, *Proceedings of the Nineteenth Annual ACM Symposium on Principles of Programming Languages*, pages 1–14, Albuquerque, New Mexico, January 1992. ACM Press.

48. Mitchell Wand. Correctness of procedure representations in higher-order assembly language. In Stephen Brookes, Michael Main, Austin Melton, Michael Mislove, and David Schmidt, editors, *Mathematical Foundations of Programming Semantics*, number 598 in Lecture Notes in Computer Science, pages 294–311, Pittsburgh, Pennsylvania, March 1991. Springer-Verlag. 7th International Conference.

49. Mark N. Wegman and F. Ken Zadeck. Constant propagation with conditional branches. *ACM Transactions on Programming Languages and Systems*, 3(2):181–210, 1991.

50. Zhe Yang. *Language Support for Program Generation: Reasoning, Implementation, and Applications*. PhD thesis, Computer Science Department, New York University, New York, New York, August 2001.

Run-Time Type Checking for Binary Programs*

Michael Burrows[1], Stephen N. Freund[2], and Janet L. Wiener[3]

[1] Microsoft Corporation, 1065 La Avenida, Mountain View, CA 94043
[2] Department of Computer Science, Williams College, Williamstown, MA 01267
[3] Hewlett-Packard Labs, 1501 Page Mill Road, Palo Alto, CA 94304

Abstract. Many important software systems are written in the C programming language. Unfortunately, the C language does not provide strong safety guarantees, and many common programming mistakes introduce type errors that are not caught by the compiler. These errors only manifest themselves at run time through unexpected program behavior, and it is often hard to isolate and identify their causes. This paper presents the Hobbes run-time type checker for compiled C programs. Our tool interprets compiled binaries, tracks type information for all memory and register locations, and reports warnings when a variety of type errors occur. Because the Hobbes type checker does not rely on source code, it is effective in many situations where similar tools are not, such as when full source code is not available or when C source is linked with program fragments written in assembly or other languages.

1 Introduction

Many software systems are written in the C programming language because it is expressive and provides precise, low-level control over the machine architecture. However, this strength is also a weakness. The expressive power of C is obtained through unsafe language features, including pointer arithmetic, explicit memory management, unchecked type casts, and so on. These features give the programmer a great deal of control but also make it difficult to ensure software reliability and to maintain large programs.

Given the importance of many systems in this category, it is essential to identify defects caused by improper use of unsafe language features. In this paper, we present Hobbes, a new run-time analysis tool that identifies a large class of errors in compiled C programs. In particular, our tool identifies *memory access errors* and *type errors*. A memory access error occurs when a program accesses an invalid memory location. Two examples of such errors are (1) reading from or writing to an unallocated location, and (2) reading from an allocated but uninitialized location. A type error occurs when an operation is performed on operands whose types are incompatible with the operation. Adding a pointer to a real number, calling a function with the wrong number or type of arguments, and dereferencing an integer as a pointer are all type errors.

---

* This work was performed, in part, while all 3 authors were employed at the Compaq Systems Research Center (now part of HP Labs).

G. Hedin (Ed.): CC 2003, LNCS 2622, pp. 90–105, 2003.

To catch errors, our tool maintains a shadow memory containing the allocation status and type of each location accessible to the target program, which it updates and checks as the target is running. Purify demonstrated the effectiveness of a shadow memory-based approach for identifying memory access errors [3]. Purify modifies the target program to maintain allocation and initialization status for each memory location, and it instruments each memory operation to check that the status information for the address being accessed is in an appropriate state. The Hobbes type checker goes beyond Purify by tracking not only memory status information, but also the type stored at each location. The type information enables our tool to check the types of the operands for each operation performed as the program executes.

The Hobbes prototype checks for errors in Linux binaries on the Intel x86 architecture. Hobbes consists of two major components: an instrumentable x86 interpreter and a run-time type checker. To check a program for type errors, the type checker maintains the shadow memory and checks each interpreted instruction for errors. Memory access and type errors are reported to the programmer, along with the call stack and the relevant data values and types.

The type checker extracts type information from the symbol tables and debug tables embedded in the binary program. It uses this information to determine the types of storage locations allocated to global variables, local variables, and parameters of functions. When debugging information is incomplete or not available, the type checker assumes more conservative types for memory locations. Even when given only partial type information for the target program, Hobbes can still identify a useful set of errors.

The Hobbes architecture provides the following benefits:

1. Hobbes uses only the binary representation of programs and does not rely on the source code for the target program or included libraries.
2. Hobbes is applicable to programs written in a mixture of any languages that compile into the standard binary format.
3. Hobbes does not modify the data representations or layout of the program.

We are not aware of other tools that provide all three of these benefits. Loginov et al. present a system similar to ours that employs source-to-source translation to insert code to maintain and check shadow memory [7]. Relying on source code translation limits their handling of libraries and mixed-language programs, and their tool does not preserve the instruction stream of the original program. Several other tools have been proposed to check for memory access errors and some type errors by extending the representation of pointers to include additional information (see, for example, [15,1]). However, we wished to avoid changing the data layout of the program since such changes are not always feasible in large systems.

Our experience indicates that the Hobbes type checker is an effective tool for finding type errors in programs. When applied to a set of programs from an undergraduate compilers class, it found a number of both memory errors and type errors, and it scaled reasonably well when checking larger programs. In particular, the false alarm rate was not a significant impediment to using the tool.

There is a substantial performance penalty for using the Hobbes type checker prototype, but we are confident that improvements we describe will significantly improve the performance of the system.

Section 2 motivates this work by demonstrating how run-time type checking can catch a number of common errors in C programs. Sections 3 and 4 describe the general Hobbes architecture and the type checker, respectively. We summarize our experiments to validate the type checker and measure performance in Section 5, and Section 6 compares the Hobbes type checker to related work. We conclude in Section 7 and outline directions for future work.

2   Motivating Examples

In this section, we present some errors that the Hobbes type checker catches, but which are not caught by the C compiler's static type checking or the allocation checking performed by tools like Purify. Figure 1 contains programs exhibiting these errors. In each case, we outline how the errors are caught.

In Example 1, the programmer writes a pointer into a union but then reads the union value as an integer. On the store to x.p, the type checker sets the shadow memory for that location to pointer. The type pointer is inferred because a lea (load effective address) instruction is used to compute &i. A multiply instruction can not be applied to an operand of type pointer, so when the multiply of x.k occurs, the type checker detects the type mismatch and generates a warning message. This example is interesting because it shows that useful type checking can be done without any help from the compiler or debugging information.

Example 2 shows an array bounds error that is not normally detected by Purify or similar systems. The programmer writes to y.a[10], which is beyond the end of the array, but still part of an allocated structure. The assignment overwrites the field y.h, which follows the array in memory. If debugging information is included in the program binary, the type checker knows that y.h should have type int. It reports an error when the program writes a value of type pointer instead. If no debugging information is available, the write is permitted, but the type checker detects an error when the value of type pointer in y.h is later used in a multiplication.

Example 3 shows a common pitfall in the use of the standard C library sorting function, qsort(). The comparison function required by qsort() is called with pointers to the elements to be compared, rather than the elements themselves. The naive programmer who wrote Example 3 omitted this extra level of indirection. A cast is almost always required when using qsort(), and the one used here, though not unusual, masks the error. Given the debugging information for the program, the type checker expects values of type int for each parameter of cmpint(). When values of type pointer are passed instead, it generates a warning.

Example 1:

```
union {
  int k;
  int *p;
} x;

void ex1() {
  int i, j;
  x.p = &i;
  j = 17 * x.k;
}
```

Example 2:

```
struct {
  int *a[10];
  int h;
} y;

void ex2() {
  int i, j;
  for (i = 0; i <= 10; i++)
    y.a[i] = &j;
  y.h *= 10;
}
```

Example 3:

```
int cmpint (int a, int b) { return ((b < a) - (a < b)); }

void ex3()
  int i;
  int array[N];
  ...
  qsort (array, N, sizeof (array[0]),
    (int (*) (const void *, const void *)) cmpint);
}
```

Fig. 1. C programs with type errors.

3 The Hobbes System Architecture

Hobbes consists of two distinct pieces: an x86 *interpreter* that runs the target program and the *type checker* analysis tool—a module that is called by the interpreter when events of interest occur in the target. The operating system kernel, in this case Linux, is unmodified. In this section, we describe the interpreter. In the next section, we describe the type checker.

The Hobbes platform is a general framework in which to build analysis tools like the Hobbes type checker. The interpreter plays the same role as a binary editor like Atom [14], or the instrumentable dynamic compiler that underlies Valgrind [12]. An analysis tool first registers interest in events that may occur while the target is running. For example, a tool may indicate that it wants notification each time the target accesses memory or executes a specific opcode. The interpreter then runs the target, which is unaware that instrumentation is taking place, and calls analysis routines provided by the tool when interesting events occur. Arguments to the analysis routines convey relevant information about the event, indicating any memory addresses, values, and registers involved.

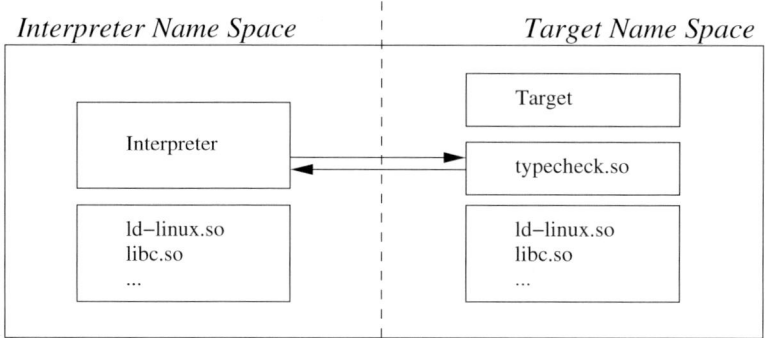

Fig. 2. The Hobbes system architecture.

A major goal of Hobbes is to provide a program environment for the target that is as close as possible to its normal execution environment. This goal influenced our design in two ways. First, we placed the components of Hobbes in normally unused parts of the address space to avoid having to relocate the target. Second, Hobbes uses two distinct name spaces, as illustrated in Figure 2. The target name space contains the target program, the type checker tool (which is a shared library) and other libraries required by the target. The interpreter name space contains the interpreter and the (potentially different) set of libraries that are linked with it. This separation prevents problems arising from name clashes or version mismatches between the libraries used in the interpreter and those used in the target, as well as potential interference problems caused by the interpreter and target sharing library data structures. Analysis tools reside in the target name space to give them access to the target dynamic loader, which is used to resolve target addresses to names.

The interpreter name space is created by the Linux kernel. To create the target name space, the Hobbes interpreter simulates the actions that the kernel would have taken to run the target, including running a new copy of the dynamic loader (`ld-linux.so`). This second loader loads the target, its shared libraries, and the analysis tools.

The Hobbes interpreter is written entirely in x86 assembly language. The main loop in the interpreter fetches instructions from the target instruction stream and performs computed jumps into tables whose entries are code fragments. The code fragment for each instruction:

1. decodes the operand specifiers and loads the addresses of the operands into specific registers,
2. performs the operation defined by the instruction opcode on those registers, and
3. moves the result, if the instruction has one, to its ultimate destination.

Except in rare circumstances, the core of the implementation for each opcode is performed by the corresponding x86 instruction. This method allows side-effects, such as the setting of condition codes, to be captured faithfully, and it improves the chances of correctly emulating the execution of unusual code sequences or instructions that behave differently on different x86 implementations.

The shared libraries for tools register analysis routines with the interpreter when the libraries are initialized as part of the loading process. If a tool has registered an analysis routine for a particular instruction opcode, a call to the analysis routine is inserted into the appropriate table entry between the first and second step above. The analysis routines are executed directly, not interpreted. The interpreter does not interpret operating system kernel code. When the interpreter encounters a system call, it executes a kernel trap in the normal way, after loading the registers with the arguments needed for the call. Some calls, notably those dealing with signals, are handled specially so as to maintain control of the target program.

Other analysis frameworks, such as Atom and Valgrind, employ binary code modification techniques to avoid the overhead of interpreting machine code. Although we could have adopted these techniques to obtain better performance, we chose to implement the interpreter for several reasons. First, interpretation preserves the layout and location of the target code and data segments, which reduces the likelihood of introducing unintended errors into the target during instrumentation. Also, no publicly available binary editor or dynamic compiler existed for x86 Linux when we started (Valgrind had not yet been released), and writing the interpreter was the simplest and fastest way to build a working prototype. In addition, the Hobbes type checker imposes a large overhead on execution beyond the interpreter's overhead, making the argument for more efficient instrumentation techniques less compelling. The large overhead is partially due to the type checker instrumenting virtually every instruction in order to track values as they pass through registers. In contrast, Purify only instruments memory accesses.

4   The Hobbes Type Checker

During startup, the Hobbes type checker shared library initializes its internal data structures and shadow memory and registers analysis routines with the interpreter. When an instruction of the target program is interpreted, the type checker tests the types of the operands and updates the type information in the shadow memory according to the instruction semantics. Any inconsistencies are reported to the user. In this section, we describe the shadow memory layout and data structures used by the type checker, demonstrate the steps to type check instructions and function calls, and describe features that reduce occurrences of false alarms. A false alarm occurs when the type checker incorrectly reports that a type error has occurred.

Shadow Memory and Type Representation. The x86 architecture provides a 4 GB address space, which the type checker divides into three sections. It uses addresses 0x00000000 – 0x5fffffff for the target program memory and addresses 0x60000000 – 0xbfffffff for the shadow memory. The Linux kernel utilizes parts of the remaining 1 GB, and we do not use it in Hobbes. Each byte in the target program is matched by a byte in the shadow memory, which encodes its type. To map from a data address to its shadow address, the type checker simply adds 0x60000000 to the data address. The interpreter places the virtual registers in the target address section so that the interpreter can shadow them like all other locations accessible to the target.

The type checker tracks primitive C types. It currently represents structures, unions, and arrays as sequences of these primitive types and does not distinguish between different pointer types. Each primitive type is encoded in the shadow memory with a bit pattern equal to the size of the type in length. For example, the four-byte integer encoding covers four bytes of shadow memory. Each byte in the shadow memory contains four fields:

c	i	v		t

The *continuation bit* c is zero if the byte is the first byte of a type encoding, and one otherwise. When c is set, the other seven bits are unused. The *initialized bit* i indicates whether the corresponding data object has been initialized. The *invariant bit* v indicates whether the type of the corresponding data object may change during execution (i.e., whether the type encoding may be overwritten with a different type encoding). The type checker marks global data and stack locations for parameters and local variables as invariant when the debugging information supports doing so. The *base type* t encodes the type of the data. The type checker currently supports the primitive types int8 (char), uint8 (unsigned char), unk8 (one byte of unknown type), int16, uint16, unk16, int32, uint32, unk32, float, double, and pointer. The unallocated base type indicates one byte of unallocated memory, and the code base type indicates one byte of code.

We present several type encodings to illustrate the layout of these structures:

initialized, unsigned char

0	1	0		uint8

uninitialized pointer

0	0	0		pointer
1				
1				
1				

initialized, invariant short

0	1	1		int16
1				

Currently, there is unused space in the encodings for multi-byte types. However, these encodings enable a fast mapping function from each data value to its shadow memory and are easy to decode. In addition, we plan to use the remaining space to encode aggregate type and pointer information in the future.

Type Checker Initialization. The type checker performs the following initialization steps before the target program begins execution.

1. The type checker reads all available debugging information in the target and shared library object code. This information includes type declarations, function prototypes, global and local variable declarations, and the mapping from names to addresses.

2. For each type, the type checker creates a template block of shadow memory that encodes it, as outlined above. Hobbes creates the template block for aggregate types by concatenating the template blocks for each element. If part of a type is unknown or ambiguous, such as when a union may contain two different primitive types, the corresponding part of the template block contains the unknown type encoding of the appropriate size.

3. For each function, the type checker creates two template blocks, one for its parameters and one for its local variables. These blocks contain the shadow memory encodings for the function's activation record. Local variable locations that may contain different types at different points in the function are assigned the unknown type. All encodings in these blocks are invariant, except those for unknown types, which are not marked as invariant.

4. The type checker initializes the shadow memory for global variables with the template blocks created in step 2. All global variables are invariant, except those which have unknown type.

5. The type checker registers analysis routines for opcodes and system calls with the interpreter.

The type checker precomputes the type representations and template blocks to avoid translating types into their encodings at run time. The types for locations originally marked as unknown are refined during execution as the type checker observes which operations are performed on the data. As described above, unknown types are introduced for locations where values of different types stored may be stored. They are also used when the target or libraries contain incomplete type information, which may occur if they are compiled without generating debugging information, if they are linked with hand-written assembly code, and so on.

The type checker also overrides `malloc`, `free`, and other memory management routines with versions that update and test the shadow memory in the obvious ways. When the interpreted program makes a system call, the interpreter copies the arguments from the virtual registers into the processor's registers and then performs the standard kernal trap. The typechecker installs built-in instrumentation callbacks to check the validity of the argument types prior to the system call and to set the type of the return value afterwards. The most common 30 system calls have been instrumented to date.

Instruction Analysis Routines. Each instruction analysis routine type checks all occurrences of a specific instruction opcode in the target execution stream. The interpreter provides the routines with the locations of the source and destination operands. Each routine

1. checks that the source operands are allocated and initialized, and that the destination is allocated;

2. checks that load and store instructions and indirect addressing modes only dereference data of type `pointer`;

3. checks the types of the source operands and computes the result type; and

4. updates the shadow memory to reflect the destination's new type, if applicable.

We elaborate on the third and fourth steps for a representative instruction. The type checker begins step 3 by extracting the type information for the sources from the shadow memory. A table is then indexed to determine the result type. To illustrate this process, we consider the instruction addl SRC, DST. This instruction adds SRC to DST, storing the result in DST. Both operands are four byte values, as indicated by the suffix l in the instruction name. For example, in addl %eax, 4(%ebp), the SRC operand is in register %eax and the DST operand is located at the address stored in register %ebp, plus 4.

The following table computes the result type for the operation, based on the types of SRC and DST. For simplicity, we include only a few of the possible operand types.

addl SRC, DST

| | DST | | | |
SRC	int8	int32	pointer	unk32
int8	error	error	error	error
int32	error	int32	pointer	unk32
pointer	error	pointer	error	unk32
unk32	error	int32	pointer	unk32

The type checker generates a warning whenever a table lookup returns error. In this example, the operands may be two integers or an integer and a pointer, but not two pointers. If DST is unknown, the result stays unknown. If SRC is unknown, the result type will be the type of DST. These heuristics for unknown types are not sound, but they reduce the false alarm rate when precise type information is not available for the operands. To aid in debugging, the type checker reports the stack trace and relevant memory and register values' types for each warning. If debugging information is available, the stack trace includes the source's file name and line number.

We show type compatibility tables for the four byte mov instruction and the lea instruction below. The lea sets DST to be the address of the SRC. These two instructions are insensitive to the original type of DST.

movl SRC, DST

SRC	DST
int8	error
int32	int32
pointer	pointer
unk32	unk32

leal SRC, DST

SRC	DST
int8	pointer
int32	pointer
pointer	pointer
unk32	pointer

Before returning control to the interpreter, the type checker writes the result type into the shadow memory for DST. If the new result type is different from the current type of DST and DST is invariant, the checker generates a warning. Otherwise, the initialized form of the result type is written into the shadow memory. Since this type may have a different size than what was there previously, the type checker assigns an unknown type to any partially overwritten type encodings immediately before and after the shadow memory for DST.

The Function Call Analysis Routine. When the interpreter invokes the analysis routine for the `call` instruction, the type checker first maps the target address of the call to the corresponding function and fetches its precomputed parameter and local variable template blocks. The type checker then compares the types of the arguments on the stack against the types in the parameter template block, reporting any mismatches. It also copies the type information for the local variable template block into the shadow memory at the appropriate offset from the frame pointer for the new function's activation record. Local variables begin as uninitialized. Full function checking can not be done if the function has a variable number of arguments or uses a non-standard activation record, which may occur when a compiler employs certain optimizations, such as tail-call elimination.

Reducing False Alarms. The initial version of our type checker reported false alarms on some common compiler idioms for the x86 architecture. For example, the `gcc` compiler may emit an `xor` instruction to clear a register containing a pointer. The compiler also uses the `lea` instruction to perform addition in certain cases. To avoid generating false alarms in situations like these, we relaxed the typing restrictions in the instruction type tables. In the case of `xor`, which originally used the same table as `add` above, we permitted two pointer operands, as long as they are the same storage location. For the `lea` instruction, we deviated from the table presented above by setting the result type to `int32` if the result value is between negative one million and one million. Numbers in this range are much more likely to be integers than addresses.

Another common source of false alarms is low-level library routines in `libc`. Handwritten assembly language implementing some of the string functions is particularly problematic because it performs integer operations on sequences of four bytes. We did not wish to relax the type rules to the point where these operations are accepted because it would weaken the checking too much. Instead, we provide a way for the programmer to supply the type checker with a list of function names and specific lines of code for which no warnings should be reported. By default, warnings are turned off for the most problematic 15 functions in `libc`, including `memcpy`, `strlen`, and `tzset`. Even though warnings are not reported for these functions, they still update the shadow memory in the expected way.

5   Evaluation

Error Detection. We begin by describing our experiences applying the Hobbes type checker to the student projects from an undergraduate compilers class at Williams College. The assignments implement a compiler for a subset of the C language. Each assignment contains 3000–6000 lines of C code, plus a 3000 line parsing library, and they use the `libc` string, file, and memory routines.

Table 1. Errors found by the Hobbes type checker in a set of compiler assignments from an undergraduate class at Williams College.

Program	LOC	Unallocated	Uninitialized	Type Error	False Alarms
p1	5,600	1	2	2	1
p2	4,033	1	2	1	1
p3	3,571	2	3	0	1
p4	4,260	1	1	1	1
p5	4,671	2	2	1	1

Table 1 summarizes the results of running each assignment on 15 sample inputs. The table shows the number of accesses to unallocated or uninitialized memory, type errors, and false alarms reported by our tool. An error reported multiple times on different inputs is only counted once in the table. In addition, Hobbes suppresses duplicate warning messages and cascading warnings caused by an error reported earlier in a run. For example, if a program reads an uninitialized value, later warnings on that memory location or the value that was read are not reported.

The type checker reported memory errors in all five programs. The causes of these errors include calling `free` on the address of a global variable, accessing memory after it was deallocated, and incorrectly assuming that a routine in the parsing library initialized fields of a structure returned to the client.

The type checker also caught a number of type errors in the programs. In p1, two type errors were found. First, due to incorrect pointer arithmetic, the program overwrote an integer stored in memory with a pointer value. When that memory location was later read and multiplied by an integer, the type checker reported a type mismatch on the operands of the multiply instruction. Purify would not have caught this error since the bad pointer arithmetic would always yield a location allocated to the program. In addition, a function in p1 passed a pointer as an argument to a function declared to take an `int` as a parameter. Inside the body of the function, the integer was cast back to a pointer and dereferenced. The type checker reported the mismatch between parameter and argument type. This code does not work properly on systems where an `int` is too small to hold a pointer, but the compiler did not warn of the problem because the programmer had not written a prototype for the function being called. A similar mistake was found in p5. The remaining two type errors, in p2 and p4, were caused by improper uses of unions similar to Example 1 in Section 2.

The type checker erroneously reported one additional type error in each of the five programs. Each program implemented a hashtable with pointer values for keys. In each program, the function to compute hash codes generated a warning because it performed arithmetic on a pointer.

Clearly, false alarms posed no serious impediment to using the Hobbes type checker on the compiler assignments. To further explore the impact of false alarms on the utility of the Hobbes type checker, we also checked a number of larger, robust UNIX utilities. In general, the false alarm rate was acceptable. For

Table 2. Performance measurements for the SPECint 2000 benchmark. All times are in seconds and are the average of three stable runs. The Ratio columns indicate performance slowdowns relative to the Base Time.

Program	Base Time	Interpreter		Instrumented		MemCheck		TypeCheck	
		Time	Ratio	Time	Ratio	Time	Ratio	Time	Ratio
164.gzip	3.0	147.9	49	219.6	73	268.0	89	470.0	157
175.vpr	3.1	279.6	90	334.1	108	385.1	124	532.5	172
176.gcc	2.3	93.5	41	136.6	59	164.5	72	286.0	124
181.mcf	0.4	8.6	22	12.0	30	15.0	38	21.0	53
186.crafty	5.5	336.8	61	473.9	86	592.8	108	1030.3	187
197.parser	5.4	178.2	33	257.3	48	311.4	58	486.1	90
252.eon	3.9	297.5	76	366.5	94	483.1	124	681.9	175
254.gap	1.4	52.9	38	76.5	55	97.8	70	160.6	115
255.vortex	9.5	472.4	50	687.9	72	889.5	94	1396.6	147
256.bzip2	13.9	587.6	42	791.3	57	930.4	67	1953.0	141
300.twolf	0.4	15.75	39	21.7	59	25.7	64	44.2	111
median			42		59		72		141

example, running `ls` with a number of different command line options netted a total of 8 spurious warnings, all of which were caused by the use of system calls not yet handled by Hobbes[1]. Several runs of `grep` generated spurious warnings, but only about uses of memory management routines in the `obstack` library, which implements a dynamic memory manager to be used in place of `malloc` and `free`. Since the `obstack` routines affect the allocation status of memory, they require special handling to be treated correctly by Hobbes and other run-time analysis tools [4]. Even in programs with much higher false alarm rates, their causes could usually be tracked to only a few problematic code sequences. Hobbes reported approximately 60 and 300 spurious warnings for runs of `vi` and `bash`, respectively. A large fraction of these false alarms are attributed to unhandled system calls, hash functions, and a small number of other code sequences.

We also verified that Hobbes could catch many classes of errors by running it on a test suite of programs with deliberate errors, all of which Hobbes found.

Hobbes catches a number of errors earlier when code is compiled without optimizations. Without optimizations, all local variables (and many intermediate values) reside on the stack, where they are marked invariant. Thus, errors can be caught as soon as an invalid value is written to a variable. In contrast, optimized code uses registers, which are not marked invariant, more heavily.

Performance. We applied the Hobbes checker to the SPECint 2000 benchmarks to evaluate the performance of our tool. Table 2 shows execution times and slowdowns for the interpreter and the interpreter instrumented with three different tools: a tool with empty analysis routines, a memory checker similar to Purify, and the type checker. All measurements are the average of three stable

---

[1] Note that without the suppression techniques for code in `libc` described in the previous chapter, this number would be higher.

runs on a dual-processor 1 GHz Pentium III machine with 1 GB of main memory running the Redhat Linux 2.4.9-smp kernel. We omit the 253.perlbmk benchmark because it creates new processes to do most of the computation and does not accurately reflect the impact of using the interpreter. The interpreter incurs a slowdown of 42 times over the base time. Most of this time is spent decoding the x86 instruction stream. Installing empty analysis routines for all opcodes increases the slowdown from 42 to 59. The interpreter spends the additional time storing registers and setting up activation records for the analysis routines.

MemCheck, a memory checker using a Purify-style checking algorithm, maintains *allocated* and *initialized* bits for each byte of memory. Unlike Purify's approach, MemCheck also shadows the registers with similar information to catch uses of uninitialized data. The memory checker increases the slowdown from 59 to 72. A slowdown of 13 relative to the base time is consistent with our own experience using a tool for Alpha executables based on binary modification and with reported measurements of Purify [3,10].

The Hobbes type checker runs roughly 140 times slower than normal execution, versus a slowdown of 59 for the empty analysis routines. The type checker has not been optimized for speed, and there are several significant ways to improve the performance of our prototype. Each instrumentation function typically checks memory safety first and then type safety. While this separation of tasks keeps the implementation straightforward, the two steps duplicate a nontrivial amount of work. We believe that restructuring the code to eliminate this overlap and further optimizing shadow memory operations will substantially improve performance. Additional improvements are also obtainable by switching from an interpreter to a binary translator and performing static analysis to reduce the number of instructions that must be instrumented. Finally, Hobbes is primarily a tool for testing a system, when performance is less important than correctness.

6   Related Work

Many projects have focused on identifying errors in C programs. We first describe other dynamic tools, and then a few static tools that target low-level code.

Purify [3], described in Section 1, was the first widely used memory access checker. Hobbes tracks a superset of the information tracked in Purify's shadow memory and is capable of identifying the same class of memory access errors. Memory errors that result from earlier type errors will be caught sooner in our system since Hobbes identifies them at the time of the type error. Valgrind is a more recent implementation of a Purify-like checker for Linux binaries [12].

Other memory access checkers change the representation of pointers in the target program to include capabilities [15,6,1,4]. For example, Austin et al. [1] extends the standard pointer representation to include a base and bounds for the block being referenced. Compiler-inserted code checks this extra information at each memory access. Such capability-based approaches can catch errors that Purify (and Hobbes) miss, such as when illegal pointer arithmetic yields a reference to some valid piece of memory. However, they are not compatible with standard compiled C code. Jones and Kelly [4] store pointer base and bounds information separately, thereby achieving a higher degree of backward compatibility.

Patil and Fisher [11] demonstrated that it is sometimes possible to perform program checking in parallel with the target program execution. They present a memory access checker that incurs a slowdown as low as 10% by using a second processor to check the correctness of pointer operations.

C-Cured [10] employs a type inference scheme to statically determine which pointers in the target are used safely and which may be used improperly. Run-time checks are then inserted to check operations involving potentially unsafe pointers. C-Cured uses an extended pointer representation for these checks. This combination of static and dynamic analysis prevents memory access errors and slows down most programs by less than a factor of two, but reliance on non-standard pointer representations limits its effectiveness in some situations.

Loginov et al. [7] present a run-time type checker that uses a shadow memory similar to ours. However, they use source-to-source translation to embed the checking and maintenance code into the target. Thus, they cannot effectively check or track types through functions in compiled libraries, and they handle only programs written entirely in C. These problems also exist in several other run-time type checkers, such as Saber C [5]. Their tool is faster than Hobbes because it instruments only source-level expressions, and not every assembly-language instruction. On standard benchmarks, their tool caused roughly a 50-fold slowdown. We believe that switching to binary translation for Hobbes would eliminate most of this performance difference. A reasonable balance between precision and performance could also be obtained by inserting source code checks wherever possible and binary code checks when source code is not available or external libraries are used.

Several recent studies present static analysis techniques for C and assembly programs that would be very useful to incorporate into Hobbes. For example, Chandra and Reps devised physical type checking to check casts between different structures [2]. They characterize safe casts and define structural subtyping for C by considering the physical layout of structures. Their checking tool can successfully identify potentially unsafe casts in large programs [13]. Xu et al. [16] focus on the related problem of inferring a valid typing for a compiled program to ensure type safety before executing it. They employ abstract interpretation to construct a static approximation of the types of registers and memory at each program point. In addition, Mycroft presents a way to reconstruct C structure declarations from their use in assembly code using type inference [9]. These last two techniques would be particularly useful for reconstructing type information in situations where it is not readily available to Hobbes. Morrisett et al. [8] present a type system for x86 assembly language, but it is very different than the one underlying the Hobbes type checker because it was designed to support compilation from a type-safe high-level language, and not from C.

7   Conclusions and Future Work

Program analysis tools to identify defects in code written in unsafe languages are necessary to improve the reliability of many software systems. The Hobbes type checker can identify a large class of type errors in such systems. While our initial experiments demonstrate the effectiveness of the Hobbes methodology, we would like to improve two key aspects of our system.

Performance.   Although the Hobbes interpreter provides a reasonable first prototype, implementing the type checker with a binary translation tool would significantly improve performance. Additional performance gains can also be obtained by eliminating the need to instrument every instruction. For example, static analysis could identify code fragments that are guaranteed to be type safe or that do not modify the program type state.

Precision.   We would like to incorporate type inference techniques similar to those of Mycroft [9] and Xu et al. [16] to improve precision when full debugging information is unavailable. In addition, we believe that distinguishing different pointer types and identifying boundaries between structure fields and array elements would allow the Hobbes type checker to find some classes of errors sooner than it currently does. We have designed extended type encodings for this information, but we have not yet evaluated how best to use it.

References

1. T. M. Austin, S. E. Breach, and G. S. Sohi. Efficient detection of all pointer and array access errors. In *Proceedings of the Conference on Programming Language Design and Implementation*, pages 290–301, 1994.
2. S. Chandra and T. W. Reps. Physical type checking for C. In *Workshop on Program Analysis For Software Tools and Engineering*, pages 66–75, 1999.
3. R. Hasting and B. Joyce. Purify: Fast detection of memory leaks and access errors. In *Proceedings of the Winter Usenix Conference*, 1992.
4. R. W. M. Jones and P. H. J. Kelly. Backwards-compatible bounds checking for arrays and pointers in C programs. In *Proceedings of the Third International Workshop on Automated Debugging*, pages 13–26. Linkoping University Electronic Press, 1997.
5. S. Kaufer, R. Lopez, and S. Pratap. Saber-C: an interpreterbased programming environment for the C language. In *Proceedings of the Summer Usenix Conference*, pages 161–171, 1988.
6. S. C. Kendall. Bcc: run–time checking for C programs. In *Proceedings of the Usenix Summer Conference*, 1983.
7. A. Loginov, S. H. Yong, S. Horwitz, and T. Reps. Debugging via run-time type checking. In *Proceedings of the Conference on Fundamental Approaches to Software Engineering*, pages 217–232, 2001.
8. J. G. Morrisett, K. Crary, N. Glew, and D. Walker. Stack-based typed assembly language. In *Types in Compilation*, pages 280–52, 1998.
9. A. Mycroft. Type-based decompilation. In *Proceedings of the European Symposium of Programming*, pages 208–223, 1999.

10. G. C. Necula, S. McPeak, and W. Weimer. CCured: type-safe retrofitting of legacy code. In *Proceedings of the Symposium on Principles of Programming Languages*, pages 128–139, 2002.
11. H. Patil and C. Fischer. Low-cost, concurrent checking of pointer and array accesses in c programs. *Software–Practice and Experience*, 27(1):87–110, January 1997.
12. J. Seward. Valgrind, an open-source memory debugger for x86-GNU/Linux, August 2002. Available from `http://developer.kde.org/~sewardj/`.
13. M. Siff, S. Chandra, T. Ball, K. Kunchithapadam, and T. W. Reps. Coping with type casts in C. In *Proceedings of ESEC/FSE '99*, pages 180–198, 1999.
14. A. Srivastava and A. Eustace. ATOM: A system for building customized program analysis tools. In *Proceedings of the Conference on Programming Language Design and Implementation*, pages 196–205, 1994.
15. J. L. Steffen. Adding run-time checking to the portable C compiler. *Software – Practice and Experience*, 22(4):305–316, 1992.
16. Z. Xu, T. Reps, and B. P. Miller. Typestate checking of machine code. In *Proceedings of the European Symposium of Programming*, pages 335–351, 2001.

Precision in Practice: A Type-Preserving Java Compiler[*]

Christopher League[1], Zhong Shao[2], and Valery Trifonov[2]

[1] Long Island University · Computer Science
1 University Plaza, Brooklyn, NY 11201
christopher.league@liu.edu
[2] Yale University · Computer Science
P.O. Box 208285, New Haven, CT 06520
flint@cs.yale.edu

Abstract. Popular mobile code architectures (Java and .NET) include verifiers to check for memory safety and other security properties. Since their formats are relatively high level, supporting a wide range of source language features is awkward. Further compilation and optimization, necessary for efficiency, must be trusted. We describe the design and implementation of a fully type-preserving compiler for Java and ML. Its strongly-typed intermediate language provides a low-level abstract machine model and a type system general enough to prove the safety of a variety of implementation techniques. We show that precise type preservation is within reach for real-world Java systems.

1 Introduction

There is increasing interest in program distribution formats that can be checked for memory safety and other security properties. The Java Virtual Machine (JVM) [1] performs conservative analyses to determine whether the byte codes of each method are safe to execute. Its *class file* format contains type signatures and other symbolic information that makes verification possible. Likewise, the Common Intermediate Language (CIL) of the Microsoft .NET platform [2] includes type information and defines verification conditions for many of its instructions.

As a general distribution format, JVM class files are very high-level and quite partial to the Java language. The byte-code language (JVML) includes no facilities for specifying data layouts or expressing the results of standard optimizations. Compiling other languages for the JVM means making foreign constructs

[*] This work was sponsored in part by the Defense Advanced Research Projects Agency ISO under the title "Scaling Proof-Carrying Code to Production Compilers and Security Policies," ARPA Order No. H559, issued under Contract No. F30602-99-1-0519, and in part by NSF Grants CCR-9901011 and CCR-0081590. The views and conclusions contained in this document are those of the authors and should not be interpreted as representing the official policies, either expressed or implied, of the Defense Advanced Research Projects Agency or the U.S. Government. Java is a registered trademark of Sun Microsystems, Inc. in the U.S. and other countries. CaffeineMark is a trademark of Pendragon Software.

G. Hedin (Ed.): CC 2003, LNCS 2622, pp. 106–120, 2003.
© Springer-Verlag Berlin Heidelberg 2003

look and act like Java classes or objects. That so many translations exist [3] is a testament to the utility of the mobile code concept, and to the ubiquity of the JVM itself. To some extent, CIL alleviates these problems. It supports user-defined value types, stack allocation, tail calls, and pointer arithmetic (which is outside the verifiable subset). Even so, a recent proposal to extend CIL for functional language interoperability [4] added no fewer than 6 new types and 12 new instructions (bringing the total number of `call` instructions to 5) and it still does not support ML's higher-order modules or Haskell's constructor classes.

Another problem with both of these formats is that they require further compilation and optimization to run efficiently on real hardware. Since these phases occur after verification, they are not guaranteed to preserve the verified safety and security properties. Bugs in the compiler may have security implications, so the entire compiler must be *trusted*.

The idea of type-preserving compilation is to remove the compiler from the trusted code base (TCB) by propagating type information through all the compilation and optimization passes. Every representation from the source down to the object code supports verification. Object formats developed in this context include Typed Assembly Language (TAL) [5] and Proof-Carrying Code (PCC) [6].

Many compilers—including Marmot [7], Intel's VM [8], and NaturalBridge BulletTrain [9]—preserve *some* kind of type information in their intermediate code, but none are rigorous enough to support verification. Lower-level code requires more sophisticated type systems. As we will demonstrate, annotations that merely distinguish between integers, floats, and objects of distinct classes are insufficient. Types must enforce subtle invariants, for which logical constructs (such as quantification) are useful.

Our previous work [10,11] developed type-theoretic encodings of many Java features. We proved useful properties, such as type preservation and decidability, but always our goal was to implement the encodings in a practical compiler. In fact, we rejected the classic object encodings [12] because their runtime penalties—superfluous indirections and function calls—were too high.

This paper describes the design and implementation of a compiler based on our encodings. It is the first practical system to use a higher-order polymorphic intermediate language to compile both functional and object-oriented source languages. Additionally, it has the following features:

- Front ends for both Standard ML [13] and JVML that share optimizations and code generators. Programs from either language run together in the same interactive runtime system.
- λJVM, our high-level intermediate language (IL) in the Java front end, uses the same primitive instructions and types as JVML, but is easier to verify and more amenable to optimization (see section 3).
- JFlint, our low-level generic IL, includes function declarations, arrays and structures, and the usual branches and numeric primitives. Its type system includes logical quantifiers (universal, existential, fixed point) and rows [14]

for abstracting over structure suffixes. The instruction stream includes explicit type operations that guide the verifier.

- Unlike the CIL extension [4], our design supports a pleasing synergy between the encodings of Java and ML. JFlint does not, for example, treat Java classes or ML modules as primitives. Rather, it provides a low-level abstract machine model and sophisticated types that are general enough to prove the safety of a variety of implementation techniques. We expand on this in section 4.
- Nothing about our instruction set should surprise a typical compiler developer. Type operations must appear periodically, but most occur in canned sequences that can easily be treated as macros. Although the detailed type information can be quite large, our graph representation maintains optimal sharing. Type annotations within the code are merely pointers into this graph. For debugging purposes, we print the type annotations using short, intuitive names such as `InstOf[java/lang/Object]`.
- All types are discarded after verification, leaving concise and efficient code, *exactly* as an untyped compiler would produce.

Our thesis, in short, is that precise type preservation is within the reach of practical Java systems.

The next section introduces a detailed example to elucidate some of the issues in certifying compilation of object-oriented languages, and to distinguish our approach from that of Cedilla Systems [15]. We postpone discussion of other related projects to section 6.

2   Background: Self-Application and Special J

We begin by attempting to compile the most fundamental operation in object-oriented programming: virtual method invocation.

```
public static void deviant (Object x, Object y)
{ x.toString(); }
```

The standard implementation adds an explicit *self* argument (`this`) to each method and collects the methods into a per-class structure called a *vtable*. Each object contains a pointer to the vtable of the class that created it. To invoke a virtual method, we load the vtable pointer from the object, load the method pointer from the vtable, and then call the method, providing the object itself as `this`.

```
public static void deviant (Object x, Object y)
{ if (x is null) throw NullPointerException;
  r1 = x.vtbl;
  r2 = r1.toString;
  call r2 (x); }
```

A certifying compiler must justify that the indirect call to `r2` is safe; this is not at all obvious. Since x might be an instance of a subclass, the method in r2 might require additional fields and methods that are unknown to the caller. Self-application works thanks to a rather subtle invariant. One way to upset that invariant is to select a method from one object and pass it *another* object as the self argument. For example, replace just the last instruction above with call r2 (y).

This might seem harmless; after all, both x and y are instances of Object. It is unsound, however, and any unsoundness can be exploited. Suppose class Int extends Object by adding an integer field; class Ref adds a byte vector and overrides toString:

```
class Ref extends Object
  {  public byte[] vec;
     public String toString()
       { vec[13] = 0xFF;  return "Ha ha!"; }
  }
```

Then, calling the deviant method as follows:

```
deviant (new Ref(...), new Int(...));
```

will jump to Ref.toString() with this bound to the Int object. Thus, we use an arbitrary integer as an array pointer. This is one reason why virtual method calls are *atomic* operations in both JVML and CIL. How to enforce the self-application invariant in lower-level code is not widely understood.

Cedilla Systems developed *Special J* [15], a proof-carrying code compiler for Java. Their paper described the design, defined some of the predicates used in verification conditions, explained their approach to exceptional control flow, and gave some experimental results. Their running example was hand-optimized code including a loop, an array field, and an exception handler.

Unfortunately, their paper did not adequately describe the safety conditions for virtual method calls. In communication with the authors, we discovered that their current system indeed does *not* properly enforce the necessary invariant on self-application [16]. It gives the type "vtable of Object" to r1 and the type "implementation of String Object.toString()" to r2. The verification condition for the call requires only that the static class of the self argument matches the static class of the object from which the method was fetched. As a result, the consumer's proof checker will *accept* the malicious code given above.

Necula claims that this hole can be patched [16], but it has still not been addressed in subsequent work [17]. One weakness in the Cedilla PCC architecture is that the rules for the *source* language are part of the trusted code base. If they are unsound, all bets are off. Moreover, the rules and the code have different levels of granularity. PCC is machine code, but its logical predicates refer specifically to Java constructs such as objects, interfaces, and methods. To support another language, an entirely new set of language-specific predicates and rules must be added to the TCB.

In the next section, we briefly survey the architecture of our compiler. Its key strongly-typed intermediate language is the topic of section 4.

3   Architecture of Our Compiler

Standard ML of New Jersey is an interactive runtime system and compiler based on a strongly-typed intermediate language called FLINT [18]. We extended the FLINT language of version 110.30 and implemented a new front end for Java class files. We updated the optimization phases to recognize the new features. The code generator and runtime system remain unchanged.

The Java front end parses class files and converts them to a high-level IL called λJVM. This language uses the same primitive instructions and types as JVML. The difference is that λJVM replaces the implicit operand stack and untyped local variables with explicit data flow and fully-typed single-assignment bindings. This alternate representation has several advantages. First, it is simpler to verify than JVML, because all the hard analyses (object initialization, subroutines, *etc.*) are performed during translation and their results preserved in type annotations. The type checker for λJVM is just 260 lines of SML code. Second, as a *functional* IL, it is (like static single assignment form) amenable to further analysis and optimization [19,20]. Although we have not implemented them, this phase would be suitable for class hierarchy analysis and various object-aware optimizations [21] because the class hierarchy and method invocations are still explicit.

We designed λJVM so that its control and data flow mimic that of JFlint. This means that the next phase of our compiler is simply an *expansion* of the JVML types and operations into more detailed types and lower-level code. For further details about λJVM, please see [22].

On JFlint, we run several contraction optimizations (inlining, common subexpression elimination, *etc.*), and type-check the code after each pass. Since method invocations are no longer atomic in JFlint, these optimizations readily lift and merge vtable accesses. A future version of the JFlint type system will even have support for optimizing array bounds checks [23].

We discard the type information before converting to MLRISC [24] for final instruction selection and register allocation. To generate typed machine code, we would need to preserve types throughout the back end. The techniques of Morrisett *et al.* [5] should apply directly, since JFlint is based on System F.

Figure 1 demonstrates the SML/JFlint system in action. The top-level loop accepts Standard ML code, as usual. The JFlint subsystem is controlled via the Java structure; its members include:

- Java.classPath : string list ref
  Initialized from the CLASSPATH environment variable, this is a list of directories where the loader will look for class files.
- Java.load : string -> unit
  looks up the named class using classPath, resolves and loads any dependencies, then compiles the byte codes and executes the class initializer.
- Java.run : string -> string list -> unit
  ensures that the named class is loaded, then attempts to call its main method with the given arguments.

```
Standard ML of New Jersey v110.30 [JFLINT 1.2]
- Java.classPath := ["/home/league/r/java/tests"];
val it = () : unit
- val main = Java.run "Hello";
[parsing Hello]
[parsing java/lang/Object]
[compiling java/lang/Object]
[compiling Hello]
[initializing java/lang/Object]
[initializing Hello]
val main = fn : string list -> unit
- main ["Duke"];
Hello, Duke
val it = () : unit
- main [];
uncaught exception ArrayIndexOutOfBounds
  raised at: Hello.main([Ljava/lang/String;)V
- ^D
```

Fig. 1. Compiling and running a Java program in SML/NJ.

The session in figure 1 sets the `classPath`, loads the `Hello` class, and binds its `main` method, using partial application of `Java.run`. The method is then invoked twice with different arguments. The second invocation wrongly accesses `argv[0]`; this error surfaces as the ML exception `Java.ArrayIndexOutOfBounds`.

This demonstration shows SML code interacting with a complete Java program. Since both run in the same runtime system, very fine-grained interactions should be possible. Benton and Kennedy [25] designed extensions to SML to allow seamless interaction with Java code when both are compiled for the Java virtual machine. Their design should work quite well in our setting also.

Ours is essentially a *static* Java compiler, as it does not handle dynamic class loading or the `java.lang.reflect` API. These features are more difficult to verify using a static type system, but they are topics of active research. The SML runtime system does not yet support kernel threads, so we have ignored concurrency and synchronization.

Finally, our runtime system does not, for now, dynamically load native code. This is a dubious practice anyway; such code has free reign over the runtime system, thus nullifying any safety guarantees won by verifying pure code. Nevertheless, this restriction is unfortunate because it limits the set of existing Java libraries that we can use.

4   Overview of the JFlint IL

To introduce the JFlint language, we begin with a second look at virtual method invocation in Java: below is the expansion into JFlint of a Java method that takes Objects x and y and calls x.toString().

```
obedient (x, y : InstOf[java/lang/Object]?) =
  switch (x)
    case null: throw NullPointerException;
    case non-null x1:
.      <f1,m1; x2 : Self[java/lang/Object] f1 m1>
.          = OPEN x1;
.      x3 = UNFOLD x2;
       r1 = x3.vtbl;
       r2 = r1.toString;
       call r2 (x2);
```

The dots at left indicate erasable type operations. The postfix ? indicates that the arguments could be null. The code contains the same operations as before: null check, two loads, and a call. The null check is expressed as a switch that, in the non-null case, binds the new identifier x1 to the value of x, but now with type InstOf[java/lang/Object] (losing the ?). It is customary to use new names whenever values change type, as this dramatically simplifies type checking.

4.1   Type Operations

The new instructions following the null check (OPEN and UNFOLD) are type operations. InstOf abbreviates a particular existential type (we clarify the meanings of the various types in section 4.4):

```
InstOf[java/lang/Object] =
      exists f0, m0: Self[java/lang/Object] f0 m0
```

OPEN eliminates the existential by binding fresh type variables (f1 and m1 in the example) to the hidden witness types. Likewise, Self abbreviates a fixed point (recursive) type:

```
Self[java/lang/Object] fi mi =
   fixpt s0: { vtbl : Meths[java/lang/Object] s0 mi;
               hash : int;
               fi }

Meths[java/lang/Object] sj mj =
           { toString : sj -> InstOf[java/lang/String];
             hashCode : sj -> int;
             mj(sj) }
```

UNFOLD eliminates the fixed point by replacing occurrences of the bound variable s0 with the recursive type itself. These operations leave us with a *structural* view of the object bound to x3; it is a pointer to a record of fields prefixed by the vtable (a pointer to a sequence of functions). Importantly, the fresh type variables introduced by the OPEN (f1 and m1) find their way into the types of the vtable functions. Specifically, r2 points to a function of type Self[java/lang/Object] f1 m1 -> InstOf[java/lang/String]. Thus the only valid self argument for r2 is x2. The malicious code of section 2 is

```
signature JFLINT = sig
 datatype value                              (* identifiers and constants *)
  = VAR of id | INT of Int32.int | STRING ...

 datatype exp
  = LETREC of fundec list * exp
  | LET    of id * exp * exp
  | CALL   of id * value list
  | RETURN of value
  | STRUCT of value list              * id * exp
  | LOAD   of value * int             * id * exp
  | STORE  of value * int * value         * exp
  ...                                 (* type manipulation instructions *)
  | INST   of id * ty list            * id * exp
  | FOLD   of value * ty              * id * exp
  | UNFOLD of value                   * id * exp
  | PACK   of ty list * (value*ty) list * id * exp
  | OPEN   of value * id list * (id*ty) list * exp
  ...
 withtype fundec = id * (id * ty) list * exp
end
```

Fig. 2. Representation of JFlint code.

rejected because opening y would introduce brand new type variables (f2 and
m2, say); these never match the variables in the type of r2. The precise typing
rules for UNFOLD and OPEN are available elsewhere [11,26].

After the final verification, the type operations are completely discarded and
the aliased identifiers are renamed. This *erasure* leaves us with *precisely* the same
operational behavior that we used in an untyped setting. Like other instructions,
type manipulations yield to simple optimizations. We can, for example, eliminate
redundant OPENs and hoist loop-invariant UNFOLDs. In fact, using *online* common
subexpression elimination, we avoid emitting redundant operations in the first
place. For a series of method calls and field accesses on the same object, we would
OPEN and UNFOLD it just once. Although the type operations have no runtime
penalty, optimizing them is advantageous. First, fewer type operations means
smaller programs and faster compilation and verification. Second, excess type
operations often hide further optimization opportunities in runtime code.

4.2 Code Representation

Our examples use a pretty-printed surface syntax for JFlint. Figure 2 contains a
portion of the SML signature for representing such code in our compiler. Identifiers and constants comprise *values*. Instructions operate on values and bind
their results to new names. Loads and stores on structures refer to the integer
offset of the field. Function declarations have type annotations on the formal
parameters. Non-escaping functions whose call sites are all in tail position are
very lightweight, more akin to basic blocks than to functions in C.

This language is closer to machine code than to JVML, but not quite as low-level as typed assembly language. Allocating and initializing a structure, for example, is one instruction: STRUCT. Similarly, the CALL instruction passes n arguments and transfers control all at once; the calling convention is not explicit. It is possible to break these down and still preserve verifiability [5], but this midpoint is simpler and still quite useful for optimization.

There are two hurdles for a conventional compiler developer using a strongly-typed IL like JFlint. The first is simply the functional notation, but it can be understood by analogy to SSA. Moreover, it has additional benefits such as enforcing the dominator property and providing homes for type annotations [19]. The second hurdle is the type operations themselves: knowing where to insert and how to optimize them. The latter is simple; most standard optimizations are trivially type-preserving. Type operations have uses and defs just like other instructions, and type variables behave (in most cases) like any other identifier.

As for knowing what types to define and where in the code to insert the type operations: we developed recipes for Java primitives [10,11]; some of these appear in figure 3. A thorough understanding of the type system is helpful for developing successful new recipes, but experimentation can be fruitful as long as the type checker is used as a safety net. Extending the type system without forfeiting soundness is, of course, a more delicate enterprise; a competent background in type theory and semantics is essential.

4.3   Interfaces and Casts

The open-unfold sequence used in method invocation appears whenever we need to access an object's structure. Getting or setting a field starts the same way: null check, open, unfold (see the first expanded primop in figure 3).

Previously, we showed the expansion of InstOf[C] as an existential type. Suppose D extends C; then, InstOf[D] is a *different* existential. In Java, any object of type D also has type C. To realize this property in JFlint, we use explicit type coercions. (This helps keep the type system simple; otherwise we would need F-bounded quantifiers [27] with 'top' subtyping [28].) λJVM marks such coercions as *upcasts*. They are expanded into JFlint code just like other operators.

An upcast should not require any runtime operations. Indeed, apart from the null test, the upcast recipe in figure 3 is nothing but type operations: open the object and repackage it to hide more of the fields and methods. Therefore, only the null test remains after type erasure: (x == null? null : x). This is easily recognized and eliminated during code generation.

In Java, casts from a class to an interface type are also implicit (assuming the class implements the interface). On method calls to objects of interface type, a compiler cannot statically know where to find the interface method. Most implementations use a dynamic search through the vtable to locate either the method itself, or an embedded *itable* containing all the methods of a given interface. This search is expensive, so it pays to cache the results. With the addition of unordered (permutable) record types and a trusted primitive for the dynamic

```
putfield C.f (x : InstOf[C]?; y : T) ⟹
 switch (x) case null: throw NullPointerException;
 case non-null x1:
.   <f3,m3; x2 : Self[C] f3 m3> = OPEN x1;
.     x3 = UNFOLD x2;
      x3.f := y;

upcast D,C (x : InstOf[D]?) ⟹
 switch (x) case null: return null : InstOf[C]?;
 case non-null x1:
.   <f4,m4; x2 : Self[D] f4 m4> = OPEN x1;
.     x2 = PACK f5=NewFlds[D] f4, m5=NewMeths[D] m4
            WITH x1 : Self[C] f5 m5;
.     return x2 : InstOf[C]?;

invokeinterface I.m (x : IfcObj[I]?; v1...vn) ⟹
 switch (x) case null: throw NullPointerException;
 case non-null x1:
.   <t; x1 : IfcPair[I] t> = OPEN x1;
      r1 = x1.itbl;
      r2 = x1.obj;
      r3 = r1.m;
      call r3 (r2, v1, ..., vn);
```

Fig. 3. Recipes for some λJVM primitives.

search, interface types pose no further problems. Verifying the searching and caching code in a static type system would be quite complex. As an experiment, we implemented a unique representation of interfaces for which the dynamic search is unnecessary [10].

In our system, interface calls are about as cheap as virtual calls (null check, a few loads and an indirect call). We represent interface objects as a pair of the interface method table and the underlying object. To invoke a method, we fetch it from the itable and pass it the object as the self argument. This implies a non-trivial coercion when an object is upcast from a class to an interface type, or from one interface to another: fetch the itable and create the pair. Since all interface relationships are declared in Java, the itables can be created when each class is compiled, and then linked into the class vtable. Since the layout of the vtable is known at the point of upcast, dynamic search is unnecessary.

The final recipe in figure 3 illustrates this technique. The new type abbreviations for representing interface objects are, for example:

```
IfcObj[java/lang/Runnable] =
     exists t . IfcPair[java/lang/Runnable] t
IfcPair[java/lang/Runnable] t =
     { itbl : { run : t -> void },  obj : t }
```

The existential hides the actual class of the object. Just as with virtual invocation, the interface invocation relies on a sophisticated invariant. A method

```
signature JTYPE = sig
 type ty
 val var     : int * int -> ty                    (* type variable *)
 val arrow   : ty list * ty -> ty                 (* function type *)
 val struct  : ty -> ty                           (* structure types *)
 val row     : ty * ty -> ty
 val empty   : int -> ty
 ...                                              (* quantified types *)
 val exists  : kind list * ty list -> ty
 val fixpt   : kind list * ty list -> ty
 val lam     : kind list * ty -> ty               (* higher-order *)
 val app     : ty * ty list -> ty
end
```

Fig. 4. Abstract interface for JFlint type representation.

from the itable must be given a compatible object as the self argument. The existential ensures that only the packaged object will be used with methods in the itable.

This scheme also supports multiple inheritance of interfaces. Suppose interface AB extends both interfaces A (with method a) and B (with method b). The itable of AB will contain pointers to itables for each of the super interfaces: To upcast from AB to B, just open the interface object, fetch itbl.B, pair it with obj, and re-package.

Unfortunately, Java's covariant subtyping of arrays (widely considered to be a misfeature) is not directly compatible with this interface representation. Imagine casting an array of class type to an array of interface type—we would need to coerce each element! For the purpose of experimentation, we ignored the covariant array subtyping rule. In the future, we would like to find a hybrid approach that allows cheap, easily verifiable invocation of interface methods, but is still compatible with the Java specification.

4.4   Type Representation

To support efficient compilation, types are represented differently from code. Figure 4 contains part of the abstract interface to our type system. Most of our types are standard: based on the higher-order polymorphic lambda calculus (see [29] for an overview).

A structure is a pointer to a sequence of fields, but we represent the sequence as a linked list of *rows*. Any *tail* of the list can be replaced with a type variable, providing a handle on suffixes of the structure. The InstOf definition used an existential quantifier [30] to hide the types of additional fields and methods; these are rows.

A universal quantifier—precisely the inverse—allows outsiders to provide types; in our encoding, it models inheritance. Subclasses provide new types for the additional fields and methods. *Kinds* classify types and provide bounds for quantified variables. They ensure that rows are composed properly by tracking the structure offset where each row begins [14].

Our object encodings rely only on standard constructs, so our type system is rooted in well-developed type theory and logic. The soundness proof for a similar system is a perennial assignment in our semantics course. The essence was even formalized in machine-checkable form using Twelf [31].

4.5   Synergy

Judging from the popular formats, it appears that there are just two ways to support different kinds of source languages in a single type-safe intermediate language. Either favor one language and make everyone else conform (JVM) or incorporate the union of all the requested features (CIL, ILX [2,4]). CIL instructions distinguish, for example, between loading functions *vs.* values from objects *vs.* classes. ILX adds instructions to load from closure environments and from algebraic data types.

JFlint demonstrates a better approach: provide a low-level abstract machine model and general types capable of proving safety of various uses of the machine primitives. Structures in JFlint model Java objects, vtables, classes, and interfaces, plus ML records and the value parts of modules. Neither Java nor ML has a universal quantifier, but it is useful for encoding both Java inheritance and ML polymorphism. The existential type is essential for object encoding but also for ML closures and abstract data types.

We believe this synergy speaks well of our approach in general. Still, it does not mean that we can support all type-safe source languages equally well. Java and ML still have much in common; they work well with precise generational garbage collection and their exceptions are similar enough. Weakly typed formats, such as C-- [32], are more ambitious in supporting a wider variety of language features, including different exception and memory models. Practical type systems to support that level of flexibility are challenging; further research is needed.

5   Implementation Concerns

If a type-preserving compiler is to scale, types and type operations must be implemented with extreme care. The techniques of Shao, et al. made the FLINT typed IL practical enough to use in a production compiler [18]. Although different type structures arise in our Java encodings, the techniques are quite successful. A full type-preserving compile of the 12 classes in the CaffeineMark 3.0 embedded series takes 2.4 seconds on a 927 MHz Intel Pentium III Linux workstation. This is about 60% more than `gcj`, the GNU Java compiler [33]. Since `gcj` is written in C and our compiler in SML, this performance gap can easily be attributed to linguistic differences. Verifying both the λJVM and the JFlint code adds another half second.

Run times are promising, but can be improved. (Our goal, of course, is to preserve type safety; speed is secondary.) CaffeineMark runs at about a third the speed in SML/NJ compared to `gcj` `-O2`. There are several reasons for this difference. First, many standard optimizations, especially on loops, have not been implemented in JFlint yet. Second, the code generator is still heavily tuned for SML; structure representations, for example, are more boxed than they should be. Finally, the runtime system is also tuned for SML; to support `callcc`, every activation record is heap-allocated and subject to garbage collection. Benchmarking is always fraught with peril. In our case, meaningful results are especially elusive because we can only compare with compilers that differ in *many* ways besides type preservation.

6   Related Work

Throughout the paper, we made comparisons to the Common Intermediate Language (CIL) of the Microsoft .NET platform [2] and ILX, a proposed extension for functional language interoperability [4]. We discussed the proof-carrying code system Special J [15] at length in section 2. We mentioned C-- [32], the portable assembly language, in section 4.5. Several other systems warrant mention.

Benton et al. built MLj, an SML compiler targeting the Java Virtual Machine [34]; we mentioned their extensions for interoperability earlier [25]. Since JVML is less expressive than JFlint, they monomorphize SML polymorphic functions and functors. On some applications, this increases code size dramatically. JVML is less appropriate as an intermediate format for functional languages because it does not model their type systems well. Polymorphic code must either be duplicated or casts must be inserted. JFlint, on the other hand, completely models the type system of SML.

Wright, et al. [35] compile a Java subset to a typed intermediate language, but they use unordered records and resort to dynamic type checks because their system is too weak to type self application. Neal Glew [36] translates a simple class-based object calculus into an intermediate language with F-bounded polymorphism [27] and a special 'self' quantifier. A more detailed comparison with this encoding is available elsewhere [11,26].

Many researchers use techniques reminiscent of those in our λJVM translation format. Marmot converts bytecode to a conventional high-level IL using abstract interpretation and type elaboration [7,37]. Gagnon et al. [38] give an algorithm to infer static types for local variables in JVML. Since they do not use a single-assignment form, they must occasionally split variables into their separate uses. Since they do not support set types, they insert explicit type casts to solve the multiple interface problem. Amme et al. [39] translate Java to SafeTSA, an alternative mobile code representation based on SSA form. Since they start with Java, they avoid the complications of subroutines and set types. Basic blocks must be split wherever exceptions can occur, and control-flow edges are added to the `catch` and `finally` blocks. Otherwise, SafeTSA is similar in spirit to λJVM.

7   Conclusion

We have described the design and implementation of our type-preserving compiler for both Java and SML. Its strongly-typed intermediate language provides a low-level abstract machine model and a type system general enough to prove the safety of a variety of implementation techniques. This approach produces a pleasing synergy between the encodings of both languages. We have shown that type operations can be implemented efficiently and do not preclude optimizations or efficient execution. We therefore believe that precise type preservation is within reach for real-world Java systems.

References

[1] Lindholm, T., Yellin, F.: The Java Virtual Machine Specification. 2nd edn. Addison-Wesley (1999)

[2] ECMA: Common language infrastructure. Drafts of the TC39/TG3 standardization process. http://msdn.microsoft.com/net/ecma/ (2001)

[3] Tolksdorf, R.: Programming languages for the JVM. http://flp.cs.tu-berlin.de/~tolk/vmlanguages.html (2002)

[4] Syme, D.: ILX: extending the .NET Common IL for functional language interoperability. In: Proc. BABEL Workshop on Multi-Language Infrastructure and Interoperability, ACM (2001)

[5] Morrisett, G., Walker, D., Crary, K., Glew, N.: From System F to typed assembly language. ACM Trans. on Programming Languages and Systems **21** (1999)

[6] Necula, G.C.: Proof-carrying code. In: Proc. Symp. on Principles of Programming Languages, Paris, ACM (1997) 106–119

[7] Fitzgerald, R., Knoblock, T.B., Ruf, E., Steensgaard, B., Tarditi, D.: Marmot: an optimizing compiler for Java. Software: Practice and Experience **30** (2000)

[8] Stichnoth, J.M., Lueh, G.Y., Cierniak, M.: Support for garbage collection at every instruction in a Java compiler. In: Proc. Conf. on Programming Language Design and Implementation, Atlanta, ACM (1999) 118–127

[9] NaturalBridge: Personal comm. with Kenneth Zadeck and David Chase (2001)

[10] League, C., Shao, Z., Trifonov, V.: Representing Java classes in a typed intermediate language. In: Proc. Int'l Conf. Functional Programming, Paris, ACM (1999)

[11] League, C., Shao, Z., Trifonov, V.: Type-preserving compilation of Featherweight Java. ACM Trans. on Programming Languages and Systems **24** (2002)

[12] Bruce, K.B., Cardelli, L., Pierce, B.C.: Comparing object encodings. Information and Computation **155** (1999) 108–133

[13] Milner, R., Tofte, M., Harper, R., MacQueen, D.: The Definition of Standard ML (Revised). MIT Press (1997)

[14] Rémy, D.: Syntactic theories and the algebra of record terms. Technical Report 1869, INRIA (1993)

[15] Colby, C., Lee, P., Necula, G.C., Blau, F., Cline, K., Plesko, M.: A certifying compiler for Java. In: Proc. Conf. on Programming Language Design and Implementation, Vancouver, ACM (2000)

[16] Necula, G.C.: Personal communication (2001)

[17] Schneck, R.R., Necula, G.C.: A gradual approach to a more trustworthy, yet scalable, proof-carrying code. In: Proc. Conf. on Automated Deduction. (2002)

[18] Shao, Z., League, C., Monnier, S.: Implementing typed intermediate languages. In: Proc. Int'l Conf. Functional Programming, Baltimore, ACM (1998) 313–323

[19] Appel, A.W.: SSA is functional programming. *ACM SIGPLAN* Notices (1998)

[20] Cytron, R., Ferrante, J., Rosen, B.K., Wegman, M.N., Zadeck, F.K.: Efficiently computing static single assignment form and the control dependence graph. ACM Trans. on Programming Languages and Systems **13** (1991) 451–490

[21] Dean, J., Grove, D., Chambers, C.: Optimization of object-oriented programs using static class hierarchy analysis. In: Proc. European Conf. Object-Oriented Programming. (1995)

[22] League, C., Trifonov, V., Shao, Z.: Functional Java bytecode. In: Proc. 5th World Conf. on Systemics, Cybernetics, and Informatics. (2001) Workshop on Intermediate Representation Engineering for the Java Virtual Machine.

[23] Shao, Z., Saha, B., Trifonov, V., Papaspyrou, N.: A type system for certified binaries. In: Proc. Symp. on Principles of Programming Languages. (2002)

[24] George, L.: Customizable and reusable code generators. Technical report, Bell Labs (1997)

[25] Benton, N., Kennedy, A.: Interlanguage working without tears: Blending ML with Java. In: Proc. Int'l Conf. Functional Programming, Paris, ACM (1999) 126–137

[26] League, C.: A Type-Preserving Compiler Infrastructure. PhD thesis, Yale University (2002)

[27] Canning, P., Cook, W., Hill, W., Olthoff, W., Mitchell, J.C.: F-bounded polymorphism for object-oriented programming. In: Proc. Int'l Conf. on Functional Programming and Computer Architecture, ACM (1989) 273–280

[28] Castagna, G., Pierce, B.C.: Decidable bounded quantification. In: Proc. Symp. on Principles of Programming Languages, Portland, ACM (1994)

[29] Barendregt, H.: Typed lambda calculi. In Abramsky, S., Gabbay, D., Maibaum, T., eds.: Handbook of Logic in Computer Science. Volume 2. Oxford (1992)

[30] Mitchell, J.C., Plotkin, G.D.: Abstract types have existential type. ACM Transactions on Programming Languages and Systems **10** (1988) 470–502

[31] Schürmann, C., Yu, D., Ni, Z.: An encoding of F-omega in LF. In: Proc. Workshop on Mechanized Reasoning about Languages with Variable Binding, Siena (2001)

[32] Peyton Jones, S., Ramsey, N., Reig, F.: C—: a portable assembly language that supports garbage collection. In Nadathur, G., ed.: Proc. Conf. on Principles and Practice of Declarative Programming. Springer (1999) 1–28

[33] Bothner, P.: A GCC-based Java implementation. In: Proc. IEEE Compcon. (1997)

[34] Benton, N., Kennedy, A., Russell, G.: Compiling Standard ML to Java bytecodes. In: Proc. Int'l Conf. Functional Programming, Baltimore, ACM (1998) 129–140

[35] Wright, A., Jagannathan, S., Ungureanu, C., Hertzmann, A.: Compiling Java to a typed lambda-calculus: A preliminary report. In: Proc. Int'l Workshop on Types in Compilation. Volume 1473 of LNCS., Berlin, Springer (1998) 1–14

[36] Glew, N.: An efficient class and object encoding. In: Proc. Conf. on Object-Oriented Programming Systems, Languages, and Applications, ACM (2000)

[37] Knoblock, T., Rehof, J.: Type elaboration and subtype completion for Java bytecode. In: Proc. Symp. on Principles of Programming Languages. (2000) 228–242

[38] Gagnon, E., Hendren, L., Marceau, G.: Efficient inference of static types for Java bytecode. In: Proc. Static Analysis Symp. (2000)

[39] Amme, W., Dalton, N., von Ronne, J., Franz, M.: SafeTSA: A type safe and referentially secure mobile-code representation based on static single assignment form. In: Proc. Conf. on Programming Language Design and Implementation, ACM (2001)

The MAGICA Type Inference Engine for MATLAB®*

Pramod G. Joisha and Prithviraj Banerjee

Department of Electrical and Computer Engineering, Northwestern University, USA.
{pjoisha, banerjee}@ece.northwestern.edu

1   Introduction

MAGICA (MAthematica system for General-purpose Inferring and Compile-time Analyses) is an extensible inference engine that can determine the types (value range, intrinsic type and array shape) of expressions in a MATLAB program. Written as a Mathematica application, it is designed as an add-on module that any MATLAB compiler infrastructure can use to obtain high-quality type inferences.

1.1   A Type Inference Using MAGICA

Lines *In[1]* and *Out[2]* below demonstrate a simple interaction with MAGICA through a notebook interface.[1] On line *In[1]*, the MAGICA type function object is applied on a representation of the MATLAB expression tanh(3.78i). MAGICA's response, shown on *Out[2]*, is the inferred type of tanh(3.78i). In this case, "type" is the expression $\{v, i, s\}$ where v, i and s are the value range, intrinsic type and array shape of tanh(3.78i); *Out[2]* indicates these to be the point 0.742071 i, the $nonreal intrinsic type designator, and the two-dimensional array shape with unit extents along both dimensions—that is, the scalar shape.

```
In[1]:= type[tanh[3.78i]]
Out[1]= {0.742071 i, $nonreal, {⟨1 , 1⟩, 2}}
```

1.2   Feature Support

The above is an example of a type inference on a single MATLAB expression. MAGICA can infer the types of whole MATLAB programs comprising an arbitrary number of user-defined functions, each having an arbitrary number of statements. User-defined functions can return multiple values, can consist of

---

* This research was supported by DARPA under Contract F30602–98–2–0144, and by NASA under Contract 276685/NAS5–00212. *Mathematica*® fonts by Wolfram Research, Inc.

[1] The outputs in this paper can be exactly reproduced by typing the code shown against each *In[n]:=* prompt into a notebook interface to version 1.0 of MAGICA, running on Mathematica 4.1.

G. Hedin (Ed.): CC 2003, LNCS 2622, pp. 121–125, 2003.

assignment statements, the `for` and `while` loops, and the `if` conditional state-ment. (All these MATLAB constructs are explained in [3].) In addition, MAGICA can handle close to 70 built-in functions in MATLAB. These include important Type II operations[2] like `subsref`, `subsasgn` and `colon` that are used in array indexing and colon expressions. For the most part, the full or nearly the full semantics of a built-in function, as specified in [3], is supported. For instance, subscripts in array indexing expressions can themselves be arrays, and arrays can be complex-valued. Not all of MATLAB's features are currently handled; these include structures, cell arrays and recent additions like function handles.

2   Representing MATLAB in MAGICA

MAGICA symbolically represents constructs in MATLAB. An example of this is the Mathematica expression `plus[a, b]`, which is MAGICA's representation of the MATLAB expression `a+b`. On line *In[1]* above, the Mathematica expression `tanh[3.78i]` was used to denote the MATLAB expression `tanh(3.78i)`. The idea of functionally representing a MATLAB expression can also be used to denote high-level constructs. For instance, the MATLAB assignment statement $1 \leftarrow \cos(3.099)$, where 1 is a MATLAB program variable, is represented in MAGICA as shown on line *In[2]* below.

> *In[2]:=* **assignment[\$\$lhs :→ 1, \$\$rhs :→ cos[3.099]]**
>
> *Out[2]=* assignment(\$\$lhs :→ 1, \$\$rhs :→ cos(3.099))

The expression's *head* is `assignment` and this is used to uniquely identify MAT-LAB assignments. The *tags* `$$lhs` and `$$rhs` serve to identify the assignment's left-hand side and right-hand side. We call 1 and `cos[3.099]` as *tag values*. A tag value can be any expression; this allows for the representation of arbitrary MATLAB assignments, including the multiple-value assignment [3].

In general, MATLAB statements are represented in MAGICA as

$$h[x_1 :\rightarrow y_1, x_2 :\rightarrow y_2, \ldots, x_n :\rightarrow y_n]$$

where the head h serves as a construct identifier, and where the delayed rules [4] $x_i :\rightarrow y_i$ $(1 \leq i \leq n)$ stand for *tag-value pairs*. MAGICA places no signif-icance on the position of a tag-value pair; this point should be kept in mind when making new definitions to extend the MAGICA system. A fair amount of documentation regarding data structure layouts has been coded into MAGICA itself as `usage` messages [4]; this provides a convenient, on-line way of pulling up layout information while interacting with MAGICA.

---

[2] MATLAB's built-in functions can be classified into one of three groups, based on how the shapes of the outputs are dependent on the shapes of the inputs [1]. Type I built-ins produce outputs whose shapes are completely determined by the shapes of the arguments, if any. Type II built-ins produce an output whose shape is *also* dependent on the elemental values of at least one input. All remaining built-ins fall into the Type III group.

In[3]:= **?if**

if[$$condition :> c_, $$then :> t_, $$else :> e_]
is the functional equivalent of an if statement in MATLAB. Forms such as
$$condition --> c, $$then --> t and $$else --> e can also be used.

3   Transitive Closure of a Graph

The two boxes in Figure 1 display a complete MATLAB program that computes the transitive closure of a graph. The graph is represented in the $N \times N$ adjacency matrix A, which is initialized arbitrarily in the function tclosure. Its transitive closure is returned in B. The shown code is directly from Alexey Malishevsky's thesis [2], with three nontrivial changes: (1) the tic and toc timing commands were removed, (2) disp was used to display B, and (3) the original monolithic script was reorganized into two files, one containing the function driver and the other containing tclosure.

3.1   M-File Contexts

Input files that constitute a MATLAB program are referred to as *M-files* in MATLAB parlance. Every M-file has its own parsed representation in MAGICA, which we call an *M-file context*. Through Mathematica's information-hiding context mechanism [4], MAGICA provides a way to save, and later retrieve, the M-file contexts of a MATLAB program. On line *In[4]* below, the M-file contexts of the two user-defined functions driver and tclosure, saved in an earlier session of MAGICA, are loaded from disk.[3]

In[4]:= **Scan[load[#, load$Disk → True]&, {"tclosure`", "driver`"}]**

An M-file context is basically a collection of Mathematica definitions that capture information about a user-defined MATLAB function. As an example, for a user-defined function f, a definition is made against the statements function object so that statements[f] expands to the function body of f. This is how the type object operates on the statements in the body of driver on line *In[5]* below.[4]

In[5]:= **type[statements[driver]] // Timing**

Out[5]= {5.47 Second, {_ **12 N1** → {512., $integer, {⟨1, 1⟩, 2}},
     _ **10 B1** → {[[0, 1]], $boolean, {⟨512, 512⟩, 2}},
     {Indeterminate, $illegal, {⟨-1, 1⟩, 2}}}}}

---

[3] These representations are in ASCII, and can be manually or automatically generated.
[4] The timings are on a 440 MHz Solaris 7 UltraSPARC-IIi having 128MB of main memory.

```
function driver        function B = tclosure(N)              end;
                       % Initialization.                      end;
N ← 512;               A ← zeros(N, N);                      end;
                       for ii = 1:N,                          B ← A;
B ← tclosure(N);         for jj = 1:N,                        % Closure.
                           if ii*jj < N/2,                     ii ← N/2;
disp(B);                     A(N-ii, ii+jj) ← 1;               while ii >= 1,
                             A(ii, N-ii-jj) ← 1;                 B ← B*B;
                           end;                                  ii ← ii/2;
                           if ii == jj,                        end;
                             A(ii, jj) ← 1;                    B ← B > 0;
```

Fig. 1. The MATLAB Transitive Closure Program

3.2   Interprocedural Type Inference

The definitions against the **type** object—currently over a 100—take care of propagating information across user-defined function interfaces. Thus the application of **type** on line *In[5]* causes type information pertaining to N to be propagated into tclosure, resulting in the shown type inference for its output variable B. On line *Out[5]*, _12N1 stands for N and _10B1 for B; this renaming is an artifact of the way in which the Mathematica representations for this program were automatically generated. *Out[5]* thus shows that the value range of B is $[[0,1]]$, its intrinsic type is $boolean, and that its shape is 512×512. The third inference on *Out[5]* represents the type of disp's outcome; the shown values reflect the fact that disp doesn't return anything.

4   Architecture

MAGICA is used through a *front-end*, which is a separate operating system process that builds a Mathematica representation of an input MATLAB program. The front-end transfers the representation to MAGICA for type analysis; the type inferences that MAGICA generates are transferred back, for use in type-related optimizations, code generation or simply for code annotation and visualization. Exchanges between the front-end and MAGICA happen across an interprocess communication link using the MathLink protocol [4]. Figure 2 shows three existing front-ends to MAGICA. Two of these—the GUI-based notebook and the text-based interface—are shipped with Mathematica. Interacting with MAGICA using them requires either the handcrafting of the program representations that are to be type inferred, or the availability of those representations on disk. (*In[1]* and *In[2]* are examples of handcrafted representations; *In[4]* uses prefabricated representations.) The third front-end, called $\mathbf{M^{AT}C}$, is a custom-built one that takes a MATLAB program in its native form and translates it to optimized C; it uses MAGICA as the inference engine to obtain the necessary type information. In fact, it was by using $\mathbf{M^{AT}C}$ that the M-file contexts for the example in

§ 3 were produced in advance. Figure 2 also shows the disk image of a sample M-file context.

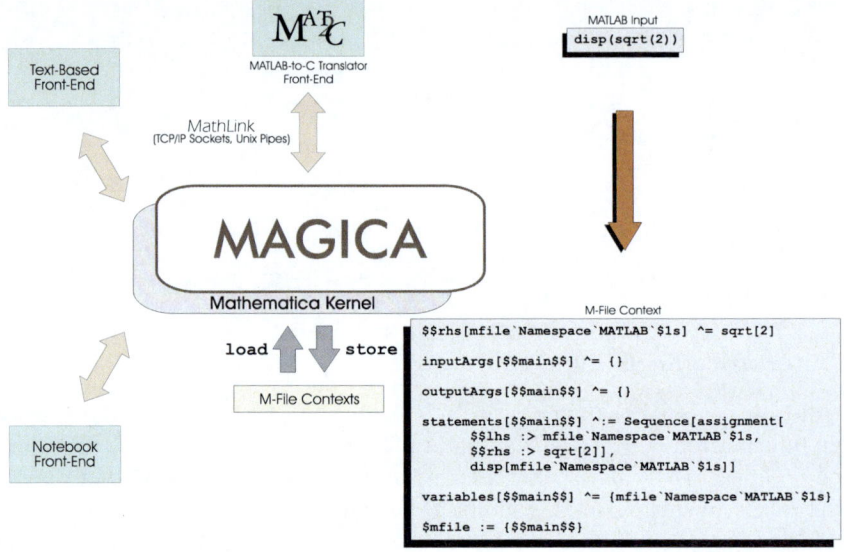

Fig. 2. The MAGICA Architecture

5 Summary

This paper briefly introduced a software tool called MAGICA that infers value ranges, intrinsic types and array shapes for the MATLAB programming language. Though shown in an interactive mode in this paper, MAGICA can also be used in a batch mode from a custom front-end. Currently, MAGICA is being used this way by $\mathbf{M}^{\text{AT}}_{\text{C}}$, a MATLAB-to-C translator that converts a MATLAB source to optimized C code.

References

1. P.G. Joisha, U.N. Shenoy, ad P. Banerjee. "An Approch to Array Shape Determination in MATLAB". Technical report CPDC-TR-2000-10-010, Department of Electrical and Computer Engineering, Northwestern University, October 2000.
2. A. Malishevsky. "Implementing a Run-Time Library for a Parallel MATLAB Compiler". M.S. report, Oregon State University, April 1998.
3. The MathWorks, Inc. *MATLAB: The Language of Technical Computing*, January 1997. Using MATLAB (Version 5).
4. S. Wolfram. The Mathematica Book, 4th ed. Wolfram Media, Inc., 1999.

Dimensions of Precision in Reference Analysis of Object-Oriented Programming Languages*

Barbara G. Ryder

Division of Computer and Information Sciences
Rutgers University
New Brunswick, New Jersey 08903 USA

Abstract. There has been approximately a ten year history of reference analyses for object-oriented programming languages. Approaches vary as to how different analyses account for program execution flow, how they capture calling context, and how they model objects, reference variables and the possible calling structure of the program. A taxonomy of analysis dimensions that affect precision (and cost) will be presented and illustrated by examples of existing reference analysis techniques.

1 Introduction

Almost 25 years after the introduction of Smalltalk-80, object-orientation is a mature, accepted technology. Therefore, it is appropriate now to take a historical look at analyses for object-oriented programming languages, examining how they have evolved, particularly with respect to ensuring sufficient precision, while preserving practical cost. Object-oriented languages allow the building of software from parts, encouraging code reuse and encapsulation through the mechanisms of inheritance and polymorphism. Commonly, object-oriented languages also allow dynamic binding of method calls, dynamic loading of new classes, and querying of program semantics at runtime using reflection.

To understand the control flow in an object-oriented program requires knowledge of the types of objects which can act as receivers for dynamic method dispatches. Thus, to know the possible calling structure in a program, the set of possible object types must be known; but to determine the set of possible types of objects, some representation of possible interprocedural calling structure must be used. Essentially the program representation (i.e., the calling structure) is dependent on the analysis solution and *vice versa*. This interdependent relationship makes analysis of object-oriented languages quite different from that of procedural languages [18]. In addition, dynamic class loading may require a runtime recalculation of some analysis results [42].

Therefore, there is a fundamental need for *reference analysis* in any analysis of object-oriented languages, in order to obtain a program representation. The term *reference analysis* is used to define an analysis that seeks to determine information about the set of objects to which a reference variable or field may point during execution. This study will discuss the dimensions of reference analysis which lead to variations in the

* This research was sponsored, in part, by NSF grant CCR: CCR-9900988.

G. Hedin (Ed.): CC 2003, LNCS 2622, pp. 126–137, 2003.
© Springer-Verlag Berlin Heidelberg 2003

precision obtained in its solution. Examining these dimensions will illustrate similarities and differences between analyses, and identify sources of precision and tradeoffs in cost. Examples of these dimensions will be discussed in the context of different analyses. Open issues not yet fully addressed will also be discussed.

Optimizing compilers and program development tools, such as test harnesses, refactoring tools, semantic browsers for program understanding, and change impact analysis tools, use reference analysis and its client analyses (e.g., side effect analysis, escape analysis, def-use analysis). There are real tradeoffs between the usability of the analysis results in terms of precision and the cost of obtaining them, the time and memory required. These tradeoffs are especially significant for interactive tools. It is important, therefore, to validate analyses by measures corresponding to their eventual use in client applications, even if a full application is not built. Use of benchmark suites which allow evaluation of different techniques using the same input data-sets is crucial; more efforts for building such suites should be encouraged by the research community.

This study is not an attempt at an encyclopedic categorization of all analyses of object-oriented languages; rather the goal is to enumerate characteristics which differentiate the precision (and affect the cost) of different analyses and to give examples of different design choices in existing analyses. There are other papers which cover many of the existing reference analyses and compare and contrast them [18,28]. This paper, by design, will be incomplete in the set of analyses mentioned.

Overview. Section 2 presents the dimensions of precision to be discussed and explain them intuitively. Section 3 discusses each dimension more fully, cites reference analysis examples of choices with respect to that dimension, and then discusses the relative influence of that dimension on reference analysis precision (and cost). Section 4 presents some open issues with regard to analysis of object-oriented programs. Finally, Section 5 summarizes these discussions.

2   Preliminaries

Recall that *reference analysis* determines information about the set of objects to which a reference variable or reference field may point during execution. Historically, various kinds of reference analyses have been developed. *Class analysis* usually involves calculation of the set of classes (i.e., types) associated with the objects to which a reference variable can refer during program execution; this information has been used commonly for call graph construction. Intuitively, class analysis can be thought of as a reference analysis in which one abstract object represents all the instantiations of a class. *Points-to analysis* of object-oriented languages is a term used often for analyses that distinguish different instantiations of a class (i.e., different objects). Points-to analyses [23,33] are often designed as extensions to earlier pointer analyses for C [43,3]. *Refers-to analysis* [45] is a term sometimes used to distinguish a points-to analysis for object-oriented languages from a points-to analysis for general-purpose pointers in C. The term *reference analysis* will be used as denoting all of these analyses for the remainder of this paper.

Most of the analyses used here as examples are reference analyses which are fundamental to understanding the semantics of object-oriented programs. Recall from Section 1, that the interprocedural control flow of an object-oriented program cannot be known without the results of these analyses. Thus, other analyses – including side effect, escape,[1] def-uses, and redundant synchronization analyses – require a reference analysis in order to obtain a representation of interprocedural flow for a program. Thus, reference analyses are crucial to any analysis of object-oriented code.

The characteristics or dimensions that directly affect reference analysis precision are presented below. The design of a specific analysis can be described by choices in each of these dimensions. After the brief description here, in Section 3 each dimension and the possible choices it offers will be illustrated in the context of existing analyses.

- **Flow sensitivity**. Informally, if an analysis is *flow-sensitive*, then it takes into account the order of execution of statements in a program; otherwise, the analysis is called *flow-insensitive*. Flow-sensitive analyses perform *strong updates* (or kills); for example, this occurs when a definition of a variable supersedes a previous definition. The classical dataflow analyses [2,25,19] are flow-sensitive, as are classical abstract interpretations [12].
- **Context sensitivity**. Informally, if an analysis distinguishes between different calling contexts of method, then it is *context-sensitive*; otherwise, the analysis is called *context-insensitive*. Classically, there are two approaches for embedding context sensitivity in an analysis, a call string approach and a functional approach [38]. *Call strings* refer to using the top sequence on the call stack to distinguish the interprocedural context of dataflow information; the idea is that dataflow information tagged with consistent call strings corresponds to the same calling context (which is being distinguished). The functional approach involves embedding information about program state at the call site, and using that to distinguish calls from one another.
- **Program representation (i.e., calling structure).** Because of the interdependence between possible program calling structure and reference analysis solution in object-oriented languages, there are two approaches to constructing an interprocedural representation for an object-oriented program. A simple analysis can obtain an approximation of the calling structure to be used by the subsequent reference analysis. Sometimes this representation is then updated using the analysis solution, when certain edges have been shown to be infeasible. Alternatively, the possible call structure can be calculated lazily, on-the-fly, interleaved with reference analysis steps. The latter approach only includes those methods in the call graph which are *reachable* from program start according to the analysis solution.
- **Object representation.** This dimension concerns the elements in the analysis solution. Sometimes one abstract object is used to represent all instantiations of a class. Sometimes a representative of each creation site (e.g., *new*) is used to represent all objects created at that site. These two naming schemes are those most often used, although alternatives exist.
- **Field sensitivity.** An object or an abstract object may have its fields represented distinctly in the solution; this is called a *field-sensitive* analysis. If the fields in an object are indistinguishable with respect to what they reference, then the analysis is termed *field-insensitive*.

---

[1] Sometimes reference analysis is performed interleaved with the client analysis, for example [36, 11,5,49,6].

- **Reference representation.** This dimension concerns whether each reference representative corresponds to a unique reference variable or to groups of references, and whether the representative is associated with the entire program or with sections of the program (e.g., a method). This dimension relates to reference variables as object representation relates to objects.
- **Directionality.** Generally, flow-insensitive analyses treat an assignment x = y as *directional*, meaning information flows from y to x, or alternatively as *symmetric* meaning subsequent to the assignment, the same information is associated with x and y. These approaches can be formulated in terms of constraints which are *unification* (i.e., equality) constraints for symmetric analyses or *inclusion* (i.e., subset) constraints for directional analyses.

By varying analysis algorithm design in each of these dimensions, it is possible to affect the precision of the resulting solution. The key for any application is to select an effective set of choices that provide sufficient precision at practical cost.

3   Dimensions of Analysis Precision

There is much in common in the design of pointer analysis for C programs and some reference analyses for Java and C^{++}. Both flow-sensitive and context-sensitive techniques were used in pointer analysis [21]. In general, the analysis community decided that flow sensitivity was not scalable to large programs. Context sensitivity for C pointer analysis also was explored independent of flow sensitivity [17,22,35], but the verdict on its effectiveness is less clear. Keeping calling contexts distinguished is of varying importance in a C program, depending on programming style, whereas in object-oriented codes it seems crucial for obtaining high precision for problems needing dependence information, for example. In general, program representation in pointer analysis was on the statement level, represented by an abstract syntax tree or flow graph. Solution methodologies included constraint-based techniques and dataflow approaches that allowed both context-sensitive and context-insensitive formulations.

Some reference analyses calculated finite sets of types (i.e., classes) for reference variables, that characterized the objects to which they may refer. The prototypical problem for which these analyses were used is *call graph construction* (i.e., dynamic dispatch resolution). More recently, reference analyses have been used for discovering redundant synchronizations, escaping objects and side-effect analysis [11,5,6,49,41,36,33,26,23, 32]. These client analyses require more precision than call graph construction and thus, provide interesting different applications for analysis comparison.

Recall that the dimensions of analysis precision include: *flow sensitivity, context sensitivity, program representation, object representation, field sensitivity, reference representation* and *directionality*. In the following discussions, each dimension is considered and examples of reference analyses using specific choices for each dimension are cited. The goal here is to better understand how these analyses differ, not to select a *best* reference analysis.

3.1 Flow Sensitivity

An early example of a flow- and context-sensitive reference analysis was presented by Chatterjee. et. al [8]. This algorithm was designed as a backwards and forwards dataflow propagation on the strongly connected component decomposition of the approximate calling structure of the program. Although the successful experiments performed on programs written in a subset of C^{++} showed excellent precision of the reference solution obtained, there were scalability problems with the approach.

Whaley and Lam [48] and Diwan et. al [15] designed techniques that perform a flow-sensitive analysis within each method, allowing kills in cases where an assignment is unambiguous. For example, an assignment p = q does allow the algorithm to re-initialize the set of objects to which p may point here only to those objects to which q may point; this is an example of a *kill* assignment. By contrast, the assignment p.f = q is not a *kill* assignment because the object whose f field is being mutated is not necessarily unique. This use of flow sensitivity has the potential of greater precision, but this potential has not yet been demonstrated for a specific analysis application.

Given that object-oriented codes generally have small methods, the expected payoff of flow sensitivity on analysis precision would seem minimal. Concerns about scalability have resulted in many analyses abandoning the use of flow sensitivity, in favor of some form of context sensitivity.

3.2 Context Sensitivity

Classically, there are two approaches to embedding context sensitivity in an analysis, using call strings and functions [38]. *Call strings* refer to using the top sequence on the runtime call stack to distinguish the interprocedural context of dataflow information; the idea is only to combine dataflow information tagged with consistent call strings (that is, dataflow information that may exist co-temporally during execution). Work in control flow analysis by Shivers [39], originally aimed at functional programming languages, is related conceptually to the Sharir and Pnueli call string approach. These control flow analyses are distinguished by the amount of calling context remembered; the analyses are called *k-CFA*, where k indicates the length of the call string maintained. The functional approach uses information about the state of computation at a call site to distinguish different call sites. Some reference analyses that solely use inheritance hierarchy information are context-insensitive [15,14,4]; some later, more precise analyses [2] are also context-insensitive to ensure scalability (according to their authors) [15,47,45,33,23,48].

Other reference analyses use both the call-string and functional notions of classical context sensitivity [38]. Palsberg and Schwartzbach presented a 1-CFA reference analysis [29]. Plevyak and Chien [30] described an incremental approach to context sensitivity, which allows them to refine an original analysis when more context is needed to distinguish parts of a solution due to different call sites; their approach seems to combine the call string and functional approaches in order to handle both polymorphic functions and polymorphic containers. Agesen [1] sought to improve upon the Palsberg and Schwartzbach algorithm by specifically adding a functional notion of context sensitivity. In his Cartesian product algorithm, he defined different contexts using tuples of

---

[2] which incorporate interprocedural flow through parameters

parameter types that could access a method; these tuples were computed lazily and memoized for possible sharing between call sites. Grove and Chambers [18] also explored the two notions of context sensitivity in different algorithms, using both call strings and tuples of parameter type sets (analogous to Agesen's Cartesian product algorithm). Milanova et. al defined *object sensitivity* [26], a functional approach that effectively allows differentiation of method calls by distinct receiver object.

This active experimentation with context sensitivity demonstrates its perceived importance in the analysis community as enabling a more precise analysis. The prevalence of method calls in an object-oriented program leads to the expectation that more precise analyses for object-oriented languages can be obtained by picking the 'right' practical embedding of context sensitivity.

3.3   Program Representation (i.e., Calling Structure)

Early reference analyses [15,14,4] were used to provide a static call graph that initialized computation for a subsequent, more precise reference analysis [29,8,23,45]. Other analyses constructed the call graph lazily, as new call edges became known due to discovery of a new object being referred to [27,31,48,33,26,23]. Grove and Chambers discuss the relative merits of both approaches and conclude that the lazy construction approach is preferred [18].

Clearly, the trend is to use the lazy construction approach so that the analysis includes a reachability calculation for further accuracy. This can be especially significant when programs are built using libraries; often only a few methods from a library are actually accessed and excluding unused methods can significantly affect analysis cost as well as precision.

3.4   Object Representation

Representation choices in analyses often are directly related to issues of precision. There are two common choices for reference analysis. First, an analysis can use one abstract object per class to represent all possible instantiations of that class. Second, objects can be identified by their creation site; in this case, all objects created by a specific *new* statement are represented by the same abstract object. Usually the reason for selecting the first representation over the second is efficiency, since it clearly leads to less precise solutions.

The early reference analyses [15,14,4,29] all used one abstract object per class. Some later reference analyses made this same choice [45,47] citing reasons of scalability. Other analyses used creation sites to identify equivalence classes of objects each corresponding to one representative object in the reference analysis solution [33,18,23,48]. There are other, more precise object naming schemes which establish finer-grained equivalence classes for objects [18,26,27,31,24].

While the use of one abstract object per class may suffice for call graph construction, for richer semantic analyses (e.g., side effect, def-use and escape analyses) the use of a representative for each object creation site is preferable.

3.5   Field Sensitivity

Another representation issue is whether or not to preserve information associated with distinct reference fields in an object. One study [33] indicated that not distinguishing object fields may result in imprecision and increased analysis cost. The majority of analyses which use representative objects also distinguish fields because of this precision improvement.

It is interesting that Liang et. al [23] reported that there appeared to be little difference in precision when fields were used either with an abstract object per class or a representative object per creation site with inclusion constraints; more experimentation is needed to understand more fully the separate effects of each of the dimensions involved in these experiments.

3.6   Reference Representation

This dimension concerns to whether or not each reference is represented by a unique representative throughout the entire program. For most reference analyses, this is the case. Sometimes, all the references of the same type are represented by one abstract reference of that type [45]. Alternatively there can be one abstract reference per method [47]. These two alternatives reduce the number of references in the solution, so that the analysis is more efficient.

Tip and Palsberg [47] explored many dimensions of reference representation. Several analyses were defined whose precision lay between RTA [4] and 0-CFA [39,18]. They experimented with abstract objects without fields and an unique reference representation (i.e., CTA analysis), abstract objects with fields and an unique reference representation (i.e., MTA analysis), abstract objects and one abstract reference per method (i.e., FTA analysis), and abstract objects with fields with one abstract reference per method (i.e., XTA analysis). The XTA analysis resulted in the best performance and precision tradeoff for call graph construction, their target application.

The VTA analysis [45] of the SABLE research project at McGill University specifically contrasted the use of unique reference representatives versus the use of one abstract reference representative per class. The latter was found to be too imprecise to be of use.

3.7   Directionality

Reference analysis usually is formulated as constraints that describe the sets of objects to which a reference can point and how these sets are mutated by the semantics of various assignments to (and through) reference variables and fields. There is a significant precision difference between symmetric and directional reference analyses, which are formulated as unification constraints or inclusion constraints, respectively. The unification constraints are similar to those used in Steensgaard's pointer analysis for C [43]; the inclusion constraints are similar to those used by Andersen's pointer analysis for C [3].

Precision differences between these constraint formulations for C pointer analysis were explained by Shapiro and Horwitz [37]. Considering the pointer assignment statement p = q, the unification analysis will union the points-to set of p with the points-to set of q, effectively saying both pointer variables can point to the same set of objects after this assignment; this union is accomplished recursively, so that if *p is also a pointer then its set is unioned to that of *q. An inclusion analysis will conclude after this same assignment statement that the points-to set of p includes the points-to set of q, maintaining the direction of the assignment.[3] Similar arguments can show why inclusion constraints can be expected to yield more a precise reference analysis solution than unification constraints as was shown by Liang et. al [23]. Ruf developed a context-sensitive analysis based on unification constraints as part of a redundant synchronization removal algorithm [36].

Solution procedures for both types of constraints are polynomial time (in the size of the constraint set), but unification constraints can be solved in almost linear worst case cost [43], whereas inclusion constraints have cubic worst case cost. Although these worst case costs are not necessarily experienced in practice, this difference has been considered significant until recently when newer techniques have shown that inclusion constraints in reference analysis can be solved effectively in practice [16,44,20,33,48, 26]. Thus, it seems that the increased precision of inclusion constraints are worth the possible additional cost, but this may depend on the accuracy needs of the specific analysis application.

4   Open Issues

There still are open issues in the analysis of object-oriented languages for which solutions must be found. Some of them are listed below.

- **Reflection.** Programs with reflection constructs can create objects, generate method calls, and access fields of objects at runtime whose declared types cannot be known at compile-time. This creates problems for analyses, because the program is effectively incomplete at compile-time. Most analyses transform a program to account for the effects of reflection before analyzing the program empirically.
- **Native methods.** Calls to native methods (i.e., methods not written in the object-oriented language, often written in C) may have dataflow consequences that must be taken into account by a safe analysis.
- **Exceptions.** In Java programs checked exceptions appear explicitly and unchecked exceptions appear implicitly; both can affect flow of control. Since obtaining a good approximation to possible program control flow is a requirement for a precise analysis, some approaches have been tried [40,7,9,10], but this is still an open problem.
- **Dynamic class loading.** Dynamic class loading may invalidate the dynamic dispatch function previously calculated by a reference analysis [42]. This suggests the possibility of designing an incremental reference analysis; however, it will be difficult to determine the previously-derived information that has been invalidated.
- **Incomplete programs.** Often object-oriented programs are either libraries or library clients, and thus partial programs. Analysis of such codes has been addressed [47,46, 34], but more work is needed. Having a good model for partial program analysis for object-oriented languages may allow analyses to be developed for component-based

---

[3] A combination of these constraints was used for C pointer analysis by Das and showed good precision in empirical experiments for practical cost [13].

programs; it is likely however, that some reliance on component-provider-based information may be necessary.
- **Benchmarks.** It is very important to use benchmark suites in testing analyses, because reproducibility is required for strong empirical validation. Some researchers have used the SPEC compiler benchmarks,[4] or have shared collected benchmark programs.[5]

5   Conclusions

Having presented an overview of the dimensions of precision in reference analysis of object-oriented languages, the current challenge in analysis research is to match the *right* analyses to specific client applications, with appropriate cost and precision. This task is aided by a clear understanding of the role of each dimension in the effectiveness of the resulting analysis solution.

The nature of object-oriented languages is that programs are constructed from many small methods and that method calls (with possible recursion) are the primary control flow structure used. Thus, it is critical to include some type of context sensitivity in an analysis, to obtain sufficient precision for tasks beyond simple dynamic dispatch. Arguably, the functional approach offers a more practical mechanism than the call-string approach embodied in k-CFA analyses and it seems to be more cost effective. It is also clear that a solution procedure using inclusion constraints can be practical and delivers increased precision over cheaper unification constraint resolution.

These opinions are held after experimentation by the community with many dimensions of analysis precision. However, no one analysis *fits* every application and many of the analyses discussed will be applicable to specific problems because their precision is sufficient *to do the job*. A remaining open question is *Can the analysis community deliver useful analyses for a problem at practical cost?* The answer is yet to be determined.

Acknowledgements. I am very grateful to my graduate student, Ana Milanova, for her insightful discussions about this topic and her enormous help with editing this paper. I also wish to thank Dr. Atanas Rountev for his editing feedback on this paper and many valuable discussions.

References

1. O. Agesen. The cartesian product algorithm: Simple and precise type inference of parametric polymorphism. In *European Conference on Object-Oriented Programming*, pages 2–26, 1995.
2. A. V. Aho, R. Sethi, and J. D. Ullman. *Compilers: Principles, Techniques, and Tools*. Addison-Wesley, 1986.

---

[4] http://www.specbench.org/osg/jvm98
[5] Examples include the programs in [47] and those found at http://prolangs.rutgers.edu/ http://www.sable.mcgill.ca/ashes/

3. L. O. Andersen. *Program analysis and specialization for the C programming language*. PhD thesis, DIKU, University of Copenhagen, 1994. Also available as DIKU report 94/19.
4. D. Bacon and P. Sweeney. Fast static analysis of C++ virtual function calls. In *Conference on Object-Oriented Programming Systems, Languages, and Applications*, pages 324–341, 1996.
5. Bruno Blanchet. Escape analysis for object-oriented languages: application to java. In *Proceedings of the 1999 ACM SIGPLAN conference on Object-oriented programming, systems, languages, and applications*, pages 20–34. ACM Press, 1999.
6. Jeff Bogda and Urs Hölzle. Removing unnecessary synchronization in java. In *Proceedings of the 1999 ACM SIGPLAN conference on Object-oriented programming, systems, languages, and applications*, pages 35–46. ACM Press, 1999.
7. R. Chatterjee. *Modular Data-flow Analysis of Statically Typed Object-oriented Programming Languages*. PhD thesis, Department of Computer Science, Rutgers University, October 1999.
8. R. Chatterjee, B. G. Ryder, and W. Landi. Relevant context inference. In *Symposium on Principles of Programming Languages*, pages 133–146, 1999.
9. Ramkrishna Chatterjee and Barbara G Ryder. Data-flow-based testing of object-oriented libraries. Department of Computer Science Technical Report DCS-TR-382, Rutgers University, March 1999.
10. Jong-Deok Choi, David Grove, Michael Hind, and Vivek Sarkar. Efficient and precise modeling of exceptions for the analysis of java programs. In *Proceedings of the 1999 ACM SIGPLAN-SIGSOFT workshop on Program analysis for software tools and engineering*, pages 21–31. ACM Press, 1999.
11. Jong-Deok Choi, Manish Gupta, Mauricio Serrano, Vugranam C. Sreedhar, and Sam Midkiff. Escape analysis for java. In *Proceedings of the 1999 ACM SIGPLAN conference on Object-oriented programming, systems, languages, and applications*, pages 1–19. ACM Press, 1999.
12. P. Cousot and R. Cousot. Abstract interpretation: A unified lattice model for static analysis of programs by construction or approximation of fixed points. In *Conference Record of the Fourth Annual ACM SIGACT/SIGPLAN Symposium on Principles of Programming Languages*, pages 238–252, January 1977.
13. Manuvir Das. Unification-based pointer analysis with directional assignments. In *Proceedings of the ACM SIGPLAN '00 Conference on Programming Language Design and Implementation*, pages 35–46, June 2000.
14. J. Dean, D. Grove, and C. Chambers. Optimizations of object-oriented programs using static class hierarchy analysis. In *European Conference on Object-Oriented Programming*, pages 77–101, 1995.
15. A. Diwan, J.Eliot B. Moss, and K. McKinley. Simple and effective analysis of statically-typed object-oriented programs. In *Conference on Object-Oriented Programming Systems, Languages, and Applications*, pages 292–305, 1996.
16. Manuel Fähndrich, Jeffrey S. Foster, Zhendong Su, and Alexander Aiken. Partial online cycle elimination in inclusion constraint graphs. In *Proceedings of the ACM SIGPLAN '98 conference on Programming language design and implementation*, pages 85–96. ACM Press, 1998.
17. J. Foster, M. Fähndrich, and A. Aiken. Polymorphic versus monomorphic flow-insensitive points-to analysis for c. In *Proceedings of International Symposium on Static Analysis*, April 2000.
18. David Grove and Craig Chambers. A framework for call graph construction algorithms. *ACM Transactions on Programming Languages and Systems (TOPLAS)*, 23(6), 2001.
19. M. S. Hecht. *Flow Analysis of Computer Programs*. Elsevier North-Holland, 1977.
20. Nevin Heintze and Olivier Tardieu. Ultra-fast aliasing analysis using cla: a million lines of c code in a second. In *Proceedings of the ACM SIGPLAN'01 Conference on Programming Language Design and Implementation*, pages 254–263, 2001.

21. Michael Hind. Pointer analysis: Haven't we solved this problem yet? In *2001 ACM SIGPLAN – SIGSOFT Workshop on Program Analysis for Software Tools and Engineering*, pages 54–61, June 2001.

22. D. Liang and M. J. Harrold. Efficient points-to analysis for whole-program analysis. In *Proceedings of the 7th Annual ACM SIGSOFT Symposium on the Foundations of Software Engineering*, LNCS 1687, pages 199–215, September 1999.

23. D. Liang, M. Pennings, and M. J. Harrold. Extending and evaluating flow-insensitive and context-insensitive points-to analyses for Java. In *Workshop on Program Analysis for Software Tools and Engineering*, pages 73–79, June 2001.
24.

24. Donglin Liang, Maikel Pennings, and Mary Jean Harrold. Evaluating the precision of static reference analysis using profiling. In *Proceedings of the international symposium on Software testing and analysis*, pages 22–32. ACM Press, 2002.

25. T. J. Marlowe and B. G. Ryder. Properties of data flow frameworks: A unified model. *Acta Informatica*, 28:121–163, 1990.

26. A. Milanova, A. Rountev, and B. Ryder. Parameterized object-sensitivity for points-to and side-effect analyses for Java. In *International Symposium on Software Testing and Analysis*, pages 1–11, 2002.

27. N. Oxhoj, J. Palsberg, and M. Schwartzbach. Making type inference practical. In *European Conference on Object-Oriented Programming*, pages 329–349, 1992.

28. J. Palsberg. Type-based analysis and applications (invited talk). In *Proceedings of 2001 ACM SIGPLAN-SIGSOFT Workshop on Program Analysis for Software Tools and Engineering*, pages 20–27. ACM Press, July 2001.

29. J. Palsberg and M. Schwartzbach. Object-oriented type inference. In *Conference on Object-Oriented Programming Systems, Languages, and Applications*, pages 146–161, 1991.

30. J. Plevyak and A. Chien. Precise concrete type inference for object oriented languages. In *Proceedings of Conference on Object-Oriented Programming Systems, Languages and Applications (OOPSLA '94)*, pages 324–340, October 1994.

31. J. Plevyak and A. Chien. Precise concrete type inference for object-oriented languages. In *Conference on Object-Oriented Programming Systems, Languages, and Applications*, pages 324–340, 1994.

32. C. Razafimahefa. A study of side-effect analyses for Java. Master's thesis, McGill University, December 1999.

33. A. Rountev, A. Milanova, and B. G. Ryder. Points-to analysis for Java using annotated constraints. In *Conference on Object-Oriented Programming Systems, Languages, and Applications*, pages 43–55, October 2001.

34. A. Rountev, A. Milanova, and B. G. Ryder. Fragment class analysis for testing of polymorphism in Java software. In *International Conference on Software Engineering*, 2003.

35. E. Ruf. Context-insensitive alias analysis reconsidered. In *Proceedings of the SIGPLAN '95 Conference on Programming Language Design and Implementation*, pages 13–22, June 1995.

36. E. Ruf. Effective synchronization removal for Java. In *Conference on Programming Language Design and Implementation*, pages 208–218, 2000.

37. M. Shapiro and S. Horwitz. Fast and accurate flow-insensitive points-to analysis. In *Conference Record of the Twenty-fourth Annual ACM SIGACT/SIGPLAN Symposium on Principles of Programming Languages*, pages 1–14, January 1997.

38. M. Sharir and A. Pnueli. Two approaches to interprocedural data flow analysis. In S. Muchnick and N. Jones, editors, *Program Flow Analysis: Theory and Applications*, pages 189–234. Prentice Hall, 1981.

39. Olin Shivers. *Control-flow Analysis of Higher-Order Languages or Taming Lambda*. PhD thesis, Carnegie-Mellon University School of Computer Science, 1991.

40. S. Sinha and M.J. Harrold. Analysis of programs that contain exception-handling constructs. In *Proceedings of International Conference on Software Maintenance*, pages 348–357, November 1998.
41. Amie L. Souter and Lori L. Pollock. Omen: A strategy for testing object-oriented software. In *Proceedings of the International Symposium on Software Testing and Analysis*, pages 49–59. ACM Press, 2000.
42. Vugranam C. Sreedhar, Michael Burke, and Jong-Deok Choi. A framework for interprocedural optimization in the presence of dynamic class loading. In *Proceedings of the ACM SIGPLAN '00 conference on Programming language design and implementation*, pages 196–207, 2000.
43. Bjarne Steensgaard. Points-to analysis in almost linear time. In *Conference Record of the Twenty-third Annual ACM SIGACT/SIGPLAN Symposium on Principles of Programming Languages*, pages 32–41, 1996.
44. Z. Su, M. Fähndrich, and A. Aiken. Projection merging: Reducing redundancies in inclusion constraint graphs. In *Conference Record of the Twenty-seventh Annual ACM SIGACT/SIGPLAN Symposium on Principles of Programming Languages*, 2000.
45. V. Sundaresan, L. Hendren, C. Razafimahefa, R. Vallee-Rai, P. Lam, E. Gagnon, and C. Godin. Practical virtual method call resolution for Java. In *Conference on Object-Oriented Programming Systems, Languages, and Applications*, pages 264–280, 2000.
46. Peter F. Sweeney and Frank Tip. Extracting library-based object-oriented applications. In *Proceedings of the 8th ACM SIGSOFT international symposium on Foundations of software engineering*, pages 98–107. ACM Press, 2000.
47. F. Tip and J. Palsberg. Scalable propagation-based call graph construction algorithms. In *Conference on Object-Oriented Programming Systems, Languages, and Applications*, pages 281–293, 2000.
48. J. Whaley and M. Lam. An efficient inclusion-based points-to analysis for strictly-typed languages. In *Static Analysis Symposium*, 2002.
49. John Whaley and Martin Rinard. Compositional pointer and escape analysis for java programs. In *Proceedings of the 1999 ACM SIGPLAN conference on Object-oriented programming, systems, languages, and applications*, pages 187–206. ACM Press, 1999.

Polyglot: An Extensible Compiler Framework for Java[*]

Nathaniel Nystrom, Michael R. Clarkson, and Andrew C. Myers

Cornell University
{nystrom,clarkson,andru}@cs.cornell.edu

Abstract. Polyglot is an extensible compiler framework that supports the easy creation of compilers for languages similar to Java, while avoiding code duplication. The Polyglot framework is useful for domain-specific languages, exploration of language design, and for simplified versions of Java for pedagogical use. We have used Polyglot to implement several major and minor modifications to Java; the cost of implementing language extensions scales well with the degree to which the language differs from Java. This paper focuses on the design choices in Polyglot that are important for making the framework usable and highly extensible. Polyglot source code is available.

1 Introduction

Domain-specific extension or modification of an existing programming language enables more concise, maintainable programs. However, programmers construct domain-specific language extensions infrequently because building and maintaining a compiler is onerous. Better technology is needed. This paper presents a methodology for the construction of extensible compilers and also an application of this methodology in our implementation of Polyglot, a compiler framework for creating extensions to Java [14]. Language extension or modification is useful for many reasons:

- **Security.** Systems that enforce security at the language level may find it useful to add security annotations or rule out unsafe language constructs.
- **Static checking.** A language might be extended to support annotations necessary for static verification of program correctness [23], more powerful static checking of program invariants [10], or heuristic methods [8].
- **Language design.** Implementation helps validate programming language designs.
- **Optimization.** New passes may be added to implement optimizations not performed by the base compiler or not permitted by the base language specification.
- **Style.** Some language features or idioms may be deemed to violate good style but may not be easy to detect with simple syntactic analysis.
- **Teaching.** Students may learn better using a language that does not expose them to difficult features (e.g., inner classes [14]) or confusing error messages [9].

---

[*] This research was supported in part by DARPA Contract F30602-99-1-0533, monitored by USAF Rome Laboratory, in part by ONR Grant N00014-01-1-0968, and in part by NSF awards 0133302 and 0208642. The views herein should not be interpreted as representing the policies or endorsement of NSF, DARPA or AFRL.

G. Hedin (Ed.): CC 2003, LNCS 2622, pp. 138–152, 2003.

We refer to the original unmodified language as the *base language*; we call the modified language a language *extension* even if it is not backwards compatible.

When developing a compiler for a language extension, it is clearly desirable to build upon an existing compiler for the base language. The simplest approach is to copy the source code of the base compiler and edit it in place. This may be fairly effective if the base compiler is carefully written, but it duplicates code. Changes to the base compiler—perhaps to fix bugs—may then be difficult to apply to the extended compiler. Without considerable discipline, the code of the two compilers diverges, leading to duplication of effort.

Our approach is different: the Polyglot framework implements an extensible compiler for the base language Java 1.4. This framework, also written in Java, is by default simply a semantic checker for Java. However, a programmer implementing a language extension may extend the framework to define any necessary changes to the compilation process, including the abstract syntax tree (AST) and semantic analysis.

An important goal for Polyglot is *scalable extensibility*: an extension should require programming effort proportional only to the magnitude of the difference between the extended and base languages. Adding new AST node types or new compiler passes should require writing code whose size is proportional to the change. Language extensions often require uniformly adding new fields and methods to an AST node and its subclasses; we require that this uniform *mixin* extension be implementable without subclassing all the extended node classes. Scalable extensibility is a challenge because it is difficult to simultaneously extend both types and the procedures that manipulate them [30,38]. Existing programming methodologies such as *visitors* [13] improve extensibility but are not a complete solution. In this paper we present a methodology that supports extension of both compiler passes and AST nodes, including mixin extension. The methodology uses abstract factories, delegation, and proxies [13] to permit greater extensibility and code reuse than in previous extensible compiler designs.

Polyglot has been used to implement more than a dozen Java language extensions of varying complexity. Our experience using Polyglot suggests that it is a useful framework for developing compilers for new Java-like languages. Some of the complex extensions implemented are Jif [26], which extends Java with security types that regulate information flow; PolyJ [27], which adds bounded parametric polymorphism to Java; and JMatch [24], which extends Java with pattern matching and iteration features. Compilers built using Polyglot are themselves extensible; complex extensions such as Jif and PolyJ have themselves been extended. The framework is not difficult to learn: users have been able to build interesting extensions to Java within a day of starting to use Polyglot. The Polyglot source code is available.[1]

The rest of the paper is structured as follows. Section 2 gives an overview of the Polyglot compiler. Section 3 describes in detail our methodology for providing scalable extensibility. Other Polyglot features that make writing an extensible compiler convenient are described in Section 4. Our experience using the Polyglot system to build various languages is reported in Section 5. Related work on extensible compilers and macro systems is discussed in Section 6, and we conclude in Section 7.

---

[1] At http://www.cs.cornell.edu/Projects/polyglot

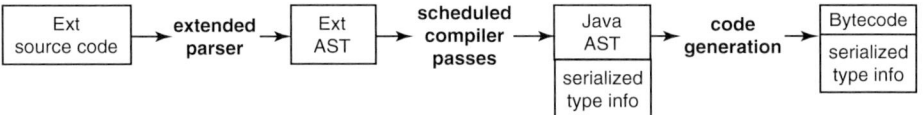

Fig. 1. Polyglot Architecture

2   Polyglot Overview

This section presents an overview of the various components of Polyglot and describes how they can be extended to implement a language extension. An example of a small extension is given to illustrate this process.

2.1   Architecture

A Polyglot extension is a source-to-source compiler that accepts a program written in a language extension and translates it to Java source code. It also may invoke a Java compiler such as `javac` to convert its output to bytecode.

The compilation process offers several opportunities for the language extension implementer to customize the behavior of the framework. This process, including the eventual compilation to Java bytecode, is shown in Fig. 1. In the figure, the name Ext stands for the particular extended language.

The first step in compilation is parsing input source code to produce an AST. Polyglot includes an extensible parser generator, PPG, that allows the implementer to define the syntax of the language extension as a set of changes to the base grammar for Java. PPG provides *grammar inheritance* [29], which can be used to add, modify, or remove productions and symbols of the base grammar. PPG is implemented as a preprocessor for the CUP LALR parser generator [17].

The extended AST may contain new kinds of nodes either to represent syntax added to the base language or to record new information in the AST. These new node types are added by implementing the `Node` interface and optionally subclassing from an existing node implementation.

The core of the compilation process is a series of compilation passes applied to the abstract syntax tree. Both semantic analysis and translation to Java may comprise several such passes. The *pass scheduler* selects passes to run over the AST of a single source file, in an order defined by the extension, ensuring that dependencies between source files are not violated. Each compilation pass, if successful, rewrites the AST, producing a new AST that is the input to the next pass. Some analysis passes (e.g., type checking) may halt compilation and report errors instead of rewriting the AST. A language extension may modify the base language pass schedule by adding, replacing, reordering, or removing compiler passes. The rewriting process is entirely functional; compilation passes do not destructively modify the AST. More details on our methodology are described in Section 3.

Compilation passes do their work using objects that define important characteristics of the source and target languages. A *type system* object acts as a factory for objects

```
1   tracked(F) class FileReader {
2     FileReader(File f) [] -> [F] throws IOException[] { ... }
3     int read() [F] -> [F] throws IOException[F] { ... }
4     void close() [F] -> [] { ... ; free this; }
5   }
```

Fig. 2. Example Coffer `FileReader`

representing types and related constructs such as method signatures. The type system object also provides some type checking functionality. A *node factory* constructs AST nodes for its extension. In extensions that rely on an intermediate language, multiple type systems and node factories may be used during compilation.

After all compilation passes complete, the usual result is a Java AST. A Java compiler such as javac is invoked to compile the Java code to bytecode. The bytecode may contain serialized extension-specific type information used to enable separate compilation; we discuss separate compilation in more detail in Section 4.

2.2   An Example: Coffer

To motivate our design, we describe a simple extension of Java that supports some of the resource management facilities of the Vault language [7]. This language, called Coffer, is a challenge for extensible compilers because it makes substantial changes to both the syntax and semantics of Java and requires identical modifications to many AST node types. Coffer allows a linear capability, or *key*, to be associated with an object. Methods of the object may be invoked only when the key is held. A key is allocated when its object is created and deallocated by a free statement in a method of the object. The Coffer type system regulates allocation and freeing of keys to guarantee statically that keys are always deallocated.

Fig. 2 shows a small Coffer program declaring a FileReader class that guarantees the program cannot read from a closed reader. The annotation tracked(F) on line 1 associates a key named F with instances of FileReader. Pre- and post-conditions on method and constructor signatures, written in brackets, specify how the set of held keys changes through an invocation. For example on line 2, the precondition [] indicates that no key need be held to invoke the constructor, and the postcondition [F] specifies that F is held when the constructor returns normally. The close method (line 4) frees the key; no subsequent method that requires F can be invoked.

The Coffer extension is used as an example throughout the next section. It is implemented by adding new compiler passes for computing and checking held key sets at each program point. Coffer's free statements and additional type annotations are implemented by adding new AST nodes and extending existing nodes and passes.

3   A Methodology for Scalable Extensibility

Our goal is a mechanism that supports scalable extension of both the syntax and semantics of the base language. The programmer effort required to add or extend a pass should be proportional to the number of AST nodes non-trivially affected by that pass; the effort required to add or extend a node should be proportional to the number of passes the node must implement in an interesting way. When extending or overriding the behavior of existing AST nodes, it is often necessary to extend a node class that has more than one subclass. For instance, the Coffer extension adds identical pre- and post-condition syntax to both methods and constructors; to avoid code duplication, these annotations should be added to the common base class of method and constructor nodes. The programmer effort to make such changes should be constant, irrespective of the number of subclasses of this base class. Inheritance is the appropriate mechanism for adding a new field or method to a single class. However, adding the same member to many different classes can quickly become tedious. This is true even in languages with multiple inheritance: a new subclass must be created for every class affected by the change. Modifying these subclasses later requires making identical changes to each subclass. *Mixin extensibility* is a key goal of our methodology: a change that affects multiple classes should require no code duplication.

Compilers written in object-oriented languages often implement compiler passes using the *Visitor* design pattern [13]. However, visitors present several problems for scalable extensibility. In a non-extensible compiler, the set of AST nodes is usually fixed. The Visitor pattern permits scalable addition of new passes, but sacrifices scalable addition of AST node types. To allow specialization of visitor behavior for both the AST node type and the visitor itself, each visitor class implements a separate callback method for every node type. Thus, adding a new kind of AST node requires modifying *all* existing visitors to insert a callback method for the node. Visitors written without knowledge of the new node cannot be used with the new node because they do not implement the callback. The Visitor pattern also does not provide mixin extensibility. A separate mechanism is needed to address this problem.

An alternative to the Visitor pattern is for each AST node class to implement a method for each compiler pass. However, this technique suffers from the dual problem: adding a new pass requires adding a method to all existing node types.

The remainder of this section presents a mechanism that achieves the goal of scalable extensibility. We first describe our approach to providing mixin extensibility. We then show how our solution also addresses the other aspects of scalable extensibility.

3.1   Node Extension Objects and Delegates

We implement passes as methods associated with AST node objects; however, to provide scalable extensibility, we introduce a delegation mechanism, illustrated in Fig. 3, that enables orthogonal extension and method override of nodes.

Since subclassing of node classes does not adequately address orthogonal extension of methods in classes with multiple subclasses, we add to each node object a field, labeled ext in Fig. 3, that points to a (possibly null) *node extension object*. The extension object (CofferExt in the figure) provides implementations of new methods and fields, thus extending the node interface without subclassing. These members are accessed by following the ext pointer and casting to the extension object type. In the example, CofferExt extends Node with keyFlow() and checkKeys() methods. Each AST node class to be extended with a given implementation of these members uses the

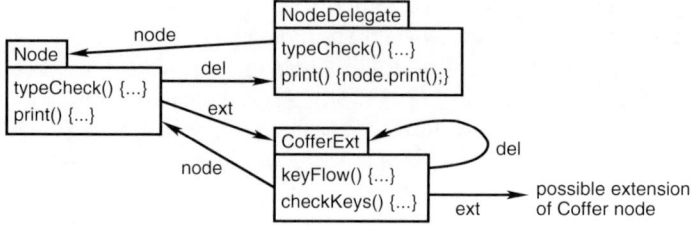

Fig. 3. Delegates and extensions

same extension object class. Thus, several node classes can be orthogonally extended with a single implementation, avoiding code duplication. Since language extensions can themselves be extended, each extension object has an `ext` field similar to the one located in the node object. In effect, a node and its extension object together can be considered a single node.

Extension objects alone, however, do not adequately handle method override when the base language is extended multiple times. The problem is that any one of a node's extension objects can implement the overridden method; a mechanism is needed to invoke the correct implementation. A possible solution to this problem is to introduce a *delegate* object for each method in the node interface. For each method, a field in the node points to an object implementing that method. Calls to the method are made through its delegate object; language extensions can override the method simply by replacing the delegate. The delegate may implement the method itself or may invoke methods in the node or in the node's extension objects.

Because maintaining one object per method is cumbersome, the solution used in Polyglot is to combine delegate objects and to introduce a single delegate field for each node object—illustrated by the `del` field in Fig. 3. This field points to an object implementing the entire `Node` interface, by default the node itself. To override a method, a language extension writer creates a new delegate object containing the new implementation or code to dispatch to the new implementation. The delegate implements `Node`'s other methods by dispatching back to the node. Extension objects also contain a `del` field used to override methods declared in the extension object interface.

Calls to all node methods are made through the `del` pointer, thus ensuring that the correct implementation of the method is invoked if the delegate object is replaced by a language extension. Thus, in our example, the node's `typeCheck` method is invoked via `n.del.typeCheck()`; the Coffer `checkKeys` method is invoked by following the node's `ext` pointer and invoking through the extension object's delegate: `((CofferExt) n.ext).del.checkKeys()`. An extension of Coffer could replace the extension object's delegate to override methods declared in the extension, or it could replace the node's delegate to override methods of the node. To access Coffer's type-checking functionality, this new node delegate may be a subclass of Coffer's node delegate class or may contain a pointer to the old delegate object. The overhead of indirecting through the `del` pointer accounts for less than 2% of the total compilation time.

3.2   AST Rewriters

Most passes in Polyglot are structured as functional AST rewriting passes. Factoring out AST traversal code eliminates the need to duplicate this code when implementing new passes. Each pass implements an *AST rewriter* object to traverse the AST and invoke the pass's method at each node. At each node, the rewriter invokes a `visitChildren` method to recursively rewrite the node's children using the rewriter and to reconstruct the node if any of the children are modified. A key implementation detail is that when a node is reconstructed, the node is *cloned* and the clone is returned. Cloning ensures that class members added by language extensions are correctly copied into the new node. The node's delegates and extensions are cloned with the node.

Each rewriter implements `enter` and `leave` methods, both of which take a node as argument. The `enter` method is invoked before the rewriter recurses on the node's children using `visitChildren` and may return a new rewriter to be used for rewriting the children. This provides a convenient means for maintaining symbol table information as the rewriter crosses lexical scopes; the programmer need not write code to explicitly manage the stack of scopes, eliminating a potential source of errors. The `leave` method is called after visiting the children and returns the rewritten AST rooted at the node.

3.3   Scalable Extensibility

A language extension may extend the interface of an AST node class through an extension object interface. For each new pass, a method is added to the extension object interface and a rewriter class is created to invoke the method at each node. For most nodes, a single extension object class is implemented to define the default behavior of the pass, typically just an identity transformation on the AST node. This class is overridden for individual nodes where non-trivial work is performed for the pass.

To change the behavior of an existing pass at a given node, the programmer creates a new delegate class implementing the new behavior and associates the delegate with the node at construction time. Like extension classes, the same delegate class may be used for several different AST node classes, allowing functionality to be added to node classes at arbitrary points in the class hierarchy without code duplication.

New kinds of nodes are defined by new node classes; existing node types are extended by adding an extension object to instances of the class. A factory method for the new node type is added to the node factory to construct the node and, if necessary, its delegate and extension objects. The new node inherits default implementations of all compiler passes from its base class and from the extension's base class. The new node may provide new implementations using method override, possibly via delegation. Methods need be overridden only for those passes that need to perform non-trivial work for that node type.

Fig. 4 shows a portion of the code implementing the Coffer key-checking pass, which checks the set of keys held when control enters a node. The code has been simplified in the interests of space and clarity. At each node in the AST, the pass invokes through the `del` pointer the `checkKeys` method in the Coffer extension, passing in the set of held keys (computed by a previous data-flow analysis pass). Since most AST nodes are not affected by the key-checking pass, a default `checkKeys` method implemented in the base

```
class KeyChecker extends Rewriter {
  Node leave(Node n) {
    ((CofferExt) n.ext).del.checkKeys(held_keys(n));
    return n;
  }
}

class CofferExt {
  Node node; CofferExt del;
  void checkKeys(Set held_keys) { /* empty */ }
}

class ProcedureCallExt extends CofferExt {
  void checkKeys(Set held_keys) {
    ProcedureCall c = (ProcedureCall) node;
    CofferProcedureType p = (CofferProcedureType) c.callee();
    if (! held_keys.containsAll(p.entryKeys()))
      error(p.entryKeys() + " not held at " + c);
  }
}
```

Fig. 4. Coffer key checking

CofferExt class is used for these nodes. For other nodes, a non-trivial implementation of key checking is required.

Fig. 4 also contains an extension class used to compute the held keys for method and constructor calls. ProcedureCall is an interface implemented by the classes for three AST nodes that invoke either methods or constructors: method calls, new expressions, and explicit constructor calls (e.g., super()). All three nodes implement the checkKeys method identically. By using an extension object, we need only to write this code once.

4   Other Implementation Details

In this section we consider some aspects of the Polyglot implementation that are not directly related to scalable extensibility.

Data-Flow Analysis. Polyglot provides an extensible data-flow analysis framework. In Java implementation, this framework is used to check the that variables are initialized before use and that all statements are reachable; extensions may perform additional data-flow analyses to enable optimizations or to perform other transformations. Polyglot provides a rewriter in the base compiler framework that constructs the control-flow graph of the program. Intraprocedural data-flow analyses can then be performed on this graph by implementing the meet and transfer functions for the analysis.

Separate Compilation. Java compilers use type information stored in Java class files to support separate compilation. For many extensions, the standard Java type information in the class file is insufficient. Polyglot injects type information into class files that can be read by later invocations of the compiler to provide separate compilation. No code need be written for a language extension to use this functionality for its extended types.

Before performing Java code generation, Polyglot uses the Java serialization facility to encode the type information for a given class into a string, which is then compressed and inserted as a final static field into the AST for the class being serialized. When compiling a class, the first time a reference to another class is encountered, Polyglot loads the class file for the referenced class and extracts the serialized type information. The type information is decoded and may be immediately used by the extension.

Quasiquoting. To generate Java output, language extensions translate their ASTs to Java ASTs and rely on the code generator of the base compiler to output Java code. To enable AST rewriting, we have used PPG to extend Polyglot's Java parser with the ability to generate an AST from a string of Java code and a collection of AST nodes to substitute into the generated AST. This feature provides many of the benefits of quasiquoting in Scheme [19].

5   Experience

More than a dozen extensions of varying sizes have been implemented using Polyglot, for example:

- Jif is a Java extension that provides information flow control and features to ensure the confidentiality and integrity of data [26].
- Jif/split is an extension to Jif that partitions programs across multiple hosts based on their security requirements [37].
- PolyJ is a Java extension that supports bounded parametric polymorphism [27].
- Param is an *abstract extension* that provides support for parameterized classes. This extension is not a complete language, but instead includes code implementing lazy substitution of type parameters. Jif, PolyJ, and Coffer extend Param.
- JMatch is a Java extension that supports pattern matching and logic programming features [24].
- Coffer, as previously described, adds resource management facilities to Java.
- PAO ("primitives as objects") allows primitive values to be used transparently as objects via automatic boxing and unboxing,
- A covariant return extension restores the subtyping rules of Java 1.0 Beta [33] in which the return type of a method could be covariant in subclasses. The language was changed in the final version of Java 1.0 [14] to require the invariance of return types.

The major extensions add new syntax and make substantial changes to the language semantics. We describe the changes for Jif and PolyJ in more detail below. The simpler extensions, such as support for covariant return types, require more localized changes.

5.1   Jif

Jif is an extension to Java that permits static checking of information flow policies. In Jif, the type of a variable may be annotated with a *label* specifying a set of principals who own the data and a set of principals that are permitted to read the data. Labels are checked by the compiler to ensure that the information flow policies are not violated.

The base Polyglot parser is extended using PPG to recognize security annotations and new statement forms. New AST node classes are added for labels and for new statement and expression forms concerning security checks. The new AST nodes and nearly all existing AST nodes are also extended with security context annotations. These new fields are added to a Jif extension class. To implement information flow checking, a labelCheck method is declared in the Jif extension object. Many nodes do no work for this pass and therefore can inherit a default implementation declared in the base Jif extension class. Extension objects installed for expression and statement nodes override the labelCheck method to implement the security typing judgment for the node. Delegates were used to override type checking of some AST nodes to disallow static fields and inner classes since they may provide an avenue for information leaks.

Following label checking, the Jif AST is translated to a Java AST, largely by erasing security annotations. The new statement and expression forms are rewritten to Java syntax using the quasiquoting facility discussed in Section 4.

Jif/split further extends Jif to partition programs across multiple hosts based on their security requirements. The syntax of Jif is modified slightly to also support integrity annotations. New passes, implemented in extension objects, partition the Jif/split program into several Jif programs, each of which will run on a separate host.

5.2   PolyJ

PolyJ is an extension to Java that supports parametric polymorphism. Classes and interfaces may be declared with zero or more type parameters constrained by *where clauses*. The base Java parser is extended using PPG, and AST node classes are added for where clauses and for new type syntax. Further, the AST node for class declarations is extended via inheritance to allow for type parameters and where clauses.

The PolyJ type system customizes the behavior of the base Java type system and introduces judgments for parameterized and instantiated types. A new pass is introduced to check that the types on which a parameterized class is instantiated satisfy the constraints for that parameter, as described in [27].

The base compiler code generator is extended to generate code not only for each PolyJ source class, but also an *adapter class* for each instantiation of a parameterized class.

5.3   Results

As a measure of the programmer effort required to implement the extensions discussed in this paper, the sizes of the code for these extensions are shown in Table 1. To eliminate bias due to the length of identifiers in the source, sizes are given in number of tokens for source files, including Java, CUP, and PPG files.

These results demonstrate that the cost of implementing language extensions scales well with the degree to which the extension differs from its base language. Simple extensions such as the covariant return extension that differ from Java in small, localized ways can be implemented by writing only small amounts of code. To measure the overhead of simply creating a language extension, we implemented an empty extension that makes

Table 1. Extension size

Extension	Token count	Percent of Base Polyglot
base Polyglot	164136	100%
Jif	126188	77%
JMatch	105269	64%
PolyJ	78159	48%
Coffer	21251	13%
PAO	3422	2%
Param	3233	2%
covariant return	1562	1%
empty	691	$< 1\%$

no changes to the Java language; the overhead includes empty subclasses of the base compiler node factory and type system classes, an empty PPG parser specification, and code for allocating these subclasses.

PolyJ, which has large changes to the type system and to code generation, requires only about half as much code as the base Java compiler. For historical reasons, PolyJ generates code by overriding the Polyglot code generator to directly output Java. The size of this code could be reduced by using quasiquoting. Jif requires a large amount of extension code because label checking in Jif is more complex than the Java type checking that it extends. Much of the JMatch overhead is accounted for by extensive changes to add complex statement and expression translations.

As a point of comparison, the base Polyglot compiler (which implements Java 1.4) and the Java 1.1 compiler, `javac`, are nearly the same size when measured in tokens. Thus, the base Polyglot compiler implementation is reasonably efficient. To be fair to `javac`, we did not count its code for bytecode generation. About 10% of the base Polyglot compiler consists of interfaces used to separate the interface hierarchy from the class hierarchy. The `javac` compiler is not implemented this way.

Implementing small extensions has proved to be fairly easy. We asked a programmer previously unfamiliar with the framework to implement the covariant return type extension; this took one day. The same programmer implemented several other small extensions within a few days.

5.4   Discussion

In implementing Polyglot we found, not surprisingly, that application of good object-oriented design principles greatly enhances Polyglot's extensibility. Rigorous separation of interfaces and classes permit implementations to be more easily extended and replaced; calls through interfaces ensure the framework is not bound to any particular implementation of an interface. The Polyglot framework almost exclusively uses *factory methods* to create objects [13], giving language extensions more freedom to change the implementation provided by the base compiler by avoiding explicitly tying code to a particular class.

We chose to implement Polyglot using only standard Java features, but it is clear that several language extensions—some of which we have implemented using Polyglot—would have made it easier to implement Polyglot. Multimethods (e.g., [5]) would have simplified the dispatching mechanism needed for our methodology. Open classes [6] might provide a cleaner solution to the extensibility problem, particularly in conjunction with multimethods. Aspect-oriented programming [20] is another technique for adding and overriding methods in an existing class hierarchy. Hierarchically extensible datatypes and functions [25] offer another solution to the extensibility problem. Multiple inheritance and, in particular, mixins (e.g., [4,11]) would facilitate application of an extension to many AST nodes at once. Built-in quasiquoting support would make translation more efficient, though the need to support several target languages would introduce some difficulties. Covariant modification of method return types would eliminate many unnecessary type casts, as would parametric polymorphism [27,28].

6   Related Work

There is much work that is related to Polyglot, including other extensible compilers, macro systems, and visitor patterns.

JaCo is an extensible compiler for Java written in an extended version of Java [39] that supports ML-style pattern matching. JaCo does not provide mixin extensibility. It relies on a new language feature—extensible algebraic datatypes [38]—to address the difficulty of handling new data types without changing existing code. Polyglot achieves scalable extensibility while relying only on features available in Java.

CoSy [1] is a framework for combining compiler phases to create an optimizing compiler. Compiler phases can be added and reused in multiple contexts without changing existing code. The framework was not designed for syntax extension. In the SUIF compiler [36], data structures can be extended with annotations, similar to Polyglot's extension objects; new annotations are ignored by existing compiler passes. Scorpion [31, 32] is a meta-programming environment that has a similar extension mechanism. Neither SUIF nor Scorpion have a mechanism like Polyglot's delegate objects to mix in method overrides.

JastAdd [16] is a compiler framework that uses aspect-oriented programming to add methods and fields into the AST node class hierarchy to implement new passes or to override existing passes. The AST node hierarchy may be extended via inheritance, but duplicate code may need to be written for each pass to support new nodes.

Macro systems and preprocessors are generally concerned only with syntactic extensions to a language. Recent systems for use in Java include EPP [18], JSE [12], and JPP [21]. Maya [2] is a generalization of macro systems that uses generic functions and multimethods to allow extension of Java syntax. Semantic actions can be defined as multimethods on those generic functions. It is not clear how these systems scale to support semantic checking for large extensions to the base language.

The Jakarta Tools Suite (JTS) [3] is a toolkit for implementing Java preprocessors to create domain-specific languages. Extensions of a base language are encapsulated as components that define the syntax and semantics of the extension. A fundamental difference between JTS and Polyglot is that JTS is concerned primarily only the syntactic analysis of the extension language, not with semantic analysis [3, section 4]. This makes JTS more like a macro system in which the macros are defined by extending the compiler rather than declaring them in the source code.

OpenJava [34] uses a meta-object protocol (MOP) similar to Java's reflection API to allow manipulation of a program's structure. OpenJava allows very limited extension of syntax, but through its MOP exposes much of the semantic structure of the program.

The original Visitor design pattern [13] has led to many refinements. Extensible Visitors [22] and Staggered Visitors [35] both enhance the extensibility of the visitor pattern to facilitate adding new node types, but neither these nor the other refinements mentioned above support mixin extensibility. Staggered Visitors rely on multiple inheritance to extend visitors with support for new nodes.

7   Conclusions

Our original motivation for developing the Polyglot compiler framework was simply to provide a publicly available Java front end that could be easily extended to support new languages. We discovered that the existing approaches to extensible compiler construction within Java did not solve to our satisfaction the problem of scalable extensibility including mixins. Our extended visitor methodology is simple, yet improves on the previous solutions to the extensibility problem. Other Polyglot features such as extensible parsing, pass scheduling, quasiquoting, and type signature insertion are also useful. Our experience using Polyglot has shown that it is an effective way to produce compilers for Java-like languages. We have used the framework for several significant language extensions that modify Java syntax and semantics in complex ways. We hope that the public release of this software in source code form will facilitate experimentation with new features for object-oriented languages.

References

1. Martin Alt, Uwe Aßmann, and Hans van Someren. Cosy compiler phase embedding with the CoSy compiler model. In Peter A. Fritzson, editor, *Proceedings of the 5th International Compiler Construction Conference (CC'94)*, volume 786 of *Lecture Notes in Computer Science*, pages 278–293, Edinburgh, UK, April 1994.
2. Jason Baker and Wilson C. Hsieh. Maya: Multiple-dispatch syntax extension in Java. In *Proc. of the ACM SIGPLAN '02 Conference on Programming Language Design and Implementation (PLDI)*, pages 270–281, Berlin, Germany, June 2002.
3. Don Batory, Bernie Lofaso, and Yannis Smaragdakis. JTS: tools for implementing domain-specific languages. In *Proceedings Fifth International Conference on Software Reuse*, pages 143–53, Victoria, BC, Canada, 1998. IEEE.
4. Gilad Bracha. *The Programming Language Jigsaw: Mixins, Modularity and Multiple Inheritance*. PhD thesis, University of Utah, 1992.
5. Craig Chambers. Object-oriented multi-methods in Cecil. In Ole Lehrmann Madsen, editor, *Proceedings of the 6th European Conference on Object-Oriented Programming (ECOOP)*, volume 615, pages 33–56, Berlin, Heidelberg, New York, Tokyo, 1992. Springer-Verlag.

6. Curtis Clifton, Gary T. Leavens, Craig Chambers, and Todd Millstein. MultiJava: Modular open classes and symmetric multiple dispatch for Java. In *OOPSLA 2000 Conference on Object-Oriented Programming, Systems, Languages, and Applications, Minneapolis, Minnesota*, volume 35(10), pages 130–145, 2000.
7. Robert DeLine and Manuel Fähndrich. Enforcing high-level protocols in low-level software. In *Proceedings of the ACM Conference on Programming Language Design and Implementation*, pages 59–69, June 2001.
8. Dawson Engler, Benjamin Chelf, Andy Chou, and Seth Hallem. Checking system rules using system-specific, programmer-written compiler extensions. In *Proceedings of Fourth Usenix Symposium on Operating Systems Design and Implementation*, San Diego, California, October 2000.
9. Robert Bruce Findler, Cormac Flanagan, Matthew Flatt, Shriram Krishnamurthi, and Matthias Felleisen. DrScheme: A pedagogic programming environment for Scheme. In *Proc. International Symposium on Programming Languages: Implementations, Logics, and Programs*, pages 369–388, 1997.
10. Cormac Flanagan, K. Rustan M. Leino, Mark Lillibridge, Greg Nelson, James B. Saxe, and Raymie Stata. Extended static checking for Java. In *Proc. of the ACM SIGPLAN '02 Conference on Programming Language Design and Implementation (PLDI)*, pages 234–245, Berlin, Germany, June 2002.
11. Matthew Flatt, Shriram Krishnamurthi, and Matthias Felleisen. Classes and mixins. In *Conference Record of POPL 98: The 25TH ACM SIGPLAN-SIGACT Symposium on Principles of Programming Languages, San Diego, California*, pages 171–183, New York, NY, 1998.
12. D. K. Frayne and Keith Playford. The Java syntactic extender (JSE). In *Proceedings of the 2001 Conference on Object Oriented Programming Systems Languages and Applications (OOPSLA '01)*, pages 31–42, Tampa, FL, USA, 2001.
13. Erich Gamma, Richard Helm, Ralph Johnson, and John Vlissides. *Design Patterns: Elements of Reusable Object-Oriented Software*. Addison Wesley, Reading, MA, 1994.
14. James Gosling, Bill Joy, and Guy Steele. *The Java Language Specification*. Addison-Wesley, August 1996. ISBN 0-201-63451-1.
15. Carl Gunter and John C. Mitchell, editors. *Theoretical aspects of object-oriented programming*. MIT Press, 1994.
16. Görel Hedin and Eva Magnusson. JastAdd—an aspect-oriented compiler construction system. *Science of Computer Programming*, 47(1):37–58, November 2002.
17. Scott E. Hudson, Frank Flannery, C. Scott Ananian, Dan Wang, and Andrew Appel. CUP LALR parser generator for Java, 1996. Software release. Located at http://www.cs.princeton.edu/~appel/modern/java/CUP/.
18. Yuuji Ichisugi and Yves Roudier. The extensible Java preprocessor kit and a tiny data-parallel Java. In *Proc. ISCOPE '97*, LNCS 1343, pages 153–160. Springer, 1997.
19. Richard Kelsey, William Clinger, and Jonathan Rees (editors). Revised^5 report on the algorithmic language Scheme. *ACM SIGPLAN Notices*, 33(9):26–76, October 1998. Available at http://www.schemers.org/Documents/Standards/R5RS.
20. Gregor Kiczales, John Lamping, Anurag Mendhekar, Chris Maeda, Cristina Videira Lopes, Jean-Marc Loingtier, and John Irwin. Aspect-oriented programming. In *Proceedings of 11th European Conference on Object-Oriented Programming (ECOOP'97)*, number 1241 in Lecture Notes in Computer Science, pages 220–242, Jyväskylä, Finland, June 1997. Springer-Verlag.
21. Joseph R. Kiniry and Elaine Cheong. JPP: A Java pre-processor. Technical Report CS-TR-98-15, California Institute of Technology, Pasadena, CA, September 1998.
22. Shriram Krishnamurthi, Matthias Felleisen, and Daniel P. Friedman. Synthesizing object-oriented and functional design to promote re-use. In *Proc. ECOOP '98*, pages 91–113, 1998.

23. Gary T. Leavens, K. Rustan M. Leino, Erik Poll, Clyde Ruby, and Bart Jacobs. JML: notations and tools supporting detailed design in Java. In *OOPSLA 2000 Companion*, pages 105–106, Minneapolis, Minnesota, 2000.

24. Jed Liu and Andrew C. Myers. JMatch: Abstract iterable pattern matching for Java. In *Proc. 5th Int'l Symp. on Practical Aspects of Declarative Languages*, New Orleans, LA, January 2003.

25. Todd Millstein, Colin Bleckner, and Craig Chambers. Modular typechecking for hierarchically extensible datatypes and functions. In *Proc. 7th ACM SIGPLAN International Conference on Functional Programming (ICFP)*, pages 110–122, Philadelphia, PA, USA, October 2002.

26. Andrew C. Myers. JFlow: Practical mostly-static information flow control. In *Proc. 26th ACM Symp. on Principles of Programming Languages (POPL)*, pages 228–241, San Antonio, TX, January 1999.

27. Andrew C. Myers, Joseph A. Bank, and Barbara Liskov. Parameterized types for Java. In *Proc. 24th ACM Symp. on Principles of Programming Languages (POPL)*, pages 132–145, Paris, France, January 1997.

28. Martin Odersky and Philip Wadler. Pizza into Java: Translating theory into practice. In *Proc. 24th ACM Symp. on Principles of Programming Languages (POPL)*, pages 146–159, Paris, France, January 1997.

29. Terence Parr and Russell Quong. ANTLR: A predicated-LL(k) parser generator. *Journal of Software Practice and Experience*, 25(7), 1995.

30. John C. Reynolds. User-defined types and procedural data structures as complementary approaches to data abstraction. In Stephen A. Schuman, editor, *New Directions in Algorithmic Languages*, pages 157–168. Institut de Recherche d'Informatique et d'Automatique, Le Chesnay, France, 1975. Reprinted in [15], pages 13–23.

31. Richard Snodgrass. The Scorpion system, August 1995. Software release. Located at ftp://ftp.cs.arizona.edu/scorpion.

32. Richard Snodgrass and Karen Shannon. Supporting flexible and efficient tool integration. In *Proceedings of the International Workshop on Advanced Programming Environments*, number 244 in Lecture Notes in Computer Science, pages 290–313, Trondheim, Norway, June 1986.

33. Sun Microsystems. *Java Language Specification*, version 1.0 beta edition, October 1995. Available at ftp://ftp.javasoft.com/docs/javaspec.ps.zip.

34. Michiaki Tatsubori, Shigeru Chiba, Marc-Oliver Killijian, and Kozo Itano. OpenJava: A class-based macro system for Java. In Walter Cazzola, Robert J. Stroud, and Francesco Tisato, editors, *Reflection and Software Engineering*, LNCS 1826, pages 119–135. Springer-Verlag, July 2000.

35. J. Vlissides. Visitors in frameworks. *C++ Report*, 11(10), November 1999.

36. R. P. Wilson, R. S. French, C. S. Wilson, S. P. Amarasinghe, J. M. Anderson, S. W. K. Tjiang, S.-W. Liao, C.-W. Tseng, M. W. Hall, M. S. Lam, and J. L. Hennessy. SUIF: An infrastructure for research on parallelizing and optimizing compilers. *SIGPLAN Notices*, 29(12):31–37, 1994.

37. Steve Zdancewic, Lantian Zheng, Nathaniel Nystrom, and Andrew C. Myers. Untrusted hosts and confidentiality: Secure program partitioning. In *Proc. 18th ACM Symp. on Operating System Principles (SOSP)*, pages 1–14, Banff, Canada, October 2001.

38. Matthias Zenger and Martin Odersky. Extensible algebraic datatypes with defaults. In *Proc. 6th ACM SIGPLAN International Conference on Functional Programming (ICFP)*, Firenze, Italy, September 2001.

39. Matthias Zenger and Martin Odersky. Implementing extensible compilers. In *ECOOP Workshop on Multiparadigm Programming with Object-Oriented Languages*, Budapest, Hungary, June 2001.

Scaling Java Points-to Analysis Using SPARK

Ondřej Lhoták and Laurie Hendren

Sable Research Group, McGill University, Montreal, Canada
{olhotak,hendren}@sable.mcgill.ca

Abstract. Most points-to analysis research has been done on different systems by different groups, making it difficult to compare results, and to understand interactions between individual factors each group studied. Furthermore, points-to analysis for Java has been studied much less thoroughly than for C, and the tradeoffs appear very different. We introduce SPARK, a flexible framework for experimenting with points-to analyses for Java. SPARK supports equality- and subset-based analyses, variations in field sensitivity, respect for declared types, variations in call graph construction, off-line simplification, and several solving algorithms. SPARK is composed of building blocks on which new analyses can be based.

We demonstrate SPARK in a substantial study of factors affecting precision and efficiency of subset-based points-to analyses, including interactions between these factors. Our results show that SPARK is not only flexible and modular, but also offers superior time/space performance when compared to other points-to analysis implementations.

1   Introduction

Many compiler analyses and optimizations, as well as program understanding and verification tools, require information about which objects each pointer in a program may point to at run-time. The problem of approximating these points-to sets has been the subject of much research; however, many questions remain unanswered [16]. As with many compiler analyses, a precision vs. time trade-off exists for points-to analysis. For analyzing programs written in C, many points between the extremes of high-precision, slow and low-precision, fast have been explored [8, 22, 6, 21, 15, 11, 19]. These analyses have been implemented as parts of distinct systems, so it is difficult to compare and combine their unique features. The design tradeoffs for doing points-to analysis for Java appear to be different than for C, and recently, several different approaches to points-to analysis for Java have been suggested [17, 20, 27]. However, once again, it is hard to compare the results since each group has implemented their analysis in a different system, and has made very different assumptions about how to handle the large Java class libraries and Java native methods.

To address these issues, we have developed the Soot Pointer Analysis Research Kit (SPARK), a flexible framework for experimenting with points-to analyses for Java. SPARK is very modular: the pointer assignment graph that it produces and simplifies can be used as input to other solvers, including those being developed by other researchers. We hope that this will make it easier for researchers to compare results. In addition, the correctness

G. Hedin (Ed.): CC 2003, LNCS 2622, pp. 153–169, 2003.

of new analyses can be verified by comparing their results to those computed by the basic analyses provided in SPARK.

In order to demonstrate the usefulness of the framework, we have also performed a substantial empirical study of a variety of subset-based points-to analyses using SPARK. We studied a wide variety of factors that affect both precision and time/space costs. Our results show that SPARK is not only flexible and modular, but also offers very good time/space performance when compared to other points-to analysis implementations.

Specific new contributions of this paper are as follows. (1) The SPARK framework itself is available as part of Soot 1.2.4 [3] and later releases under the LGPL for the use of all researchers. (2) We present a study of a variety of representations for points-to sets and of a variety of solving strategies, including an incremental, *worklist-based*, field-sensitive algorithm which appears to scale well to larger benchmarks. (3) We report on an empirical evaluation of many factors affecting the precision, speed, and memory requirements of subset-based points-to analysis algorithms. We focus on improving the speed of the analysis without significant loss of precision. (4) We make recommendations to allow analyses to scale to programs on the order of a million lines of code. Even trivial Java programs are becoming this large as the standard class library grows.

The structure of this paper is as follows. In Section 2 we examine some of the challenges and factors to consider when designing an effective points-to analysis for Java. In Section 3 we introduce the SPARK framework and discuss the important components. Section 4 shows SPARK in action via a large empirical study of a variety of subset-based pointer analyses. In Section 5 we discuss related work and in Section 6 we provide our conclusions and discuss future work.

2   Points-to Analysis for Java

Although some of the techniques developed for C have been adapted to Java, there are significant differences between the two languages that affect points-to analysis. In C, points-to analysis can be viewed as two separate problems: analysis of stack-directed pointers, and analysis of heap-directed pointers. Most C programs have many more occurrences of the address-of (&) operator, which creates stack-directed pointers, than dynamic allocation sites, which create heap-directed pointers. It is therefore important for C points-to analyses to deal well with stack-directed pointers. Java, on the other hand, allows no stack-directed pointers whatsoever, and Java programs usually have many more dynamic allocation sites than C programs of similar size. Java analyses therefore have to handle heap-directed pointers well. Another important difference is the strong type checking in Java, which limits the sets of objects that a pointer could point to, and can therefore be used to improve analysis speed and precision. Diwan et. al. have shown the benefits of type-based alias analysis for Modula-3 [10]. Our study shows that using types in Java is very useful for improving efficiency, and also results in a small improvement in precision.

The object-oriented nature of Java also introduces new complexities in dealing with any whole program analysis. In order to build a call graph, some approximation of the targets of virtual method calls must be used. There are two basic approaches. The first approach is to use an approximation of the call graph built by another analysis.

The second approach is to construct the call graph on-the-fly, as the pointer analysis proceeds. In our empirical study, Section 4, we compare the two approaches.

Related to the problem of finding a call graph is finding the set of methods that must be analyzed. In sequential C programs, there is one entry point, `main`, and a whole program analysis can start at this entry point and then incrementally (either ahead-of-time or during analysis) add all called methods. In Java the situation is much more complicated as there are many potential entry points including static initializers, finalizers, thread start methods, and methods called using reflection. Further complicating matters are native methods which may impact points-to analysis, but for which we do not have the code to analyze. Our SPARK framework addresses these points.

Another very important point is the large size of the Java libraries. Even small application programs may touch, or appear to touch, a large part of the Java library. This means that a whole program analysis must be able to handle large problem sizes. Existing points-to analyses for Java have been successfully tested with the 1.1.8 version of the Java standard libraries [17, 20], consisting of 148 thousand lines of code (KLOC). However, current versions of the standard library are over three times larger (eg. 1.3.1_01 is 574 KLOC), dwarfing most application programs that use them, so it is not clear that existing analyses would scale to such large programs. Our framework has been designed to provide the tools to develop efficient and scalable analyses which can effectively handle large benchmarks using the large libraries.

3   SPARK Framework

3.1   Overview

The Soot Pointer Analysis Research Kit (SPARK) is a flexible framework for experimenting with points-to analyses for Java. Although SPARK is very competitive in efficiency with other points-to analysis systems, the main design goal was not raw speed, but rather the flexibility to make implementing a wide variety of analyses as easy as possible, to facilitate comparison of existing analyses and development of new ones.

SPARK supports both subset-based [6] and equality-based [22] analyses, as well as variations that lie between these two extremes. In this paper, we focus on the more precise, subset-based analyses. Although SPARK is limited to flow-insensitive analyses, most of the benefit of flow-sensitivity is obtained by splitting variables.

SPARK is implemented as part of the Soot bytecode analysis, optimization, and annotation framework [26]. Soot accepts Java bytecode as input, converts it to one of several intermediate representations, applies analyses and transformations, and converts the results back to bytecode. SPARK uses as its input the Jimple intermediate representation, a three-address representation in which local (stack) variables have been split according to DU-UD webs, and declared types have been inferred for them. The results of SPARK can be used by other analyses and transformations in Soot. Soot also provides an annotation framework that can be used to encode the results in classfile annotations for use by other tools or runtime systems [18].

The execution of SPARK can be divided into three stages: pointer assignment graph construction, pointer assignment graph simplification, and points-to set propagation. These stages are described in the following subsections.

3.2   Pointer Assignment Graph

SPARK uses a *pointer assignment graph* as its internal representation of the program being analyzed. The first stage of SPARK, the pointer assignment graph builder, constructs the pointer assignment graph from the Jimple input. Separating the builder from the solver makes it possible to use the same solution algorithms and implementations to solve different variations of the points-to analysis problem.

The pointer assignment graph consists of three types of nodes. Allocation site nodes represent allocation sites in the source program, and are used to model heap locations. Simple variable nodes represent local variables, method parameters and return values, and static fields. Field dereference nodes represent field access expressions in the source program; each is parametrized by a variable node representing the variable being dereferenced by the field access. The nodes in the pointer assignment graph are connected with four types of edges reflecting the pointer flow, corresponding to the four types of constraints imposed by the pointer-related instructions in the source program (Table 1). In this table, a and b denote allocation site nodes, src and dst denote variable nodes, and $src.f$ and $dst.f$ denote field dereference nodes.

Table 1. The four types pointer assignment graph edges.

	Allocation	Assignment	Field store	Field load
Instruction	$a : dst := new\ C$	$dst := src$	$dst.f := src$	$dst := src.f$
Edge	$a \rightarrow dst$	$src \rightarrow dst$	$src \rightarrow dst.f$	$src.f \rightarrow dst$
Rules	$\dfrac{a \rightarrow dst}{a \in pt(dst)}$	$\dfrac{src \rightarrow dst \quad a \in pt(src)}{a \in pt(dst)}$	$\dfrac{src \rightarrow dst.f \quad a \in pt(src) \quad b \in pt(dst)}{a \in pt(b.f)}$	$\dfrac{src.f \rightarrow dst \quad a \in pt(src) \quad b \in pt(a.f)}{b \in pt(dst)}$

Later, during the propagation of points-to sets, a fourth type of node (denoted $a.f$ and $b.f$) is created to hold the points-to set of each field of objects created at each allocation site. These nodes are parameterized by allocation site and field. However, they are not part of the initial pointer assignment graph.

Depending on the parameters to the builder, the pointer assignment graph for the same source code can be very different, reflecting varying levels of precision desired of the points-to analysis. As an example, the builder may make assignments directed for a subset-based analysis, or bi-directional for a equality-based analysis. Another example is the representation of field dereference expressions in the graph, as discussed next.

Field Dereference Expressions: A field expression $p.f$ refers to the field f of the object pointed to by p. There are three standard ways of dealing with fields. A *field-sensitive* interpretation, which is the most precise, considers $p.f$ to represent only the field f of only objects in the points-to set of p. A less precise, *field-based* interpretation approximates each field f of all objects using a single set, ignoring the p. The key advantage of this is that points-to sets can be propagated along a pointer assignment graph of only simple variable nodes *in one single iteration*, by first merging strongly-connected components of nodes, then propagating in topological order. Many C points-to analyses use a *field-independent* interpretation, which ignores the f, and approximates all the fields of objects in the points-to set of p as a single location. In Java, the field information is readily available, and different fields are guaranteed not to be aliased, so a field-independent interpretation makes little sense. SPARK supports field-sensitive and field-based analyses, and field-independent analyses would be trivial to implement.

3.3   Call Graph Construction

An interprocedural points-to analysis requires an approximation of the call graph. This can be constructed in advance using a technique such as CHA [9], RTA [7] or VTA [24], or it can be constructed on-the-fly as the points-to sets of call site receivers are computed. The latter approach gives somewhat higher precision, but requires more iteration as edges are added to the pointer assignment graph.

SPARK supports all of these variations, but in this paper, our empirical study focuses on CHA and on-the-fly call graph construction. SPARK always uses the CHA call graph builder included in Soot to determine which methods are reachable for the purposes of *building* the pointer assignment graph. However, on-the-fly call graph construction can be achieved at *solving* time by excluding interprocedural edges from the initial graph, and then adding only the reachable edges as the points-to sets are propagated.

In theory, determining which methods are possibly reachable at run-time is simple: start with a root set containing the main method, and transitively add all methods which are called from methods in the set. Java is not this simple, however; execution can also start at static initializers, finalizers, thread start methods, and dynamic call sites using reflection. Soot considers all these factors in determining which methods are reachable. For the many call sites using reflection inside the standard class library, we have compiled, by hand, a list of their possible targets, and they are automatically added to the root set.

In addition, native methods may affect the flow of pointers in a Java program. SPARK therefore includes a native method simulation framework. The effects of each native method are described in the framework using abstract Java code, and SPARK then creates the corresponding pointer flow edges. The native method simulation framework was designed to be independent of SPARK, so the simulations of native methods should be usable by other analyses.

3.4   Points-to Assignment Graph Simplification

Before points-to sets are propagated, the pointer assignment graph can be simplified by merging nodes that are known to have the same points-to set. Specifically, all the nodes in a strongly-connected component (cycle) will have equal points-to sets, so they can be merged to a single node. A version of the off-line variable substitution algorithm given in [19] is also used to merge equivalence sets of nodes that have a single common predecessor.[1]

---

[1] If types are being used, then only nodes with compatible types can be merged; the interaction of types and graph simplification is examined in Section 4.

SPARK uses a fast union-find algorithm [25] to merge nodes in time almost linear in the number of nodes. This is the same algorithm used for equality-based [22] analyses. Therefore, by making all edges bidirectional and merging nodes forming strongly-connected components, we can implement a equality-based analysis in SPARK. In fact, we can easily implement a hybrid analysis which is partly equality-based and partly subset-based by making only *some* of the edges bidirectional. One instance of a similarly hybrid analysis is described in [8]. Even when performing a fully subset-based analysis, we can use the same unification code to simplify the pointer assignment graph.

3.5 Set Implementations

Choosing an appropriate set representation for the points-to sets is a key part of designing an effective analysis. The following implementations are currently included as part of SPARK; others should be easy to add. *Hash Set* is a wrapper for the `HashSet` implementation from the standard class library. It is provided as a baseline against which the other set implementations can be compared. *Sorted Array Set* implements a set using an array which is always kept in sorted order. This makes it possible to compute the union of two sets in linear time, like in a merge sort. *Bit Set* implements a set as a bit vector. This makes set operations very fast regardless of how large the sets get (as long as the size of the universal set stays constant). The drawback is that the many sparse sets use a large amount of memory. *Hybrid Set* represents small sets (up to 16 elements) explicitly using pointers to the elements themselves, but switches to a bit vector representation when the sets grow larger, thus allowing both small and large sets to be represented efficiently.

3.6 Points-to Set Propagation

After the pointer assignment graph has been built and simplified, the final step is propagating the points-to sets along its edges according to the rules shown in Table 1. SPARK provides several different algorithms to implement these rules.

Iterative Algorithm: SPARK includes a naive, baseline, iterative algorithm (Algorithm 1) that can be used to check the correctness of the results of the more complicated algorithms.[2] Note that for efficiency, all the propagation algorithms in SPARK consider variable nodes in topological order (or pseudo-topological order, if cycles have not been simplified).

Worklist Algorithm: For some of our benchmarks, the iterative algorithm performs over 60 iterations. After the first few iterations, the points-to sets grow very little, yet each iteration is as expensive as the first few. A better, but more complex solver based on worklists is also provided as part of SPARK and is outlined in Algorithm 2. This solver maintains a worklist of variable nodes whose points-to sets need to be propagated to their successors, so that only those nodes are considered for propagation.

---

[2] For clarity, the algorithms are presented here without support for on-the-fly call graph construction. However, both variations are implemented in SPARK and evaluated in Section 4.

Algorithm 1 Iterative Propagation

```
 1: initialize sets according to allocation edges
 2: repeat
 3:    propagate sets along each assignment edge p → q
 4:    for each load edge p.f → q do
 5:       for each a ∈ pt(p) do
 6:          propagate sets pt(a.f) → pt(q)
 7:    for each store edge p → q.f do
 8:       for each a ∈ pt(q) do
 9:          propagate sets pt(p) → pt(a.f)
10: until no changes
```

Algorithm 2 Worklist Propagation

```
 1: for each allocation edge o₁ → p do
 2:    pt(p) = {o₁}
 3:    add p to worklist
 4: repeat
 5:    repeat
 6:       remove first node p from worklist
 7:       propagate sets along each assignment edge p → q,
             adding q to worklist whenever pt(q) changes
 8:       for each store edge q → r.f where p = q or p = r do
 9:          for each a ∈ pt(r) do
10:             propagate sets pt(q) → pt(a.f)
11:          for each load edge p.f → q do
12:             for each a ∈ pt(p) do
13:                propagate sets pt(a.f) → q
14:                add q to worklist if pt(q) changed
15:    until worklist is empty
16:    for each store edge q → r.f do
17:       for each a ∈ pt(r) do
18:          propagate sets pt(q) → pt(a.f)
19:       for each load edge p.f → q do
20:          for each a ∈ pt(p) do
21:             propagate sets pt(a.f) → q
22:             add q to worklist if pt(q) changed
23: until worklist is empty
```

In the presence of field-sensitivity, however, the worklist algorithm is not so simple. Whenever a variable node p appears in the worklist (which means that its points-to set has new nodes in it that need to be propagated), the algorithm propagates along edges of the form $p \to q$, but also along loads and stores involving p (those of the form $p \to q.f$, $q \to p.f$, and $p.f \to q$), since they are likely to require propagation. However, this is not sufficient to obtain the complete solution. For example, suppose that a is in the points-to sets of both p and q, so that p and q are possible aliases. After processing any store into

$q.f$, we should process all loads from $p.f$. However, there is no guarantee that p will appear in the worklist. For this reason, the algorithm must still include an outer iteration over *all* the load and store edges. To summarize, lines 16 to 22 in the outer loop are necessary for correctness; lines 8 to 14 could be removed, but including them greatly reduces the number of iterations of the outer loop and therefore reduces the analysis time.

Incremental Sets: In certain implementations of sets (hash set and sorted array set), each set union operation takes time proportional to the size of the sets being combined. While iterating through an analysis, the contents of one set are repeatedly merged into the contents of another set, often adding only a small number of new elements in each iteration. We can improve the algorithm by noting that the elements that have already been propagated must be found in the set in every subsequent iteration.

Thus, as an optional improvement, SPARK includes versions of the solvers that use incremental sets. Each set is divided into a "new" part and an "old" part. During each iteration, elements are propagated only between the new parts, which are likely to be small. At the end of each iteration, all the new parts are flushed into their corresponding old part. An additional advantage of this is that when constructing the call graph on-the-fly, only the smaller, new part of the points-to set of the receiver of each call site needs to be considered in each iteration.

4   Using SPARK for Subset-Based Points-to Analysis

In order to demonstrate that SPARK provides a general and effective means to express different points-to analyses, we have done an extensive empirical study of a variety of subset-based points-to analyses. By expressing many different variations within the same framework we can measure both precision and cost of the analyses.

4.1   Benchmarks

We tested SPARK on benchmarks from the SPECjvm [4] suite, along with `sablecc` and `soot` from the Ashes [1] suite, and `jedit` [2], a full-featured editor written in Java. The last three were selected because they are non-trivial Java applications used in the real world, and they were also used in other points-to analysis studies [20, 27, 17]. The complete list of benchmarks appears in the summary in Table 5 at the end of this section, along with some characteristics of the benchmarks, and measurements of the effectiveness of SPARK on them. All benchmarks were analyzed with the Sun JDK 1.3.1_01 standard class library, on a 1.67 GHz AMD Athlon with 2GB of memory running Linux 2.4.18. In addition, we also tested the `javac` benchmark with the Sun JDK 1.1.8 standard class library for comparison with other studies.

We chose four representative benchmarks for which to present the detailed results of our experiments on individual factors affecting precision and efficiency of points-to analysis. We chose `compress` as a small SPECjvm benchmark, `javac` as a large SPECjvm benchmark, and `sablecc` and `jedit` as large non-SPECjvm benchmarks written by distinct groups of people. We observed similar trends on the other benchmarks.

Table 2. Analysis precision.

		Dereference Sites (% of total)							Call Sites (% of total)			
		0	1	2	3-10	11-100	101-1000	1001+	0	1	2	3+
compress	nt-otf-fs	35.2	23.4	6.3	14.1	5.9	0.1	14.9	53.8	42.6	1.6	1.9
	at-otf-fs	35.3	32.7	8.0	17.4	4.3	2.2	0.0	53.8	42.6	1.6	1.9
	ot-otf-fs	36.9	32.1	7.8	17.0	4.3	1.8	0.0	54.6	42.3	1.3	1.8
	ot-cha-fs	20.5	39.6	10.1	21.8	6.0	2.1	0.0	40.8	51.7	2.6	4.9
	ot-otf-fb	26.3	38.1	9.4	19.2	5.1	1.9	0.0	48.0	47.4	2.0	2.6
	ot-cha-fb	16.0	41.6	10.9	22.9	6.4	2.2	0.0	37.5	54.3	2.9	5.2
javac	nt-otf-fs	31.4	22.2	6.0	12.9	5.8	6.4	15.2	50.1	45.3	1.9	2.7
	at-otf-fs	31.6	33.9	8.7	17.7	5.7	2.4	0.0	50.1	45.3	1.9	2.7
	ot-otf-fs	33.0	33.3	8.6	17.3	5.7	2.0	0.0	50.8	45.2	1.5	2.5
	ot-cha-fs	18.4	40.0	10.5	21.5	7.2	2.3	0.0	38.0	53.9	2.6	5.5
	ot-otf-fb	23.6	38.6	10.0	19.2	6.5	2.1	0.0	44.6	49.9	2.1	3.3
	ot-cha-fb	14.5	41.7	11.3	22.5	7.6	2.4	0.0	34.9	56.3	3.0	5.8
sablecc	nt-otf-fs	31.6	24.2	5.9	12.7	9.5	0.2	15.8	49.9	45.8	2.1	2.2
	at-otf-fs	31.7	37.9	7.4	16.2	4.9	2.0	0.0	49.9	45.8	2.1	2.2
	ot-otf-fs	33.1	37.4	7.3	15.7	4.9	1.6	0.0	50.8	45.5	1.6	2.0
	ot-cha-fs	18.4	44.1	9.2	20.1	6.4	1.9	0.0	37.9	54.2	2.9	5.0
	ot-otf-fb	23.6	42.6	8.7	17.7	5.7	1.7	0.0	44.7	50.3	2.2	2.8
	ot-cha-fb	14.4	45.8	10.0	21.0	6.8	1.9	0.0	34.9	56.6	3.3	5.2
jedit	nt-otf-fs	25.6	29.6	6.6	12.7	3.8	1.5	20.2	43.8	52.0	1.9	2.2
	at-otf-fs	25.7	42.4	9.0	16.3	4.7	2.0	0.0	43.8	52.0	1.9	2.2
	ot-otf-fs	27.1	42.0	8.9	15.9	4.3	1.9	0.0	44.6	51.9	1.4	2.1
	ot-cha-fs	14.5	47.9	10.7	19.4	5.5	2.1	0.0	33.2	59.3	2.3	5.1
	ot-otf-fb	18.9	46.7	10.0	17.6	4.8	2.0	0.0	38.6	56.7	1.9	2.8
	ot-cha-fb	12.1	49.0	11.0	20.1	5.7	2.1	0.0	30.7	61.5	2.5	5.3

4.2   Factors Affecting Precision

We now discuss three factors that affect not only the efficiency of the analysis, but also the precision of its result. These factors are: (1) how types are used in the analysis, (2) whether we use a CHA-based call graph or build the call graph on the fly, and (3) whether the analysis is field-sensitive or field-based.

Table 2 gives the results. For each benchmark we experiment with five different points-to analyses, where each analysis is named by a triple of the form xx-yyy-zz which specifies the setting for each of the three factors (a complete explanation of each factor is given in the subsections below). For each benchmark/points-to analysis combination, we give a summary of the precision for dereference sites and call sites.

For dereference sites, we consider all occurrences of references of the form p.f and we give the percentage of dereference sites with 0, 1, 2, 3-10, 11-100, 101-1000 and more than 1000 elements in their points-to sets. Dereference sites with 0 items in the set correspond to statements that cannot be reached (i.e. the CHA call graph conservatively indicated that it was in a reachable method, but no allocation ever flows to that statement).

For call sites, we consider all `invokevirtual` and `invokeinterface` calls and report the percentage of such call sites with with 0, 1, 2, and more than two target methods, where the target methods are found using the types of the allocation sites pointed to by the receiver of the method call. For example, for a call of the form `o.m()`, the types of allocation sites pointed to by `o` would be used to find the target methods. Calls with 0 targets correspond to unreachable calls and calls with 1 target are guaranteed to be monomorphic at run-time.

Note that since the level of precision required is highly dependent on the application of the points-to results, this table is not intended to be an absolute measure of precision; rather, we present it only to give some idea of the relative precision of different analysis variations, and to give basic insight into the effect that different levels of precision have on the analysis.

Respecting Declared Types: Unlike in C, variables in Java are strongly-typed, limiting the possible set of objects to which a pointer could point. However, many points-to analyses adapted from C do not take advantage of this. For example, the analyses described in [20, 24] ignore declared types as the analysis proceeds; however, objects of incompatible type are removed after the analysis completes.

The first three lines of each benchmark in Table 2 show the effect of types. The first line shows the precision of an analysis in which declared types are ignored, *notypes* (abbreviated nt). The second line shows the results of the same analysis after objects of incompatible type have been removed after completion of the analysis, *aftertypes* (abbreviated at). The third line shows the precision of an analysis in which declared types are respected throughout the analysis, *on-the-fly types* (abbreviated ot).

We see that removing objects based on declared type after completion of the analysis (at) achieves almost the same precision as enforcing the types during the analysis (ot). However, notice that during the analysis (nt), between 15% and 20% of the points-to sets at dereference sites are over 1000 elements in size. These large sets increase memory requirements prohibitively, and slow the analysis considerably. We therefore recommend enforcing declared types as the analysis proceeds, which eliminates almost all of these large sets. Further, based on this observation, we focus on analyses that respect declared types for the remainder of this paper.

Call Graph Construction: As we have already mentioned, the call graph used for an inter-procedural points-to analysis can be constructed ahead of time using, for example, CHA [9], or on-the-fly as the analysis proceeds [20], for greater precision. We abbreviate these variations as cha and otf, respectively. As the third and fourth lines for each benchmark in Table 2 show, computing the call graph on-the-fly increases the number of points-to sets of size zero (dereference sites determined to be unreachable), but has a smaller effect on the size distribution of the remaining sets.

Field Dereference Expressions: We study the handling of field dereference expressions in a field-based (abbreviated fb) and field-sensitive (abbreviated fs) manner. Comparing rows 3 and 5 (on-the-fly call graph), and rows 4 and 6 (CHA call graph), for each benchmark, we see that field-sensitive analysis is more precise than the field-based analysis. Thus, it is probably worthwhile to do field-sensitive analysis if the cost of the analysis is reasonable. As we will see later, in Table 4, with the appropriate solver, the field-sensitive analysis can be made to be quite competitive to the field-based analysis.

4.3   Factors Affecting Performance

Set Implementation: We evaluated the analyses with the four different implementations of points-to sets described in Section 3. Table 3 shows the efficiency of the implementations using two of the propagation algorithms: the naive, iterative algorithm, and the incremental worklist algorithm. For both algorithms, we respected declared types during the analysis, used a CHA call graph, and simplified the pointer assignment graph by collapsing cycles and variables with common predecessors as described in [19]. The "Graph space" column shows the space needed to store the original pointer assignment graph, and the remaining space columns show the space needed to store the points-to sets. The data structure storing the graph is designed for flexibility rather than space efficiency; it could be made smaller if necessary. In any case, its size is linear in the size of the program being analyzed.

Table 3. Set Implementation (time in seconds, space in MB).

		Graph space	Hash time	space	Array time	space	Bit time	space	Hybrid time	space
	Algorithm									
compress	Iterative	31	3448	311	1206	118	36	75	24	34
	Incremental Worklist	31	219	319	62	57	14	155	9	53
javac	Iterative	34	3791	361	1114	139	50	88	33	41
	Incremental Worklist	34	252	369	61	68	19	181	13	65
sablecc	Iterative	36	4158	334	1194	132	50	93	32	42
	Incremental Worklist	36	244	342	54	62	17	193	11	66
jedit	Iterative	42	6502	583	2233	229	91	168	59	77
	Incremental Worklist	42	488	597	135	114	38	349	24	128

The terrible performance of the hash set implementation is disappointing, as this is the implementation provided by the standard Java library. Clearly, anyone serious about implementing an efficient points-to analysis in Java must write a custom set representation.

The sorted array set implementation is prohibitively expensive using the iterative algorithm, but becomes reasonable using the incremental worklist algorithm, which is designed explicitly to limit the size of the sets that must be propagated.

The bit set implementation is much faster still than the sorted array set implementation. However, especially when used with the incremental worklist algorithm, its memory usage is high, because the many small sets are represented using the same size bit-vector as large sets. In addition, the incremental worklist algorithm splits each points-to set into two halves, making the bit set implementation use twice the memory.

Finally, the hybrid set implementation is even faster than the bit set implementation, while maintaining modest memory requirements. We have found the hybrid set implementation to be consistently the most efficient over a wide variety of settings of the other parameters, and therefore recommend that it always be used.

Points-to Set Propagation Algorithms: Table 4 shows the time and space requirements of the propagation algorithms included in SPARK. All measurements in this table were made using the hybrid set implementation, and without any simplification of the pointer assignment graph.[3] Again, the "Graph space" column shows the space needed to store the original pointer assignment graph, and the remaining space columns show the space needed to store the points-to sets.

Table 4. Propagation Algorithms (time in seconds, space in MB).

		Graph space	Iterative time	space	Worklist time	space	Incr. Worklist time	space
compress	nt-otf-fs	32	1628	357	992	365	399	605
	ot-otf-fs	37	133	52	58	51	**52**	**69**
	ot-cha-fs	36	49	68	15	63	**13**	**91**
	ot-otf-fb	35	158	54	86	52	**66**	**66**
	ot-cha-fb	34	17	62	**10**	**56**	13	76
javac	nt-otf-fs	34	2316	502	1570	512	715	856
	ot-otf-fs	40	201	69	103	66	**90**	**90**
	ot-cha-fs	39	64	83	22	77	**18**	**109**
	ot-otf-fb	37	218	70	123	66	**102**	**84**
	ot-cha-fb	37	22	75	**11**	**67**	15	90
sablecc	nt-otf-fs	35	2190	462	1382	472	635	772
	ot-otf-fs	41	274	72	104	70	**95**	**94**
	ot-cha-fs	41	66	88	20	83	**18**	**117**
	ot-otf-fb	38	255	74	138	72	**114**	**90**
	ot-cha-fb	38	52	81	**14**	**74**	18	97
jedit	nt-otf-fs	oom	oom	oom	oom	oom	oom	oom
	ot-otf-fs	49	313	121	142	117	**101**	**169**
	ot-cha-fs	48	107	141	59	131	**38**	**196**
	ot-otf-fb	47	298	104	178	99	**111**	**126**
	ot-cha-fb	45	28	109	**21**	**98**	27	128

The nt-otf-fs line shows how much ignoring declared types hurts efficiency (the "oom" for `jedit` signifies that the analysis exceeded the 1700MB of memory allotted); we recommend that declared types be respected. Results from the recommended algorithms are in bold.

---

[3] The time and space reported for the hybrid set implementation in Table 3 are different than in Table 4 because the former were measured with off-line pointer assignment graph simplification, and the latter without.

The iterative algorithm is consistently slowest, and is given as a baseline only. The worklist algorithm is usually about twice as fast as the iterative algorithm. For the CHA field-based analysis, this algorithm is consistently the fastest, faster even than the incremental worklist algorithm. This is because the incremental worklist algorithm is designed to propagate only the newly-added part of the points-to sets in each iteration, but the CHA field-based analysis requires only a single iteration. Therefore, any benefit from its being incremental is outweighed by the overhead of maintaining two parts of every set. However, both field-sensitivity and on-the-fly call graph construction require iteration, so for these, the incremental worklist algorithm is consistently fastest. We note that the speedup comes with a cost in the memory required to maintain two parts of every set.

Note also that while the field-based analysis is faster than field-sensitive with a CHA call graph, it is slower when the call graph is constructed on the fly (with all propagation algorithms). This is because although a field-based analysis with a CHA call graph completes in one iteration, constructing the call graph on-the-fly requires iterating regardless of the field representation. The less precise field-based representation causes more methods to be found reachable, increasing the number of iterations required.

Graph Simplification: Rountev and Chandra [19] showed that simplifying the pointer assignment graph by merging nodes known to have equal points-to sets speeds up the analysis. Our experience agrees with their findings.

When respecting declared types, a cycle can only be merged if all nodes in the cycle have the same declared type, and a subgraph with a unique predecessor can only be merged if all its nodes have declared types that are supertypes of the predecessor. On our benchmarks, between 6% and 7% of variable nodes were removed by collapsing cycles, compared to between 5% and 6% when declared types were respected. Between 59% and 62% of variable nodes were removed by collapsing subgraphs with a unique predecessor, compared to between 55% and 58% when declared types were respected. Thus, the effect of respecting declared types on simplification is minor.

On the other hand, when constructing the call graph on-the-fly, no inter-procedural edges are present before the analysis begins. This means that any cycles spanning multiple methods are broken, and the corresponding nodes cannot be merged. The 6%-7% of nodes removed by collapsing cycles dropped to 1%-1.5% when the call graph was constructed on-the-fly. The 59%-62% of nodes removed by collapsing subgraphs with a unique predecessor dropped to 31%-33%. When constructing the call graph on-the-fly, simplifying the pointer assignment graph before the analysis has little effect, and on-the-fly cycle detection methods should be used instead.

4.4   Overall Results

Based on our experiments, we have selected three analyses that we recommend as good compromises between precision and speed, with reasonable space requirements:
ot-otf-fs is suitable for applications requiring the highest precision. For this analysis, the incremental worklist algorithm works best.
ot-cha-fs is much faster, but with a drop in precision as compared to ot-otf-fs (mostly

because it includes significantly more call edges). For this analysis, the incremental worklist algorithm works best.

ot-cha-fb is the fastest analysis, completing in a single iteration, but it is also the least precise. For this analysis, the non-incremental worklist algorithm works best.

Each of the three analyses should be implemented using the hybrid sets.

Table 5. Overall Results (time in seconds, space in MB, precision in precent).

Benchmark	methods (CHA)	stmts (CHA)	types	ot-otf-fs time	space	prec.	ot-cha-fs time	space	prec.	ot-cha-fb time	space	prec.
compress	15183	278902	2770	52	106	69.1	13	127	60.1	10	90	57.6
db	15185	278954	2763	52	107	68.9	14	128	59.9	11	90	57.4
jack	15441	288142	2816	54	112	68.7	14	132	60.1	11	94	57.6
javac (1.1.8)	4602	86454	874	8	27	63.6	3	24	57.4	1	16	55.1
javac	16307	301801	2940	89	131	66.3	18	148	58.4	11	104	56.2
jess	15794	288831	2917	57	115	68.1	15	136	59.2	10	97	56.8
mpegaudio	15385	283482	2782	56	112	68.6	16	134	59.7	11	93	57.4
raytrace	15312	281587	2789	53	107	68.5	13	129	59.6	11	91	57.1
sablecc	16977	300504	3070	95	136	70.5	18	158	62.5	14	112	60.3
soot	17498	310935	3435	88	143	68.3	19	162	60.4	18	116	58.4
jedit	19621	367317	3395	100	218	69.1	38	244	62.3	21	143	61.1

Table 5 shows the results of these three analyses on our full set of benchmarks. The first column gives the benchmark name (javac is listed twice: once with the 1.1.8 JDK class library, and once with the 1.3.1_01 JDK class library). The next two columns give the number of methods determined to be reachable, and the number of Jimple[4] statements in these methods. Note that because of the large class library, these are the largest Java benchmarks for which a subtype-based points-to analysis has been reported, to our knowledge. The fourth column gives the number of distinct types encountered by the subtype tester. The remaining columns give the analysis time, total space, and precision for each of the three recommended analyses. The total space includes the space used to store the pointer assignment graph as well as the points-to sets; these were reported separately in previous tables. The precision is measured as the percentage of field dereference sites at which the points-to set of the pointer being dereferenced has size 0 or 1; for a more detailed measurement of precision, see Table 2.

5   Related Work

The most closely related work are various adaptations of points-to analyses for C to Java.

Rountev, Milanova and Ryder [20] based their field-sensitive analysis for Java on Soot [26] and the BANE [5] constraint solving toolkit, on which further points-to analysis work has been done [12,23]. Their analysis was field-sensitive, constructed the call graph

---

[4] Jimple is the three-address typed intermediate representation used by Soot.

on-the-fly, and ignored declared types until after the analysis completed. They reported empirical results on many benchmarks using the JDK 1.1.8 standard class library. Since they do not handle declared types during the analysis, their implementation suffers from having to represent large points-to sets, and is unlikely to scale well to large class libraries. They do not report results for the JDK 1.3.1 library, but their results for javac (1.1.8) show 350 seconds and 125.5 MB of memory (360 MHz Sun Ultra-60 machine with 512 MB of memory, BANE solver written in ML), compared to 8 seconds and 27 MB of memory (1.67 GHz AMD Athlon with 2GB memory, solver written in Java) for the ot-otf-fs analysis using SPARK. The precision of our results should be very slightly better, since the Rountev et. al. method is equivalent to our at-otf-fs analysis, which we showed to be slightly less precise that the ot-otf-fs analysis.

Whaley and Lam's [27] approach is interesting in that it adapts the demand-driven algorithm of Heintze and Tardieu [15, 14] (see below) to Java. The intermediate representation on which their analysis operates is different from Jimple (on which our and Rountev, Milanova and Ryder's analyses are based) in that it does not split stack locations based on DU-UD webs; instead, it uses intra-method flow-sensitivity to achieve a similar effect. In contrast with other work that used a conservative (safe) approximation of reachable methods which to analyze, Whaley and Lam's experiments used optimistic assumptions (not safe) about which methods need to be analyzed. In particular, the results presented in their paper [27] are for a variation of the analysis that does not analyze class initializers and assumes that all native methods have no effect on the points-to analysis. Their optimistic assumptions about which methods are reachable lead to reachable method counts almost an order of magnitude lower than reported in other related work, such as the present paper, and [20, 24]; in fact, they analyze significantly fewer methods than can be observed to be executed at run-time in a standard run of the benchmarks. As a result of the artificially small number of methods that they analyze, they get fast execution times. Even so, when looking at the jedit benchmark, the only benchmark for which they analyze at least half of the number of methods analyzed by SPARK, their analysis runs in 614 seconds and 472 MB of memory (2 GHz Pentium 4, 2GB of memory, solver written in Java), compared to 100 seconds and 218 MB for the most precise analysis in SPARK (1.67 GHz AMD Athlon, 2GB memory, solver written in Java).

Our comparison with these two other previous works for points-to analysis for Java illustrates two important things. First, it would be nice if we could compare the analyses head to head, on the same system, with the same assumptions about what code needs to be analyzed. Second, it appears that SPARK allows one to develop efficient analyses that compare very favourably with previous work.

Liang, Pennings and Harrold [17] tested several variations of Java points-to analyses, including subset-based and equality-based variations, field-based and field-sensitive variations, and constructing the call graph using CHA [9] and RTA [7]. Instead of analyzing benchmarks with the standard class library, they hand-coded a model of the most commonly used JDK 1.1.8 standard classes. Thus, we cannot make direct comparisons, since our results include all the library code.

Heintze and Tardieu [15, 14] reported very fast analysis times using their analysis for C. The main factor making it fast was a demand-driven algorithm that also collapsed cycles in the constraint graph on-the-fly. Such a demand-driven algorithm is particularly useful when the points-to sets of only a subset of pointer variables are required; we plan to implement it in a future version of SPARK for such applications. In addition, in an unpublished report [13], Heintze discusses an implementation of sets using bit-vectors which are shared, so that copies of an identical set are only stored once. We are also considering implementing this set representation in SPARK.

Since points-to analysis in general is a very active area of research, we can only list the work most closely related to ours. A more complete survey appears in [16].

6   Conclusions and Future Work

We have presented SPARK, a flexible framework for experimenting with points-to analysis for Java. Our empirical results have shown that SPARK is not only flexible, but also competitive with points-to analyses that have been implemented in other frameworks. Using SPARK, we studied various factors affecting the precision and efficiency of points-to analysis. Our study led us to recommend three specific analyses, and we showed that they compare favourably to other analyses that have been described in the literature. We plan several improvements to SPARK. First, we would like to create an on-the-fly pointer assignment graph builder, so that the entire pointer assignment graph need not be built for an on-the-fly call graph analysis. Second, we would like to add Heintze and Tardieu's demand-driven propagation algorithm to SPARK.

We have several studies in mind that we would like to perform using SPARK. First, we are implementing points-to analysis using Reduced Ordered Binary Decision Diagrams to store the large, often duplicated sets. Second, we plan to study the effects of various levels of context-sensitivity on Java points-to analysis. Third, we will experiment with various clients of the points-to analysis.

Acknowledgements. We are grateful to Feng Qian for work on the native method simulator, to Navindra Umanee for help producing the list of methods called using reflection by the standard class library, to Marc Berndl and John Jorgensen for helpful discussions, to Atanas Rountev, Ana Milanova, and Barbara Ryder for providing details about how their points-to analysis determines the reachable call graph, and to John Whaley for answering our questions about the assumptions made by his analysis, and the settings he used in his experiments.

References

1. Ashes suite collection. http://www.sable.mcgill.ca/software/.
2. jEdit: Open source programmer's text editor. http://www.jedit.org/.
3. Soot: a Java optimization framework. http://www.sable.mcgill.ca/soot/.
4. SPEC JVM98 benchmarks. http://www.spec.org/osg/jvm98/.
5. A. Aiken, M. Fähndrich, J. S. Foster, and Z. Su. A toolkit for constructing type- and constraint-based program analyses. In *Types in Compilation, Second International Workshop, TIC '98*, volume 1473 of *LNCS*, pages 78–96, 1998.

6. L. O. Andersen. *Program Analysis and Specialization for the C Programming Language.* PhD thesis, University of Copenhagen, May 1994. (DIKU report 94/19).
7. D. F. Bacon and P. F. Sweeney. Fast static analysis of C++ virtual function calls. In *Proceedings of the 1996 OOPSLA*, pages 324–341, 1996.
8. M. Das. Unification-based pointer analysis with directional assignments. In *Proceedings of PLDI'00*, volume 35.5 of *ACM Sigplan Notices*, pages 35–46, June 2000.
9. J. Dean, D. Grove, and C. Chambers. Optimization of object-oriented programs using static class hierarchy analysis. In *ECOOP'95—Object-Oriented Programming, 9th European Conference*, volume 952 of *LNCS*, pages 77–101, Aug. 1995.
10. A. Diwan, K. S. McKinley, and J. E. B. Moss. Type-based alias analysis. In *Proceedings of PLDI'98*, pages 106–117, 1998.
11. M. Emami, R. Ghiya, and L. J. Hendren. Context-sensitive interprocedural points-to analysis in the presence of function pointers. In *Proceedings of PLDI'94*, pages 242–256, 1994.
12. M. Fähndrich, J. S. Foster, Z. Su, and A. Aiken. Partial online cycle elimination in inclusion constraint graphs. In *Proceedings of PLDI'98*, pages 85–96, June 1998.
13. N. Heintze. Analysis of large code bases: The compile-link-analyze model. `http://cm.bell-labs.com/cm/cs/who/nch/cla.ps`, 1999.
14. N. Heintze and O. Tardieu. Demand-driven pointer analysis. In *Proceedings of PLDI'01*, pages 24–34, 2001.
15. N. Heintze and O. Tardieu. Ultra-fast aliasing analysis using CLA: A million lines of C code in a second. In *Proceedings of PLDI'01*, volume 36.5 of *ACM SIGPLAN Notices*, pages 254–263, June 2001.
16. M. Hind. Pointer analysis: Haven't we solved this problem yet? In *Proceedings of PASTE'01*, pages 54–61, June 2001.
17. D. Liang, M. Pennings, and M. J. Harrold. Extending and evaluating flow-insensitive and context-insensitive points-to analyses for Java. In *Proceedings of PASTE'01*, pages 73–79, 2001.
18. P. Pominville, F. Qian, R. Vallée-Rai, L. Hendren, and C. Verbrugge. A framework for optimizing Java using attributes. In *Compiler Construction (CC 2001)*, volume 2027 of *LNCS*, pages 334–554, 2001.
19. A. Rountev and S. Chandra. Off-line variable substitution for scaling points-to analysis. In *Proceedings of PLDI'00*, pages 47 – 56, Jun 2000.
20. A. Rountev, A. Milanova, and B. G. Ryder. Points-to analysis for Java using annotated constraints. In *Proceedings of the 2001 OOPSLA*, pages 43–55, 2001.
21. M. Shapiro and S. Horwitz. Fast and accurate flow-insensitive points-to analysis. In *Conference Record of 24th POPL '97*, pages 1–14, Jan. 1997.
22. B. Steensgaard. Points-to analysis in almost linear time. In *Conference Record of 23rd POPL'96*, pages 32–41, Jan. 1996.
23. Z. Su, M. Fähndrich, and A. Aiken. Projection merging: reducing redundancies in inclusion constraint graphs. In *Proceedings of the 27th POPL'00*, pages 81–95, 2000.
24. V. Sundaresan, L. Hendren, C. Razafimahefa, R. Vallée-Rai, P. Lam, E. Gagnon, and C. Godin. Practical virtual method call resolution for Java. In *Proceedings of the 2000 OOPSLA*, pages 264–280, 2000.
25. R. E. Tarjan. Efficiency of a good but not linear set union algorithm. *Journal of the ACM (JACM)*, 22(2):215–225, 1975.
26. R. Vallée-Rai, E. Gagnon, L. J. Hendren, P. Lam, P. Pominville, and V. Sundaresan. Optimizing Java bytecode using the Soot framework: Is it feasible? In *Compiler Construction (CC 2000)*, volume 1781 of *LNCS*, pages 18–34, 2000.
27. J. Whaley and M. Lam. An efficient inclusion-based points-to analysis for strictly-typed languages. In *Static Analysis 9th International Symposium, SAS 2002*, volume 2477 of *LNCS*, pages 180–195, 2002.

Effective Inline-Threaded Interpretation of Java Bytecode Using Preparation Sequences*

Etienne Gagnon[1] and Laurie Hendren[2]

[1] Sable Research Group
Université du Québec à Montréal, etienne.gagnon@uqam.ca
[2] McGill University
Montreal, Canada, hendren@cs.mcgill.ca

Abstract. Inline-threaded interpretation is a recent technique that improves performance by eliminating dispatch overhead within basic blocks for interpreters written in C [11]. The dynamic class loading, lazy class initialization, and multi-threading features of Java reduce the effectiveness of a straight-forward implementation of this technique within Java interpreters. In this paper, we introduce preparation sequences, a new technique that solves the particular challenge of effectively inline-threading Java. We have implemented our technique in the SableVM Java virtual machine, and our experimental results show that using our technique, inline-threaded interpretation of Java, on a set of benchmarks, achieves a speedup ranging from 1.20 to 2.41 over switch-based interpretation, and a speedup ranging from 1.15 to 2.14 over direct-threaded interpretation.

1 Introduction

One of the main advantages of interpreters written in high-level languages is their simplicity and portability, when compared to static and dynamic compiler-based systems. One of their main drawbacks is poor performance, due to a high cost for dispatching interpreted instructions. In [11], Piumarta and Riccardi introduced a technique called *inlined-threading* which reduces this overhead by dynamically inlining instruction sequences within basic blocks, leaving a single instruction dispatch at the end of each sequence. To our knowledge, *inlined-threading* has not been applied to Java interpreters before. Applying this *inline-threaded* technique within an interpreter-based Java virtual machine (JVM) is unfortunately difficult, as Java has features that conflict with a straight-forward implementation of the technique. In particular, the JVM specification [9] mandates lazy class initialization, permits lazy class loading and linking, and mandates support for multi-threading. Efficient implementation of laziness requires in-place code replacement which is a delicate operation to do within a multi-threaded environment. In this paper, we introduce a technique called *preparation sequences* which solves the synchronization and shorter sequence problems caused by in-place code replacement within an inline-threaded interpreter-based JVM.

* This research was partly supported by NSERC, FCAR and Hydro-Québec.

G. Hedin (Ed.): CC 2003, LNCS 2622, pp. 170–184, 2003.
© Springer-Verlag Berlin Heidelberg 2003

This paper is structured as follows. In Section 2 we briefly describe some interpreter instruction dispatch techniques, including inline-threading. Then, in Section 3 we discuss the difficulty of applying the inline-threaded technique in a Java interpreter. Next, in section 4 we introduce our *preparation sequences* technique. In Section 5, we present our experimental results within the *SableVM* framework. In Section 6 we discuss related work. Finally, in Section 7, we present our conclusions.

2   Dispatch Types

In this section, we describe three dispatch mechanisms generally used for implementing interpreters.

Switching. A typical bytecode interpreter loads a bytecode program from disk using standard file operations, and stores instructions into an array. It then dispatches instructions using a simple loop-embedded *switch* statement, as shown in Figure 1(a). This approach has performance drawbacks. Dispatching instructions is very expensive. A typical compilation of the dispatch loop requires a minimum of 3 control transfer machine instructions per iteration: one to jump from the previous bytecode implementation to the head of the loop, one to test whether the bytecode is within the bounds of handled switch-case values, and one to transfer control to the selected case statement. On modern processors, control transfer is one of the main obstacles to performance [7], so this dispatch mechanism causes significant overhead.

Direct-Threading. This technique was popularized by the Forth programming language [5]. Direct-threading improves on switch-based dispatch by eliminating central dispatch. In the executable code stream, each bytecode is replaced by the address of its associated implementation. This reduces, to one, the number of control transfer instructions per dispatch. Direct-threading is illustrated in Figure 1(b)[1].

Inline-Threading. This technique, recently introduced in [11], improves upon direct-threading by eliminating dispatch overhead for instructions within a *basic block* [1]. The general idea is to identify instruction sequences forming basic blocks, within the code array, then to dynamically create a new implementation for the whole sequence by sequentially copying the body of each implementation into a new buffer, then copying the dispatch code at the end. Finally a pointer to this sequence implementation is stored into the code array, replacing the original bytecode of the first instruction in the sequence. Figure 2 illustrates the creation of an instruction sequence implementation and shows an abstract *source code* representation of the resulting inlined instruction sequence implementation.

---

[1] Figure 1(b) uses the *label-as-value* GNU C extension, but direct-threading can also be implemented using a couple of macros containing inline assembly.

(a) Pure Switch-Based Interpreter	(b) Direct-Threaded Interpreter

```char code[CODESIZE];```
```char *pc = code;```
```int stack[STACKSIZE];```
```int *sp = stack;```
 	
```/* load bytecodes from file and```
```   store them in code[] */```
```...```
```/* dispatch loop */```
```while(true) {```
``` switch(*pc++) {```
```   case ICONST_1: *sp++ = 1; break;```
```   case ICONST_2: *sp++ = 2; break;```
```   case IADD: --sp; sp[-1] += *sp; break;```
```   ...```
```   case END: exit(0);```
```}}```
	```/* code */```
	```void *code[] = {```
	``` &&ICONST_2, &&ICONST_2,```
	``` &&ICONST_1, &&IADD, ...```
	```}```
	```void **pc = code;```
	
	```/* dispatch first instruction */```
	```goto **(pc++);```
	
	```/* implementations */```
	```ICONST_1: *sp++ = 1; goto **(pc++);```
	```ICONST_2: *sp++ = 2; goto **(pc++);```
	```IADD: --sp; sp[-1] += *sp;```
	``` goto **(pc++);```
	```...```

Fig. 1. Switch and Direct-Threaded Interpreters

Inline-threading improves performance by reducing the overhead due to dispatch. This is particularly effective for sequences of simple instructions, which have a high *dispatch to real work* ratio. Unfortunately, not all instructions can be inlined. Inlining instructions that contain C function calls, hidden (compiler generated) function calls, or even simple conditional expressions (in presence of some compiler optimizations) can prevent inlining[2].

3   The Difficulty of Inline-Threading Java

Lazy Loading and Preparation. In Java, classes are dynamically loaded. The JVM Specification [9] allows a virtual machine to *eagerly* or *lazily* load classes (or anything in between). But this flexibility does not extend to *class initialization*[3]. Class initialization must occur at specific execution points, such as the first invocation of a static method or the first access to a static field of a class. Lazily loading classes has many advantages: it saves memory, reduces network traffic, and reduces startup overhead.

Inline-threading requires analyzing a bytecode array to determine *basic blocks*, allocating and preparing implementation sequences, and lastly preparing a code array. As this preparation is time and space consuming, it is advisable to only prepare methods that will actually be executed. This can be achieved through lazy method preparation.

Performance Issue. Lazy preparation (and loading), which aims at improving performance, can pose a performance problem within a multi-threaded[4] environ-

---

[2] The target of a relative branch instruction might be invalid in the inlined instruction copy.

[3] Class initialization consists of initializing static fields and executing static class initializers.

[4] Note that *multi-threading* is a concurrent programming technique which is inherently supported in Java, whereas *inline-threading* is an instruction dispatch technique.

(a) Instruction Implementations	(c) Inlined Instruction Sequence
ICONST_1_START: *sp++ = 1; ICONST_1_END: goto **(pc++); INEG_START: sp[-1] = -sp[-1]; INEG_END: goto **(pc++); DISPATCH_START: goto **(pc++); DISPATCH_END: ;	 ICONST_1 body: *sp++ = 1; INEG body : sp[-1] = -sp[-1]; DISPATCH body: goto **(pc++);

(b) Sequence Computation
| ```
/* Implement the sequence ICONST_1 INEG */
size_t iconst_size = (&&ICONST_1_END - &&ICONST_1_START);
size_t ineg_size = (&&INEG_END - &&INEG_START);
size_t dispatch_size = (&&DISPATCH_END - &&DISPATCH_START);

void *buf = malloc(iconst_size + ineg_size + dispatch_size);
void *current = buf;

memcpy(current, &&ICONST_START, iconst_size); current += iconst_size;
memcpy(current, &&INEG_START, ineg_size); current += ineg_size;
memcpy(current, &&DISPATCH_START, dispatch_size);
...
/* Now, it is possible to execute the sequence using: */
goto **buf;
``` |

Fig. 2. Inlining a Sequence

ment. The problem is that, in order to prevent corruption of the internal data structure of the virtual machine, concurrent preparation of the same method (or class) on distinct Java threads should not be allowed.

The natural approach, for preventing concurrent preparation, is to use synchronization primitives such as *pthread mutexes*[5]. But, this approach can have a very high performance penalty; in a naive implementation, it adds synchronization overhead to every method call throughout a program's execution, which is clearly unacceptable, specially for multi-threaded Java applications.

Broken Sequences. An important performance factor of inline-threading is the length of inlined instruction sequences. Longer sequences reduce the dispatch-to-real work ratio and lead to improved performance. Lazy class initialization mandates that the first call to a static method (or access to a static field) must cause initialization of a class. This implies (in a naive Java virtual machine implementation) that instructions such as GETSTATIC must use a conditional to test whether the target class must be initialized prior to performing the static field access. If initialization is required, a call to the initialization function must be made. The conditional and the C function call prevent inlining of the GETSTATIC instruction.

What we would like, is to use two versions of the GETSTATIC instruction, as shown in Figure 3 and replace the slow synchronized version by the fast version after initialization. Unfortunately this does not completely solve our performance problem. Even though this technique eliminates synchronization overhead from most executions of the GETSTATIC instruction, it inhibits the removal of dispatch code in an instruction which has very little *real work* to do. In fact, the cost can

---

[5] POSIX Threads mutual exclusive locks.
```

be as high as the execution of two additional dispatches. To measure this, we compare the cost of two inline-threaded instruction sequences that only differ in their respective use of `ILOAD` and `GETSTATIC` in the middle of the sequence.

Synchronized GETSTATIC	Unsynchronized GETSTATIC

`GETSTATIC_INIT: /* pseudo-code */`
 	
`pthread_mutex_lock(...);`
 	
`/* lazily load class */`
`...`
`/* conditional & function call */`
`if (must_initialize)`
`   initialize_class(...);`
`/* do the real work */`
`*sp++ = class.static_field;`
`/* replace by fast version */`
`code[pc -1] = &&GETSTATIC_NO_INIT;`
 	
`pthread_mutex_unlock(...);`
 	
`/* dispatch */`
`goto **(pc++);`
	`GETSTATIC_NO_INIT: /* pseudo-code */`
	
	`/* do the real work */`
	`*sp++ = class.static_field;`
	
	`/* dispatch */`
	`goto **(pc++);`

Fig. 3. `GETSTATIC` With and Without Initialization

Broken Sequence Cost. If we had the sequence of instructions `ICONST2-`-`ILOAD-IADD`, we could build a single inlined sequence for these three instructions, adding a single dispatch at the end of this sequence. Cost: $3 \times realwork + 1 \times dispatch$. If, instead, we had the sequence of instructions `ICONST2-GETSTATIC-`-`IADD`, we would not be allowed to create a single inlined sequence for the three instructions. This is because, in the prepared code array, we would need to put 3 distinct instructions: `ICONST2`, `GETSTATIC_INIT`, and `IADD`, where the middle instruction cannot be inlined. Even though the `GETSTATIC_INIT` will eventually be replaced by the more efficient `GETSTATIC_NO_INIT`, the performance cost, after replacement, will remain: $3 \times realwork + 3 \times dispatch$. So, the overhead of a broken sequence can be as high as two additional dispatches.

Two-Values Replacement. In reality, the problem is even a little deeper. The *pseudo-code* of Figure 3 hides the fact that `GETSTATIC_INIT` needs to replace two values, in the code array: the instruction opcode and its operand. The idea is that we want the address of the static variable as an operand (not an indirect pointer) to achieve maximum efficiency, as shown in Figure 4. But this pointer is unavailable at the time of preparation of the code array, as lazy class loading only takes place later, within the implementation of the `GETSTATIC_INIT` instruction.

Replacing two values without synchronization creates a race condition. Here is a short illustration of the problem. A first Java thread reads both initial values, does the instruction work, then replaces the first of the two values. At this exact point of time (before the second value is replaced), a second Java thread reads the two values (instruction and operand) from memory. The second Java thread

Fast Instruction	Code Array

`GETSTATIC_NO_INIT:`
`{ int *pvalue =`
`    (pc++)->pvalue;`
`  *sp++ = *pvalue;`
`}`
`/* dispatch */`
`goto **(pc++);`
	`/* Initially */`
	`...`
	`[GETSTATIC_INIT]`
	`[POINTER_TO_FIELD_INFO]`
	`...`
	`/* After first execution */`
	`...`
	`[GETSTATIC_NO_INIT]`
	`[POINTER_TO_FIELD]`
	`...`

Fig. 4. Two-Values Replacement in Code Array

will thus get the fast instruction opcode and the old field info pointer. This can of course lead to random execution problems.

4   Preparation Sequences

In this section, we first introduce an incomplete solution to the problems discussed in Section 3, then we introduce our *preparation sequences* technique.

Incomplete Solution. The two problems we face are *two-values replacement*, and *shorter sequences* caused by the slow preparation version of instructions such as `GETSTATIC`. Of course, there is a simple solution to two-values replacement that consists of using single-value replacement[6] and an indirection in the *fast* version of instructions, as shown in Figure 5. Note how this implementation differs from Figure 4; in particular the additional `fieldinfo` indirection. This simple solutions comes at a price, though: that of an additional indirection in a very simple instruction. Furthermore, this solution does not solve the shorter sequences problem.

Fast Instruction with Indirection	Code Array

`GETSTATIC_NO_INIT:`
`{ int *pvalue =`
`    (pc++)->fieldinfo->pvalue;`
`  *sp++ = *pvalue;`
`}`
`/* dispatch */`
`goto **(pc++);`
	`/* Initially */`
	`...`
	`[GETSTATIC_INIT]`
	`[POINTER_TO_FIELD_INFO]`
	`...`
	`/* After first execution */`
	`...`
	`[GETSTATIC_NO_INIT]`
	`[POINTER_TO_FIELD_INFO]`
	`...`

Fig. 5. Single-Value Replacement of `GETSTATIC`

---

[6] Single-value replacement does not require synchronization when there is a single aligned word to change.

The Basic Idea. Instead, we propose a solution that solves both problems. This solution consists of adding *preparation sequences* in the code array. The basic idea of preparation sequences is to duplicate certain portions of the code array, leaving fast inlined-sequences in the main copy, and using slower, synchronized, non-inlined preparation version of instructions in the copy. Single-value replacement is then used to direct control flow appropriately.

Single-Instruction Preparation Sequence. *Preparation sequences* are best explained using a simple illustrative example. We continue with our GETSTATIC example. We assume, for the moment, that the GETSTATIC instruction is preceded and followed by non-inlinable instructions, in the code array. An appropriate instruction sequence would be MONITORENTER-GETSTATIC-MONITOREXIT, as neither monitor instruction is inlinable.

Figure 6, (a) and (b), illustrates the initial content of a prepared code array containing the above 3-instructions sequence. The GETSTATIC *preparation sequence* appears at the end of the code array. The initial content of the code array is as follows. After the MONITORENTER, we insert a GOTO instruction followed by two operands: (i) the address of the GETSTATIC preparation sequence, and (ii) an additional word (initially NULL) which will eventually hold a pointer to the static field. At the end of the code array, we add a preparation sequence, which consists of 3 instructions (identified by a *) along with their operands.

(a) Original Bytecode	(b) Initial Content of Code Array	(c) GETSTATIC_INIT
... MONITORENTER GETSTATIC INDEXBYTE1 INDEXBYTE2 MONITOREXIT	``` ... ... [MONITORENTER]* OPCODE_1: [GOTO]* [@ SEQUENCE_1] OPERAND_1: [NULL_POINTER] NEXT_1: [MONITOREXIT]* ... SEQUENCE_1: [GETSTATIC_INIT]* [POINTER_TO_FIELDINFO] [@ OPERAND_1] [REPLACE]* [GETSTATIC_NO_INIT] [@ OPCODE_1] [GOTO]* [@ NEXT_1] Opcodes followed by a * are instructions. ```	``` GETSTATIC_INIT: { fieldinfo_t *fieldinfo = (pc++)->fieldinfo; int **destination = (pc++)->ppint; pthread_mutex_lock(...); /* lazily load and initialize class, and resolve field */ ... /* store field information in code array */ *destination = fieldinfo->pvalue; /* do the real work */ *sp++ = *(fieldinfo->pvalue); pthread_mutex_unlock(...); } /* dispatch */ goto **(pc++); ```

(d) GETSTATIC_NO_INIT	(e) GOTO	(f) REPLACE
``` GETSTATIC_NO_INIT: /* skip address */ pc++; { int *pvalue = (pc++)->pvalue; /* do the real work */ *sp++ = *pvalue; } /* dispatch */ goto **(pc++); ```	``` GOTO: { void *address = (pc++)->address; pc = address; } /* dispatch */ goto **(pc++); ```	``` REPLACE: { void *instruction = (pc++)->instruction; void **destination = (pc++)->ppvoid; *destination = instruction; } /* dispatch */ goto **(pc++); ```

Fig. 6. Single GETSTATIC Preparation Sequence

Figure 6, (c) to (f), shows the implementation of four instructions: GOTO, REPLACE, GETSTATIC_INIT, and GETSTATIC_NO_INIT. Notice that in the preparation sequence, the GETSTATIC_NO_INIT opcode is used as an operand to the REPLACE instruction.

We used labels (e.g. SEQUENCE_1:) to represent the address of specific opcodes. In the real code array, absolute addresses are stored in opcodes such as [@ SEQUENCE_1].

Here is how execution proceeds. On the first execution of this portion of the code, the MONITORENTER instruction is executed. Then, the GOTO instruction is executed, reading its destination in the following word. The destination is the SEQUENCE_1 label, or more accurately, the GETSTATIC_INIT opcode, at the head of the *preparation sequence*.

The GETSTATIC_INIT instruction then reads two operands: (a) a pointer to the field information structure, and (b) a destination pointer for storing a pointer to the resolved static field. It then proceeds normally, loading and initializing the class, and resolving the field, if it hasn't yet been done[7]. Then, it stores the address of the resolved field in the destination location. Notice that, in the present case, this means that the pointer-to-field will *overwrite* the NULL value at label OPERAND_1. Finally, it executes the *real work* portion of the instruction, and dispatches to the next instruction.

The next instruction is a special one, called REPLACE, which simply stores the value of its first operand into the address pointed-to by its second operand. In this particular case, a pointer to the GETSTATIC_NO_INIT *instruction* will be stored at label OPCODE_1, overwriting the former GOTO instruction pointer. This constitutes, in fact, our *single-value* replacement.

The next instruction is simply a GOTO used to exit the *preparation sequence*. It jumps to the instruction following the original GETSTATIC bytecode, which in our specific case is the MONITOREXIT instruction.

Future executions of the same portion of the code array will see a GETSTATIC_NO_INIT instruction (at label OPCODE_1), instead of a GOTO to the *preparation sequence*. Two-values replacement is avoided by leaving the GOTO operand address in place. Notice how the implementation of GETSTATIC_NO_INIT in Figure 6 (d) differs from the implementation in Figure 4, by an additional pc++ to skip the address operand.

Some Explanations. Our single-instruction preparation sequence has avoided two-values replacement by using an extra word to permanently store a *preparation sequence address* operand, even though this address is useless after initial execution.

This approach adds some overhead in the fast version of the *overloaded* instruction; that of a program-counter increment, to skip the preparation sequence address. One could easily question whether this gains any performance improve-

---

[7] Each field is only resolved once, yet there can be many GETSTATIC instructions accessing this field. The same holds for class loading and initialization.

ment over that of using an indirection as in Figure 5. This will be answered by looking at longer preparation sequences.

The strangest looking thing, is the usage of 3 distinct instructions in the preparation sequence. Why not use a single instruction with more operands? Again, the answer lies in the implementation of longer *preparation sequences*.

Full Preparation Sequences. We now proceed with the full implementation of preparation sequences. Our objective is two-fold: (a) we want to avoid two-values replacement, and (b) we want to build longer inlined instruction sequences for our inlined-threaded interpreter, for reducing dispatch overhead as much as possible.

To demonstrate our technique, we use the three instruction sequence: IC-ONST2-GETSTATIC-ILOAD.

Figure 7, (a) and (b), shows the initial state of the code array, the content of the dynamically constructed ICONST2-GETSTATIC-ILOAD inlined instruction sequence, some related instruction implementations, and the content of the code array after first execution.

This works similarly to the single-instruction preparation sequence, with two major differences: (a) the jump to the *preparation sequence* initially replaces the ICONST_2 instruction, instead of the GETSTATIC instruction, and (b) the REPLACE instruction stores a pointer to an *inlined instruction sequence*, overwriting the GOTO instruction.

Here is how execution proceeds in detail. On the first execution of this portion of the code, the GOTO instruction is executed. Its destination is the ICONST_2 opcode, at the head of the *preparation sequence*.

Next, the ICONST_2 instruction is executed. Next, the GETSTATIC_INIT instruction reads two operands: (a) a pointer to the field information structure, and (b) a destination pointer for storing a pointer to the resolved static field. It then proceeds normally, loading and initializing the class, and resolving the field, if it hasn't yet been done. Then, it stores the address of the resolved field in the destination location. Finally, it executes the *real work* portion of the instruction, and dispatches to the next instruction.

The next instruction is a REPLACE, which simply stores a pointer to the dynamically *inlined instruction sequence* ICONST2-GETSTATIC-ILOAD at label OPCODE_1, overwriting the former GOTO instruction, and performing a *single-value* replacement.

Next, the ILOAD instruction is executed. Finally, the tail GOTO exits the *preparation sequence*.

Future executions of the same portion of the code array will see the ICONST2--GETSTATIC-ILOAD instruction sequence (at label OPCODE_1), as shown in Figure 7(f). Notice that the *inlined implementation* of GETSTATIC_NO_INIT in Figure 7(c) does not add any overhead to the fast implementation shown in Figure 4.

Thus, we have achieved our goals. In particular, we have succeeded at inlining an instruction sequence, even though it had a complex two-modes (preparation

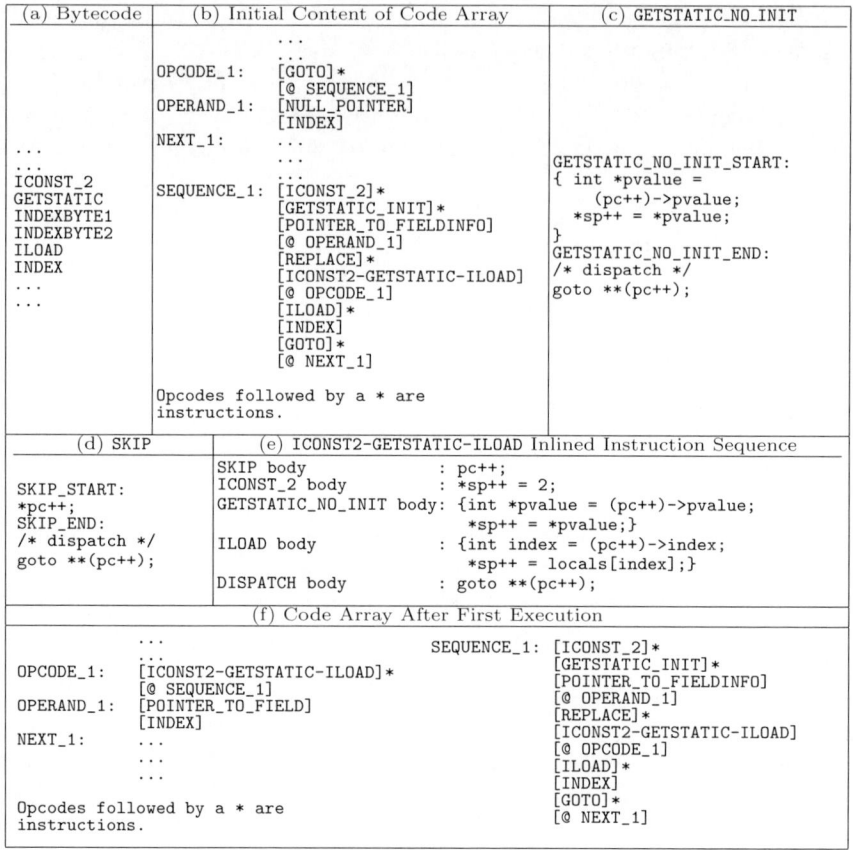

Fig. 7. Full Preparation Sequence

/ fast) instruction in the middle, while avoiding two-values replacement. All of this with minimum overhead in post-first execution of the code array.

Detailed Preparation Procedure. Preparation of a code array, in anticipation of inline-threading, proceeds as follows:

1. Instructions are divided in three groups: inlinable, two-modes-inlinable (such as GETSTATIC), and non-inlinable.
2. Basic blocks (determined by control-flow and non-inlinable instructions) are identified.
3. Basic blocks of inlinable instructions, without two-modes-inlinable instructions, are inlined normally.
4. Every basic block containing two-modes-inlinable instructions causes the generation of an additional *preparation sequence* at the end of the code array, and the construction of a related *inlined instruction sequence*.

The construction of a *preparation sequence* proceeds as follows:

1. Instructions are copied sequentially into the preparation sequence.
   - Inlinable instructions and their operands are simply copied as-is.
   - The *preparation* version of two-modes-inlinable instructions is copied into the preparation sequence, along with the destination address for resolved operands.
2. A `REPLACE` instruction with appropriate operands is inserted just after the last two-modes-inlinable instruction.
3. A final `GOTO` instruction with appropriate operand is added at the end of the preparation sequence.

The motivation for adding the replace instruction just after the the last two-modes-inlinable instruction, is that it is the earliest safe place to do so. Replacing sooner could cause the execution (on another Java thread) of the fast version of an upcoming two-modes instruction before it is actually prepared. Replacing later can also be a problem, specially if some upcoming inlinable instruction is a conditional (or unconditional) branch instruction. This is because, if the branch is taken, then single-value replacement will not take place, forcing the next execution to take the slow path[8].

The construction of an *inlined instruction sequence* containing two-modes-inlinable instructions proceeds as follows:

1. The body of the `SKIP` instruction is copied at the beginning of the sequence implementation.
2. Then, all instruction bodies are sequentially copied.
3. Finally, the body of the `DISPATCH` instruction is copied at the end of the sequence implementation.

Note that a single preparation sequence can contain multiple two-modes instructions. Yet, on the fast execution path, there is a single program-counter increment (i.e. `SKIP` body) per inlined instruction sequence.

5   Experimental Results

We have implemented 3 flavors of threaded interpretation, in the *Sable VM* framework [6]: switch-threading, direct-threading and inline-threading. *Switch-threading* differs from simple switch-based bytecode interpretation in that it is applied on a *prepared* code array of word-size elements. To avoid the two-values replacement problem, *single-instruction preparation sequences* are in use within the switch-threaded and direct-threaded engines. We have performed execution time measurements with *Sable VM* to measure the efficiency of inline-threading

---

[8] Multiple executions of the same *preparation sequence* is allowed, but suffers from high dispatch overhead. It *can* happen in the normal operation of the inline-threaded interpreter as the result of an exception thrown before single-value replacement, while executing a *preparation sequence*.

Java, using our technique. We have performed our experiments on a 1.5 GHz Pentium IV based Debian GNU/Linux workstation with 1.5 Gb RAM, and a 7200 RPM disk, running SPECjvm98 benchmarks and two object-oriented applications: Soot version 1.2.3[9] and SableCC version 2.17.3[10].

In a first set of experiments, we have measured the relative performance of the switch-threaded, direct-threaded and inline-threaded engines. Results are shown in Table 1. To do these experiments, three separate versions of *SableVM* were compiled with identical configuration options, except for the interpreter engine type.

Table 1. Inline-Threading Performance Measurements

benchmark	switch-threaded	direct-threaded	inline-threaded
compress	317.72 sec.	281.78 sec. (1.13)	131.64 sec. (2.41) (2.14)
db	132.15 sec.	119.17 sec. (1.11)	87.64 sec. (1.51) (1.36)
jack	45.65 sec.	46.78 sec. (0.98)	38.16 sec. (1.20) (1.23)
javac	110.10 sec.	105.24 sec. (1.05)	89.37 sec. (1.23) (1.17)
jess	74.79 sec.	68.12 sec. (1.10)	53.57 sec. (1.40) (1.27)
mpegaudio	285.77 sec.	242.90 sec. (1.18)	136.97 sec. (2.09) (1.77)
mtrt	142.87 sec.	115.34 sec. (1.24)	100.39 sec. (1.42) (1.15)
raytrace	166.19 sec.	134.06 sec. (1.24)	113.55 sec. (1.46) (1.18)
soot	676.06 sec.	641.96 sec. (1.05)	548.13 sec. (1.23) (1.17)
sablecc	40.12 sec.	36.95 sec. (1.09)	26.09 sec. (1.54) (1.41)

Columns of Table 1 contain respectively: (a) the name of the executed benchmark, (b) the execution time in seconds using the switch-threaded engine, (c) the execution time in seconds using the direct-threaded engine, and the speedup over the switch-threaded engine in parentheses, and (d) the execution time in seconds using the inline-threaded engine, and the speedup over both switch-threaded and direct-threaded engines respectively in parentheses.

The *Inline-threaded* engine does deliver significant performance improvement. It achieves a speedup of up to 2.41 over the switch-threaded engine. The smallest measured speedup, over the *fastest* of the two other engines on a benchmark, is of 1.15 on the *mtrt* benchmark, where it still delivers a speedup of 1.42 over the second engine.

It is important to note that the switch-threaded engine already has some advantages over a pure switch-based bytecode interpreter. It benefits from word alignment and other performance improving features of the *SableVM* framework. So, it is likely that the performance gains of inline-threading over pure bytecode interpretation are even bigger than those measured against switch-threading.

In a second set of tests, we measured the performance improvement due to the inlining of two-modes instructions (e.g. GETSTATIC), within the inlined-

---

[9] http://www.sable.mcgill.ca/soot/
[10] http://www.sablecc.org/

threaded engine. To do so, we compiled a version of SableVM with a special option that prevents inlining of two-modes instructions, and compared its speed to the normal inline-threaded engine. Results are shown in Table 2.

Table 2. Preparation Sequences Performance Measurements

benchmark	shorter sequences	full sequences	speedup
compress	195.50 sec.	131.64 sec.	1.49
db	108.22 sec.	87.64 sec.	1.24
jack	40.46 sec.	38.16 sec.	1.06
javac	99.99 sec.	89.37 sec.	1.12
jess	62.91 sec.	53.57 sec.	1.17
mpegaudio	157.38 sec.	136.97 sec.	1.16
mtrt	105.39 sec.	100.39 sec.	1.05
raytrace	133.12 sec.	113.55 sec.	1.17
soot	617.42 sec.	548.13 sec.	1.13
sablecc	32.35 sec.	26.09 sec.	1.24

Columns of Table 2 contain respectively: (a) the name of the executed benchmark, (b) the execution time in seconds using the special inline-threaded engine that does not inline two-modes instructions, (c) the execution time in seconds using the normal inline-threaded engine implementing full preparation sequences, and (d) the speedup achieved by the normal inline-threaded engine over the atrophied version.

Our performance measurements show that the speedup due to longer sequences ranges between 1.05 and 1.49, which is quite significant.

6   Related Work

The most closely related work to the work of this paper is the work of I. Piumarta and F. Riccardi in [11]. We have already discussed the inline-threading technique introduced in this paper in Section 2. Our work builds on top of this work, by introducing techniques to deal with *multi-threaded* execution environments, and inlining of *two-modes* instructions. Inline-threading, in turn, is the result of combining the Forth-like *threaded interpretation* technique [5] (which we have already discussed in Section 2) with the idea of *template-based* dynamic compilation [2,10]. The main advantage of inline-threading over that of template based compilation is its simplicity and portability.

A related system for dynamic code generation is that of *vcode*, introduced by D. Engler [4]. The *vcode* system is an architecture-neutral runtime assembler. It can be used for implementing *just-in-time* compilers. It is in our future plans to experiment with *vcode* for constructing an architecture-neutral *just-in-time* compiler for *SableVM*, offering an additional choice of performance-portability tradeoff.

Other closely related work is that of *dynamic patching*. The problem of potential high cost synchronization costs for concurrent modification of executed code is also faced by dynamically adaptive Java systems. In [3], M. Cerniac *et al.* describe a technique for *dynamic inline patching* (a similar technique is also described in [8]). The main idea is to store a self-jump (a jump instruction to itself) in the executable code stream before proceeding with further modifications of the executable code. This causes any concurrent thread executing the same instruction to spin-wait for the completion of the modification operation.

Our technique of using explicit synchronization in preparation sequences and single value replacement has the marked advantage of causing no spin-wait. Spinning can have, in some cases, a highly undesirable side effect, that of *almost* dead-locking the system when the spinning thread has much higher priority than the *code patching* thread. This is because, while it is spinning, the high priority does not make any progress in code execution and, depending on the thread scheduling policy of the host operating system, might be preventing the patching thread from making noticeable progress.

7   Conclusions

In this paper we have explained the difficulty of using the *inline-threaded* interpretation technique in a Java interpreter. Then, we introduced a new technique, *preparation sequences*, that not only makes it possible, but also effective. This technique uses efficient single-word replacement for managing lazy class-loading and preparation in a multi-threaded environment, and increases the length of *inlined instruction sequences*, reducing *dispatch* overhead. We then presented our experimental results, showing that an inline-threaded interpreter engine, implementing our technique, achieves significant performance improvements over that of switch-threaded and direct-threaded engines. Our results also show that longer inlined instructions sequences, due solely to preparation sequences, can yield a speedup ranging between 1.05 and 1.49.

References

1. A. V. Aho, R. Sethi, and J. D. Ullman. *Compilers: principles, techniques, and tools*. Addison-Wesley Longman Publishing Co., Inc., 1986.
2. J. Auslander, M. Philipose, C. Chambers, S. J. Eggers, and B. N. Bershad. Fast, effective dynamic compilation. In *Proceedings of the ACM SIGPLAN '96 conference on Programming language design and implementation*, pages 149–159. ACM Press, 1996.
3. M. Cierniak, G.-Y. Lueh, and J. N. Stichnoth. Practicing JUDO: Java under dynamic optimizations. In *Proceedings of the ACM SIGPLAN '00 Conference on Programming Language Design and Implementation*, pages 13–26, Vancouver, British Columbia, June 2000. ACM Press.
4. D. R. Engler. Vcode: a retargetable, extensible, very fast dynamic code generation system. In *Proceedings of the ACM SIGPLAN '96 conference on Programming language design and implementation*, pages 160–170. ACM Press, 1996.

5. A. M. Ertl. A portable Forth engine. http://www.complang.tuwien.ac.at/forth/threaded-code.html.
6. E. M. Gagnon and L. J. Hendren. SableVM:A Research Framework for the Efficient Execution of Java Bytecode. In *Proceedings of the Java Virtual Machine Research and Technology Symposium (JVM-01)*, pages 27–40. USENIX Association, Apr. 2001.
7. J. L. Hennessy and D. A. Patterson. *Computer architecture (2nd ed.): a quantitative approach.* Morgan Kaufmann Publishers Inc., 1996.
8. K. Ishizaki, M. Kawahito, T. Yasue, H. Komatsu, and T. Nakatani. A study of devirtualization techniques for a Java Just-In-Time compiler. In *Proceedings of the ACM SIGPLAN '00 conference on Object-oriented programming, systems, languages, and applications*, pages 294–310. ACM Press, 2000.
9. T. Lindholm and F. Yellin. *The Java Virtual Machine Specification.* Addison-Wesley, second edition, 1999.
10. F. Noel, L. Hornof, C. Consel, and J. L. Lawall. Automatic, template-based runtime specialization: Implementation and experimental study. In *Proceedings of the IEEE Computer Society International Conference on Computer Languages 1998*, pages 132–142. IEEE Computer Society Press, Apr. 1998.
11. I. Piumarta and F. Riccardi. Optimizing direct threaded code by selective inlining. In *Proceedings of the ACM SIGPLAN '98 Conference on Programming Language Design and Implementation*, pages 291–300. ACM Press, June 1998.

Integrating Generations with Advanced Reference Counting Garbage Collectors

Hezi Azatchi[1]* and Erez Petrank[2]**

[1] IBM Haifa Research Labs,
Haifa University Campus,
Mount Carmel, Haifa 31905, Israel
`hezia@cs.technion.ac.il`
[2] Dept. of Computer Science,
Technion – Israel Institute of Technology,
Haifa 32000, Israel
`erez@cs.technion.ac.il`

Abstract. We study an incorporation of generations into a modern reference counting collector. We start with the two on-the-fly collectors suggested by Levanoni and Petrank: a reference counting collector and a tracing (mark and sweep) collector. We then propose three designs for combining them so that the reference counting collector collects the young generation or the old generation or both. Our designs maintain the good properties of the Levanoni-Petrank collector. In particular, it is adequate for multithreaded environment and a multiprocessor platform, and it has an efficient write barrier with no synchronization operations. To the best of our knowledge, the use of generations with reference counting has not been tried before.

We have implemented these algorithms with the Jikes JVM and compared them against the concurrent reference counting collector supplied with the Jikes package. As expected, the best combination is the one that lets the tracing collector work on the young generation (where most objects die) and the reference counting work on the old generation (where many objects survive). Matching the expected survival rate with the nature of the collector yields a large improvement in throughput while maintaining the pause times around a couple of milliseconds.

Keywords: Runtime systems, Memory management, Garbage collection, Generational Garbage Collection.

1   Introduction

Automatic memory management is well acknowledged as an important tool for fast development of large reliable software. It turns out that the garbage collection process has an important impact on the overall runtime performance.

* Most of this work was done while the author was at the Computer Science Dept., Technion – Israel Institue of Technology.
** This research was supported by the E. AND J. BISHOP RESEARCH FUND and by the FUND FOR PROMOTION OF RESEARCH at the Technion.

G. Hedin (Ed.): CC 2003, LNCS 2622, pp. 185–199, 2003.

Thus, clever design of efficient memory management and garbage collection is an important goal in today's technology.

1.1   Reference Counting

Reference counting is the most intuitive method for automatic storage management known since the sixties (c.f. [8].) The main idea is that we keep for each object a count of the number of references to the object. When this number becomes zero for an object o, we know that o can be reclaimed. Reference counting seems very promising to future garbage collected systems, especially with the spread of the 64 bit architectures and the increase in usage of very large heaps. Tracing collectors must traverse all live objects, and thus, the bigger the usage of the heap (i.e., the amount of live objects in the heap), the more work the collector must perform. Reference counting is different. The amount of work is proportional to the amount of work done by the user program between collections plus the amount of space that is actually reclaimed. But it does not depend on the space consumed by live objects in the heap.

Historically, the study of concurrent reference counting for modern multithreaded environments and multiprocessor platforms has not been as extensive and thorough as the study of concurrent and parallel tracing collectors. However, recently, we have seen several studies and implementations of modern reference counting algorithms on modern platforms building on and improving on previous work. Levanoni and Petrank [17] following DeTreville [9] have presented an on-the-fly reference counting algorithms that overcome the concurrency problems of reference counting. Levanoni and Petrank have completely eliminated the need for synchronization operations in the write barrier. In addition, the algorithm of Levanoni and Petrank drastically reduces the number of counter updates (for common benchmarks).

1.2   Generational Collection

Generational garbage collection was introduced by Lieberman and Hewitt [18], and the first published implementation was by Ungar [24]. Generational garbage collectors rely on the assumption that many objects die young. The heap is partitioned into two parts: the young generation and the old generation. New objects are allocated in the young generation, which is collected frequently. Young objects that survive several collections are "promoted" to the older generation. If the generational assumption (i.e., that most objects die young) is indeed correct, we get several advantages. Pauses for the collection of the young generation are short; collections are more efficient since they concentrate on the young part of the heap where we expect to find a high percentage of garbage; and finally, the working set size is smaller both for the program (because it repeatedly reuses the young area) and for the collector (because most of the collections trace over a smaller portion of the heap).

Since in this paper we discuss an on-the-fly collector, we do not expect to see reduction of the pause time: they are extremely low already. Our goal is to keep the low pauses of the original algorithm. However, increased efficiency and better locality may give us a better overall collection time and a better throughput. This is indeed what we achieve.

1.3   This Work

In this work, we study how generational collection interacts with reference counting. Furthermore, we employ a modern reference counting algorithm adequate for running on a modern environment (i.e., multithreaded) and modern platform (i.e., multiprocessor). We study three alternative uses of reference counting with generations. In the first, both the young and the old generations are collected using reference counting. In the second, the young generation is collected via reference counting and the collector of the old generation is a mark-and-sweep collector. The last alternative we explore is a use of reference counting to collect the old generation and mark-and-sweep to collect the young generation. As building blocks, we use the Levanoni-Petrank sliding view collectors [17]: the reference counting collector and the mark-and-sweep collector. Our new generational collectors are on-the-fly and employ a write barrier that uses no synchronization operation (like the original collectors).

Note that one combination is expected to win the race. Normally, the percentage of objects that survive is small in the young generation and high in the old generation. If we look at the complexity of the involved algorithms, reference counting has complexity related to the number of dead objects. Thus, it matches the death rate of the old generation. Tracing collectors do better when most objects die - thus, they match the death rate of the young generation. Indeed the combination employing tracing for the young generation and reference counting for the old yields the best results.

In addition to the new study of generations with reference counting, our work is also interesting as yet another attempt to run generations with an on-the-fly collector. The only other work that we are aware of that uses generations with an on-the-fly collector is the work of Domani, Kolodner, and Petrank in which generations are used with a mark and sweep collector [15][1].

1.4   Generational Collection without Moving Objects

Usually, on-the-fly garbage collectors do not move objects; the cost of moving objects while running concurrently with program threads is too high. Demers, et al. [2] presented a generational collector that does not move objects. Their motivation was to adapt generations for conservative garbage collection. Here

---

[1] A partial incorporation of generations with an mark and sweep collector, used only for immutable objects was used by Doligez, Leroy and Gonthier [13,12]. The whole scheme depends on the fact that many objects in ML are immutable. This is not true for Java and other imperative languages. Furthermore, the collection of the young generation is not concurrent. Each thread has its own private young generation (used only for immutable objects), which is collected while that thread is stopped.

we exploit their ideas: instead of partitioning the heap physically and keeping the young objects in a separate area we partition the heap logically. For each object, we keep one bit indicating if it is young or old.

1.5   Implementation and Results

We have implemented our algorithms on Jikes - a Research Java Virtual Machine version 2.0.3 (upon Linux Red-Hat 7.2). The entire system, including the collector itself is written in Java (extended with unsafe primitives to access raw memory). We have taken measurements on a 4-way IBM Netfinity 8500R server with a 550MHz Intel Pentium III Xeon processor and 2GB of physical memory. The benchmarks used were the SPECjvm98 benchmark suite and the SPECjbb2000 benchmark. These benchmarks are described in detail in SPEC's Web site[23]. In Section 5 we report the measurements we ran with our collectors. We tested our new collectors against the Jikes concurrent collector distributed with the Jikes Research Java Virtual Machine package. This collector is a reference counting concurrent collector developed at IBM and reported in [3]. Our most efficient collector (the one that uses reference counting for the old generation) achieves excellent performance measures. The throughput is improved by up to 40% for the SPECjbb2000 benchmark. The pauses are also smaller. These results hold for the default heap size of the benchmarks. Running the collectors on tight heaps show that our generational collector is not suitable for very small heaps. In such conditions, the original Jikes algorithm performs better. A possible explanation to this phenomena is that reference counting is more efficient than the tracing collection (of the young generation) when the collections are too frequent. In this case, the tracing collector must trace the live (young) objects repeatedly, whereas the reference counting only spends time proportional to the work done in between the collections.

1.6   Cycle Collection

A major disadvantage of reference counting is that it does not collect cycles. If the old generation is collected with a mark-and-sweep collector, there is no issue, since the cycles will be collected then. When reference counting is used for the old generation we also use the mark-and-sweep collector occasionally to collect the full heap and reclaim garbage cycles[2].

1.7   Organization

In Section 2 we review reference counting developments through recent years and mention related work. In section 3 we present the Levanoni-Petrank collectors we build on. In section 4 we present the generational algorithms. In section in section 5 we discuss our implementation and present our measurements. We conclude in section 6.

---

[2] Another option was to use the cyclic structures collector of Bacon and Rajan [4] but from their measurements it seems that tracing collectors should be more efficient. Thus, we chose to use the readily available tracing collector.

2   An Overview on Reference Counting Algorithms

The traditional method of reference counting, was first developed for Lisp by Collins [8]. The idea is to keep a reference count field for each object telling how many references exist to the object. Whenever a pointer is updated the system invokes a *write barrier* that keeps the reference counts updated. In particular, if the pointer is modified from pointing to O_1 into pointing to O_2 then the write barrier decrements the count of O_1 and increments the count of O_2. When the counter of an object is decreased to zero, it is reclaimed. The reference counts of all its predecessors (its children values at the previous sliding-view) are then decremented as well and the reclamation may continue recursively. Improvements to the naive algorithm were suggested in several subsequent papers. Weizman [25] studied ameliorating the delay introduced by recursive deletion. Several works [22,26] use a single bit for each reference counter with a mechanism to handle overflows. The idea being that most objects are singly-referenced, except for the duration of short transitions.

Deutsch and Bobrow [10] noted that most of the overhead on counter updates originates from the frequent updates of local references (in stack and registers). They suggested to use the write barrier only for pointers on the heap. Now, when a reference count decreases to zero, the object can not be reclaimed since it may still be reachable from local references. To collect objects, a collection is invoked. During the collection one can reclaim all objects with zero heap reference count that are not accessible from local references. Their method is called *deferred reference counting* and it yields a great saving in the write barrier overhead. It is used in most modern reference counting collectors. In particular, this method was later adapted for Modula-2+ [9]. Further study on reducing work for local variables can be found in [6] and [19].

Reference counting seemed to have an intrinsic problem with multithreading implying that a semaphore must be used for each pointer update. The problems were dealt with a series of paper [9,20,3,17]. The sliding views algorithm of Levanoni and Petrank [17] presented a reference counting collector that completely eliminated the need for a synchronization operation in the write barrier. In this work, we use the sliding views algorithms as the basic clock for the generational algorithms. A detailed description of the Levanoni Petrank collectors follow.

3   The Levanoni-Petrank Collectors

In this section we provide a short overview of the Levanoni-Petrank collectors. Due to space limitations we omit the pseudo code. More details appear in our technical report [1]. The full algorithm is described in the original paper [17].

3.1   The Sliding-View Reference Counting Algorithm

The Levanoni-Petrank collectors [17] are based on computing differences between heap snapshots. The algorithms operate in cycles. A cycle begins with a collection and ends with another. Let us describe the collector actions during cycle

k. Using a write barrier, the mutators records all heap objects whose pointer slots are modified during cycle k. The recorded information is the address of the modified object as well as the values of the object's pointer slots before the current modification. A dirty flag is used to let only one record be kept for any modified slot. The analysis shows that (infrequent) races may cause more than one record be created for an object, but all such records contain essentially the same information. The records are written into a local buffer with no synchronization. The dirty flag is actually implemented as a pointer, being either null when the flag is clear, or a pointer $o.LogPointer$ to the logging location in the local buffer if the flag is set.

All created objects are marked dirty during creation. There is no need to record their slots values as they are all null at creation time (and thus, also during the previous collection). But objects that will be referenced by these slots during the next collection must be noted and their reference counts must be incremented.

A collection begins by taking a sliding-view of the heap. A sliding-view is essentially a non-atomic snapshot of the heap. It is obtained incrementally, i.e. the mutators are not stopped simultaneously. A snooping mechanism is used to ensure that the sliding view of the heap does not confuse the collector into reclaiming live objects: while the view is being read from the heap, the write-barrier mark any object that is assigned a new reference in the heap. These objects are marked as $Snooped$ by ascribing them to the threads' local buffer: $Snooped_i$, thus, preventing them from being collected in this collection cycle mistakenly.

Getting further into the details, the Levanoni-Petrank collector employs four handshakes during the collection cycle. The collection starts with the collector raising the $Snoop_i$ flag of each thread, signaling to the mutators that it is about to start computing a sliding-view. During the first handshake, mutator local buffers are retrieved and then are cleared. The objects which are listed in the buffers are exactly those objects that have been changed since the last cycle. Next, the dirty flags of the objects listed in the buffers are cleared while the mutators are running. This step may clear dirty marks that have been concurrently set by the running mutators. The logging in the threads' local buffers is being used in order to keep these dirty bits set in the second handshake. The third handshake is carried out to assure the reinforcement is visible to all mutators. During the fourth handshake threads local states are scanned and objects directly reachable from the roots are marked as $Roots$. After the fourth handshake the collector proceeds to adjust rc fields due to differences between the sliding views of the previous and current cycle. Each object which is logged to one of the mutator's local buffers was modified since the previous collection cycle, thus we need to decrement the rc of its slots values in the previous sliding-view and increment the rc of its slots values in the current sliding-view. The rc decrement operation of each modified object is done using the objects' replica at the retrieved local buffers. Each object replica contains the object slots' value at the time the previous sliding-view was taken. The rc increment operation of each modified object is more complicated as the mutators can change the current sliding-view values of the object's slots while the collector tries to increment their *rc* field. This race is solved by taking a replica of the object to be adjusted and committing it. First, we check if the object's dirty flag, *o.LogPointer*, is set. If it is set it points already to a committed replica (taken by some mutator) of the object's slots at the time the current sliding-view was taken. Otherwise, we take a temporary replica of the object and commit it by checking afterwards that the object's dirty flag is still not set. If it is committed the replica contains the object's slots value at the time the current sliding-view was taken and can be used to increment the *rc* of the object's slots value. Otherwise, if the dirty flag is set, we use the replica pointed by the set dirty flag in order to adjust the *rc* of the object's slots. A collection cycle ends with reclamation which recursively free any object with zero *rc* field which is not marked as *local*.

3.2   The Sliding-View Tracing Algorithm

"Snapshot at the beginning" [16] mark&sweep collectors exploit the fact that a garbage object remains garbage until the collector recycles it. i.e., being garbage is a stable property. The Levanoni-Petrank sliding-view tracing collector takes the idea of "Snapshot at the beginning" one logical step further and show how it is possible to trace and sweep given a "sliding view at the beginning". The collector computes a sliding-view exactly as in the previous reference counting algorithm. After the Mark-Roots stage, the collector starts tracing according to the sliding view associated with the cycle. When in needs to trace through an object the collector tries to determine its value in the sliding view as was done in the previous algorithm, i.e. by checking if the object's *LogPointer* (the dirty flag) is set. If it is set each object's slot sliding-view value can be found directly from the already committed (by some mutator) replica which is pointed to by the object's *LogPointer*. If it is not set, a temporary replica of the object is taken and is committed by checking again if the object's dirty flag is still not set. If the replica is committed the collector continues by tracing through the object's replica. Finally, the collector proceeds to reclaim garbage objects by sweeping the heap.

4   The Generational Collectors

In this section we describe the collectors we have designed. Due to lack of space, we concentrate on the winning collector. The description of the other two collectors appears in our technical report [1].

Our generational mechanism is simple. The young generation holds all objects allocated since the previous collection and each object that survives a young (or full) collection is immediately promoted to the old generation. This naive promotion policy fits nicely into the algorithms we use. Recall that generations are not segregated in the heap since we do not move objects in the heap. In order to quickly determine if an object is young or old, we keep a bitmap (1 bit for each 8 bytes) telling which objects are old. All objects are created young and promotion modifies this bit. By the experience of Domani et al [15] we believe that spending more collection efforts on an aging mechanism does not pay. See [15] for more the details of this experience.

4.1   Reference Counting for the Full Collection

Here, we describe the algorithm that worked best: using reference counting for the full collections and tracing (mark-and-sweep) for the minor collections.

The minor (mark and sweep) collection. The mark and sweep minor collection marks all reachable young objects at the current sliding view and then sweeps all young unmarked objects. The young generation contains all the objects that were created since the *previous* collection cycle and were logged by the i-th mutator to its local $Young\text{-}Objects_i$ buffer. These local buffers hold addresses of all newly created objects since the recent collection and can be also viewed as holding pointers to all objects in the young generation to be processed by the next collection. These buffers are retrieved by the collector in the first handshake of the collection and their union $Young\text{-}Objects$ buffer of the collector is the young generation to be processed(swept) in this minor collection cycle.

Recall that we are using the Levanoni-Petrank sliding view collectors as the basis for this work. The sliding view algorithm uses a dirty flag for each object to tell if it was modified since the previous collection. All modified objects are kept in a $Updates$ buffer (which is essentially the union of all mutator's local buffers) so that the rc fields of objects referenced by these objects' slots can later be updated by the collector. Since we are using the naive promotion policy, we may use these buffers also as our remembered set: The young generation contains only objects that have been created since the last collection, thus it follows that inter-generational pointers may only be located in pointer slots that have been modified since the last collection. Clearly, objects in the old generation that point to young objects must have been modified since the last collection cycle, since the young objects did not exist previous to this collection. Thus, the addresses of all the inter-generational pointers must appear in the $Updates$ buffer of the collector at this collection cycle. At first glance it may appear that this is enough. However, the collection cycle is not atomic in the view of the program. It runs concurrently with the run of the program. Thus, referring to the time of the last collection cycle is not accurate. During the following discussion, we assume that the reader is familiar with the Levanoni-Petrank [17] original collectors. There are two cases in which inter-generational pointers are created but do not appear in the $Updates$ buffer read by the collector in the first handshake.

Case 1: Mutator M_j creates a new object O after responding to the first handshake. Later, Mutator M_i, who has not yet seen the first handshake executes an update operation assigning a pointer in the old generation to reference the object O. In this case, an inter-generational pointer is created: the object O was not reported to the collector in the first handshake and thus, will not be reclaimed or promoted in the current collection. It will be reported as a young object to the collector only in the next collection. But the update is recorded in the current collection (the update was executed before the first handshake in the view of Mutator M_i) and will not be seen in the next collection. Thus, an inter-generational pointer will be missing from the view of the next collection.

Case 2: Some mutator updates a pointer slot in an object O to reference a young object. The object O is currently dirty because of the previous collection cycle, i.e., the first handshake has occurred, but the clear dirty flags operation has not yet executed for that object. In this case, an inter-generational pointer is created but it is not logged to the i-th mutator *Updates* local buffer. Indeed, this pointer slot must appear in the *Updates* buffer of the previous collection and correctness of the original algorithm is not foiled, yet in the next cycle the *Updates* buffer might not contain this pointer, thus an inter-generational pointer may be missing from the view of next collection.

In order to correctly identify inter-generational pointers that are created in one of the above two manners, each minor collection records into a special buffer called *IGP-Buffer*, all the addresses of objects that had to do with updates to a young objects in the uncertainty period from before the first handshake has begun until after the clear dirty flags operation is over for all the modified(logged) objects. The next collection cycle will use that *IGP-Buffer* buffer that was appended in the *previous* collection cycle as its *PrevIGP-Buffer* buffer in order to scan the potential inter-generational pointers that might have not appeared in the *Updates* buffer. In this way, we are sure to have all inter-generational pointers covered for each minor collection.

Finally, we note that the sweep phase processes only young objects. It scans each object's color in the *Young-Buffer*. Objects which are marked with *white* color are reclaimed, otherwise, they are promoted by setting their *old* flag as true.

The full (reference counting) collection. The *Major-Young-Objects* and *Major-Updates* buffers are full collection buffers that correspond to the minor collection's *Young-Objects* and *Updates* buffers. These buffers are prepared by the minor collections to serve the full collection. Only those objects which promoted by the minor collections should be logged to the major buffers as these objects will live till the next full collection. The minor collection avoids repetition in these buffers using an additional bitmap called *LoggedToMajorBuffers*. Other than the special care required with the buffers, the major collection cycle is similar to the original reference counting collector besides. The rc field adjustments are executed for each modified object, thus, logged to *Major-Updates* buffer or *Updates* buffer. The rc of the object's previous sliding-view slots values is decremented and the object's current sliding-view slots values rc is incremented. As for young objects, the same procedure needs only to increment the rc fields of the current sliding-view slots values for each young object, thus, logged to *Major-Young-Objects* or *Young-Objects*. No decrement operation should be taken on the rc field of *Young-Objects* objects slots because their object did not exist in the previous collection cycle and was created only afterwards and their value then was null.

Using deferred reference counting ([17] following [10]), we employ a *zero count table* denoted ZCT to hold each young object whose count decreases to zero during the counter updates. All these candidates are checked after all the updates are done. If their reference count is still zero and they are not referenced from the roots, then they may be reclaimed. Note that all newly created (young) objects must be checked since they are created with reference count zero. (They are only referenced by local variables in the beginning.) Thus, all objects in the *Young-Objects* as well as in the *Major-New-Objects* buffer are appended to the ZCT that is reclaimed by the collector.

The inability of reference counters algorithms to reclaim cyclic structures is being treated with an auxiliary mark-and-sweep algorithm used infrequently during the full collection.

5   Implementation and Results

We have implemented our collectors into Jikes. We have decided to use the non-copying allocator of Jikes, which is based on the allocator of Boehm Demers and Shenker [7]. This allocator is suitable for collectors that do not move objects. It keeps the fragmentation low and allows both efficient sporadic reclamation of objects (as required by the reference counting) and efficient linear reclamation of objects (as required by the sweep procedure). A full heap collection will be triggered when the amount of available memory drops below a predefined threshold. A minor heap collection will be triggered after every 200 new allocator-block allocations. This kind of triggering strategy emulates allocations from a young generation whose size is limited.

We have taken measurements on a 4-way IBM Netfinity 8500R server with 550MHz Intel Pentium III Xeon processors and 2GB of physical memory. We also measured the run of our collector on a client machine: a single 550MHZ Intel Pentium III processor and 2GB of physical memory. The benchmarks we used were the SPECjvm98 benchmark suite and the SPECjbb2000 benchmark. These benchmarks are described in detail in SPEC's Web site[23].

The Jikes concurrent collector. Our collectors measurements are compared with the concurrent reference counting collector supplied with the Jikes package and reported in [3]. The Jikes concurrent collector is an advanced on-the-fly pure reference-counting collector and it has similar characteristics as our collectors, namely, the mutators are loosely synchronized with the collector, allowing very low pause times.

Testing procedure. We used the benchmark suite using the test harness, performing standard automated runs of all the benchmarks in the suite. Our standard automated run runs each benchmark five times for each of the JVM's involved (each implementing a different collector). To get an additional multi-threaded benchmark, we have also modified the _227_mtrt benchmark from the SPECjvm98 suite to run on a varying number of threads. We measured its run

Max Pauses[ms] with SPECjvm98 and SPECjbb2000(1-3 threads)								
Collector	jess	javac	db	mtrt	jack	jbb-1	jbb-2	jbb-3
Generational: RC for full	2.6	3.2	1.3	1.8	2.2	2.3	3.5	4.2
Jikes-Concurrent	2.7	2.8	1.8	1.8	1.6	2.3	3.1	5.5

Fig. 1. Max pause time measurements for SPECjvm98 and SPECjbb2000 benchmarks on a multiprocessor. SPECjbb2000 was measured with 1, 2, and 3 warehouses.

with 2, 4, 6, 8 and 10 threads. Finally, to understand better the behavior of these collectors under tight and relaxed conditions, we tested them on varying heap sizes. For the SPECjvm98 suite, we started with a 32MB heap size and extended the sizes by 8MB increments until a final large size of 96MB. For SPECjbb2000 we used larger heaps, as reported in the graphs. In the results, we concentrate on the best collector, i.e., the collector that uses reference-counting for the full collection. In our technical report [1] we provide measurements for all collectors. Also, in our technical report, we provide a systematic report on how we selected our parameters, such as the triggering policy, the allocator parameters, the size of the young generation, etc. We omit these reports from this short paper for lack of space.

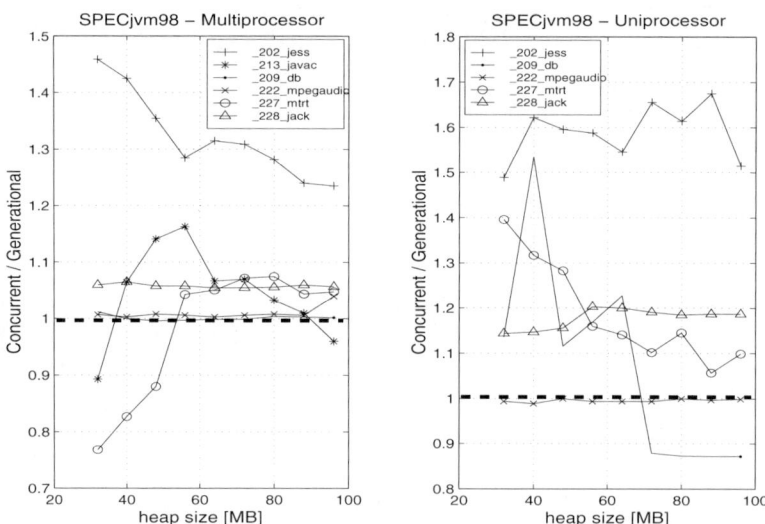

Fig. 2. Running time ratios (Jikes-Concurrent/Generational) for the SPECjvm98 suite with varying heap sizes. The graph on the left shows results on a multiprocessor and the graph on the right reports results for a uniprocessor.

Server measurements. The SPECjvm98 benchmarks (and so also the _227_mtrt modified benchmark) provide a measure of the elapsed running time which we report. We report in figure 2 the running time ratio of our collector

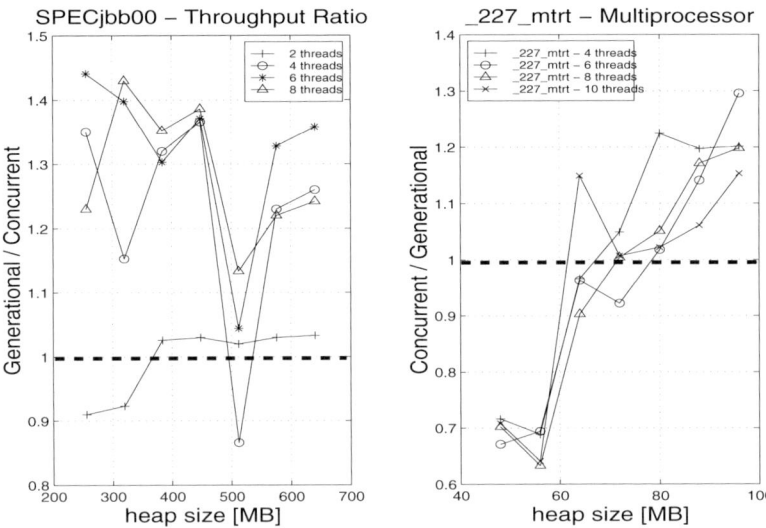

Fig. 3. The graph on the left shows SPEC_jbb2000 throughput ratios (Generational/Jikes-Concurrent) on a multiprocessor and the graph on the right reports running time ratio (Jikes-Concurrent/Generational) for the _227_mtrt benchmarks on a multiprocessor.

and the Jikes concurrent collector. The higher the number, the better our collector performs. In particular, a value above 1 means our collector outperforms the Jikes concurrent collector.

We ran each of the SPECjvm98 benchmarks on a multiprocessor, allowing a designated processor to run the collector thread. We report these results in figure 2 (graph on left). These results demonstrate performance when the system is not busy and the collector may run concurrently on an idle processor. In practically all measurements, our collector did better than the Jikes concurrent collector, up to an improvement of 48% for _202_jess on small heaps. The behavior of the collector on a busy system may be tested when the number of application threads exceeds the number of (physical) processors. A special case is when the JVM is run on a uniprocessor. In these cases, the efficiency of the collector is important: the throughput may be harmed when the collector spends too much CPU time. We have modified the _227_mtrt benchmark to work with varying number of threads (4, 6, 8, 10 threads) and the resulting running time measures are reported in the right graph of figure 3. The measurements show an improved performance for almost all parameters with typical to large heaps, with the highest improvement being 30% for _227_mtrt with 6 threads and heap size 96MBytes. However, on small heaps the Jikes concurrent collector does better.

The results of SPECjbb2000 are measured a bit differently. The run of SPECjbb2000 requires a multi-phased run with an increasing number of threads. Each phase lasts for two minutes with a ramp-up period of half a minute before each phase. Again, we report the throughput ratio improvement. Here the result

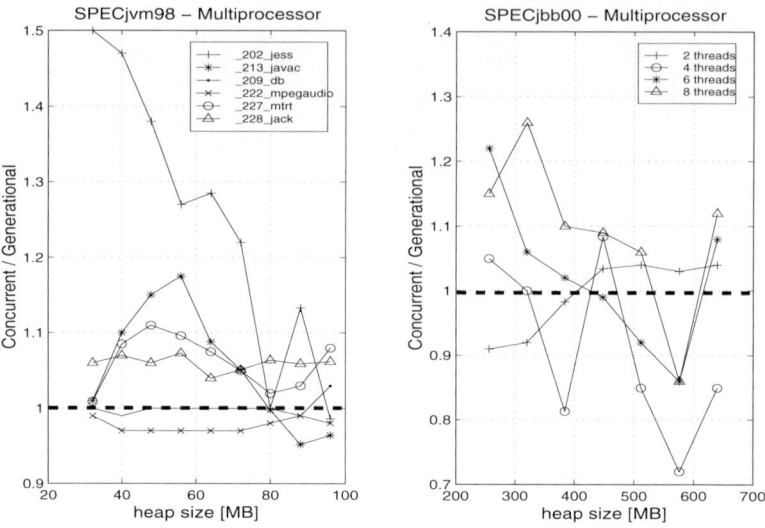

Fig. 4. The results of the second generational algorithm which uses reference counting for the minor generation. The graph on the left shows SPEC_jvm98 running time ratios (Jikes-Concurrent/Generational) on a multiprocessor and the graph on the right reports throughput ratio (Generational/Jikes-Concurrent) for SPEC_jbb2000 on a multiprocessor.

is throughput and not running-time. For clarity of representation, we report the inverse ratio, so that higher ratios still show better performance of our collector, and ratios larger than 1 imply our collector outperforming the Jikes concurrent collector. The measurements are reported for a varying number of threads (and varying heap sizes) in the left graph of Figure 3. When the system has no idle processor for the collector (4,6, and 8 warehouses), our collector clearly outperforms the Jikes concurrent collector. The typical improvement is 25% and the highest improvement is 45%. In the case in which 2 warehouses are run and the collector is free to run on an idle processor, our collector performs better when the heap is not tight, whereas on tighter heaps, the Jikes concurrent collector wins.

The maximum pause times for the SPECjvm98 benchmarks and the SPECjbb2000 benchmark are reported in figure 1. The SPECjvm98 benchmarks were run with heap size 64MBytes and those of SPECjbb2000 (with 1,2,3 threads) with heap size 256MBytes. Note that if the number of threads exceed the number of processors, then long pause times appear because threads lose the CPU to other mutators or the collector. Hence the reported settings. It can be seen that the maximum pause times (see figure 1) are as low as those of the Jikes concurrent collector and they are all below 5ms.

We go on with a couple of graphs presenting measurements of the second best collector: the one that runs reference counting for the young generation and mark and sweep for the full collection. In figure 4 we report the running time and throughput ratio of this collector. As seen from these graphs this collector does not perform significantly worse. In most measurements, it did better than the Jikes concurrent collector, up to an improvement of 50% for _202_jess on small heaps and 25% for the SPECjbb2000 benchmark with 8 number of threads. More measurements appear in our technical report.

Client measurements. Finally, we have also measured our generational collector on a uniprocessor to check how it handles a client environment with the SPECjvm98 benchmark suite. We report the uniprocessor tests in figure 2 (graph on right). It turns out that the generational algorithm is better than the Jikes concurrent collector in almost all tests. Note the large improvement of around 60% for the _202_jess benchmark.

6   Conclusions

We have presented a design for integrating generations with an on-the-fly reference counting collector: using reference counting for the full collection and mark and sweep for collecting the young generation. A tracing collector is infrequently used to collect cyclic garbage structures. We used the Levanoni-Petrank sliding view collectors as the building blocks for this design. The collector was implemented on Jikes and was run on a 4-way IBM Netfinity server.

Our measurements against the Jikes concurrent collector show a large improvement in throughput and the same low pause times. The collector presented here is the best among the three possible incorporation of generations into reference counting collectors.

References

1. Hezi Azatchi and Erez Petrank. Integrating Generations with Advanced Reference Counting Garbage Collectors. Technical Report, Faculty of Computer Science, Technion, Israel Institute of Technology, October 2002. Available at http://www.cs.technion.ac.il/~erez/publications.html.
2. Alan Demers, Mark Weiser, Barry Hayes, Hans Boehm, Daniel G. Bobrow, and Scott Shenker. Combining generational and conservative garbage collection: Framework and implementations. In Conference Record of the *Seventeenth Annual ACM Symposium on Principles of Programming Languages*, ACM SIGPLAN Notices, January 1990. ACM Press, pages 261–269.
3. D. Bacon, C. Attanasio, H. Lee, V. Rajan, and S. Smith. Java without the coffee breaks: A nonintrusive multiprocessor garbage collector. *ACM SIGPLAN Conference on Programming Language Design and Implementation (PLDI)*, Snowbird, Utah, June 20–22 2001.
4. D. Bacon and V. Rajan. Concurrent Cycle Collection in Reference Counted Systems. *Fifteenth European Conference on Object-Oriented Programming* (ECOOP), University Eötvös Lorand, Budapest, Hungary, June 18–22 2001.
5. Henry G. Baker. List processing in real-time on a serial computer. *Communications of the ACM*, 21(4):280–94, 1978.

6. Henry G. Baker. Minimising reference count updating with deferred and anchored pointers for functional data structures. *ACM SIGPLAN Notices*, 29(9), September 1994.
7. Hans-Juergen Böhm, Alan J. Demers, and Scott Shenker. Mostly parallel garbage collection. collector. *ACM SIGPLAN Conference on Programming Language Design and Implementation (PLDI, 1991), ACM SIGPLAN Notices*, 26(6):157–164, 1991.
8. George E. Collins. A method for overlapping and erasure of lists. *Communications of the ACM*, 3(12):655–657, December 1960.
9. John DeTreville. Experience with concurrent garbage collectors for Modula-2+. Technical Report 64, DEC Systems Research Center, Palo Alto, CA, August 1990.
10. L. Peter Deutsch and Daniel G. Bobrow. An efficient incremental automatic garbage collector. *Communications of the ACM*, 19(9):522–526, September 1976.
11. Edsgar W. Dijkstra, Leslie Lamport, A. J. Martin, C. S. Scholten, and E. F. M. Steffens. On-the-fly garbage collection: An exercise in cooperation. *Communications of the ACM*, 21(11):965–975, November 1978.
12. Damien Doligez and Georges Gonthier. Portable, unobtrusive garbage collection for multiprocessor systems. In *POPL* 1994.
13. Damien Doligez and Xavier Leroy. A concurrent generational garbage collector for a multi-threaded implementation of ML. In *POPL* 1993.
14. Tamar Domani, Elliot K. Kolodner, Ethan Lewis, Elliot E. Salant, Katherine Barabash, Itai Lahan, Yossi Levanoni, Erez Petrank, and Igor Yanover. Implementing an On-the-fly Garbage Collector for Java. *ISMM*, 2000.
15. Tamar Domani, Elliot K. Kolodner, and Erez Petrank. Generational On-the-fly Garbage Collector for Java. *ACM SIGPLAN 2000 Conference on Programming Language Design and Implementation* (PLDI) 2000.
16. Shinichi Furusou, Satoshi Matsuoka, and Akinori Yonezawa. *Parallel conservative garbage collection with fast allocation*. In Paul R. Wilson and Barry Hayes, editors, GC workshop at OOPSLA, October 1991.
17. Yossi Levanoni and Erez Petrank. An On-the-fly Reference Counting Garbage Collector for Java, *proccedings of the ACM Conference on Object-Oriented Programming, Systems, Languages, and Applications (OOPSLA '01)*. See also the Technical Report CS-0967, Dept. of Computer Science, Technion, Nov. 1999.
18. H. Lieberman and C. E. Hewitt. A Real Time Garbage Collector Based on the Lifetimes of Objects. *Communicaitons of the ACM*, 26(6), pages 419–429, 1983.
19. Young G. Park and Benjamin Goldberg. Static analysis for optimising reference counting. *IPL*, 55(4):229–234, August 1995.
20. Manoj Plakal and Charles N. Fischer. Concurrent Garbage Collection Using Program Slices on Multithreaded Processors.
21. Tony Printezis and David Detlefs. A generational mostly-concurrent garbage collector. *ISMM* 2000.
22. David J. Roth and David S. Wise. One-bit counts between unique and sticky. *ACM SIGPLAN Notices*, pages 49–56, October 1998. ACM Press.
23. Standard Performance Evaluation Corporation, http://www.spec.org/
24. D. Ungar. Generation Scavenging: A Non-disruptive High Performance Storage Reclamation Algorithm. ACM SIGPLAN Notices Vol. 19, No. 5, May 1984, pp. 157–167.
25. J. Weizenbaum. Symmetric list processor. *Communications of the ACM*, 6(9):524–544, September 1963.
26. David S. Wise. Stop and one-bit reference counting. Technical Report 360, Indiana University, Computer Science Department, March 1993.

The Interprocedural Express-Lane Transformation

David Melski[1] and Thomas Reps[2]

[1] GrammaTech, Inc., melski@grammatech.com
[2] Comp. Sci. Dept., Univ. of Wisconsin, reps@cs.wisc.edu

Abstract. The express-lane transformation isolates and duplicates frequently executed program paths, aiming for better data-flow facts along the duplicated paths. An express-lane p is a copy of a frequently executed program path such that p has only one entry point at its beginning; p may have branches back to the original code, but the original code never branches into p. Classical data-flow analysis is likely to find sharper data-flow facts along an express-lane, because there are no join points.

This paper describes several variants of interprocedural express-lane transformations; these duplicate hot interprocedural paths, i.e., paths that may cross procedure boundaries. The paper also reports results from an experimental study of the effects of the express-lane transformation on interprocedural range analysis.

1 Introduction

In path profiling, a program is instrumented with code that counts the number of times particular finite-length path fragments of the program's control-flow graph—or *observable paths*—are executed. One application of path profiling is to transform the profiled program by isolating and optimizing frequently executed, or *hot*, paths. We call this transformation the *express-lane transformation*. An *express-lane* p is a copy of a hot path such that p has only one entry point at its beginning; p may have branches back to the original code, but the original code never branches into p. Classical data-flow analysis is likely to find sharper data-flow facts along the express lanes, since there are no join points. This may create opportunities for program optimization.

We use the interprocedural express-lane transformation together with range analysis to perform program optimization. Our approach differs from the literature on profile-driven optimization in one or more of the following aspects:

1. We duplicate interprocedural paths. This may expose correlations between branches in different procedures, which can lead to more optimization opportunities [5].
2. We perform code transformation before performing data-flow analysis. This allows us to use classic data-flow analyses.
3. We guide path duplication using interprocedural path profiles. This point may sound redundant, but [7], for example, uses edge profiles to duplicate intraprocedural paths. The advantage of using interprocedural path profiles is that we get more accuracy in terms of which paths are important.
4. We perform interprocedural range analysis on the transformed graph.
5. We attempt to eliminate duplicated code when there was no benefit to range analysis. This can help eliminate code growth.

G. Hedin (Ed.): CC 2003, LNCS 2622, pp. 200–216, 2003.

This paper describes algorithms and presents experimental results for the approach to profile-driven optimization described above. Specifically, our work makes the following contributions:

1. [3] provides an elegant solution for duplicating intraprocedural paths based on an intraprocedural path profile; this paper generalizes that work by providing algorithms that take a program supergraph (an interprocedural control-flow graph) and an interprocedural path profile and produce an *express-lane supergraph*.
2. We show that interprocedural express-lane transformations yield benefits for range analysis: programs optimized using an interprocedural express-lane transformation and range analysis resolve (a) 0–7% more dynamic branches than programs optimized using the intraprocedural express-lane transformation and range analysis, and (b) 1.5–19% more dynamic branches than programs optimized using range analysis alone.
3. We show that by using range analysis instead of constant propagation, the intraprocedural express-lane transformation can lead to greater benefit than previously reported. We also show that code growth due to the intraprocedural express-lane transformation is not always detrimental to program performance.
4. Our experiments show that optimization based on an interprocedural express-lane transformation does benefit performance, though usually not enough to overcome the costs of the transformation. These results suggest that software and/or hardware support for *entry* and *exit* splitting may be a profitable research direction; entry and exit splitting are described in Section 3.1.

The remainder of the paper is organized as follows: Section 2 describes the relevant details of the interprocedural path-profiling techniques. Section 3 describes the interprocedural express-lane transformations. Section 4 presents experimental results. Section 5 describes related work.

2   Path Profiling Overview

To understand the interprocedural express-lane transformation, it is helpful to understand the interprocedural paths that are duplicated. This section summarizes the relevant parts of [10] and [11]. In these works, the Ball-Larus technique [4] is extended in several directions:

1. **Interprocedural vs. Intraprocedural:** [10] presents interprocedural path-profiling techniques in which the observable paths can cross procedure boundaries. Interprocedural paths tend to be longer and to capture correlations between the execution behavior of different procedures.
2. **Context vs. Piecewise:** In piecewise path profiling, each observable path corresponds to a path that may occur as a subpath (or piece) of an execution sequence. In context path profiling, each observable path corresponds to a pair $\langle C, p \rangle$, with an *active-suffix* p that corresponds to a subpath of an execution sequence, and a *context-prefix* C that corresponds to a context (*e.g.*, a sequence of pending calls) in which p may occur. A context path-profiling technique generally has longer observable paths and maintains finer distinctions than a piecewise technique.

In this paper, we use three kinds of path profiles: Ball-Larus path profiles (*i.e.*, intraprocedural piecewise path profiles) and the interprocedural piecewise and context path profiles of [10,11]. (Our techniques could be applied to other types of path profiles.)

Interprocedural path profiling works with an interprocedural control-flow graph called a *supergraph*. A program's supergraph G^* consists of a unique entry vertex $Entry_{global}$, a unique exit vertex $Exit_{global}$, and a collection of control-flow graphs.

The flowgraph for procedure P has a unique entry vertex, $Entry_P$, and a unique exit vertex, $Exit_P$. The other vertices of the flowgraph represent statements and predicates in the usual way, except that each procedure call in the program is represented a *call* vertex and a *return-site* vertex. For each procedure call to procedure P (represented, say, by call vertex c and return-site vertex r), G^* contains a *call-edge*, $c \rightarrow Entry_P$, and a *return-edge*, $Exit_P \rightarrow r$. The supergraph also contains the edges $Entry_{global} \rightarrow Entry_{main}$ and $Exit_{main} \rightarrow Exit_{global}$.

As in the Ball-Larus technique, the observable paths in the interprocedural path-profiling techniques are not allowed to contain backedges. Furthermore, an observable path cannot contain a call-edge or return-edge from a recursive call-site. (Recursive call-sites are those that are the source of a backedge in the call graph.)

An observable path in an interprocedural context path profile may contain *surrogate edges*; surrogate edges are required because observable paths are not allowed to contain backedges. Unlike other edges in an observable path, a surrogate edge is not an edge in the supergraph. A surrogate edge $Entry_P - \rightarrow v$ in an observable path p represents an unknown path fragment q that starts at the entry vertex $Entry_P$ of a procedure P and ends with a backedge to vertex v in procedure P. An observable path from an interprocedural path profiling technique may also contain *summary edges*. A summary edge connects a call vertex with its return-site vertex.

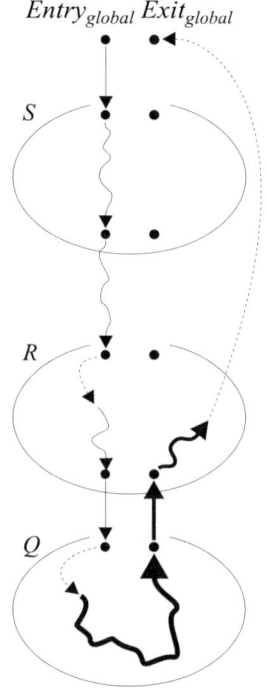

Fig. 1. Example of an interprocedural context path. The active-suffix is shown in bold and surrogate edges are shown using dashed-lines.

In the context path-profiling technique, a context-prefix is a sequence of path fragments in the supergraph, each fragment connected to the next by a surrogate edge. The context-prefix summarizes both the sequence of pending call-sites and some information about the path taken to each pending call-site. Fig. 1 shows a schematic of an observable path from an interprocedural context path profile.

Fig. 2 shows the average number of SUIF1 instructions in an observable path for several SPEC95 benchmarks. (For technical reasons discussed in [11], there are some situations where an interprocedural piecewise path is considered to have a context-prefix, cf. m88ksim, li, perl, and vortex.)

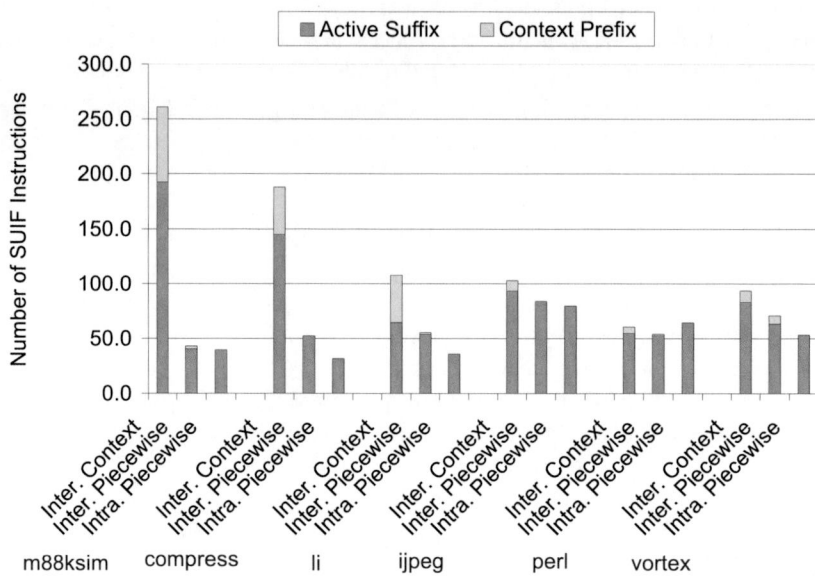

Fig. 2. Graph of the average number of SUIF instructions in an observable path for interprocedural context, interprocedural piecewise, and intraprocedural piecewise path profiles of SPEC95 benchmarks when run on their reference inputs. Each observable path was weighted by its execution frequency.

3   The Interprocedural Express-Lane Transformation

The intraprocedural express-lane transformation takes a control-flow graph and an intraprocedural, piecewise path profile and creates an express-lane graph [3]. In this section, we describe how to extend this algorithm to take as input the program supergraph and an interprocedural path profile, and produce as output an express-lane supergraph.

There are several issues that must be addressed. The definition of an express-lane must be extended. In a context path profile, a path may consist of a non-empty context-prefix as well as an active-suffix. Also, an observable path may contain "gaps" represented by surrogate edges. An express-lane version of an observable path may have a context-prefix and an active-suffix, and may have gaps just as the observable path does.

There are also technical issues that must be resolved. The interprocedural express-lane transformation requires a mechanism for duplicating call-edges and return-edges. We will use a straightforward approach that duplicates a call edge $c \rightarrow Entry_P$ by creating copies of c and $Entry_P$ and duplicates a return edge $Exit_P \rightarrow r$ by creating copies of $Exit_P$ and r.

Many modifications of the intraprocedural algorithm are required to obtain an algorithm for performing the interprocedural express-lane transformation. The Ammons-Larus express-lane transformation uses a *hot-path automaton* — a deterministic finite automaton (DFA) for recognizing hot-paths — and takes the cross product of this automaton with the control-flow graph (CFG), which can be seen as another DFA.

To create an automaton that recognizes a set of interprocedural hot-paths, we require a *pushdown* automaton (PDA). The supergraph can be seen as a second PDA. Thus, if we mimic the approach in [3], we would need to combine two pushdown automata, a problem that is uncomputable, in general. Instead, we create a collection of deterministic finite automata, one for each procedure; the automaton for procedure P recognizes hot-paths that start in P.

3.1   Entry and Exit Splitting

The algorithm for performing the interprocedural express-lane transformation uses entry splitting to duplicate call-edges and exit splitting to duplicate return-edges [5,6]. Entry splitting allows a procedure P to have more than one entry. Exit splitting allows a procedure P to have multiple exits, each of which is assigned a number. Normally, when a procedure call is made, the caller provides a return address. In the case where a procedure has multiple exits, the caller provides a vector of return addresses. When the callee reaches the ith exit vertex, it branches to the ith return address. Our implementation uses a semantically equivalent but inferior method of entry (and exit) splitting: each call vertex sets an entry number before making a normal procedure call; the called procedure (calling procedure) then executes a switch on the entry (exit) number to jump to the proper entry (return) point.

3.2   Defining the Interprocedural Express-Lane

In this section, we give a definition of an interprocedural express-lane. First we consider a simple example to develop intuition about what should happen when we duplicate an observable path from an interprocedural context path profile.

Example 1. Consider the supergraph shown in Fig. 3. Suppose we wish to create an express-lane version of the observable path $p = [Entry_{main} \rightarrow a \rightarrow b \rightarrow d \rightarrow Entry_{foo} - \rightarrow F \rightarrow H \rightarrow I]$ The context-prefix $[Entry_{main} \rightarrow a \rightarrow b \rightarrow d \rightarrow Entry_{foo}]$ indicates a path taken in main to the call-site on *foo*. The active-suffix of p is $[F \rightarrow H \rightarrow I]$. The principal difficulty in duplicating p has to do with the edge $Entry_{foo} - \rightarrow F$: this surrogate-edge appears in the middle of the observable path, but does not appear in the supergraph. What does it mean to duplicate this edge?

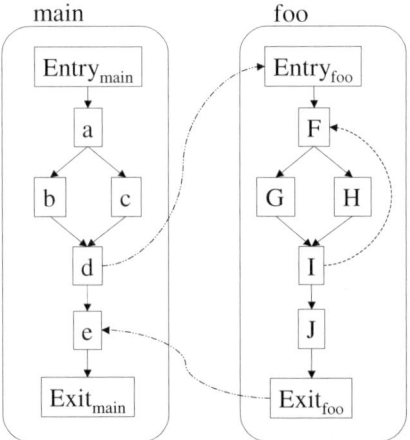

Fig. 3. Example supergraph.

Peeking ahead, Fig. 9 shows an express-lane graph with an express-lane version of p. When we create an express-lane version of p, we create copies of the path's context-prefix and its active-suffix. The copy of the context-prefix ends at a copy

$[Entry_{foo}, 4]$ of vertex $Entry_{foo}$. The copy of the active-suffix begins at a copy $[F, 8]$ of vertex F. We desire that any time execution reaches $[F, 8]$, it came along a path from $[Entry_{foo}, 4]$: we want to make sure that the duplicated active-suffix executes in the context of the duplicated context-prefix.□

We can now give a technical definition of an interprocedural express-lane: let G^* be a supergraph and let p be an observable path. Let H^* be a supergraph where every vertex of H^* is a copy of a vertex in G^*. Then an *express-lane* version of p is a sequence of vertices $[a_1, a_2, \ldots, a_n]$ in H^* such that the following properties are satisfied:

Duplication property: a_i is a copy of the ith vertex in p.

Minimal predecessor property: A vertex a_i may have multiple predecessors if $a_i \equiv a_1$, or the $(i-1)^{th}$ edge of p is a surrogate edge, or a_i is a copy of a return-site vertex; otherwise a_i has exactly one predecessor, which is a_{i-1}. If a_i is a copy of return-site vertex r then let c be the call vertex associated with r:

  – If there is a copy of c in $[a_1 \ldots a_{i-1}]$, then a_i is associated with one call vertex, the last copy of c in $[a_1 \ldots a_{i-1}]$; otherwise, a_i may be associated with many call vertices.
  – If a_{i-1} is a copy of an exit vertex, then a_i is targeted by exactly one return-edge, $a_{i-1} \to a_i$. If a_i is a_1 or a_{i-1} is a copy of a call vertex, then a_i may be targeted by multiple return-edges.

Context property: For a vertex a_i in procedure P, if there is a copy of $Entry_P$ in $[a_1 \ldots a_i]$, then a_i can reached by an intraprocedural path from the last copy of $Entry_P$ in $[a_1 \ldots a_i]$ and not from any other copy of $Entry_P$.

These properties sometimes allow a vertex on an express-lane to have multiple predecessors (*i.e.*, there may be branches into the middle of an express-lane). This is necessary because: (1) a surrogate edge $u \to v$ does not specify a direct predecessor vertex of v in the supergraph; (2) a return-site vertex always has both an intraprocedural predecessor (the call site vertex) and an interprocedural predecessor.

3.3   Performing the Interprocedural Express-Lane Transformation

We now present two algorithms for performing the interprocedural express-lane transformation, one for interprocedural piecewise path profiles, and one for interprocedural context path profiles.

Our approach to constructing the express-lane supergraph consists of three phases:

1. Construct a family $\mathcal{A}$ of automata with one automaton A_p for each procedure P. The automaton A_P is specified as a DFA that recognizes (prefixes of) hot-paths that begin in P.
2. Use the Interprocedural Hot-path Tracing Algorithm (see below) to combine $\mathcal{A}$ with the supergraph G^* to generate an initial express-lane supergraph.
3. Make a pass over the generated express-lane supergraph to add return-edges and summary-edges where appropriate. This stage finishes connecting the intraprocedural paths created in the previous step.

The two algorithms for performing the interprocedural express-lane transformation differ slightly in the first step.

The Hot-path Tracing Algorithm treats the automata in $\mathcal{A}$ as DFAs, though technically they are not: an interprocedural hot path p may contain "gaps" that are represented by surrogate- or summary-edges. These gaps may be filled by *same-level valid paths*, or SLVPs; an SLVP is a path in which every return-edge can be matched with a previous call-edge, and vice versa. An automaton that recognizes the hot-path p requires the ability to skip over SLVPs in the input string, which requires a PDA. However, we can treat the hot-path automata as DFAs for the following reasons:

1. The automata in $\mathcal{A}$ have transitions that are labeled with summary-edges. A transition $(q_i, c \to r, q_j)$ that is labeled with a summary-edge $c \to r$ is considered to be an "oracle" transition that is capable of skipping over an SLVP in the input string. The oracle required to skip an SLVP is the supergraph-as-PDA.
2. When we combine a hot-path automaton with the supergraph, an oracle transition $(q_i, c \to r, q_j)$ will be combined with the summary-edge $c \to r$ of the supergraph to create the vertices $[c, q_i]$ and $[r, q_j]$ and the summary-edge $[c, q_i] \to [r, q_j]$ in the express-lane supergraph. The justification for this is that the set of SLVPs that an oracle transition $(q_i, c \to r, q_j)$ should skip over is precisely the set of SLVPs that drive the supergraph-as-PDA from c to r.

Throughout the following sections, our examples use the program shown in Fig. 3.

The Hot-Path Automata for Interprocedural Piecewise Paths In this section, we show how to construct the set $\mathcal{A}$ of hot-path automata for recognizing hot interprocedural piecewise paths. We expand our definition of $\mathcal{A}$ to allow each automaton $A_P \in \mathcal{A}$ to transition to other automata in $\mathcal{A}$; thus, it is more accurate to describe $\mathcal{A}$ as one large automaton with several sub-automata.

As in [3], we build a hot-path automaton for recognizing a set of hot paths by building a trie A of the paths and defining a failure function that maps a vertex of the trie and a supergraph edge to another vertex of the trie [2]. We then consider A to be a DFA whose transition function is given by the edges of the trie and the failure function.

For each procedure P, we create a trie of the hot paths that start in P. Hot paths that can only be reached by following a backedge $u \to v$ are prefixed with the special symbol $\bullet_v$ before they are put in the trie. A transition that is labeled by $\bullet_v$ can match any backedge that targets v. Fig. 4 shows the path tries for the supergraph in Fig. 3 and the following paths:

$$Entry_{main} \to a \to b \to d \to Entry_{foo} \to F \to G \to I$$
$$\bullet_F \; F \to H \to I$$
$$\bullet_F \; F \to G \to I \to J \to Exit_{foo} \to e \to Exit_{main}$$

Every hot-path prefix corresponds to a unique state in a path trie. If a hot-path prefix ends at a vertex v and drives an automaton to state q, we say that q represents v; the root of the path trie for procedure P is said to represent $Entry_P$. The fact that q represents vertex v is important, since for a vertex $[v, q]$ in the express-lane supergraph, either $[v, q]$ is not on an express-lane and q represents an entry vertex, or q represents v.

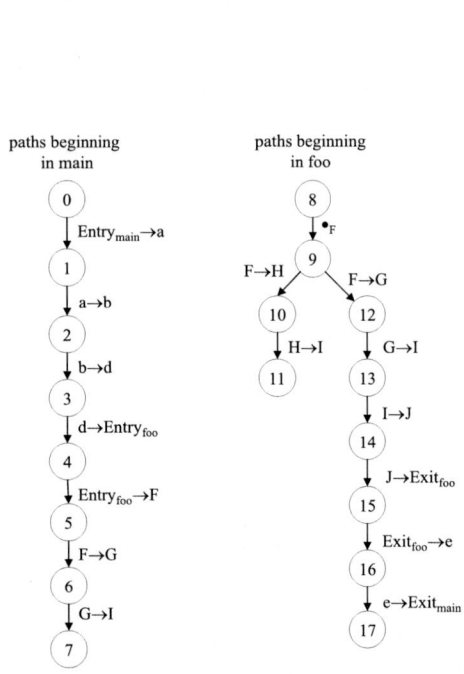

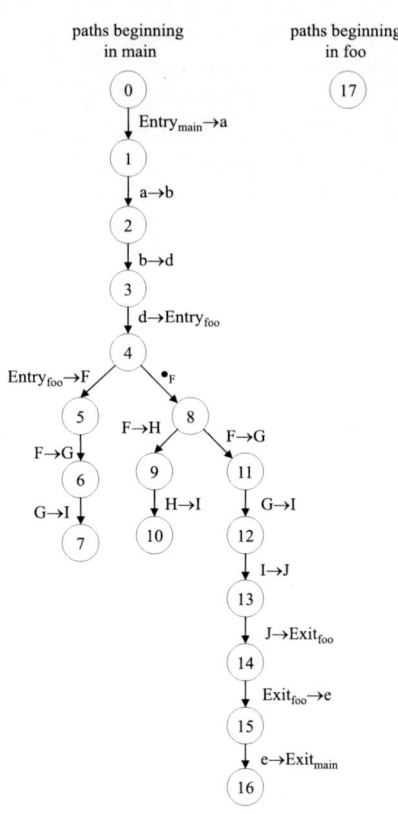

Fig. 4. Path trie for an interprocedural piecewise path profile of the supergraph in Fig. 3. For $i \in [4..15]$ and a backedge e in *foo*, $h(q_i, e) = q_9$; For $i \in [4..15]$ and a non-backedge e in *foo*, $h(q_i, e) = q_8$. For $i \in ([0..3] \cup [16..17])$ and an edge e in *main*, $h(q_i, e) = q_0$.

Fig. 5. Path trie for an interprocedural context path profile of the supergraph in Fig. 3. For $i \in ([0..3] \cup [15..16])$ and an edge e in *main*, $h(q_i, e) = q_0$. For $i \in [4..14]$ and a backedge e in *foo*, $h(q_i, e) = q_4$; for $i \in [4..14]$ and a non-backedge e in *foo*, $h(q_i, e) = q_8$. For q_{17} and any edge e in *foo*, $h(q_{17}, e) = q_{17}$.

As in [3], we define a failure function $h(q, u \to v)$ for a state q of any trie and an intraprocedural or summary-edge $u \to v$; the failure function is not defined for interprocedural edges. If q represents a vertex w of procedure P and $u \to v$ is not a backedge, then $h(q, u \to v) = root\_trie_P$, where $root\_trie_P$ is the root of the trie for hot paths beginning in P. If $u \to v$ is a backedge, then $h(q, u \to v) = q_{\bullet_v}$, where $q_{\bullet_v}$ is the target state in the transition $(root\_trie_P, \bullet_v, q_{\bullet_v})$; if there is no transition $(root\_trie_P, \bullet_v, q_{\bullet_v})$, then $q_{\bullet_v} = root\_trie_P$.

The later phases of the express-lane transformation make use of two functions, *LastActiveCaller* and *LastEntry*, which map trie states to trie states. For a state q that represents a vertex in procedure P, *LastActiveCaller*(q) maps to the most recent ancestor of q that represents a call vertex that makes a non-recursive call to P. *LastEntry*(q)

maps to the most recent ancestor of q that represents $Entry_P$. $LastActiveCaller(q)$ and $LastEntry(q)$ are undefined for q if there is no appropriate ancestor of q in the trie.

The Hot-Path Automata for Interprocedural Context Paths The principal difference with the previous section is in how the failure function is defined. As above, a path trie is created for each procedure. Before a path is put into a trie, each surrogate edge $u \to v$ is replaced by an edge labeled with $\bullet_v$. As before, $\bullet_v$ matches any backedge that targets v. Fig. 5 shows the path tries for the supergraph in Fig. 3 and the paths:

$$Entry_{main} \to a \to b \to d \to Entry_{foo} \to F \to G \to I$$
$$Entry_{main} \to a \to b \to d \to Entry_{foo} \; \bullet_F \; F \to H \to I$$
$$Entry_{main} \to a \to b \to d \to Entry_{foo} \; \bullet_F \; F \to G \to I \to J \to Exit_{foo} \to e$$
$$\to Exit_{main}$$

A state q that represents an entry vertex $Entry_P$ corresponds to a hot-path prefix p that describes a calling context for procedure P. For this reason, states in the trie that represent entry vertices take on special importance in this section. Also, the map $LastEntry$ will be important.

The maps $LastActiveCaller$ and $LastEntry$ are defined as in the last section. The failure function is defined as follows: if $u \to v$ is not a backedge, then $h(q, u \to v) = LastEntry(q)$. If $u \to v$ is a backedge, then $h(q, u \to v) = q'$, where q' is the state reached by following the transition labeled $\bullet_v$ from $LastEntry(q)$; if there is no such state, then $q' = LastEntry(q)$.

We now give some intuition for how the Hot-path Tracing Algorithm interacts with an automaton for interprocedural context paths. For any context-prefix p that leads to a procedure P, the Interprocedural Hot-path Tracing Algorithm may have to clone parts of P. This is required to make sure that the Context Property is guaranteed for express-lanes that begin with p (see Example 1). To accomplish this, the Hot-path Tracing Algorithm may generate many vertices $[x, q]$, where q is the automaton state in hot-path automaton A that corresponds to the context-prefix p: when the hot-path automaton A is in the state q and is scanning a path $[u \to v \to w \ldots]$ in procedure P that is cold in the context described by p, the automaton will stay in state q. Thus, the Interprocedural Hot-path Tracing Algorithm generates the path $[[u, q] \to [v, q] \to [w, q] \ldots]$. Only when the tracing algorithm begins tracing a path that is hot in the context of p does the hot-path automaton move out of state q.

Phase 2: Hot-Path Tracing of Intraprocedural Path Pieces This section describes the hot-path tracing algorithm that combines the family $\mathcal{A}$ of hot-path automata with the supergraph. A state q is a *reset state* if $h(q, u \to v) = q$ for some non-backedge $u \to v$. Reset states are important for several reasons: (1) a context-prefix p always drives a hot-path automaton to a reset-state; (2) for every vertex $[v, q]$ in the express-lane supergraph that is *not* part of an express-lane (*i.e.*, $[v, q]$ is part of residual, cold code), q is a reset state; and (3) for a reset state q and an express-lane supergraph vertex $[v, q]$, either v is an entry vertex represented by q, or $[v, q]$ is a cold vertex. We use these facts to determine whether an express-lane supergraph vertex $[v, q]$ is part of an express-lane.

G^* is the input supergraph.

$\mathcal{A}$ is a family of hot-path automata, with one automaton for each procedure in G^*

$A_P \in \mathcal{A}$ denotes the automaton for procedure P

T_P denotes the transition relation of A_P

$\mathcal{T}$ is the disjoint union of all T_P

$root\_trie_{main}$ is the start state of A_{main}

W is a worklist of express-lane supergraph vertices

$H^* \equiv (V, E)$ is the express-lane supergraph

Main()

/* First, create all the vertices that might begin a hot-path */

1:     $V = \{Entry'_{global}, Exit'_{global}\}$

2:     **Foreach** procedure P

3:         $Create Vertex([Entry_P, root\_trie_P])$ /* See Figure 8 */

4:         **If** there is a transition $(root\_trie_P, \bullet_r, q')$ where r is a return-site vertex

           /* For hot-paths that begin at return-sites, start the express-lane. */

5:             $Create Vertex([r, q'])$

6:     $E = \{Entry'_{global} \rightarrow [Entry_{main}, root\_trie_{main}]\}$

8:     **While** $W \neq \emptyset$

9:         $[v, q] = Take(W)$ /* select and remove an element from W */

10:        **If** v is a call vertex

11:            $ProcessCallVertex([v, q])$

12:        **Else If** v is an exit vertex

13:            **ForeachEdge** $v \rightarrow r$ in G^*

14:                /* $v \rightarrow r$ is a return-edge */

15:                **If** there is a transition $(q, v \rightarrow r, q') \in \mathcal{T}$.

16:                    $Create Vertex([r, q'])$ /* See Figure 8 */

17:        **Else**

18:            **ForeachEdge** $v \rightarrow v'$ in G^*

19:                Let q' be the unique state such that $(q, v \rightarrow v', q') \in \mathcal{T}$.

20:                $Create Vertex([v', q'])$

21:                $E = E \cup \{[v, q] \rightarrow [v', q']\}$

22:    **Foreach** vertex $[Exit_{main}, q] \in V$

23:        $E = E \cup \{[Exit_{main}, q] \rightarrow Exit'_{global}\}$

    End Main

Fig. 6. Interprocedural Hot-Path Tracing Algorithm.

Fig. 6 and 7 show the Interprocedural Hot-path Tracing Algorithm. The bulk of the work of the Interprocedural Hot-Path Tracing Algorithm is done by lines 19–21 of Fig. 6: these process each express-lane supergraph vertex $[v, q]$ that is not a call or exit vertex. This part of the algorithm is very similar to [3]: given an express-lane supergraph vertex $[v, q]$, a supergraph edge $v \rightarrow v'$ (which represents the transition $(v, v \rightarrow v', v')$ in the supergraph-as-PDA), and a transition $(q, v \rightarrow v', q')$, lines 19–21 "trace out" a new edge $[v, q] \rightarrow [v', q']$ in the express-lane supergraph. If necessary, a new vertex $[v', q']$ is added to the express-lane supergraph and the worklist W.

The Interprocedural Hot-Path Tracing Algorithm differs from its intraprocedural counterpart in the processing of call and exit vertices. Fig. 7 shows the function *ProcessCallVertex* that is used to process a call-vertex $[c, q]$. *ProcessCallVertex* has two responsibilities: (1) it creates call-edges from $[c, q]$; and (2) it must creates return-site vertices $[r, q']$ that could be connected to $[c, q]$ by a summary-edge in Phase 3 of the con-

CreateVertex($[v, q]$)
24:      **If** $[v, q] \notin V$
25:          $V = V \cup \{[v, q]\}$
26:          $Put(W, [v, q])$
End CreateVertex

ProcessCallVertex($[c, q]$) /* c is a call vertex */
27:      Let r be the return-site vertex associated with c
         /* Create call edges to all appropriate entry vertices */
28:      **ForeachEdge** $c \rightarrow Entry_P$
            /* v may have many callees if it is an indirect call-site */
29:          **If** $(q, c \rightarrow Entry_P, q') \in T$
               /* There is a hot path continuing from c along the edge $c \rightarrow Entry_P$ */
30:              $Create\,Vertex([Entry_P, q'])$
31:              $E = E \cup \{[c, q] \rightarrow [Entry_P, q']\}$
32:              Label $[c, q] \rightarrow [Entry_P, q']$ with "$(_{[c,q]}$"
33:          **Else**
               /* Hook up $[c, q]$ to a cold copy of $Entry_P$ */
34:              $Create\,Vertex([Entry_P, root\_trie_P])$
35:              $E = E \cup \{[c, q] \rightarrow [Entry_P, root\_trie_P]\}$
36:              Label the call-edge $[c, q] \rightarrow [Entry_P, root\_trie_P]$ with "$(_{[c,q]}$"
            /* Create every return-site vertex $[r,q']$ that could be needed in phase 3 */
37:          Let q' be the unique state such that $(q, v \rightarrow r, q') \in T$
38:          $Create\,Vertex([r, q'])$
End ProcessCallVertex

Fig. 7. The procedures *CreateVertex* and *ProcessCallVertex* used in Fig. 6.

struction. If Phase 3 does not create the summary-edge $[c, q]$, then $[r, q']$ is unnecessary and will be removed from the graph in Phase 3.

Phase 3: Connecting Intraprocedural Path Pieces The third phase of the interprocedural express-lane transformation is responsible for completing the express-lane supergraph H^*. It must add the appropriate summary-edges and return-edges. Formally, this phase of the interprocedural express-lane transformation ensures the following:

> For each call vertex $[c, q]$
>   For each call-edge $[c, q] \rightarrow [Entry_P, q']$
>   For each exit vertex $[Exit_P, q'']$ reachable from $[Entry_P, q']$ by an SLVP
>   There must be a return-site vertex $[r, q''']$ such that
>   1. There is a summary-edge $[c, q] \rightarrow [r, q''']$
>   2. There is a return-edge $[Exit_P, q''] \rightarrow [r, q''']$

The algorithm for Phase 3 is given in [11], Section 7.3.4.

4 Experimental Results

This section is broken into two parts. Section 4.1 discusses the effects of the various express-lane transformations on interprocedural range analysis. Section 4.2 presents experimental results on using the express-lane transformation and range analysis to perform program optimization.

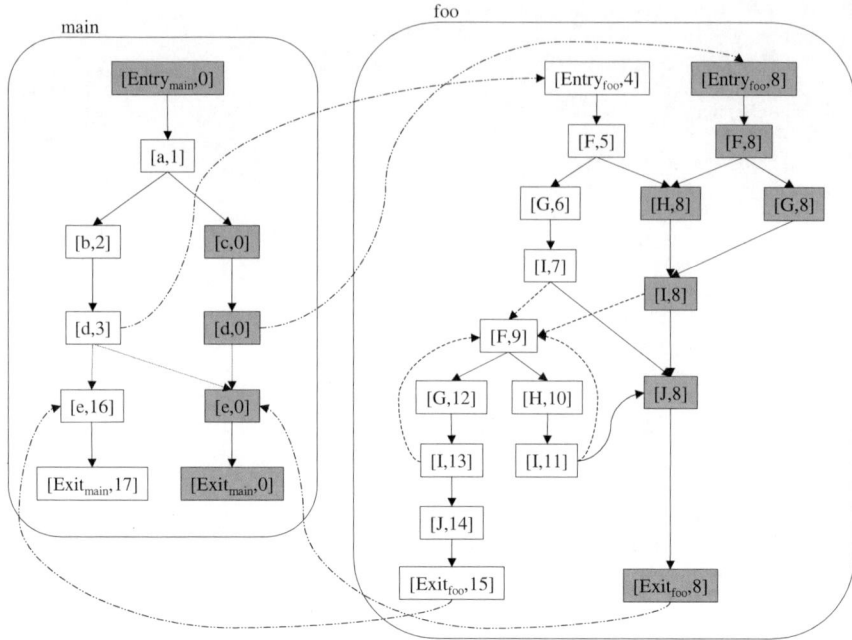

Fig. 8. Express-lane supergraph for the supergraph in Fig. 3 and the hot-path automaton in Fig. 4. Most of the graph is constructed during Phase 2 of the construction. The edges $[d,3] \rightarrow [e,16]$, $[d,3] \rightarrow [e,16], [d,3] \rightarrow [e,0], [d,0] \rightarrow [e,0]$, and $[Exit_{foo}, 8] \rightarrow [e,0]$ are added during Phase 3. Each shaded vertex $[v,q]$ has a state q that is a reset state; except for $[Entry_{main}, 0]$ and $[Entry_{foo}, 4]$, these are cold vertices.

4.1 Effects of the Express-Lane Transformation on Range Analysis.

We have written a tool in SUIF 1.3.0.5 called the Interprocedural Path Weasel (IPW) that performs the interprocedural express-lane transformation.[1] The program takes as input a set of C source files for a program P and a path profile pp for P. IPW first identifies the smallest subset pp' of pp that covers 99% of the SUIF instructions executed.[2] Next, IPW performs the appropriate express-lane transformation on P, creating an express-lane version of each path in pp'. Finally, IPW performs interprocedural range analysis on the express-lane (super)graph.

The experiments with IPW were run on a 550 MhZ Pentium III with 256M RAM running Solaris 2.7. IPW was compiled with GCC 2.95.3 -O3. Each test was run 3 times, and the run times averaged. Cols. 3–5 of Table 1 compare the code growth and the increase in range-analysis time for the different express-lane transformations.

To evaluate the results of range analysis on a program P, we weighted each data-flow fact in vertex v by the execution frequency of v. Columns 6–8 of Table 1 compare

---

[1] The tool is named after, and based on, Glenn Ammons's tool Path Weasel, which performs the intraprocedural express-lane transformation [3].

[2] The value 99% was arrived at experimentally; duplicating more paths does not cause a greater benefit for range analysis, but it does cause a significant increase in code growth [11].

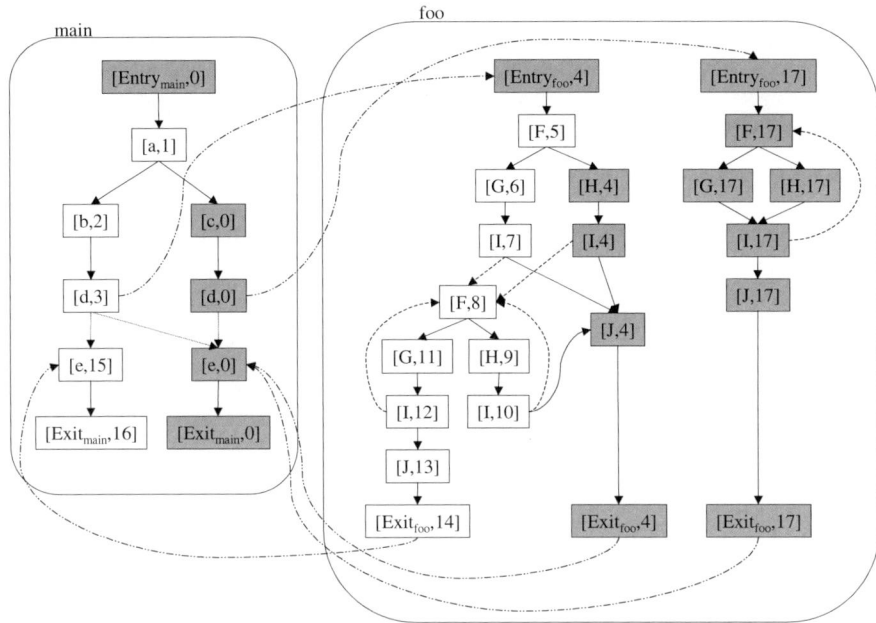

Fig. 9. Express-lane supergraph for the hot-path automaton in Fig. 5 and the supergraph in Fig. 3. Most of the graph is constructed during Phase 2. The edges $[d, 3] \rightarrow [e, 15]$, $[d, 3] \rightarrow [e, 0]$, $[d, 0] \rightarrow [e, 0]$, and $[Exit_{foo}, 17] \rightarrow [e, 0]$ are added during Phase 3. Each shaded vertex $[v, q]$ has a state q that is a reset state; except for $[Entry_{main}, 0]$ and $[Entry_{foo}, 4]$, these are cold vertices.

the results of range analysis after the express-lane transformations have been performed. Three comparisons are made: the percentage of instruction operands that have a constant value; the percentage of instructions that have a constant result; and the percentage of *decided branches*, or conditional branch instructions that are determined to have only one possible outcome. In all cases, the interprocedural express-lane transformations do better than the intraprocedural express-lane transformation.

The range analysis we use allows the upper bound of a range to be increased once before it widens the upper bound to $(\text{MaxVal} - 1)$. Lower bounds are treated similarly. Our range analysis is similar to Wegman and Zadeck's conditional constant propagation [14] in that (1) it simultaneously performs dead code analysis and (2) it uses conditional branches to refine the data-flow facts.

4.2   Using the Express-Lane Transformation for Program Optimization

As mentioned in the introduction, it is possible to reduce the express-lane graph while preserving "valuable" data-flow facts. We used three different reduction strategies:

1. Strategy 1 preserves data-flow facts that determine the outcome of a conditional branch. Strategy 1 is based on the Coarsest Partitioning Algorithm [1,11].

Table 1. Columns 3–5 show a comparison of the (compile-time) cost of performing various express-lane transformations and the (compile-time) cost of performing interprocedural range analysis after an express-lane transformation has been performed; times are measured in seconds. Columns 6–8 show a comparison of the results of range analysis after various express-lane transformations have been performed.

Benchmark	E-Lane Transform.	Transform. Time (sec)	# Vertices in E-Lane Graph	Range Prop. Time (sec)	% const. operands	% const. results	% decided branches
124.m88ksim	Inter., Context	9.8	24032	569.5	28.5	33.1	19.7
	Inter., Piecewise	4.9	15113	508.4	28.6	33.2	20.0
	Intra., Piecewise	3.0	14218	734.2	27.7	32.3	17.5
	None	-	11455	300.8	25.9	31.1	0.8
129.compress	Inter., Context	1.4	2610	14.7	21.3	26.9	9.8
	Inter., Piecewise	0.3	1014	9.4	21.3	26.9	9.8
	Intra., Piecewise	0.2	696	10.2	21.3	26.2	2.2
	None	-	522	5.2	20.8	25.8	0.0
130.li	Inter., Context	12.9	23125	99.1	24.1	27.3	4.0
	Inter., Piecewise	5.3	11319	73.2	24.1	27.3	3.9
	Intra., Piecewise	1.9	7940	35.7	23.6	26.8	2.2
	None	-	7240	29.0	23.3	26.5	0.0
132.ijpeg	Inter., Context	13.0	18087	628.8	16.8	23.6	4.0
	Inter., Piecewise	8.5	13768	526.1	16.8	23.6	4.0
	Intra., Piecewise	7.1	12955	504.3	16.6	23.3	1.4
	None	-	12192	488.2	15.9	22.7	0.0
134.perl	Inter., Context	10.3	33863	713.8	24.3	28.8	3.3
	Inter., Piecewise	9.0	30189	655.2	24.2	28.8	3.0
	Intra., Piecewise	6.7	29309	718.6	24.1	28.7	2.8
	None	-	27988	573.9	23.0	28.5	1.3

2. Strategy 2 preserves all data-flow facts. Strategy 2 is based on the Coarsest Partitioning Algorithm and the Edge Redirection Algorithm given in [11].
3. Strategy 3 is similar to Strategy 2, but only preserves data-flow facts that decide conditional branches (as in Strategy 1).

[11] contains more details, and more discussion of the trade-offs between these strategies. Fig. 10 compares the amount of reduction achieved by these strategies.

Tables 2 through 4 show the results of using various forms of the express-lane transformation together with Range Analysis to optimize SPEC95Int benchmarks. Specifically, we followed these steps:

1. Perform an express-lane transformation.
2. Perform interprocedural range analysis on the express-lane (super)graph.
3. Reduce the express-lane (super)graph.
4. Eliminate decided branches and replace constant expressions.
5. Emit C source code for the transformed program.
6. Compile the C source code using GCC 2.95.3 -O3.
7. Compare the runtime of the new program with the runtime of the original program.

For a base case, we performed range analysis without any express-lane transformation (repeated as Col. 2 in Tables 2 through 4). We ran experiments with three different express-lane transformations. For each of the transformations, we tried the three reduction strategies listed above. We also ran experiments where we performed an express-lane

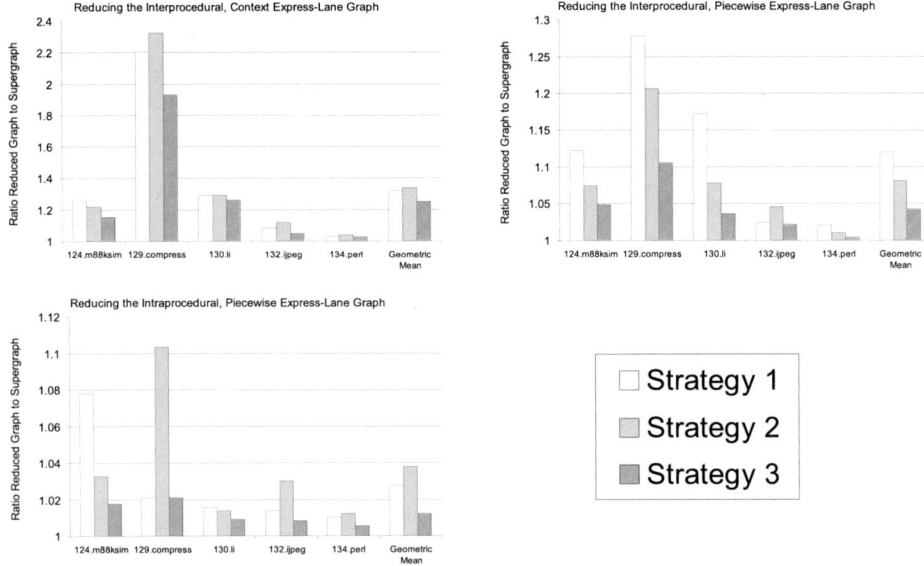

Fig. 10. Comparison of the strategies for reducing the express-lane supergraph.

transformation, then used Strategy 1 to reduce the express-lane (super)graph and then skipped Step 4 above. The reported run time is always the average of three runs.

The best results were for the intraprocedural express-lane transformation (Tables 4). The intraprocedural express-lane transformation together with the range analysis optimizations has a benefit to performance even when no reduction strategy is used to limit code growth. In fact, aggressive reduction strategies can destroy the performance gains. There are several possible reasons for this:

1. GCC may be able to take advantage of the express-lane transformation to perform its own optimizations (*e.g.*, code layout [7]).
2. Reduction of the hot path graphs may result in poorer code layout that requires more unconditional jumps along critical paths [12].
3. The more aggressive reduction strategies seek only to preserve decided branches, and may destroy data-flow facts that show an expression to have a constant value.
4. The code layout for the reduced graph may interact poorly with the I-cache.

The results shown in Tables 4 and 5 are often (but not always) negative. There are two likely reasons for this:

1. It would have been difficult to modify an x86 code generator or a hardware simulator to support entry and exit splitting; instead, we used a straightforward implementation in software. This incurred overhead on each procedure entry and exit.
2. There is a significant increase in code growth.

Col. 4 of Tables 4 and 5 (and 6) show the performance overhead incurred by the transformations. Fig. 10 shows reasonable code growth for the interprocedural express-lane

Table 2. Program speedups due to the **interprocedural, context** express-lane transformation and range propagation. For the base run times shown in Col. 2, the benchmarks were optimized by removing decided branches and constant expressions (but without any express-lane transformation) and then compiled using GCC 2.95.3 -O3.

Benchmark	Base run time (sec)	Reduction Strategy				
		None	Strategy 1	Strategy 1, No Step 4	Strategy 2	Strategy 3
124.m88ksim	146.70	-34.7%	-9.3%	-29.5%	-13.1%	-11.4%
129.compress	135.46	-14.0%	**1.0%**	-4.3%	**2.4%**	**2.0%**
130.li	125.81	-57.2%	-20.4%	-27.8%	-30.4%	-25.4%
132.ijpeg	153.83	-7.5%	-1.6%	-1.2%	-4.5%	-4.8%
134.perl	109.04	-21.3%	**4.9%**	**6.0%**	-3.1%	-3.0%

Table 3. Program speedups due to the **interproc., piecewise** express-lane trans. and range prop.

Benchmark	Base run time (sec)	Reduction Strategy				
		None	Strategy 1	Strategy 1, No Step 4	Strategy 2	Strategy 3
124.m88ksim	146.70	-13.6%	-0.7%	-11.4%	**5.7%**	**5.4%**
129.compress	135.46	-14.0%	**0.5%**	-4.5%	-0.2%	**2.0%**
130.li	125.81	-68.1%	-26.7%	-40.1%	-11.4%	**2.5%**
132.ijpeg	153.83	-2.3%	-2.2%	-0.8%	-2.2%	-4.2%
134.perl	109.04	-19.4%	2.8%	2.7%	**6.1%**	**3.6%**

transformation, and we assume that most of the performance degredation is due to entry and exit splitting. Using the reduction strategies with the interprocedural express-lane transformations usually helps performance. (Graph reduction may eliminate the need for entry and exit splitting.) With aggressive reduction, the interprocedural piecewise express-lane transformation usually leads to performance gains (see Col. 6 of Table 3).

It should also be noted that the interprocedural express-lane transformations combined with the range-analysis optimizations do have a strong positive impact on program performance, although it is usually not as great as the costs incurred by the transformations. This can be seen in the experiments where we did not eliminate branches and replace constants: cf. Columns 3 and 4 of the Tables 4 and 5. (In those few cases where

Table 4. Program speedups due to the **intraproc., piecewise** express-lane trans. and range prop.

Benchmark	Base run time (sec)	Reduction Strategy				
		None	Strategy 1	Strategy 1, No Step 4	Strategy 2	Strategy 3
124.m88ksim	146.70	**10.6%**	**13.0%**	1.2%	**11.6%**	**7.4%**
129.compress	135.46	**6.4%**	**5.5%**	-2.1%	**2.1%**	**0.1%**
130.li	125.81	**8.1%**	**10.3%**	**7.2%**	-1.7%	-0.6%
132.ijpeg	153.83	**1.0%**	**0.7%**	-0.1%	-1.6%	-2.0%
134.perl	109.04	**9.7%**	**10.0%**	**6.3%**	**9.9%**	**5.4%**

performance showed a slight improvement, we assume there was a change in code layout that had instruction cache effects.) This suggests that software and/or hardware support for entry and exit splitting would be a profitable research direction.

5   Related Work and Conclusions

The work in this paper is an interprocedural extension of the work in [3]. This paper and [3] are related to other work that focuses on improving the performance of particular program paths. A partial list of such works includes [8,7,9,13,6,15]. A more detailed discussion of related work can be found in [11]. As stated in the introduction, the interprocedural express-lane transformation differs from other techniques in the literature on one or more of the following points:

1. We duplicate interprocedural paths before performing analysis.
2. We guide path duplication using interprocedural path profiles.
3. We perform interprocedural range analysis on the transformed graph.
4. We eliminate duplicated code when there was no benefit to range analysis.

We have shown that the interprocedural express-lane transformations have a beneficial effect on interprocedural range analysis. The performance gains from the interprocedural express-lane transformation are slight or negative — but we have shown that it has potential. Specifically, we have shown that a greater percentage of dynamic branches can be decided statically, and that performance improvements are likely with a better hardware and/or software implementation of entry and exit splitting.

References

1. A. V. Aho, J.E. Hopcroft, and J.D. Ullman. *The design and analysis of computer algorithms.* Addison-Wesley, 1974.
2. Alfred V. Aho. *Algorithms for finding patterns in strings*, chapter 5, pages 255–300. MIT Press, 1994.
3. G. Ammons and J. Larus. Improving data-flow analysis with path profiles. In *PLDI98.*
4. T. Ball and J. Larus. Efficient path profiling. In *MICRO 1996*, 1996.
5. R. Bodik, R. Gupta, and M.L. Soffa. Interprocedural conditional branch elimination. In *PLDI'97.*
6. Rastislav Bodik. *Path-sensitive, value-flow optimizations of programs.* PhD thesis, University of Pittsburg, 2000.
7. P.P. Chang, S.A. Mahlke, and W.W. Hwu. Using profile information to assist classic code optimizations. *Software practice and experience*, 1(12), Dec. 1991.
8. J. A. Fisher. Trace scheduling: A technique for global microcode compaction. In *IEEE Trans. on Computers*, volume C-30, pages 478–490, 1981.
9. R.E. Hank. *Region-Based Compilation.* PhD thesis, UIUC, 1996.
10. D. Melski and T. Reps. Interprocedural path profiling. In CC99.
11. D.G. Melski. *Interprocedural Path Profiling and the Interprocedural Express-Lane Transformation.* PhD thesis, University of Wisconsion, 2002.
12. F. Mueller and D. B.Whalley. Avoiding unconditional jumps by code replication. In *PLDI92.*
13. M. Poletto. *Path splitting: a technique for improving data flow analysis*, 1995.
14. M.N. Wegman and F.K. Zadeck. Constant propagation with conditional branches. In *POPL85.*
15. Reginald Clifford Young. *Path-based Compilation.* PhD thesis, Harvard University, 1998.

Automatic Detection of Uninitialized Variables

Thi Viet Nga Nguyen, François Irigoin, Corinne Ancourt, and Fabien Coelho

Ecole des Mines de Paris, 77305 Fontainebleau, France
{nguyen,irigoin,ancourt,coelho}@cri.ensmp.fr

Abstract. One of the most common programming errors is the use of a variable before its definition. This undefined value may produce incorrect results, memory violations, unpredictable behaviors and program failure. To detect this kind of error, two approaches can be used: compile-time analysis and run-time checking. However, compile-time analysis is far from perfect because of complicated data and control flows as well as arrays with non-linear, indirection subscripts, etc. On the other hand, dynamic checking, although supported by hardware and compiler techniques, is costly due to heavy code instrumentation while information available at compile-time is not taken into account.

This paper presents a combination of an efficient compile-time analysis and a source code instrumentation for run-time checking. All kinds of variables are checked by PIPS, a Fortran research compiler for program analyses, transformation, parallelization and verification. Uninitialized array elements are detected by using imported array region, an efficient inter-procedural array data flow analysis. If exact array regions cannot be computed and compile-time information is not sufficient, array elements are initialized to a special value and their utilization is accompanied by a value test to assert the legality of the access. In comparison to the dynamic instrumentation, our method greatly reduces the number of variables to be initialized and to be checked. Code instrumentation is only needed for some array sections, not for the whole array. Tests are generated as early as possible. In addition, programs can be proved to be free from used-before-set errors statically at compile-time or, on the contrary, have real undefined errors. Experiments on SPEC95 CFP show encouraging results on analysis cost and run-time overheads.

1 Introduction

Used-before-set refers to the error occurring when a program uses a variable which has not been assigned a value. This uninitialized variable, once used in a calculation, can be quickly propagated throughout the entire program and anything may happen. The program may produce different results each time it runs, or may crash for no apparent reason, or may behave unpredictably. This is also a known problem for embedded software. Some programming languages such as Java and C++ have built-in mechanisms that ensure memory to be initialized to default values, which make programs work consistently but may not give intended results.

G. Hedin (Ed.): CC 2003, LNCS 2622, pp. 217–231, 2003.

To detect this kind of error, two approaches can be used: compile-time analysis and run-time checking. However, compile-time analysis is far from perfect because complicated data and control flows result in a very large imprecision. Furthermore, the use of global variables and arrays with non-linear, indirection subscripts, etc sometimes makes static checking completely ineffective, leading to many spurious warnings. In addition, some other program analyses such as points-to analysis [1], alias analysis and array bound checking [2] are prerequisite for the detection of uninitialized variable uses.

On the other hand, pure dynamic checking is costly due to heavy code instrumentation while information available at compile-time is not taken into account. The slowdown between instrumented and uninstrumented codes has been measured to be up to 130 times in [3]. Dynamic checking is not so effective that, as shown in a report comparing Fortran compilers [4], only some Lahey/Fujitsu and Salford compilers offer run-time checking for all kinds of variables. The other compilers such as APF version 7.5, G77 version 0.5.26, NAS version 2.2 and PGI version 3.2-4 do not have this option. Intel Fortran Compiler version 6.0 and NAGWare F95 version 4.1 only check for local and formal scalar variables; array and global variables are omitted. The code instrumentation degrades the execution performance so it can only be used to create a test version of the program, not a production version. In addition, run-time checking only validates the code for a specific input.

With the growth of hardware performance - processor speed, memory bandwidth - software systems have become more and more complicated to solve better real application problems. Debugging several million lines of code becomes more difficult and time-consuming. Execution time overheads of dynamic checking or a large number of possibly undefined variable warnings issued by static checking are not highly appreciated. Efficient compile-time analysis to prove the safety of programs, to detect statically program errors, or to reduce the number of run-time checks is necessary. The question is, by using advanced program analyses, i.e interprocedural array analysis, can static analysis be an adequate answer to the used-before-set problem for the scientific codes? If not, can a combination of static and dynamic analyses reduce the cost of uninitialized variable checking? The goal of our research is to provide a more precise and efficient static analysis to detect uninitialized variables, and if sufficient information is not available, run-time checks are added to guarantee the program correctness.

The paper is organized as follows. Section 2 presents some related work on uninitialized variable checking. Section 3 describes the imported array regions analysis. Our used-before-set verification is presented in Section 4. Experimental results obtained with the SPEC95 CFP benchmark are given in Section 5. Conclusions are drawn in the last section.

2   Related Work

To cope with the used-before-set problem, some compilers silently initialize variables to a predefined value such as zero, so that programs work consistently, but give incorrect results. Other compilers provide a run-time check option to spot uses of undefined values. This run-time error detection can be done by initializing each variable with a special value, depending on the variable type. If this value is encountered in a computation, a trap is activated. This technique was pioneered by Watfor, a Fortran debugging environment for IBM mainframes in the 70's, and then used in Salford, SGI and Cray compilers.

For example, the option *trap_uninitialized* of SGI compilers forces all real variables to be initialized with a NaN value (Not a Number - IEEE Standard 754 Floating Point Numbers) and when this value is involved in a floating-point calculation, it causes a floating-point trap. This approach raise several problems. Exception handler functions or compiler debugging options can be used to find the location of the exception but they are platform- and compiler-dependent. Furthermore, the IEEE invalid exception can be trapped for other reasons, not necessarily an uninitialized variable. In addition, when no floating-point calculation is done, e.g in the assignment X = Y, no used-before-set error is detected which makes tracking the origin of an error detected later difficult. Other kinds of variables such as integer and logical are not checked for uninitialization. In conclusion, the execution overhead of this technique is low but the used-before-set debugging is almost impossible.

Other compilers such as Lahey/Fujitsu compilers, SUN dbx debugger, etc use a *memory coloring algorithm* to detect run-time errors. For example, Valgrind, an open-source memory debugger (*http://devel-home.kde.org/sewardj*) tracks each byte of memory in the original program with nine status bits, one of which tracks the addressability of that byte, while the other eight track the validity of the byte. As a result, it can detect the use of single uninitialized bits, and does not report spurious errors on bit-field operations. The object code instrumentation method is used in Purify, a commercial memory access checking tool. Each memory access is intercepted and monitored. The advantage of this method is that it does not require recompilation and it supports libraries. However, the method is instruction set and operating system dependent. The memory usage is bigger than other methods. Furthermore, the program semantics is lost. An average slowdown of 5.5 times between the generated code and the initial code is reported for Purify in [5].

The plusFORT toolkit (*http://www.polyhedron.com*) instruments source code with probe routines so that uninitialized data can be spotted at run-time using any compiler and platform. There are functions to set variables to undefined, and functions to verify if a data item is defined or not. Variables of all types are checked. The amount of information about violations provided by plusFORT is precise and useful for debugging. The name of the subprogram, the line where the reference to an uninitialized variable occurred is reported in a log-file. However, the instrumentation is not so effective because of inserted code. Fig. 1 shows that plusFORT can detect bugs which depend on external data, but the execution time is greatly increased with such dynamic tests.

To reduce the execution cost, illegal uses of an uninitialized variable can be detected at compile-time by some compilers and static analyzers. LCLint [6] is

```
SUBROUTINE QKNUM(IVAL, POS)
INTEGER IVAL, POS, VALS(50), IOS
CALL SB$ENT('QKNUM', 'DYNBEF.FOR')
CALL UD$I4(IOS)
CALL UD$AI4(50, VALS)
READ (11, *, IOSTAT = IOS) VALS
CALL QD$I4('IOS', IOS, 4)
IF (IOS .EQ. 0) THEN
    DO POS = 1,50
        CALL QD$I4('VALS(POS)',VALS(POS),6)
        CALL QD$I4('IVAL', IVAL, 6)
        IF (IVAL .EQ. VALS(POS)) GOTO 10
    ENDDO
ENDIF
POS = 0
10      CALL SB$EXI
END
```

Fig. 1. Example with plusFORT probe routines

an advanced C static checker that uses formal specification written in the LCL language to detect instances where the value of a location may be used before it is defined. Although few spurious warnings are generated, there are cases where LCLint cannot determine if a use-before-definition error is present, so a message may be issued for a non-existing problem. In other cases, a real problem may go undetected because of some simplified assumptions.

The static analyzer ftnchek (*http://www.dsm.fordham.edu/ftnchek*) gives efficient warnings about possible uninitialized variables, but the analysis is not complete. Warnings about common variables are only given for cases in which a variable is used in some routine but not set in any other routine. It also has the same problems as LCLint about non-existing or undetected errors, because of, for example the simplified rule about equivalenced arrays.

Reps et al. [7] consider the possibly uninitialized variable as an IFDS (*interprocedural, finite, distributive, subsets*) problem. A precise interprocedural data flow analysis via graph reachability is implemented with the Tabulation Algorithm to report the uses of possibly uninitialized variables. They compare the accuracy and time requirement of the Tabulation Algorithm with a naive algorithm that considers all execution paths, not only interprocedurally realizable ones. The number of possibly uninitialized variables detected by their algorithm ranges from 9% to 99% of that detected by the naive one. However, this is only an over-approximation that does not give an exact answer if there are really use-before-set errors in the program or not. The number of possibly undefined variables is rather high, 543 variables for a 897 line program, 894 variables for a 1345 line program.

PolySpace technologies (*http://www.polyspace.com*) apply abstract interpretation, the theory of semantic language approximations, to detect automatically read accesses to non-initialized data. This technique predicts efficiently run-time errors and information about maybe non-initialized variables can be useful for the debugging process of C and Ada programs. But no data is given by the PolySpace group so we cannot compare with them.

Another related work of Feautrier [8] proposes to compute for each use of a scalar or array cell its *source function*, the statement that is the source of the value contained therein at a given instant of the program execution. Uninitialized variable checking can be done by verifying in the source the presence of the sign $\perp$, which indicates access to an undefined memory cell. Unfortunately, the input language in this paper is restricted to assignment statements, FOR loops, affine indices and loop limits.

The main difficulties encountered by static analysis for the used-before-set verification are complicated data and control flows with different kinds of variables. This explains why only a small set of variables such as scalar and local variables is checked by some static analyzers and compilers. Our motivation is to develop a more efficient program analysis to the used-before-set problem by using imported array regions.

3   Imported Array Region Analysis

Array region analyses collect information about the way array elements used and defined by programs. A *convex array region*, as defined in [9,10], is a set of array elements described by a convex polyhedron [11]. Its constraints link the region parameters that represent the array dimensions to the values of the program integer scalar variables. A region has the approximation MUST if every element in the region is accessed with certainty, MAY if its elements are simply potentially accessed and EXACT if the region exactly represents the requested set of array elements. There were two kinds of array regions, READ and WRITE regions, that represent the effects of program statements on array elements. For instance, A-WRITE-EXACT-{PHI1==1,PHI2==I} is the array region of statement A(1,I)=5. The region parameters PHI1 and PHI2 respectively represent the first and second dimensions of A.

The order in which references to array elements are executed, array data flow information, is essential for program optimizations. IN array regions are introduced in [10,12] to summarize the set of array elements whose values are *imported* (or *locally upward exposed*) by the current piece of code. One array element is imported by a fragment of code if there exists at least one use of the element whose value has not been defined earlier in the fragment itself. For instance, in the illustrative example in Fig. 2, the element B(J,K) in the second statement of the second J loop is read but its value is not imported by the loop body because it is previously defined by the first statement. On the contrary, the element B(J,K-1) is imported from the first J loop. The propagation of IN regions begins from the elementary statements to compound statements such as conditional statements, loops and sequences of statements, and through procedure calls. The input language of our analysis is Fortran.

```
K = FOO()
DO I = 1,N
   DO J = 1,N
      B(J,K) = J + K
   ENDDO
   K = K + 1
   DO J = 1,N
      B(J,K) = J*J - K*K
      A(I) = A(I) + B(J,K) + B(J,K-1)
   ENDDO
ENDDO
```

Fig. 2. Imported array region example

Elementary Statement. The IN regions of an assignment are all read references of the statement. Each array reference on the right hand side is converted to an elementary region. Array references in the subscript expressions of the left hand side reference are also taken into account. These regions are EXACT if and only if the subscripts are affine functions of the program variables. To save space, regions of the same array are merged by using the union operator.

The IN regions of an input/output statement are more complicated. The input/output status, error and end-of-file specifiers are handled with respect to the Fortran standard [13]. The order of variable occurrences in the input list is used to compute the IN regions of an input statement. For example, in the input statement READ *,N,(A(I),I=1,N), N is not imported since it is written before being referenced in the implied-DO expression (A(I),I=1,N).

Conditional Statement. The IN regions of a conditional statement contain the READ regions of the test condition, plus the IN regions of the true branch if the test condition is evaluated true, or the IN regions of the false branch if the test condition is evaluated false. Since the test condition value is not always known at compile-time, the IN regions of the true and false branches, combined with the test condition, are unified in the over-approximated regions.

Loop Statement. The IN regions of a loop contain array elements imported by each iteration but not previously written by the preceding iterations. Given the IN and WRITE regions of the loop body, the loop IN regions contain the imported array elements of the loop condition, plus the imported elements of the loop body if this condition is evaluated true. Then, when the loop is executed again, in the program state resulting from the execution of the loop body, they are added to the set of loop imported array elements in which all elements written by the previous execution are excluded.

Sequence of Statements. Let s be the sequence of instructions $s_1; s_2; ..s_n;$. The IN regions of the sequence contain all elements imported by the first statement s_1, plus the elements imported by $s_2; ..s_n;$ after the execution of s_1, but not written by the latter.

Control Flow Graph. Control flow graphs are handled in a very straightforward fashion: the IN regions of the whole graph are equal to the union of the

IN regions imported by all the nodes in the graph. Every variable modified at a node is projected from the regions of all other nodes. All approximations are decreased to `MAY`.

Interprocedural Array Region. The interprocedural propagation of `IN` regions is performed by a reverse invocation order traversal on the program call graph: a procedure is processed after its callees. For each procedure, the summary `IN` regions are computed by eliminating local effects from the `IN` regions of the procedure body. Information about formal parameters, global and static variables are preserved. The resulting summary regions are stored in the database and retrieved each time the procedure is invoked. At each call site, the summary `IN` regions of the called procedure are translated from the callee's name space into the caller's name space, using the relationships between actual and formal parameters, and between the declarations of global variables in both routines.

Fig. 3 shows the `IN` regions computed for the running example. In the body of the second J loop, array elements `A(I)`, `B(J,K)` and `B(J,K-1)` are imported by the second statement. Since `B(J,K)` is defined by the first statement, only `A(I)` and `B(J,K-1)` are imported by the loop body. The IN regions of the second J loop are `<B(PHI1,PHI2)-IN-EXACT-{1<=PHI1,PHI1<=N,PHI2==K-1}>` and `<A(PHI1)-IN-EXACT-{PHI1==I}>`. After propagating upward these IN regions through statement K=K+1, region of array B becomes `<B(PHI1,PHI2)-IN-EXACT-{1<=PHI1,PHI1<=N,PHI2==K}>`. Once again, all array elements in this region are defined by the first J loop, so only array elements of A are imported by the code fragment in this example.

Array analysis is also studied in many papers [14,15,16,17,18,19]. The convex array regions implemented in PIPS are based on the Regions method [20] where `IN` region, the set of imported array elements, is somewhat similar to ExposedRead region in [15], UE set in [16], USE(s) in [17] and input effects in [19]. However, our `IN` region and the others differ. For example, in [15], array element sets are represented by lists of polyhedra and there is no exact representation, only under- and over-approximations. The ExposedRead sets contain array elements which are used in the continuation of the whole program before being defined, while `IN` regions are restricted to the current level in the hierarchical control flow graph. In [16], an array element set is a list of Regular Section Descriptors with bounds and step, guarded by predicates derived from IF conditions. When insufficient information is available, our `MAY` regions should be more accurate because we can keep more information about `PHI` variables. Input effects [19] give for each array element its first use in the considered fragment of code. This is similar to our `IN` regions but the precise statement instance in which the reference is performed is kept in the summary. The implementation choice really is the trade-off between efficiency and precision. The `IN` regions developed by [12] are used in this paper, with some improvements.

```
        K = FOO()
C       <A(PHI1)-IN-EXACT-{1<=PHI1, PHI1<=N}>
        DO I = 1,N
C       <A(PHI1)-IN-EXACT-{PHI1==I}>
            DO J = 1,N
                B(J,K) = J + K
            ENDDO
C       <B(PHI1,PHI2)-IN-EXACT-{1<=PHI1, PHI1<=N, PHI2==K}>
C       <A(PHI1)-IN-EXACT-{PHI1==I}>
            K = K + 1
C       <B(PHI1,PHI2)-IN-EXACT-{1<=PHI1, PHI1<=N, PHI2==K-1}>
C       <A(PHI1)-IN-EXACT-{PHI1==I}>
            DO J = 1,N
C       <B(PHI1,PHI2)-IN-EXACT-{PHI1==J, PHI2==K-1}>
C       <A(PHI1)-IN-EXACT-{PHI1==I}>
                B(J,K) = J*J - K*K
C       <B(PHI1,PHI2)-IN-EXACT-{PHI1==J, K-1<=PHI2, PHI2<=K}>
C       <A(PHI1)-IN-EXACT-{PHI1==I}>
                A(I) = A(I) + B(J,K) + B(J,K-1)
            ENDDO
        ENDDO
```

Fig. 3. Computed IN regions

4   Used-Before-Set Analysis

Our used-before-set analysis is directly based on IN array regions. These regions
are computed for arrays, but scalar variables also carry the same kind of information which is cheaper to compute. In fact, the region of a scalar has an
empty predicate, i.e <V-IN-EXACT-{}>. Information about imported array elements and scalar variables are propagated interprocedurally, from the elementary
statements to the compound statements. We traverse the program call graph in
the invocation order, in which a procedure is processed after all its callers.

procedure Used_Before_Set_Analysis(p)
    p : current procedure
begin
    s := entry statement of p
    l := list of variables having IN region at s
    for each $v \in l$
        if local_variable(v, p) or global_variable_in_main_program(v, p) **then**
            if the IN region of v at s is MUST or EXACT **then**
                error: "Variable v is used before set"
            else /* MAY IN region */
                insert an initialization on v before s
                go_down_and_verify(v, s)
        else /* v is a formal parameter or a global variable in a called procedure*/
            if must_be_checked(v, p) **then**
                go_down_and_verify(v, s)

end
procedure go_down_and_verify(v, s)
begin
    for each sub-statement s_i of s
        if the IN region of v at s_i is **EXACT then**
            insert a verification on v before s_i
        else /* MAY IN region*/
            if call_statement(s_i) **then**
                mark must_be_checked for the corresponding
                formal or global variables in the called procedure
            else
                go_down_and_verify(v, s_i)
end

The list of IN regions at the module entry statement gives us the set of all possibly undefined variables of the module, and vice-versa, only variables in this list may be used before set. So at the entry statement, if the list of IN regions is empty, there is no used-before-set error in this module. Otherwise, each variable in the list is checked. In Fortran, a variable scope is always a module. The scope of a global variable declared in a module is that module but the scope of the common block where the variable is located is the whole program. So the IN regions of all global variables are propagated to the main program, although the variables are not declared in it. Depending on the variable type (local, formal or global) and the current module, we have two cases:

Case 1: Local or global variable in the main program. Depending on the region approximation, we have two sub-cases:

- If the IN region has the approximation MUST or EXACT, the variable must be used somewhere in the module before being defined and an error is detected.
- Otherwise, the region is MAY; we instrument the code by inserting an initialization function before the entry statement and go down to the sub-statements where the IN region is propagated from. Before each statement where we know with certainty that the variable must be imported, a verification function is inserted. We continue to go down for each statement with MAY regions. If this statement is a procedure call, information is added to mark that the corresponding formal parameters of the actual variable, or the corresponding global variables must be checked at the callee's level. To help the debugging process, information about the call path is added to locate the run-time error.

Case 2: Formal parameter or global variable in a called procedure. If this variable is marked as *must be checked*, we repeat the process as for local variables, but no initialization is needed since it has been performed earlier in one of the callers.

To trap premature usage, the initialization is implemented by assigning a special value to the maybe uninitialized scalar variable or array element. The verification checks whether the variable value is equal to this special value, and reports the error if one has occurred. If the variable is an array, the instrumented code is a DO loop associated to the corresponding IN region, whereas it is a simple assignment and test for the scalar variables. All array elements in the MAY IN region are marked uninitialized and all array elements in the EXACT IN region are checked. We use the algorithm described in [21] to compute loop bounds from the region predicate, which is a polyhedron. This algorithm scans the polyhedron and uses the Fourier pairwise elimination to find loop bounds for each dimension. The generated loops have the following form:

```
IF (condition) THEN                    IF (condition) THEN
   DO PHI1 = LOWER1, UPPER1               DO PHI1 = LOWER1, UPPER1
      A(PHI1) = special_value                IF (A(PHI1).EQ.special_value) STOP
   ENDDO                                  ENDDO
ENDIF                                  ENDIF
   a. Marking initialization                  b. Initialization verification
```

However, there are some implementation problems related to the special value and the type of variable. We can use a SNaN (Signaling Not a Number) for floating variables but it is not evident for integer and logical variables. Currently, we choose the maximal integral value for integer variables, a value different from 0 and 1 for logical variables. This may raise false positive warnings when program computations really involve these special values. This is also a problem for other compiler implementations. Some memory coloring techniques can be used to avoid this problem, but at the expense of memory usage.

The efficiency of our analysis depends on the accuracy of array region analyses. The more precise the imported array regions are, the smaller the number of variables to be checked is, and code instrumentation is only used when we do not have enough information. Only array elements in the MAY IN regions are initialized and checked. Initialization and verification statements are inserted in the source code and the program is then compiled and executed normally. The executable code appears to the user to operate as the original, but if a used-before-set error is detected, the program is stopped with a message to indicate the name of the variable, the module and the call path where this error occurred. Another implemented option is that when a use before definition takes place, we do not stop the program but write details to a log-file for later analysis in order to catch several bugs in one run.

To illustrate the used-before-set analysis, we use the example of plusFORT. Fig. 4 shows the IN regions computed for module QKNUM. At the module entry, there is one IN region for variable IVAL which means that only this formal variable may be used without initialization. The variable POS is not imported by the loop because it is defined as the loop index. Neither is IOS imported by the module because its value has been defined by the READ statement, before being used in the test condition.

Array regions of the input statement are computed by taking into account the Fortran standard [13]: if the input/output status equals to zero, neither an error condition nor an end-of-file condition is encountered by the processor, all data in the input/output list are transfered. If the input/output status is not

```
          SUBROUTINE QKNUM(IVAL, POS)
          INTEGER IVAL, POS, VALS(50), IOS
C         <IVAL-IN-MAY-{}>
          READ (11, *, IOSTAT = IOS) VALS
C         <IOS-IN-EXACT-{}>
C         <IVAL-IN-MAY-{}>
C         <VALS(PHI1)-IN-MAY-{1<=PHI1, PHI1<=50, IOS==0}>
          IF (IOS .EQ. 0) THEN
C         IF (IVAL.EQ.MAXINT) STOP "IVAL is undefined in module QKNUM ..."
C         <IVAL-IN-EXACT-{}>
C         <VALS(PHI1)-IN-MAY-{1<=PHI1, PHI1<=50}>
             DO POS = 1,50
C         <IVAL-IN-EXACT-{}>
C         <POS-IN-EXACT-{}>
C         <VALS(PHI1)-IN-EXACT-{PHI1==POS}>
                IF (IVAL .EQ. VALS(POS)) GOTO 10
             ENDDO
          ENDIF
          POS = 0
10        END
```

Fig. 4. Used-before-set analysis example

equal to zero and there is no error or end-of-file specifier, execution of the executable program is terminated, no array element is defined. This is a language implementation feature but it must be respected to detect the uninitialized errors correctly. The set of array elements written by the input statement is exactly: `<VALS(PHI1)-WRITE-EXACT-{1<=PHI1, PHI1<=50, IOS==0}>` and when propagating the IN region of array `VALS` backward, we have: `<VALS(PHI1)-IN-MAY-{1<=PHI1, PHI1<=50, IOS==0}>` - `<VALS(PHI1)-WRITE-EXACT-{1<=PHI1, PHI1<=50, IOS==0}>` = `<VALS(PHI1)-IN-EXACT-{}>`. So all the elements of array `VALS` are well defined before they are used. There is no used-before-set error for the local variables in this module. By using static analysis, we prove that no instrumentation is needed, which is a big advantage with respect to the code generated by plus-FORT (Fig. 1). Since we do not have any calling context, it is not possible to conclude whether the variable `IVAL` is already initialized by the callers of `QKNUM`. If the whole program was given, and following some call paths, `IVAL` may not be initialized, a verification would be inserted before the loop and inside the conditional statement, as shown in the fifth comment line in Fig. 4.

5   Experimental Results

We used the SPEC95 CFP benchmarks [22] that contain all kinds of variables: scalar and array, local, formal and global, with complicated data and control flow graphs. The experiments consist of two steps: IN array region computation and used-before-set analysis. Table 1 summarizes relevant information for each

Table 1. SPEC95 CFP: number of lines, modules, scalar variables (total, maybe uninitialized and percentage), array variables (total, maybe uninitialized and percentage), compilation time (total and the used-before-set phase) and execution slowdown.

Bench	Line	Mod	Scalar			Array			Compilation		Slowdown
			Tot	May	Percen	Tot	May	Percen	Total	UBS	
tomcatv	190	1	24	0	0.00%	9	5	55.56%	0:08	0:01	4.42
swim	429	6	42	0	0.00%	14	13	92.86%	0:15	0:01	4.19
su2cor	2332	35	276	12	4.35%	118	63	53.39%	5:35	0:02	5.43
hydro2d	4292	42	226	11	4.87%	34	7	20.59%	1:47	0:05	5.07
mgrid	484	12	49	0	0.00%	10	4	40.00%	1:50	0:14	3.77
applu	3868	16	200	1	0.50%	33	10	30.30%	20:48	1:32	6.06
turb3d	2101	23	246	14	5.69%	32	31	96.88%	2:03	0:17	6.41
apsi	7361	96	1035	125	12.08%	19	11	57.89%	21:05	0:05	1.06
fpppp	2784	38	919	331	36.02%	40	26	65.00%	6:39	0:29	12.92
wave5	7764	105	1192	74	6.21%	162	33	20.37%	26:46	2:95	UBS

benchmark. We report the total numbers of scalar and array variables (Columns 4 and 7), the numbers of maybe uninitialized variables detected by the static analysis (Columns 5 and 8) and the corresponding percentages (Columns 6 and 9). On average, the percentages of maybe uninitialized variables to be checked at run-time are 3.1% for scalar variables and 37.96% for array variables. No used-before-set error is detected at compile-time, which is expected for benchmarks. All scalar variables in *tomcatv*, *swim* and *mgrid* are proved to be well initialized. One initialization and several verifications (single tests for scalar variables and loops for arrays) are added for each maybe uninitialized variable.

Column 10 shows the total compilation time (in minutes and seconds) required by PIPS to parse, compute imported array regions, analyze and generate code with used-before-set checks. The used-before-set analysis phase only takes a very small fraction of this compilation time, which is shown in Column 11. These times are measured on a UltraSparc II 440MHz, 256 Mo RAM. The code instrumented with PIPS initializations and verifications is then compiled with the SUN Workshop F77 version 5.0 compiler to generate executable files. This experiment is reported with the optimizing options turned on, using the SPEC95 CFP measurement guidelines (f77 -fast -xarch=v8plusa -fsimple=2 -xprefetch). Uninitialized variables are detected in *wave5*. In subroutine PARTBL, the local and static variables LCMMAX and LCMR are used before initialization.

The execution time slowdown with the standard input data for other SPEC95 CFP benchmarks is shown in the last column. We did not measure the slowdown when all references have to be instrumented, without help of static analysis, to show the contribution of the combined analysis, because we think that the slowdown given in this paper is more important in order to compare with the other work. On average, the instrumented code is 5.48 times slower than the initial code. There is only a 6% overhead for *apsi*. The overhead is rather high for *fpppp* (about 13 times) because of irreducible control flow graphs in this benchmark. Information is lost and the approximation of array regions becomes MAY.

It corresponds to 36.02% of checked scalar variables and 65% of checked array variables . To improve the results, we can use a more sophisticated treatment on irreducible control flow graphs when computing array regions. On the other hand, some program transformations are needed for several benchmarks. For instance, we can reduce the total number of variables to be checked from 18 to 14 for *hydro2d* by cloning the subroutine ADLEN which has two totally different behaviors for two parameter values: "half" and "full" steps. This optimization makes the array region analysis more precise, since interprocedural information helps to narrow down the scope of possible effects of the called procedure.

Other solutions are used in different compilers such as the undefined bit pattern or the NaN floating point trap, which can reduce greatly the execution time overheads. The verification on real variables can be omitted and replaced by the NaN exception trap. However, the origin of the uninitialized errors is not easy to locate with this method. Since the primary objective of this work is to reduce the number of possibly undefined variables by using static analysis, we do not intend to implement these techniques at the moment. Experimental results show that SPEC95 CFP are in general well-debugged programs. Used-before-set errors have been found in only one benchmark with its given input.

6   Conclusion

Static and dynamic analyses complement each other. Static analysis can discover automatically run-time errors and reduce the instrumentation or debugging cost. Dynamic checking takes into account program control flows and real input data that sometimes make static checking completely ineffective. Our used-before-set analysis combines these two approaches in order to reduce the overall cost while assuring the correctness of program.

PIPS is a source-to-source compiler that can be used for program analyses, transformation, parallelization and verification. By reusing advanced interprocedural analyses, the verification task becomes more efficient. READ and WRITE regions are already used to analyze program dependencies. IN regions are exploited for program optimizations such as array privatization, compile-time optimization of local memory or cache behavior in hierarchical memory machines, etc. Their precision is improved to target the verification. Only about 600 additional lines of C code are needed to implement the used-before-set analysis phase.

By using the IN region analysis, the static phase can improve one's confidence of the program correctness by showing that the program is free from used-before-set errors. Or, an error can be detected statically and the bug can be fixed right after the analysis. A small number of maybe uninitialized variables pointed by our compile-time analysis can help the testing and validation process to save debugging time. Run-time checks are generated only when information is not available to monitor the verification process. When executing the code, if a used-before-set error happens, the message error provides information about what occurred prior to the error, which can be of great help when trying to identify the fragment of code that actually caused the error. Furthermore, we could have an appropriate exception handling mechanism which is very important for safety-critical systems.

Experimental results also show that poor code quality can make static analysis insufficient; run-time checks remain and run-time failures cannot be eliminated. In addition to SPEC95 CFP suite, our analysis is applied to some large scale industrial applications to enhance the debugging process. We have encountered other problems with used-before-set checking, e.g the type mismatch. The actual variable is of integer type and the corresponding formal variable is declared of real type. In the called procedure, we verify if the formal variable is initialized by a NaN value check, which is in fact a check on integer variable and this may give false results. In addition, the compiler and platform dependences of initialization and verification functions are also implementation problems.

To obtain better results with static analysis, we are planning to improve the accuracy of IN array regions on an arbitrary control flow graph by using a more precise analysis, based on the control flow graph restructuring algorithm of Bourdoncle [23]. In addition, other approaches of array analysis such as input effects of Leservot [19] can give the exact statement where the used-before-set error occurs. Or, as in [24], the list of complementary array sections can be kept when performing some convex operators on array regions, in order to have more precise analysis on array usage. The source function [8] can also be applied to the used-before-set checking problem. The question is to study the trade-off between precision and summarization, as well as the complexity in space and time. Our method can be applied to other programming languages, with appropriate language construct handling. For example, the procedure call recursion can be handled with fixed point analysis on the call graph when computing imported array regions. Other problems such as pointer analysis must be studied to improve the precision of the static analysis in order to have an effective combined approach. The PIPS software and documentation as well as the used before set checking are available on *http://www.cri.ensmp.fr/ pips*.

References

1. Steensgaard, B.: Points-to analysis in almost linear time. In: ACM Symposium on Principles of Programming Languages, (1996) 32–41
2. Nguyen, T.V.N.: Efficient and Effective Software Verifications for Scientific Applications using Static Analyses and Code Instrumentation. PhD thesis, Ecole des Mines de Paris (2002)
3. Loginov, A., Yong, S.H., Horwitz, S., and Reps, T.W.: Debugging via run-time type checking. In Fundamental Approaches to Software Engineering (2001) 217–232
4. Appleyard, J.: Comparing Fortran compilers. ACM SIGPLAN – Fortran Forum **20** (2001) 6–10
5. Hasting, R., Joyce, B.: Purify: fast detection of memory leaks and access errors. In: Winter USENIX Conference (1992) 125–136
6. Evans, D., Guttag, J., Horning, J., Tan, Y.M.: LCLint: A tool for using specifications to check code. In: ACM SIGSOFT Symposium on Foundations of Software Engineering (1994) 87–96

 7. Reps, T., Horwitz, S., Sagiv, M.: Precise interprocedural dataflow analysis via graph reachability. In: ACM Symposium on Principles of Programming Languages (1995) 49–61
 8. Feautrier, P.: Dataflow analysis of array and scalar references. International Journal of Parallel Programming **20** (1991) 23–53
 9. Irigoin, F., Jouvelot, P., Triolet, R.: Semantical interprocedural parallelization: an overview of the PIPS project. In: International Conference on Supercomputing (1991) 144–151
10. Creusillet, B., Irigoin, F.: Interprocedural array region analyses. In: International Workshop on Languages and Compilers for Parallel Computing. Volume 1033 of Lecture Notes in Computer Science, Springer-Verlag (1995) 46–60
11. Schrijver, A.: Theory of Linear and Integer Programming. John Wiley & Sons, Chichester (1986).
12. Creusillet, B.: IN and OUT array region analyses. In: Workshop on Compilers for Parallel Computers. (1995) 233–246
13. ANSI: Programming Language FORTRAN, ANSI X3.9-1978, ISO 1539-1980. American National Standard Institute, New York (1983).
14. Duesterwald, E., Gupta, R., Soffa, M.L.: A practical data flow framework for array reference analysis and its application in optimization. In: ACM SIGPLAN Conference on Programming Language Design and Implementation (1993) 68–77
15. Hall, M.W., Amarasinghe, S.P., Murphy, B.R., Liao, S.W., Lam, M.S.: Detecting coarse-grain parallelism using an interprocedural parallelizing compiler. Super-Computing (1995)
16. Gu, J., Li, Z., Lee, G.: Symbolic array dataflow analysis for array privatization and program parallelization. In: Supercomputing (1995)
17. Tu, P., Padua, D.A.: Gated SSA-based demand-driven symbolic analysis for parallelizing compilers. In: International Conference on Supercomputing (1995)414–423
18. Duesterwald, E., Gupta, R., Soffa, M.L.: Demand-driven computation of interprocedural data flow. In: ACM Symposium on Principles of Programming Languages (1995) 37–48
19. Leservot, A.: Analyses interprocédurales du flot des données. PhD thesis, Université Paris VI (1996)
20. Triolet, R., Feautrier, P., Irigoin, F.: Automatic parallelization of Fortran programs in the presence of procedure calls. In: European Symposium on Programming (1986)
21. Ancourt, C., Irigoin, F.: Scanning polyhedra with DO loops. In: ACM SIGPLAN Symposium on Principles and Practice of Parallel Programming (1991) 39–50
22. Dujmovic, J.J., Dujmovic, I.: Evolution and evaluation of SPEC benchmarks. ACM SIGMETRICS **26** (1998) 2–9
23. Bourdoncle, F.: Sémantiques des langages impératifs d'ordre supérieur et interprétation abstraite. PhD thesis, Ecole Polytechnique, France (1992)
24. Manjunathaiah, M., Nicole, D.A.: Precise analysis of array usage in scientific programs. Scientific Programming **6** (1997) 229–242
25. Ami, T.L., Reps, T., Sagiv, L., Wilhelm, R.: Putting static analysis to work for verification: A case study. In: International Symposium on Software Testing and Analysis, (2000) 26–38
26. Arnold, M., Ryder, B.G.: A framework for reducing the cost of instrumented code. In: ACM SIGPLAN Conference on Programming Language Design and Implementation (2001) 168–179

Generalised Regular Parsers

Adrian Johnstone and Elizabeth Scott

Royal Holloway, University of London
{A.Johnstone,E.Scott}@rhul.ac.uk

Abstract. Aycock and Horspool have given an algorithm which improves the efficiency of GLR parsers. A grammar is 'reduced' so that there is no recursion apart from non-hidden left recursion, an FA recogniser is then constructed and a stack is used when the recursive parts of the original grammar are required. Aycock and Horspool then give an algorithm which performs all possible traversals of the resulting PDA on a given input string. This mirrors the approach taken by Tomita to perform all traversals of an LR(0) FA. However, Aycock and Horspool's algorithm does not terminate in the case where the grammar contains hidden left recursion. In this paper we give a different method for constructing an FA which recognises the language generated by the grammar provided that the only recursion in the grammar arises from left or right recursion. Using this FA allows us to reduce the number of places that the stack is required. We also give a different algorithm for constructing all traversals of the final PDA which is correct in all cases, including grammars with hidden left recursion. Thus we can apply our algorithm to all context free grammars.

1 Introduction

It is well known that a language is regular if and only if it is defined by a one-way deterministic finite automaton (FA) (see for instance [1], pp 118–120) and that the context free languages are similarly defined by the one-way nondeterministic pushdown automata (PDA). Intuitively, the context free languages include those with properly nested bracket structures. A deterministic FA is unable to guarantee that brackets are paired correctly (the slogan has it that 'regular expressions can't count') but the addition of a stack enables correct nesting to be tested.

The Chomsky hierarchy shows that a regular language may be described by a Context Free Grammar (CFG) and, although it is in general undecidable whether a particular CFG generates a regular language it is useful to think informally of CFGs as having some productions which are regular and some which are necessarily context free. Left and right recursion ($A\overset{*}{\Rightarrow}A\beta$, $A\overset{*}{\Rightarrow}\alpha A$) produce iterated constructs in the generated language which may be described by regular productions. The context free parts of the language arise from those productions which contain *embedded* recursion such as $A\overset{*}{\Rightarrow}\gamma A\delta$ where γ and δ are markers for left and right hand bracketing constructs. In detail, of course, embedded recursion may not be immediately obvious since the recursion may be

G. Hedin (Ed.): CC 2003, LNCS 2622, pp. 232–246, 2003.

indirect. To further complicate matters, embedded recursion may be intertwined with left or right recursion.

The usefulness of separating out iterative language constructs from necessarily recursive ones is clearly demonstrated by the widespread use of *extended* context free grammars [2] which directly support the use of regular expressions in rules. In recursive descent parsers it is usual to parse these regular expressions using iteration.

It is reasonable to ask if we can algorithmically discover the context free core of a grammar, automatically replacing left and right recursion with regular expressions, providing an optimal BNF to EBNF conversion. The motivation here is to reduce stack activity during the parse and thus speed up the parser. Although such a technique would be of general application (allowing recursive descent parsers to replace recursive function calls with iteration, for instance) it is particularly interesting to analyse the behaviour of LR shift-reduce parsers from this vantage point since the LR languages correspond to those defined by deterministic PDA's. Regular languages, in the form of the deterministic handle-finding automaton are at the heart of the standard LR parsing scheme. A stack is used to handle self-embedded recursion and right recursion. Interestingly, left recursion is absorbed into the handle finding automaton. In the case of general (non-deterministic) CFG's multiple stacks may be needed to keep track of multiple putative derivations.

Tomita [3] gave an algorithm for recognising any context free language by maintaining a compact representation of these multiple stacks in a 'graph structured stack', allowing all traversals of an LR FA to be performed together. (Note, Tomita's basic algorithm does not work for all context free *grammars* since the grammars must have had their cycles and, in some cases, their ϵ-productions removed. Tomita modified his algorithm to handle ϵ-rules but this algorithm still fails on hidden right recursion. An inelegant fix was subsequently provided by Farshi [4]. We have described elsewhere a modification of Tomita's basic algorithm which works for all context free grammars [5] which is more efficient than the Tomita and Farshi variants.)

Aycock and Horspool [6,7] have given a parsing method in which a grammar is 'reduced' so that there is no recursion apart from non-hidden left recursion. An FA recogniser for the reduced grammar is then constructed, and a stack is used when the recursive parts of the original grammar are required. Aycock and Horspool also give an algorithm which performs all possible traversals of the resulting PDA on a given input string. This mirrors the approach taken by Tomita to perform all traversals of an LR FA.

Aycock and Horspool's algorithm does not terminate in the case where the grammar contains 'hidden' left recursion. This is also the case for Tomita's algorithm but the reasons for the failure to terminate in the two cases are different. Tomita's algorithm really failed on hidden right recursion but he introduced a modification to correct the problem. It was this modification which in turn failed with respect to hidden left recursion (for further discussion of this issue see [8]). In Aycock and Horspool's case if a grammar non-terminal, A say, has the property that $A\overset{*}{\Rightarrow}\alpha A\beta$, where $\alpha \neq \epsilon$ then the automaton which recognises the language generated by A calls itself recursively. If $\alpha\overset{*}{\Rightarrow}\epsilon$ (that is, the grammar contains hidden left recursion) then the automaton will repeatedly call itself without consuming any input, and hence will fail to terminate.

In this paper we describe the construction of a *reduction incorporated automaton* from a grammar which we can prove (see [9]) correctly recognises the language generated by the grammar provided that the only recursion in the grammar essentially arises from left or right recursion. Using this automaton rather than the one constructed by Aycock and Horspool allows us to reduce the number of places that the stack is required in the final algorithm. We give a new algorithm for constructing all traversals of the final PDA and we can prove that this algorithm is correct in all cases, including grammars with hidden left recursion. Thus we can apply our modified parsing method to all context free grammars. The theorems in this paper are stated without proof, but full formal proofs can be found in the techincal report [9] on which this paper is based.

2   Initial Definitions

A *context free grammar* consists of a set $\mathbf{N}$ of non-terminal symbols, a set $\mathbf{T}$ of terminal symbols, an element $S \in \mathbf{N}$ called the start symbol, and a set of grammar rules of the form $A ::= \alpha$ where $A \in \mathbf{N}$ and α is a (possibly empty) string of terminals and non-terminals. We assume that there is an augmented start rule, $S' ::= S$, so that S' does not appear on the right hand side of any grammar rule.

A *derivation step* is an element of the form $\gamma A\delta \Rightarrow \gamma\alpha\delta$ where γ and δ are strings of terminals and non-terminals and $A ::= \alpha$ is a grammar rule. A *derivation* of τ from σ is a sequence of derivation steps $\sigma \Rightarrow \beta_1 \Rightarrow \beta_2 \Rightarrow \ldots \Rightarrow \beta_{n-1} \Rightarrow \tau$. We write $\sigma\overset{*}{\Rightarrow}\tau$ and $\sigma\overset{+}{\Rightarrow}\tau$ if $n > 0$.

A *sentential form* is any string α such that $S\overset{*}{\Rightarrow}\alpha$ and a *sentence* is a sentential form which contains only elements of $\mathbf{T}$. The set, $L(\Gamma)$, of sentences which can be derived from the start symbol of a grammar Γ, is defined to be the *language* generated by Γ.

A string α is *nullable* if $\alpha\overset{*}{\Rightarrow}\epsilon$ and *null* if $\alpha\overset{*}{\Rightarrow}u \in \mathbf{T}^*$ implies that $u = \epsilon$. We say that a grammar has *left (or right) recursion* if there is a non-terminal A and a derivation $A\overset{*}{\Rightarrow}\alpha A\beta$ where α is nullable (or β is nullable). We say that the recursion is *hidden* if $\alpha \neq \epsilon$ (or $\beta \neq \epsilon$). A grammar has *proper self embedding* if there is some non-terminal, A, and non-null strings α, β such that $A\overset{*}{\Rightarrow}\alpha A\beta$.

A *finite automaton* (FA) consists of a set of states and a set of transitions between these states. One of the states is singled out to be the *start* state, and one or more states are designated as *accepting* states. The transitions are labelled with grammar symbols together with the empty string ϵ. For technical reasons we shall want to label some of the transitions with special versions of ϵ which correspond to 'performing a reduction by rule i'. We denote these as $\mathcal{R}i$.

A *path* is a sequence $\theta_1 \ldots \theta_k$ of transitions in the FA such that the source state of θ_{i+1} is the target state of θ_i, for $1 \leq i \leq k - 1$. A *path through the FA* is a path $\theta_1 \ldots \theta_k$ such that the source state of θ_1 is the start state and the target state of θ_k is an accepting state. For a path θ, we write $\bar{\theta}$ for the string of terminal and non-terminal symbols obtained by taking the labels of the transitions in θ and removing the ϵ and $\mathcal{R}$ symbols. We say that a string μ of grammar symbols is *accepted* by an FA, N, if there is a path θ through N such that $\bar{\theta} = \mu$.

3   Reduction Incorporated Automata

Parsing involves comparing a sentential form with the rules of a grammar so as to detect derivation steps and thus derivations. It is natural to render a grammar as an FA in which the states correspond to *slots* in the grammar, that is positions between grammar symbols, and the edges to the matching of grammar symbols. The standard non-deterministic LR(0) automaton is based on this approach: a slot is represented as an *item*, a rule of the form $X ::= \alpha \cdot \beta$, where $X ::= \alpha\beta$ is a grammar production rule. The automaton includes a state for each item, $X ::= \alpha \cdot x\beta$ and $X ::= \alpha x \cdot \beta$ are connected via an edge labelled x, and $X ::= \alpha \cdot A\beta$ and $A ::= \cdot \gamma$ are connected via an edge labelled ϵ. The accepting states of the FA are those with no out-edges, corresponding to items of the form $A ::= \gamma \cdot$. The final LR(0) automaton is then obtained by performing the subset construction.

Aycock and Horspool's central idea is to add additional 'reduction' transitions from accepting states of the FA to the state which would be reached after the corresponding reduction had been performed. Precisely how these reductions should be introduced is slightly subtle and a full discussion is given in [9]. It turns out that we cannot simply use the LR(0) automaton. Aycock and Horspool give a method for constructing their FA which uses *tries* [6]. We use a different approach based on our Reduction Incorporated Automaton (RIA). The following is an informal description; a formal definition is given in Section 3.1.

(i)   Create an expanded LR(0) automaton by 'multiplying out': each occurrence of a nonterminal on the RHS of a production causes the entire set of items for that non-terminal to be added afresh. In the case of recursive rules, add an ϵ-edge back to the most recent instance of the target item on a path from the start state to the current state.

(ii) Add Aycock and Horspool style 'reduction' transitions (labelled with $\mathcal{R}$) from the leaves of the multiplied out FA (which would correspond to accepting states in the LR(0) automaton) to the state corresponding to the consumption of the accepted non-terminal. The resulting automaton is called the first stage, or initial RIA (IRIA).

(iii) Remove transitions labelled with non-terminals, since the final RIA will only be used to match strings of terminals.

(iv) Perform the subset construction, with $\mathcal{R}$-transitions treated as non-ϵ edges, to remove some non-determinism.

Example 1 Given Γ_1, a right recursive grammar:

0. $S' ::= S$	1. $S ::= \epsilon$	2. $S ::= aA$
3. $A ::= bS$	4. $A ::= Dg$	5. $D ::= b$

the IRIA resulting from construction steps (i) and (ii) is

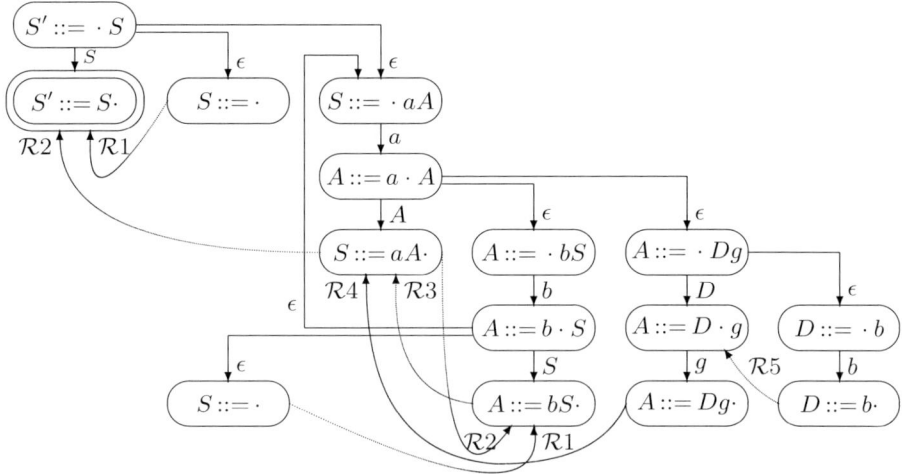

In this case the difference between this and the standard LR(0) approach is that there are two states labelled $S ::= \cdot$.

The back-edge from state $A ::= b \cdot S$ to $S ::= \cdot aA$ and the corresponding $\mathcal{R}2$ transition from $S ::= aA\cdot$ to $A ::= bS\cdot$ arise from the recursive occurrence of S in the rule $A ::= bS$. These recursion back-edges indicate the points at which the 'multiplying-out' of the LR(0) automaton would yield an infinite automaton unless a cycle is created.

After application of construction steps (iii) and (iv) we obtain $\text{RIA}(\varGamma_1)$:

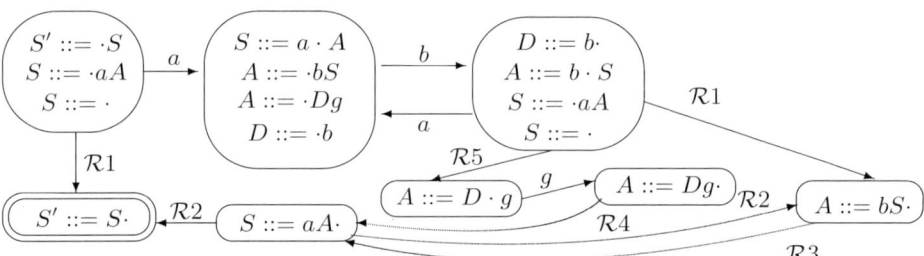

The existence of the $\mathcal{R}$-transitions means that the automaton is still non-deterministic. We could reduce the non-determinism further by assigning 'lookahead' sets to the $\mathcal{R}$ transitions. However, this would still not always resolve all non-determinism, so we shall discuss the addition of lookahead symbols to the final push down automaton rather than introduce them at this intermediate stage.

3.1   Formal RIA Construction Algorithm

The results given in this paper (and the corresponding proofs given in [9]) are based on the following formal RIA construction algorithm.

Given an augmented grammar $\varGamma$ we construct an RIA as follows:

Step 1: Create the start node labelled $S' ::= \cdot S$.

Step 2: While there are nodes in the FA which are not marked as dealt with, carry out the following:

1. Pick a node K labelled $X ::= \mu \cdot \gamma$ which is not marked as dealt with.

2. If $\gamma \neq \epsilon$ then let $\gamma = x\gamma'$ where $x \in \mathbf{N} \cup \mathbf{T}$, create a new node, M, labelled $X ::= \mu x \cdot \gamma'$, and add an arrow labelled x from K to M. This arrow is defined to be a *primary edge*.

3. If $x = Y$, where Y is a non-terminal, for each rule $Y ::= \delta$:

   if there is a node L, labelled $Y ::= \cdot \delta$, and a path θ from L to K which consists of only primary edges and primary ϵ-edges (θ may be empty), add an arrow labelled ϵ from K to L,

   otherwise, create a new node with label $Y ::= \cdot \delta$ and add an arrow labelled ϵ from K to this new node. This arrow is defined to be a *primary ϵ-edge*.

4. Mark K as dealt with.

Step 3: Remove all the 'dealt with' marks from all nodes and mark the node labelled $S' ::= S\cdot$ as the accepting node.

Step 4: While there are nodes labelled $Y ::= \gamma\cdot$ that are not dealt with: pick a node K labelled $X ::= x_1 \ldots x_n\cdot$ which is not marked as dealt with. Let $Y ::= \gamma$ be rule i. If $X \neq S'$ then find each node L labelled $Z ::= \delta \cdot X\rho$ such that there is a path labelled $(\epsilon, x_1, \ldots, x_n)$ from L to K, then add an arrow labelled $\mathcal{R}i$ from K to the child of L labelled $Z ::= \delta X \cdot \rho$. Mark K as dealt with. (The new edge is called a reduction edge).

Step 5: Remove all arrows labelled with nonterminals (this does not make any node unreachable because there is a reduction arrow with the same target as each removed arrow).

Step 6: Perform the subset construction with edges labelled $\mathcal{R}i$ treated as non-ϵ edges.

Theorem 1 *Let Γ be an augmented grammar and let $RIA(\Gamma)$ be the associated automaton constructed as above. If α is a non-trivial sentential form of Γ then α is accepted by $RIA(\Gamma)$.*

Furthermore, if Γ does not contain any proper self embedding and $u \in \mathbf{T}^*$ is accepted by $RIA(\Gamma)$ then $S' \overset{*}{\Rightarrow} u$.

In the next section we will describe how to deal with grammars which do contain proper self embedding.

4   Generalised Regular Parsing

In this section we describe how to build a PDA which can be used to recognise sentences in a language generated by a given context free grammar. The method is an extension of the construction given by Aycock and Horspool [6].

As we mentioned in the introduction, the problem with Aycock and Horspool's method is that, like any recursion based method, if a process makes a recursive call to itself without consuming any input then the method will ultimately fail to terminate unless special terminating measures, such as limiting the number of recursive calls, are introduced. An automaton constructed by Aycock and Horspool's method can make a recursive call to itself without consuming any input if and only if the original grammar contains hidden left recursion. (Non-hidden left recursion does not generate a recursive call because it is absorbed into the appropriate state when the automaton is constructed. This is exactly analogous to LR(0) FAs which, for the same reason, admit direct left recursion but not hidden left recursion.) Elsewhere, [5], we have given an extension of Tomita's original algorithm which allows ϵ-productions and can cope with grammars which contain hidden left recursion because the algorithm checks whether a path in the GSS already exists before adding it again. Using a similar idea, we have modified the call structure used by Aycock and Horspool to allow us to determine when a call is being repeated without any input having been consumed, thus ensuring that our algorithm always terminates.

In the rest of this section we shall describe our generalised regular parsing algorithm. We begin by modifying the grammar to remove most of the recursion (which changes the language generated by the grammar). We then construct the RIA for the modified grammar as described in the previous section, together with RIAs for certain subgrammars. We describe how to construct, from these automata, an automaton, called a recursion call automaton (RCA), for the original grammar Γ which, together with a stack, can be used to recognise sentences of Γ. We then give our algorithm for computing the results of all possible traversals of the RCA for a given input string.

4.1   Recursive Call Automata

Given a grammar, Γ, if there is a non-terminal A and a derivation $A \overset{+}{\Rightarrow} \alpha A \beta$, where α and β are not null, then pick one such A and replace an instance of A on the RHS of a rule with a special terminal of the form $A^{\perp}$ so that this derivation is no longer possible. Repeat this process until the derived grammar, Γ_S, has no proper self embedding, and construct RIA(Γ_S).

For each special terminal $A^{\perp}$ in Γ_S construct the grammar Γ_A which has the same rules as Γ_S but with the addition of a new start rule $S_A ::= A$, and then construct RIA(Γ_A) in such a way that all the state labels are disjoint from the state labels of any other automaton we have constructed during this process. We link all these automata together as follows: for each transition anywhere in any of the automata labelled $A^{\perp}$ let the source node be labelled h and the target node be labelled k. Remove this transition from the automaton and add a new transition from node h to the start node of the automaton Γ_A, labelling the new transition $p(k)$. Label the accepting node of RIA(Γ_A) with pop. The start and accepting states of the RCA are the start and acceptiing states, respectively, of RIA(Γ_S). We shall refer to this new automaton as the *recursion call automaton (RCA) associated with* Γ, RCA(Γ).

We can reduce the non-determinism in RCA(Γ) by adding lookahead symbols to the transitions. All reduction and push transitions whose target has a transition labelled $x \in \mathbf{T}$ or a transition with x in its lookahead set have x in their lookahead sets. The *pop* action has a lookahead set which is the union of all the lookahead sets associated with all the transitions from states which can be reached when this pop action is performed (i.e. the targets of the transitions labelled $A^\perp$ in the reduction incorporated automaton). Also, actions whose target is an accepting state have $ in their lookahead sets.

Example 2 Consider the grammar Γ which contains proper self embedding on B and hidden left and right recursion on S. (Note the string A is null so the derivation $S \Rightarrow BSA$ does not constitute proper self embedding.)

$$
\begin{array}{llll}
S' & ::= & S & \qquad B \quad ::= \quad DBb \mid \epsilon \qquad A \quad ::= \quad \epsilon \\
S & ::= & BSA \mid \epsilon & \qquad D \quad ::= \quad a \mid \epsilon
\end{array}
$$

We remove the proper self embedding by replacing the second instance of B with a special terminal, $B^\perp$, resulting in the grammar Γ_S

$$
\begin{array}{llll}
0.\ S' & ::= & S & \qquad 3.\ B \quad ::= \quad DB^\perp b \qquad 6.\ D \quad ::= \quad \epsilon \\
1.\ S & ::= & BSA & \qquad 4.\ B \quad ::= \quad \epsilon \qquad\qquad\quad 7.\ A \quad ::= \quad \epsilon \\
2.\ S & ::= & \epsilon & \qquad 5.\ D \quad ::= \quad a
\end{array}
$$

The first stage reduction incorporated FA, IRIA(Γ_S) is

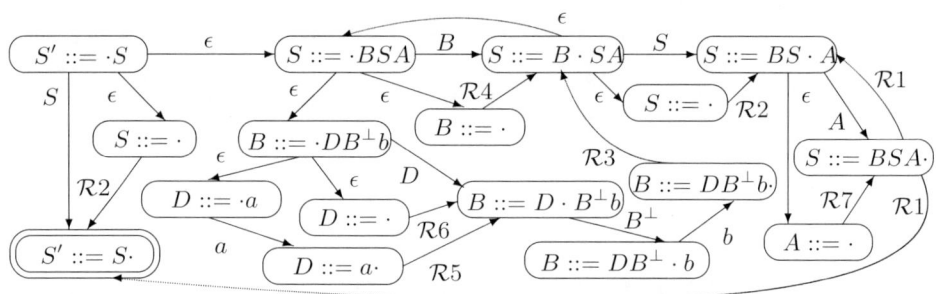

Building and combining RIA(Γ_S) and RIA(Γ_B) gives

(Here $X = \{a, b\}$ and $Y = \{a, b, \$\}$.)

A traversal of an RCA starts in the start state with a base node on the call stack. Then, if we have reached state h and the next input symbol is a, either,

- move to state k along a transition labelled $(\mathcal{R}i, Z)$ where $a \in Z$, or
- move to state k along a transition labelled $(p(l), Z)$ where $a \in Z$, and push l on to the top of the call stack, or
- if h is labelled (pop, Z) and $a \in Z$, pop a symbol, l, off the top of the call stack and move to state l, or
- move to state k along a transition labelled a and read the next input symbol.

If we have reached an accepting state of $RCA(\Gamma)$ and all the input has been consumed, report that the input has been accepted. Otherwise, if no further transitions are possible, report that this traversal has not been successful.

Theorem 2 *A string, u, of terminals is in the language generated by Γ if and only if there is a traversal of $RCA(\Gamma)$ which accepts the input u.*

4.2   Traversing an RCA

We now consider how to determine whether or not there is a traversal of $RCA(\Gamma)$ on a given input string $u = a_1 \ldots a_n$. The basic idea is to traverse the RCA and record the states we can reach on the input that we have seen so far. The process proceeds in steps, one step for each input symbol and one for the last symbol, \$. We start in the start state and construct the set of all states which can be reached without consuming any input. We then start a new set which contains all states which can be reached from a state in the first set along a transition labelled a_1. We then add all the states which can be reached without consuming any further input. If we encounter a transition labelled with a push action then we need to move to the state which is the target of this transition and to record the state we need to move back to, the argument of the push label, to be used when we reach the corresponding pop action. Thus we instead of just states, we maintain a set U of (state, node) pairs which can be reached from the currently read input.

The possibility of nested calls and multiple alternatives where the RCA is non-deterministic mean that we need an efficient method of recording the return states. Following Aycock and Horspool we create a call graph which is structured in a similar way to Tomita's graph structured stack and associate each state we reach in a traversal with a node in the call graph. When a *push* transition is used we find or create a node in the call graph which is labelled with the return state and we record the corresponding node with the state. We begin all traversals by creating a base node in the call graph, q_0, labelled -1 (which is not the label of any RCA node). We need to record the set of call graph nodes constructed at each step in order to check whether a node with a particular label has already been constructed, because in this case the node is reused. For this we use a set P.

We shall see that left and right recursion in Γ_S cause loops of reductions in $RCA(\Gamma)$. We ensure that the traversal construction process terminates in such cases by only adding each pair (k, q) to the set U once at any given step in the process. It is also possible to have loops which consume no input if in the grammar Γ_S we have $A \overset{*}{\Rightarrow} \alpha A^\perp \beta$ where $\alpha \overset{*}{\Rightarrow} \epsilon$. In this case the loop involves a push to the start state of Γ_A and is the source of the problem with algorithm given in [6]. We deal with this problem using an idea similar to that used by Farshi in his modification of Tomita's algorithm: we introduce loops in the call graph. Before giving the formal algorithm we illustrate our approach with two examples.

Computing Traversals Using Example 2

Recall the grammar from Example 2 above and consider traversing the RCA with input string $ab\$$.

We begin in the start state with lookahead symbol a and single stack node q_0, so $U = \{(0, q_0)\} = P$. From state 0 we can reach states 3 and 4 along reduction transitions, so $U = \{(0, q_0), (3, q_0), (4, q_0)\}$. From state 3 we can return to state 3 along a reduction but as $(3, q_0)$ is already in U we do not add it again, to ensure that this step terminates. State 4 has a push transition so we create a new call graph node, q_1, labelled with the argument of this transition, 8, and we make q_1 a parent of the node, q_0, and we add $(12, q_1)$ to U and P.

With lookahead symbol a from state 12 we can reach state 14 along a reduction transition, so we add $(14, q_1)$ to U. From state 14 there is a push transition $p(15)$ so we create a new call graph node q_2 labelled 15 and an edge from q_2 to q_1, and add $(12, q_2)$ to U and P. From $(12, q_2)$ we add $(14, q_2)$ to U, then from $(14, q_2)$ we traverse the push transition labelled $p(15)$. There is already a call graph node, q_2, labelled 15 so we reuse this node and create an edge from it to q_2. Since $(12, q_2)$ is already in U we do not add it again.

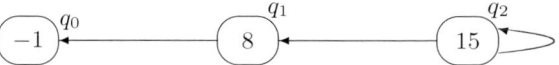

This step of the construction is now complete and we have $U = \{(0, q_0), (3, q_0), (4, q_0), (12, q_1), (14, q_1), (12, q_2), (14, q_2)\}$. We then read the input symbol, a, and check each of the elements in U for transitions labelled a. The states reachable in this way form the basis of the new set U for this step. Thus we have $U = \{(2, q_0), (13, q_1), (13, q_2)\}$ and $P = \emptyset$. We then traverse the reductions from 2 and 13, adding $(4, q_0)$, $(14, q_1)$ and $(14, q_2)$ to U. States 4 and 14 have push transitions, so we create new call graph nodes, q_3, q_4 labelled 8 and 15 (see the diagram below), and add $(12, q_3)$ and $(12, q_4)$ to U and P. We then traverse the transitions from state 12 and add $(14, q_3)$, $(14, q_4)$, $(11, q_3)$ and $(11, q_4)$ to U. When we process $(14, q_3)$ and $(14, q_4)$ we see that $(12, q_4) \in P$ and q_4 has label 15, so we reuse this node and just add edges from q_4 to q_3 and q_4.

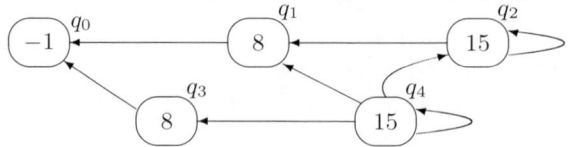

State 11 has an associated *pop* action thus, when we process $(11, q_3)$, for all nodes which are children of q_3, in this case q_0, we pop the label, 8, of q_3 off the stack and move to state 8 with the new stack, whose top node is q_0, i.e. we add $(8, q_0)$ to U. Similarly, for $(11, q_4)$ we add $(15, q_4)$, $(15, q_3)$, $(15, q_2)$ and $(15, q_1)$ to U. This step is then complete with
$U = \{(2, q_0), (13, q_1), (13, q_2), (4, q_0), (14, q_1), (14, q_2), (12, q_3), (12, q_4), (14, q_3),$
$(14, q_4), (11, q_3), (11, q_4), (8, q_0), (15, q_4), (15, q_3), (15, q_2), (15, q_1)\}$.

Finally we read the b and set $U = \{(9, q_0), (16, q_4), (16, q_3), (16, q_2), (16, q_1)\}$. With lookahead \$ there is a reduction from state 9 to 3, then to states 5, 6 and 10. So $U = \{(9, q_0), (16, q_4), (16, q_3), (16, q_2), (16, q_1), (3, q_0), (5, q_0), (6, q_0), (10, q_0)\}$. We have now completed the process, the lookahead symbol is \$ and there is an element $(10, q_0) \in U$ whose state is an accepting state of the RCA and whose call graph node is the base node. Thus we accept the input string, i.e. $ab \in L(\Gamma)$.

There is one further issue that we need to address before we give the formal algorithm. When we perform a pop action on a node, q labelled k, in the call graph we need to create elements in U for each of the children of q. If we subsequently add a new child p to q then we need to ensure that (k, p) is added to U. Thus when we create new edge from q to p we check to see if U contains any elements which result in a pop action from q. If such elements exist then we ensure that U contains (k, p).

Example 3

Consider the grammar Γ, $S' ::= S$ $S ::= SSSb \mid \epsilon$.
We remove the proper self embedding, resulting in the grammar Γ_S

$$0.\ S'\ :=\ S \qquad 1.\ S\ ::=\ SS^{\perp}S^{\perp}b \qquad 2.\ S\ ::=\ \epsilon$$

Then RIA(Γ_S) and RCA(Γ) are

We traverse RCA(Γ) with input string $b\$$. Starting with the element $(0, q_0)$ we traverse the reduction and add the element $(1, q_0)$ to U. We then traverse the push transition, creating a new call graph node q_1 labelled 2 and adding $(0, q_1)$ to U and to P. We then traverse the reduction from $(0, q_1)$ and add $(1, q_1)$ to U. The pop action in state 1 causes $(2, q_0)$ to be added to U, and, as there is already a call graph node labelled 2 which has been constructed at this step, the push transition from $(1, q_1)$ results in the construction of an edge from q_1 to itself (see the diagram below). This creates a new edge from q_1 down which the pop action associated with $(1, q_1)$ must be applied, and thus the element $(2, q_1)$ is added to U. If we then traverse the push transition from $(2, q_0)$ we create a call graph node, q_2 labelled 3 with child q_0, and add $(0, q_2)$ to U and P. When we traverse the push transition from $(2, q_1)$ we find that there is already a call graph node labelled 3 so we just add an edge from q_2 to q_1. We then traverse the reduction from $(0, q_2)$, adding $(1, q_2)$ to U, and perform the pop action for each of q_2's children, so that

$$U = \{(0, q_0), (1, q_0), (0, q_1), (1, q_1), (2, q_0), (2, q_1), (0, q_2), (1, q_2), (3, q_0), (3, q_1)\}.$$

The push transition from $(1, q_2)$ causes an edge to be added from q_1 to q_2, and then the pop action associated with $(1, q_1)$ is applied down this edge, adding $(2, q_2)$ to U. Finally, the push transition from $(2, q_2)$ causes a new edge to be added from q_2 to itself, and the pop action associated with $(1, q_2)$ then causes $(3, q_2)$ to be added to U.

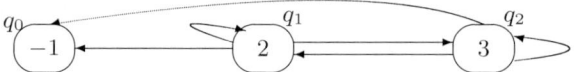

This completes the first step of the process. We then read the next input symbol, b, and continue traversing the RCA. Ultimately, when this step is complete we have

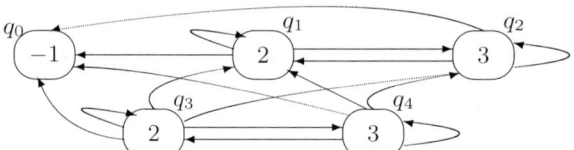

$$U = \{(4, q_0), (4, q_1), (4, q_2), (1, q_0), (1, q_1), (1, q_2), (2, q_0), (2, q_1), (2, q_2), (3, q_0),$$
$$(3, q_1), (3, q_2), (0, q_3), (0, q_4), (1, q_3), (1, q_4), (2, q_3), (2, q_4), (3, q_3), (3, q_4)\}.$$

Since the next input symbol is $\$$ and U contains $(1, q_0)$, where 1 is an accepting state of RCA(Γ), the string b is accepted.

4.3   A Formal Recognition Algorithm for RCA(Γ)

We shall now give the algorithm which computes the results of all possible traversals of an RCA for a given input. We shall assume that the RCA is given in the form of a table, $\mathcal{T}$, whose rows are indexed by the state numbers of the RCA, with the start state by convention being numbered 0, and whose columns are indexed by the terminal symbols of the grammar and the end-of-string symbol, $\$$. The entries in the table are sets of actions. If there is a transition in RCA(Γ) from state h to state k labelled with the terminal a, then $\mathcal{T}(h, a)$ contains the action sk. If there is a transition in RCA(Γ) from state h to state k labelled $(\mathcal{R}i, Z)$, $(p(l), Z)$ or (pop, Z) then, for all $x \in Z$, $\mathcal{T}(h, x)$ contains the action $(\mathcal{R}i, k)$, $(p(l), k)$ or pop respectively.

We begin with the RCA, input $a_1 \ldots a_n \$$, and a recursion call graph which contains a single node labelled -1 which is not the label of any state in the RCA. At the end of each step in the process we have a set U of RCA nodes which can be reached using the portion of input consumed so far, together with the node which is the top of the associated call stacks. In the algorithm we shall call this set U_i to facilitate the exposition. At the beginning of each step we have a set $U_{i-1}a_i$ of nodes which can be reached from the previous set via a shift action on the input symbol, a_i, which has just been read.

The nodes of the recursion call graph are all labelled with state numbers from the RCA, except for a unique base node which is labelled -1. For every node in the call graph there will be a path from this node to the base node. In practice the labels on the call graph nodes will all be states in the RCA which appear as parameters to $p()$ transitions.

Input: an RCA written as a table $\mathcal{T}$, and a string $a_1 \ldots a_n \$$
$a_{n+1} = \$$, $U_0 = P_0 = \emptyset, \ldots, U_n = P_n = \emptyset$
create a base node, q_0, in the call graph
create a process node, u_0, in U_0 labelled $(0, q_0)$ and add $(0, q_0)$ to P_0
for $i = 0$ to n do {
  add all the elements of U_i to A

  while $A \neq \emptyset$ {
    remove $u = (h, q)$ from A
    if $sk \in \mathcal{T}(h, a_{i+1})$ { if there is no node labelled (k, q) in U_{i+1} {
                    create a process node v labelled (k, q)
                    add v to U_{i+1} } }
    for each $(\mathcal{R}i, k) \in \mathcal{T}(h, a_{i+1})$ { if there is no $v \in U_i$ labelled (k, q) {
                      create a process node v labelled (k, q)
                      add v to A and to U_i } }
    if $pop \in \mathcal{T}(h, a_{i+1})$ { let k be the label of q and Z be the successors of q
                  for each $p \in Z$ {
                    if there is no $v \in U_i$ labelled (k, p) {
                      create a process node v labelled (k, p)
                      add v to A and to U_i } } }
    for each $(p(l), k) \in \mathcal{T}(h, a_{i+1})$ {
        if there is $(k, t) \in P_i$ such that t has label l {
          if there is no edge from t to q {
            add an edge from t to q
            if there is no node in U_i with label (l, q) {
                if there is $v \in U_i \backslash A$ with label of the form (f, t)
                    and $pop \in \mathcal{T}(f, a_{i+1})$ {
                  create a process node v labelled (l, q)
                  add v to A and to U_i } } } }
        else { create a node t with label l in the call graph
           make q a successor of t
           create a process node v labelled (k, t)
           add v to A, to U_i and to P_i } } } } }

if U_n contains a node whose label is (h_∞, q_0) where h_∞ is an accept state
    of the RCA and q_0 is the base node of the call graph { report success }
else { report failure }

Theorem 3 *Given RCA(Γ) and an input string $a_1 \ldots a_n\$$, Algorithm 4.3 terminates and reports success if $a_1 \ldots a_n$ is in the language generated by Γ and terminates and reports failure if $a_1 \ldots a_n$ is not in the language.*

5   Conclusion

The techniques described in this paper form a two-level generalisation of the finite automata that underlie parsing. We construct an FA (the Reduction Incorporated Automaton) which recognises the regular parts of a language and use this as a basis for another FA (the Recursive Call Automaton) which uses a stack when we need to recognise recursive parts of the language.

The RCA is nondeterministic, and so we need to manage multiple stacks. Tomita's GSS is a general-purpose structure for maintaining multiple stacks which may share prefixes and, by virtue of there being a finite set of values that may appear at the top of those stacks, may also be merged. In a Tomita parser, merging occurs when two stacks have the same LR state on top. In the RCA, merging occurs when two stacks have the same RCA state on top. A key difference is that Tomita must maintain a complete trace of all stack activity because the GSS is used to manage reductions, and during a reduction the parser needs to be able to look down into the stacks to see which state to go to. This is unnecessary in the case of the RCA which only ever needs to look one level back to find the state it needs to go to.

The use of a GSS-like structure, and the applicability of our approach to generalised parsing might create the impression that our parser is Tomita-like. Indeed Aycock and Horspool whose reduction transitions inspired this work describe their algorithm as an optimisation of Tomita's algorithm. In fact, the short-circuiting of the reduction path search by the reduction transitions means that there are few points of contact between the approaches. Tomita's algorithm and the variations of it, for example those given by Farshi [4] and Rekers [10], are generalised LR algorithms in the sense that if they are given an LR grammar then they essentially behave like a traditional stack based LR parser. In our case, and that of Aycock and Horspool, the parsers behave like FAs on regular grammars.

We would like to be able to produce an efficient version of what could be called *a generalised regular parser* in the sense that the algorithm is essentially an FA in the case where the input grammar defines a regular language. However, with the method described here this cannot be fully achieved because it is possible to have a grammar which contains non-trivial self embedding but whose language is still regular, for example $S ::= aSa \mid \epsilon$. For this grammar the RIA would accept, for example, a^3. Thus, following Aycock and Horspool, our algorithm has an initial phase which modifies the input grammar if it contains proper self-embedding and in some cases the algorithm uses a stack even though the underlying language is regular.

We have said little about the production of derivations from our parser since the scheme presented here is essentially just a recogniser. We have investigated two approaches: the production of Tomita-like Shared Packed Parse Forests and the construction of an FA whose language is essentially the set of all possible right-most derivations of the sentence. Space precludes a full discussion here, but the main issue is to ensure that production of derivations does not significantly compromise the efficiency gains from the reduction in stack activity. For this reason we prefer the second of the two approaches, see [9] for further details.

References

1. Aho, A.V., Ullman, J.D.: The Theory of Parsing, Translation and Compiling. Volume 1 – Parsing of Series in Automatic Computation. Prentice-Hall Inc. (1972)
2. Wirth, N.: What can we do about the unnecessary diversity of notation for syntactic definitions? Communications of the ACM **20** (1977)
3. Tomita, M.: Efficient parsing for natural language. Kluwer Academic Publishers, Boston (1986)
4. Nozohoor-Farshi, R.: GLR parsing for ϵ-grammars. In Tomita, M., ed.: Generalized LR parsing. Kluwer Academic Publishers, Netherlands (1991) 61–75
5. Johnstone, A., Scott, E.: Generalised reduction modified LR parsing for domain specific language prototyping. In: Proc. 35th Annual Hawaii International Conference On System Sciences (HICSS02). IEEE Computer Society, IEEE, New Jersey (2002)
6. Aycock, J., Horspool, N.: Faster generalised LR parsing. In: Compiler Construction: 8th International Conference, CC'99. Volume 1575 of Lecture Notes in computer science., Springer-Verlag (1999) 32–46
7. Aycock, J., Horspool, R.N., Janousek, J., Metichar, B.: Even faster generalised LR parsing. Acta Informatica **37** (2001) 633–651
8. Johnstone, A., Scott, E.: Tomita-style generalised LR parsers. Technical Report TR-00-12, Royal Holloway, University of London, Computer Science Department (2000)
9. Scott, E., Johnstone, A.: Table based parsers with reduced stack activity. Technical Report TR-02-08, Royal Holloway, University of London, Computer Science Department (2002)
10. Rekers, J.G.: Parser generation for interactive environments. PhD thesis, University of Amsterdam (1992)

Rapid and Robust Compiler Construction Using Template-Based Metacompilation

C. van Reeuwijk

Delft University of Technology
Mekelweg 4, 2628 CD Delft, The Netherlands
C.vanReeuwijk@cs.tudelft.nl

Abstract. We have developed Tm, a template-based metacompiler. Given a set of data-structure definitions and a template, Tm generates files that instantiate the template for the given data structures. With this process, Tm is able to generate program code to manipulate these data structures. Since it uses templates, the generated code is not restricted to a specific programming language: any sufficiently powerful programming language can be targeted.

Tm has been used for a wide variety of tasks and languages. However, it was designed to support compiler construction, and most applications have been in that area.

In this paper we outline Tm, and describe our experiences with using it to construct a static compiler for Java. As we will show, it has significantly accelerated implementation of the compiler. Almost 75% of its source code is generated by Tm, allowing us to rapidly implement a much more robust and sophisticated compiler than would have been possible otherwise.

1 Introduction

In an earlier paper [6] we described Tm (short for Template Manager), a template code generator. Given a set of data-structure definitions and a template, Tm generates an output file that is an expansion of the template using the data structure definitions (Fig. 1).

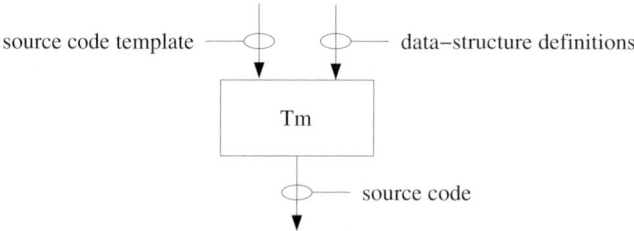

Fig. 1. Given a source code template file and a set of data-structure definitions, Tm generates a source code file.

G. Hedin (Ed.): CC 2003, LNCS 2622, pp. 247–261, 2003.

For example, the following definitions could be used to represent connections between electronic components:

```
connection = Wire: { name:string } | Bundle: { l:[connection] };
```

A connection is either a single wire or a bundle of connections, represented by types Wire or Bundle respectively. Both are subtypes of connection. A Wire contains a string field, a Bundle contains a list of connections.

Now consider the following Tm template:

```
.foreach t ${typelist}
typedef str_$t *$t;
.endforeach
```

The two lines starting with a dot form a Tm command that iterates over the defined types, and assigns the current type to variable t. The remaining line is written to the output in each iteration. The two $t expressions are references to variable t that are substituted by Tm.

Executing this template using the type definitions shown above results in:

```
typedef str_Wire *Wire;
typedef str_Bundle *Bundle;
typedef str_connection *connection;
```

Tm templates are programs for the Tm macro language. When executed, these programs can generate source code for another programming language. This process is called *metaprogramming*, since it is a metalevel above 'normal' programming. The approach that Tm uses is called *static metacompilation* or *template metaprogramming* since it is done at compile time, not at runtime.

Because it uses templates, Tm is neutral with respect to the target language of the generated files. Various users have written templates for programming languages such as Miranda, Pascal, C, C++, Lisp, Clean and Java, but also for targets such as Unix shells, the Unix streaming editor (sed), and configuration files for various programs. The most common target is the C programming language.

Tm supports file inclusion in its templates, so code can be shared between projects, and standard templates can be provided for common code. An extensive set of standard templates have been developed for C, and for many programs the code provided by these templates is sufficient.

Tm has proved to be very useful in a large variety of projects. To illustrate this, we will examine the use of Tm and its C templates in the construction of Timber [9,10], a parallelizing Spar/Java compiler. Using Tm has had a profound impact on the implementation of Timber. Nearly 75% of its source code is generated by Tm. Code templates strongly encourage code reuse, since a code template section is repeatedly expanded, and entire code templates are re-used between projects. Moreover, code templates can automate a number of error-prone tasks, such as dependency calculations between node types. For all these reasons, using Tm has allowed us to implement a far more robust, powerful and adaptable compiler than otherwise would have been possible.

The source code of the Timber compiler is available for downloading from [4], the source code of Tm itself is available for downloading from the Tm website [5].

The paper is organized as follows: In Section 2 we describe related work. In Sections 3 and 4 we give an overview of Tm. In Section 5 we describe the C templates of Tm. In

Section 6 we describe the Timber compiler and the impact of Tm on its implementation, and in Section 7 we draw some conclusions.

2   Metaprogramming Languages

In a sense, the most popular metaprogramming language is formed by the directives of the C/C++ preprocessor. Unfortunately, it is a very weak language lacking even simple features such as iteration or string manipulation. Generic macro processors such as the Unix tool 'm4' have also been used for metaprogramming, but such a macro processor has no knowledge about the data-structure definitions for which code must be generated. However, for effective metaprogramming the metaprogramming language must know the data-structure definitions of a program, and the relation between them. This allows the metaprogram to generate code that is tailor-made for a specific data structure.

Knowledge about the data-structure definitions can be provided at run time or at compile time. At run time, the knowledge can be provided through a set of inquiry functions that list the types in a program, list members of a type, etc. Such inquiry functions are available in languages like Java, Smalltalk, and Python. This approach is called *dynamic metaprogrammimg*. For example, Java associates a java.lang.Class object with every object in a program. Query methods of the Class object allow the program to list methods, constructors and fields of the class, and to obtain detailed information about these methods.

The advantage of dynamic metaprogramming is that the same language is used for programming and metaprogramming, obviating the need to learn a new language. However, since the metaprogramming is done at run time, is difficult to compile the output of the metaprogram. The alternative, interpretation, results in slower execution. Also, dynamic metaprogramming languages are usually not designed for large-scale metaprogramming, so that extensive templates are cumbersome to implement. Finally, dynamic metaprogramming is inherently restricted to a single programming language.

When the knowledge about the data-structure definitions is provided at compile time, this is called *static metaprogramming* or *static metacompilation*. Knowledge about the data-structure definitions can be extracted from the target language, or can be provided as definitions in the metaprogramming language. The first approach requires tight integration with the programming language under it. It is used, for example, in Willink's Flexible Object Generator [11,12] (FOG). He replaces the standard preprocessor of C++ with a much more powerful metacompiler integrated with C++. Unfortunately, although FOG can access C++ class definitions, it does not allow computations on the relations between classes. This is a restriction of FOG, not one that is inherent to the used approach. The approach *is* inherently restricted to a single programming language.

It is also possible to construct a static metacompiler that is independent of the underlying programming language. With this approach, the data-structure definitions are part of the metalanguage, and metaprograms must generate data-structure definitions for the target language. This makes the metacompiler fully independent of the target language. This is the approach used by Tm, although we strictly separate the macrolanguage and the data-structure definition language.

The same approach is used by AutoGen [1]. It shares many features with Tm, but was designed for general code construction tasks. In contrast, Tm was designed to generate manipulation code for data structures, and in particular to assist in compiler construction. AutoGen's macro language does not have Tm's rich set of functions and commands to access and manipulate data-structure definitions. Also, it lacks the rich set of C templates that Tm provides.

3   Tm Data-Structure Definitions

A Tm data-structure definition file, such as the one shown in Fig. 2, consists of a series of definitions of Tm *types*. A Tm type is either a *class*, or a *tuple*. For example, in Fig. 2 origin is a tuple type, all others are class types. Both classes and tuples can contain an arbitrary number of fields.

```
expr = { org:origin } +
    VarExpr: { nm:string } |
    AddExpr: { l:expr, r:expr } |
    SubExpr: { l:expr, r:expr } |
    NegExpr: { x:expr } |
    ConstExpr: { n:int } |
    CallExpr: { fn:string, parms:[expr] };

origin == ( file:string, line:int );
```

Fig. 2. A typical set of Tm type definitions to represent expressions in a programming language.

3.1   Fields

Each field of a tuple or class consists of a *name* and a *type*. The type can be either a simple type, written as the name of the type; or a list type, written by surrounding a type with a square bracket pair ('[' and ']'). List types denote lists of arbitrary length, whose length can change at run-time. For example, the following are all valid fields:

```
line:int          file:string
points:[point]    words:[[char]]
```

3.2   Class Types

In its simplest form, a class type consists of a list of fields separated by commas, and surrounded by curly braces. Like all type definitions, it must be terminated by a semicolon (';'). For example:

```
origin = { file:string, line:int };
```

A class can also inherit from other types. For example:

```
ifStatement = statement + { cond:expr, then:block, else:block };
```

means that the ifStatement class inherits the fields of the statement class.

A class can be defined to be *virtual* by using the '~=' operator instead of the '=' operator. This indicates that the class itself will never be created, only subclasses of this class. For example:

```
statement ~= { org:origin };
```

To allow compact and clear specification of a class with many subclasses, subclasses can be specified in the class itself. For example:

```
statement = { org:origin } +
    ifStatement: { cond:expr, then:block, else:block } |
    whileStatement: { cond:expr, body:block } |
    forStatement: { var:string, bound:expr, body:block } |
    assignStatement: { lhs:expr, rhs:expr }
    ;
```

Every labeled component is called an *alternative*; every alternative defines a subclass with the name of its label. A class containing alternatives is always virtual. Thus, the definition above is equivalent with:

```
statement ~= { org:origin };
ifStatement = statement + { cond:expr, then:block, else:block };
whileStatement = statement + { cond:expr, body:block };
forStatement = statement + { var:string, bound:expr, body:block };
assignStatement = statement + { lhs:expr, rhs:expr };
```

3.3   Tuple Types

A *tuple* consists of a list of fields separated by commas and surrounded with parentheses. Like all type definitions, it must be terminated by a semicolon ('; '). For example:

```
origin == ( file:string, line:int );
```

The '==' operator introduces a tuple type.

A tuple can inherit from other types. For example, the following tuple inherits from `statement`:

```
ifStatement == statement + ( cond:expr, then:block, else:block );
```

A tuple statement cannot contain alternatives or multiple lists of fields.

A tuple type can always be converted to an equivalent class type; tuples are provided for compactness and efficiency.

3.4   Restrictions

A number of restrictions are enforced on the type definitions:

- A type can not have the same name as a previously defined type.
- A type can not, directly or indirectly, inherit from itself.
- A type can not, directly or indirectly, inherit the same type twice.
- A type can not have two fields with the same name, or inherit a field with the same name as one of its own fields.

4   The Tm Template Language

The Tm template language is an untyped interpreted programming language to manipulate Tm type definitions and text. It is powerful enough to generate code for arbitrary programming languages, and for metalevel computations such as generating sequence numbers, calculating the dependencies between types, and calculate the transitive closure of these dependencies.

In Tm templates, all lines starting with a dot ('.') are commands. Lines that do not start with a dot are copied to the output. In both command lines and output lines, expressions starting with a $ are expanded. Expressions of the form $() denote variable references, expressions of the form $[] denote arithmetic expressions, expressions of the form ${} denote function invocations, and all other expressions of the form $<letter> denote variable references to the variable <letter>. For example, the template:

```
.set n 4
.set words for while goto
int br[$n,${len $(words)}];
int ht[$[$n*${len $(words)]}]];
```

will produce:

```
int br[4,3];
int ht[12];
```

The function len calculates the length of the list it is given, in this case the list assigned to variable words. The $[] expression in the declaration of ht multiplies the calculated length by n.

There are also functions to list the defined types, list the field names of a given type, retrieve the type of a given field, manipulate strings, etc. There are also commands to include files, define macros, etc. For further details see [7].

5   The Tm C Templates

As part of the core Tm distribution a number of templates for the C programming language are provided. These templates have been used in a large range of programs, including Tm itself and in the Timber compiler described below. It is useful to distinguish three different types of template: *administration* templates, which generate code for general-purpose administration of types, *tree walker* templates, that generate code to visit particular nodes in a tree, and *analysis* templates, that generate code to traverse a tree and collect information about the nodes in the tree.

For example, using the type definitions of Fig. 2 consider the following template:

```
.set wantdefs rdup_origin
.set basename demo
.include tmc.ct
```

The variable wantdefs is set to the list of functions that should be generated. In this case only the function rdup_origin is requested. The last line includes the standard administration template file tmc.ct. The code in this file will generate the requested function.

From this template, Tm will generate a function `rdup_origin` that creates a duplicate of an `origin` instance. The C templates automatically generate other functions when they are necessary to implement the requested functions. In this case, the template will also generate a function `new_origin` that, given a string and an integer, creates a new instance of `origin`.

5.1   Administration

The C administration code templates can generate code to:

- Create and destroy instances of the defined types.
- Read and write an ASCII representation of instances of these types.
- Compare two instances.
- Manipulate lists: append to, insert in, delete from, reverse, concatenate.
- Duplicate type instances.

For example, to create new instances of the types of Fig. 2, the following functions can be generated:

```
origin new_origin( int line, string file );
expr new_VarExpr( origin org, string nm );
expr new_AddExpr( origin org, expr l, expr r );
expr new_CallExpr( origin org, string fn, expr_list parms );
expr_list new_expr_list();
```

To recursively free instances of these types, the following functions can be generated:

```
void rfre_origin( origin e );
void rfre_expr( expr e );
void rfre_expr_list( expr_list l );
```

As explained above, the C templates automatically generate other functions if they are necessary to implement the requested functions.

5.2   Tree Walkers

It is often necessary to traverse ('walk') a tree, and visit all nodes of a specific type. For example, in the types of Fig. 2 we might want to visit all `NegExpr` nodes containing a `ConstExpr`, and replace them with a new `ConstExpr`. The action to be performed on each node must be written by the user. However, code is also needed to traverse the tree and ensure that all instances of the target nodes are visited, and Tm can take care of that. Appendix A shows a tree walker to implement our example, here we only briefly describe its requirements and features.

The tree walker template requires the following from the programmer:

- A list of node types to start the walk from, and a list of node types to visit.
- Action functions for all node types that must be visited.
- Macros for generating signatures and invocations of the walker functions.

From this information Tm computes the set of nodes to walk, and generates appropriate walker functions. The action functions provided by the user are copied to the output file, and together they form a complete tree walker.

By letting the user specify the signature of the walker and action functions, the tree walkers are flexible enough to pass arbitrary information into the tree walk, and to accumulate arbitrary information during the tree walk.

Using a tree walker has the usual advantages of code templates: extensive code re-use. Moreover, the tree-walker template automates the calculation of the required traversal. Since that is an error-prone task that must be repeated after every change or addition to the data structures, automation greatly improves the reliability of the traversal code.

A tree walker is similar in concept to the *visitor pattern* that has been proposed as a design pattern for object-oriented programming [3]. In both cases we wish to apply operations on a set of node types in a tree. The visitor pattern is implemented by adding a method to all node types. These methods implement a walk over the entire tree. During the walk, nodes are passed to a visitor method that applies the appropriate method for that type of node. A different type of walk over the tree only requires the definition of a different visitor method.

Although the visitor pattern has some of the advantages of a Tm template, it also has a number of drawbacks. In particular, it is still necessary to implement the (generic) tree walk by hand. Moreover, the visitor methods are often complicated since the correct action for every type of node must be determined and executed. Finally, the entire tree is always visited, even if a particular walk does not require it.

In contrast, for a Tm tree walker all tree traversal and type inspection code is generated; the user only needs to supply the code for the operations on the visited types.

5.3 Analyzers

One specific type of tree walker is used to collect information about a tree. For example, we might want to estimate the size of the generated code, determine whether an expression has side-effects, or collect the variables that are used in a code fragment. We call such tree walkers *analyzers*, and we provide a specialized template to generate them. An analyzer must not modify the tree it walks, and its operation must be a *reduction* operation. Typical reduction operators are boolean *and* and *or*, summation (for example to calculate the estimated size of a code fragment), and list concatenation (for example to collect all variable names in a code fragment).

The analyzer template requires the following from the programmer:

- A list of node types to start the walk from, and a list of node types to visit.
- For all the node types to visit, a classification of the node. The method can be `ignore` (do not visit this node), `reduction` (the value is the reduction of the values of its fields, possibly combined with a given constant), `constant` (the value is the given constant), or `function` (the value is computed by a user-supplied function).
- The type of the analysis result (e.g. `int`).
- The reduction operator to apply (e.g. addition).
- The neutral element of the reduction (e.g. 0).
- A macro to generate walker function signatures.
- Optionally, a termination test expression.

From this information the set of nodes to walk is computed, and appropriate walker functions are generated. The termination test expression allows useless tree walks to be cut off. For example, once the intermediate result of a boolean *and* reduction is *false*, the traversal can stop, since the result will always be *false*.

6   Application of Tm in the Timber Compiler

Tm and its C templates are used extensively in the Timber compiler [9,10], a static compiler for a superset of Java [4]. To illustrate the usefulness of Tm we will describe the impact that the use of Tm has had on the compiler.

Internally, the Timber compiler consists of three modules (Fig. 3): a frontend that translates Spar/Java to an intermediate representation called Vnus [2,8], a number of parallelization engines that rewrite Vnus, and a backend that translates Vnus to C++ code.

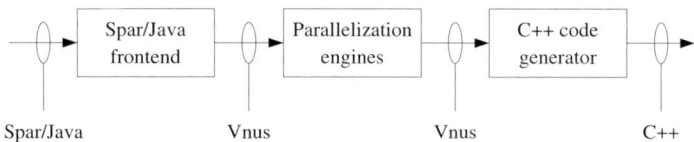

Fig. 3. Data flow in the Timber compiler.

To give an indication of the amount of work Tm has saved us, we will show statistics comparing the number of lines of hand-written and generated code[1]. We calculate the amount of generated code by counting the lines in the generated source files, and subtracting the number of lines in the template file. For the amount of hand-written code we count the lines in the non-generated source files, and in the template files.

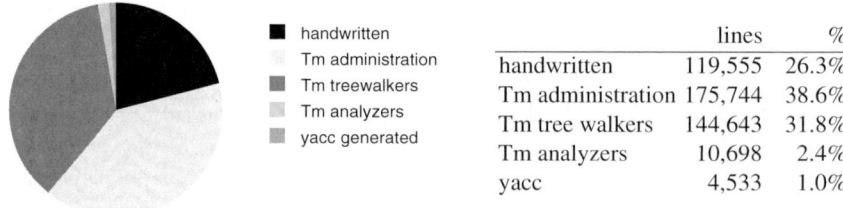

	lines	%
handwritten	119,555	26.3%
Tm administration	175,744	38.6%
Tm tree walkers	144,643	31.8%
Tm analyzers	10,698	2.4%
yacc	4,533	1.0%

Fig. 4. Code origin for the entire Timber compiler.

---

[1] This comparison is meaningful because the style of the code generated by our Tm templates is similar to what we write ourselves.

We assign each line of code that is passed to the C compiler to one of the following five categories: hand-written, generated by yacc, or generated by a Tm administration, tree walker or analysis template.

Figure 4 shows the statistics for the entire compiler. In subsequent sections we will show the statistics for the individual compiler phases.

As these figures show, nearly 75% of the compiler code is generated by Tm. Roughly half of the generated code is for administration, and the other half implements tree walkers. Only a small fraction of the generated code is devoted to analyzer tree walkers. One reason for this is that analyzer tree walkers are a fairly recent development; some analysis operations are still done in hand-written code, even though in a new implementation an analyzer tree walker would be used.

The Timber compiler has taken an estimated five person-years to implement: three person-years to implement a static Java compiler, and two to implement the language extensions and the parallelization engines. The resulting compiler is able to compile large programs and large parts of the standard Java library to efficient executables.

6.1   Communication between Engines

The Timber compiler consists of independent programs, called *engines*, that are 'glued' together with a shell script. Internally, each engine represents the program as a tree of Tm types. Communication between the compiler engines is implemented using Tm-generated functions. These functions print a tree to a textual representation in a file, and convert this textual representation back into a tree.

6.2   The Spar/Java Frontend

Figure 5 shows the code generation statistics for the Spar/Java frontend.

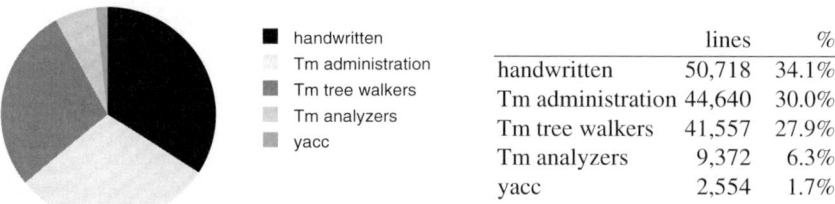

	lines	%
handwritten	50,718	34.1%
Tm administration	44,640	30.0%
Tm tree walkers	41,557	27.9%
Tm analyzers	9,372	6.3%
yacc	2,554	1.7%

Fig. 5. Origin of the frontend code.

The frontend parses Spar/Java, applies the semantic checks required by Java on the program, applies a number of optimizations, and generates Vnus. A number of tree walkers implement distinct compiler phases. In order of their application they do the following:

- Rewrite some constructs to simplify the remaining phases.
- Register class declarations in the symbol table.
- Register methods and constructors in the symbol table.
- Bind variables, types, methods and constructors.
- Check correctness of the program.
- Apply a number of code optimizations, e.g. inlining, constant folding.
- Add garbage-collection administration code.
- Eliminate unused variable declarations.

Other tree walkers implement auxiliary operations that work on fragments of code instead of an entire program. They do the following:

- Mark variables that are only read as 'final'.
- Rename variable references (used in method inlining).
- List the scope names of a code fragment.
- List variables that are not bound in the given code fragment.
- Do constant folding on an expression.
- List the assigned variables of a code fragment.
- Update the use count of the methods used in a code fragment.
- Rewrite 'return' statements to 'goto' statements (used in method inlining).

A number of analyzer tree walkers are also used, which do the following:

- Estimate the size of a given code fragment.
- Determine whether an expression is constant.
- Determine whether an expression requires the garbage-collection administration to be up-to-date.
- Determine whether a code fragment alters the state of the garbage-collection administration.
- Determine whether an expression has side effects.
- Determine whether an expression evaluates to zero.

6.3   The Parallelization Engines

Figure 6 shows the code generation statistics for the parallelization engines.

The parallelization engines transform implicitly parallel Vnus programs (sequential programs with parallelization annotations) to explicitly parallel Vnus programs. The engines are implemented as a set of 57 rules that each apply a simple rewrite operation on the Vnus program. These rules are implemented as tree walkers. Some example rules are:

- Search for loops that only contain a communication statement for a single element, and replace them by code that communicates all elements in a single message.
- Exchange loops in a loop nest when this is profitable.
- Simplify `if` statements with a constant `true` or `false` condition.

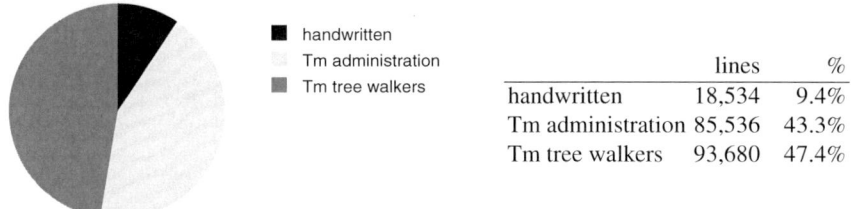

	lines	%
handwritten	18,534	9.4%
Tm administration	85,536	43.3%
Tm tree walkers	93,680	47.4%

Fig. 6. Origin of the parallelization code.

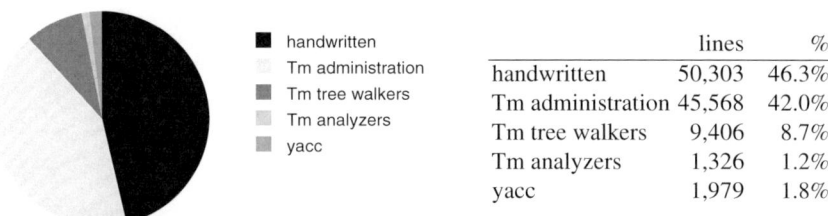

	lines	%
handwritten	50,303	46.3%
Tm administration	45,568	42.0%
Tm tree walkers	9,406	8.7%
Tm analyzers	1,326	1.2%
yacc	1,979	1.8%

Fig. 7. Origin of the backend code.

6.4   The Vnus Backend

Figure 7 shows the code generation statistics for the Vnus backend.

The backend translates Vnus code to C++ code. Similar to the frontend, a number of tree walkers implement distinct compilation phases (checking, optimization), and a number of other tree walkers serve as auxiliary functions (constant folding, tests, etc.).

7   Conclusions

Our template-based metacompiler Tm is able to generate an extensive range of functions to manipulate data structures. Since it uses templates, the generated code is not restricted to a specific programming language.

Since Tm provides a full programming language for template implementation, it is possible to write highly sophisticated templates, for example the tree walker templates described in Section 5.2, and the analyzers described in Section 5.3.

As we have shown, the use of Tm has had a profound impact on the implementation of Timber, our Spar/Java compiler. Nearly 75% of the source code of the compiler is generated by Tm, allowing rapid implementation of the compiler, and resulting in a much more robust and sophisticated compiler than would have been possible otherwise. Consequently, in three person-years we have been able to implement a Java compiler that is able to correctly compile large parts of the standard library to efficient executables. Our extensions to Java, and the parallelization engines were implemented in two person-years.

References

[1] AutoGen website. URL: autogen.sourceforge.net.
[2] P.F.G. Dechering, J.A. Trescher, J.P.M. de Vreught, and H.J. Sips. V-cal: a calculus for the compilation of data parallel languages. In C.-H. Huang et. al., editor, *8th Intl. Workshop, Languages and Compilers for Parallel Computing*, number 1033 in LNCS, pages 388–395, Columbus, Ohio, USA, August 1995. Springer Verlag.
[3] Erich Gamma, Richard Helm, Ralph Johnson, and John Vlissides. *Design Patterns: Elements of Reusable Object-Oriented Software*. Addison Wesley, January 1995.
[4] C. van Reeuwijk. Timber download page. www.pds.twi.tudelft.nl/timber/downloading.html.
[5] C. van Reeuwijk. Tm website. www.pds.twi.tudelft.nl/~reeuwijk/software/Tm.
[6] C. van Reeuwijk. Tm: a code generator for recursive data structures. *Software – Practice and Experience*, 22(10):899–908, October 1992.
[7] C. van Reeuwijk. Template manager reference manual. PDS Technical Report PDS-2000-003, Delft University of Technology, May 2000. www.pds.twi.tudelft.nl/reports/2000/PDS-2000-003.
[8] C. van Reeuwijk. The Vnus language specification, version 2.1. PDS Technical Report PDS-2000-002, Delft University of Technology, May 2000. www.pds.twi.tudelft.nl/reports/2000/PDS-2000-002.
[9] C. van Reeuwijk, A. van Gemund, and H.J. Sips. Spar: A programming language for semi-automatic compilation of parallel programs. *Concurrency – Practice and Experience*, 11(9):1193–1205, November 1997.
[10] C. van Reeuwijk, F. Kuijlman, and H.J. Sips. Spar: a set of extensions of Java for scientific computation. *Concurrency and Computation: Practice and Experience*, accepted for publication.
[11] Edward D. Willink. *Meta-Compilation for C++*. PhD thesis, Computer Science Research Group, University of Surrey, UK, June 2001.
[12] Edward D. Willink and Vyacheslav B. Muchnick. An object-oriented preprocessor fit for C++. *IEE Proceedings – Software*, 147:49–58, April 2000.

A   Example Tree Walker

Given the data structures of Fig. 2, the following tree walker template generates code to rewrite all `NegExpr` instances containing a `ConstExpr` to a new constant expression. To do this, an action function `fold_NegExpr_action` is defined. See the comments in the template and the generated code for further explanation.

```
.macro generate_walker_declaration v t
static $t fold_$t_walker( $t $v );
.endmacro
.macro generate_walker_signature v t
static $t fold_$t_walker( $t $v )
.endmacro
.. Given an indent, an expression, its real type and its
.. perceived type, generate invocation of an action.
.macro generate_action_call i x t n
.if ${eq $t $n}
$i$v = ($t) fold_$t_action( $x );
.else
$i$v = ($t) fold_$t_action( ($t) $x );
.endif
.endmacro
.. Given an indent, an expression, its real type and its
```

```
.. perceived type, generate invocation of a walker.
.macro generate_walker_call i v t n
.if ${eq $t $n}
$i$v = ($t) fold_$t_walker( $v );
.else
$i$v = ($t) fold_$t_walker( ($t) $v );
.endif
.endmacro
.. If 't' has an action, invoke it, else invoke its walker
.macro generate_descent_call i v t n
.if ${member $t $(actors)}
.call generate_action_call "$i" "$v" "$t" "$n"
.else
.call generate_walker_call "$i" "$v" "$t" "$n"
.endif
.endmacro
.set actors NegExpr
.. Insert the macros required for tree walking.
.insert tmcwalk.t
.. Calculate which types must be visited.
.set visit_types ${call calc_treewalk "expr" "$(actors)"}
.. Generated forward declarations for the walker functions
.call generate_walker_forwards "$(visit_types)"

static expr fold_NegExpr_action( NegExpr x )
{
.call generate_walker_call "    " x NegExpr NegExpr
    if( x->x->tag == TAGConstExpr ){
        ConstExpr res = (ConstExpr) (x->x);
        x->x = exprNIL;
        rfre_expr( x );
        res->n = -res->n;
        return (expr) res;
    }
    return x;
}

.. Generate the walker functions.
.call generate_walker "$(visit_types)"
```

When this template is executed, the following code is generated:

```
/* ---------- Generated forward declarations start here ---------- */

/* Forward declarations. */
static AddExpr fold_AddExpr_walker( AddExpr e );
static SubExpr fold_SubExpr_walker( SubExpr e );
static NegExpr fold_NegExpr_walker( NegExpr e );
static expr_list fold_expr_list_walker( expr_list e );
static CallExpr fold_CallExpr_walker( CallExpr e );
static expr fold_expr_walker( expr e );

/* ---------- Generated forward declarations end here ---------- */

static expr fold_NegExpr_action( NegExpr x )
{
    x = (NegExpr) fold_NegExpr_walker( x );
    if( x->x->tag == TAGConstExpr ){
        ConstExpr res = (ConstExpr) (x->x);
        x->x = exprNIL;
        rfre_expr( x );
        res->n = -res->n;
        return (expr) res;
    }
    return x;
}

/* ---------- Generated code starts here ---------- */
```

```
/* Walker for class AddExpr. */
static AddExpr fold_AddExpr_walker( AddExpr e )
{
    e->l = (expr) fold_expr_walker( e->l );
    e->r = (expr) fold_expr_walker( e->r );
}

/* Walker for class SubExpr. */
static SubExpr fold_SubExpr_walker( SubExpr e )
{
    e->l = (expr) fold_expr_walker( e->l );
    e->r = (expr) fold_expr_walker( e->r );
}

/* Walker for class NegExpr. */
static NegExpr fold_NegExpr_walker( NegExpr e )
{
    e->x = (expr) fold_expr_walker( e->x );
}

/* Walker for list expr_list. */
static expr_list fold_expr_list_walker( expr_list e )
{
    {
        unsigned int ix;

        for( ix=0; ix<e->sz; ix++ ){
            e->arr[ix] = (expr) fold_expr_walker( e->arr[ix] );
        }
    }
}

/* Walker for class CallExpr. */
static CallExpr fold_CallExpr_walker( CallExpr e )
{
    e->parms = (expr_list) fold_expr_list_walker( e->parms );
}

/* Walker for class expr. */
static expr fold_expr_walker( expr e )
{
    switch( e->tag ){
        case TAGAddExpr:
            e = (AddExpr) fold_AddExpr_walker( (AddExpr) e );
            break;

        case TAGSubExpr:
            e = (SubExpr) fold_SubExpr_walker( (SubExpr) e );
            break;

        case TAGNegExpr:
            e = (NegExpr) fold_NegExpr_action( (NegExpr) e );
            break;

        case TAGCallExpr:
            e = (CallExpr) fold_CallExpr_walker( (CallExpr) e );
            break;

        default:
            break;

    }
}


/* ----------- Generated code ends here ----------- */
```

The Verifying Compiler: A Grand Challenge for Computing Research

Tony Hoare

Microsoft Research Ltd., 7 JJ Thomson Ave, Cambridge CB3 0FB, UK
thoare@microsoft.com

Abstract. I propose a set of criteria which distinguish a grand challenge in science or engineering from the many other kinds of short-term or long-term research problems that engage the interest of scientists and engineers. As an example drawn from Computer Science, I revive an old challenge: the construction and application of a verifying compiler that guarantees correctness of a program before running it.

1 Introduction

The primary purpose of the formulation and promulgation of a grand challenge is to contribute to the advancement of some branch of science or engineering. A grand challenge represents a commitment by a significant section of the research community to work together towards a common goal, agreed to be valuable and achievable by a team effort within a predicted timescale. The challenge is formulated by the researchers themselves as a focus for the research that they wish to pursue in any case, and which they believe can be pursued more effectively by advance planning and co-ordination. Unlike other common kinds of research initiative, a grand challenge should not be triggered by hope of short-term economic, commercial, medical, military or social benefits; and its initiation should not wait for political promotion or for prior allocation of special funding. The goals of the challenge should be purely scientific goals of the advancement of skill and of knowledge. It should appeal not only to the curiosity of scientists and to the ambition of engineers; ideally it should appeal also to the imagination of the general public; thereby it may enlarge the general understanding and appreciation of science, and attract new entrants to a rewarding career in scientific research.

An opportunity for a grand challenge arises only rarely in the history of any particular branch of science. It occurs when that branch of study first reaches an adequate level of maturity to predict the long-term direction of its future progress, and to plan a project to pursue that direction on an international scale. Much of the work required to achieve the challenge may be of a routine nature. Many scientists will prefer not to be involved in the co-operation and co-ordination involved in a grand challenge. They realize that most scientific advances, and nearly all break-throughs, are accomplished by individuals or small teams, working competitively and in relative isolation. They value their privilege of pursuing bright ideas in new directions at short

G. Hedin (Ed.): CC 2003, LNCS 2622, pp. 262–272, 2003.

notice. It is for these reasons that a grand challenge should always be a minority interest among scientists; and the greater part of the research effort in any branch of science should remain free of involvement in grand challenges.

A grand challenge may involve as much as a thousand man-years of research effort, drawn from many countries and spread over ten years or more. The research skill, experience, motivation and originality that it will absorb are qualities even scarcer and more valuable than the funds that may be allocated to it. For this reason, a proposed grand challenge should be subjected to assessment by the most rigorous criteria before its general promotion and wide-spread adoption. These criteria include all those proposed by Jim Gray [1] as desirable attributes of a long-range research goal.   The additional criteria that are proposed here relate to the maturity of the scientific discipline and the feasibility of the project. In the following list, the earlier criteria emphasize the significance of the goals, and the later criteria relate to the feasibility of the project, and the maturity of the state of the art.

- **Fundamental.** It arises from scientific curiosity about the foundation, the nature, and the limits of an entire scientific discipline, or a significant branch of it.
- **Astonishing.** It gives scope for engineering ambition to build something useful that was earlier thought impractical, thus turning science fiction to science fact.
- **Testable.** It has a clear measure of success or failure at the end of the project; ideally, there should be criteria to assess progress at intermediate stages too
- **Inspiring.** It has enthusiastic support from (almost) the entire research community, even those who do not participate in it, and do not benefit from it.
- **Understandable.** It is generally comprehensible, and captures the imagination of the general public, as well as the esteem of scientists in other disciplines.
- **Useful.** The understanding and knowledge gained in completion of the project bring scientific or other benefits; some of these should be attainable, even if the project as a whole fails in its primary goal.
- **Historical.** The prestigious challenges are those which were formulated long ago; without concerted effort, they would be likely to stand for many years to come.
- **International.** It has international scope, exploiting the skills and experience of the best research groups in the world. The cost and the prestige of the project is shared among many nations, and the benefits are shared among all.
- **Revolutionary.** Success of the project will lead to radical paradigm shift in scientific research or engineering practice. It offers a rare opportunity to break free from the dead hand of legacy.
- **Research-directed.** The project can be forwarded by the reasonably well understood methods of academic research. It tackles goals that will not be achieved solely by commercially motivated evolution of existing products.
- **Challenging.** It goes beyond what is known initially to be possible, and requires development of understanding, techniques and tools unknown at the start.
- **Feasible.** The reasons for previous failure to meet the challenge are well understood and there are good reasons to believe that they can now be overcome.
- **Incremental.** It decomposes into identified intermediate research goals, which can be shared among many separate teams over a long time-scale.
- **Co-operative.** It calls for planned co-operation among identified research teams and research communities with differing specialized skills.

- **Competitive.** It encourages and benefits from competition among individuals and teams pursuing alternative lines of enquiry; there should be clear criteria announced in advance to decide who is winning, or who has won.
- **Effective.** Its promulgation changes the attitudes and activities of research scientists and engineers.
- **Risk-managed.** The risks of failure are identified, symptoms of failure will be recognized early, and strategies for cancellation or recovery are in place.

The tradition of grand challenges is common in many branches of science. If you want to know whether a challenge qualifies for the title 'Grand', compare it with

–	Prove Fermat's last theorem	(accomplished)
–	Put a man on the moon within ten years	(accomplished)
–	Cure cancer within ten years	(failed in 1970s)
–	Map the Human Genome	(accomplished)
–	Map the Human Proteome	(too difficult for now)
–	Find the Higgs boson	(under investigation)
–	Find Gravity waves	(under investigation)
–	Unify the four forces of Physics	(under investigation)
–	Hilbert's programme for mathematical foundations	(abandoned in 1930s)

All of these challenges satisfy many of the criteria listed above in varying degrees, though no individual challenge could be expected to satisfy all the criteria. The first in the list was the oldest and in some ways the grandest challenge; but being a mathematical challenge, my suggested criteria are considerably less relevant for it.

In Computer Science, the following examples may be familiar from the past. That is the reason why they are listed here, **not as recommendations,** but just as examples

–	Prove that P is not equal to NP	(open)
–	The Turing test	(outstanding)
–	The verifying compiler	(abandoned in 1970s)
–	A championship chess program	(completed)
–	A GO program at professional standard	(too difficult)
–	Automatic translation from Russian to English	(failed in 1960s)

The first of these challenges is of the mathematical kind. It may seem to be quite easy to extend this list with new challenges. The difficult part is to find a challenge that passes the tests for maturity and feasibility. The remainder of this contribution picks just one of the challenges, and subjects it to detailed evaluation according to the seventeen criteria.

2   The Verifying Compiler: Implementation and Application

A verifying compiler [2] uses automated mathematical and logical reasoning methods to check the correctness of the programs that it compiles. The criterion of correctness is specified by types, assertions, and other redundant annotations that are associated with the code of the program, often inferred automatically, and increasingly often supplied by the original programmer. The compiler will work in combination with other program development and testing tools, to achieve any desired degree of confidence in the structural soundness of the system and the total correctness of its more critical components. The only limit to its use will be set by an evaluation of the cost and benefits of accurate and complete formalization of the criterion of correctness for the software.

An important and integral part of the project proposal is to evaluate the capabilities and performance of the verifying compiler by application to a representative selection of legacy code, chiefly from open sources. This will give confidence that the engineering compromises that are necessary in such an ambitious project have not damaged its ability to deal with real programs written by real programmers. It is only after this demonstration of capability that programmers working on new projects will gain the confidence to exploit verification technology in new projects.

Note that **the verifying compiler itself does not itself have to be verified.** It is adequate to rely on the normal engineering judgment that errors in a user program are unlikely to be compensated by errors in the compiler. Verification of a verifying compiler is a specialized task, forming a suitable topic for a separate grand challenge.

This proposed grand challenge is now evaluated under the seventeen headings listed in the introduction.

Fundamental.   Correctness of computer programs is the fundamental concern of the theory of programming and of its application in large-scale software engineering. The limits of application of the theory need to be explored and extended. The project is self-contained within Computer Science, since it constructs a computer program to solve a problem that arises only from the very existence of computer programs.

Astonishing.   Most of the general public, and even many programmers, are unaware of the possibility that computers might check the correctness of their own programs; and it does so by the same kind of logical methods that for thousands of years have conferred a high degree of credibility to mathematical theorems.

Testable.   If the project is successful, a verifying compiler will be available as a standard tool in some widely used programming productivity toolset. It will have been tested in verification of structural integrity and security and other desirable properties of millions of lines of open source software, and in more substantial verification of critical parts of it. This will lead to removal of thousands of errors, risks, insecurities and anomalies in widely used code. Proofs will be subjected to check by rival proof tools. The major internal and external interfaces in the software will be documented by assertions, to make existing components safer to use and easier to reuse [3]. The benefits will extend also to the evolution and enhancement of legacy code, as well as the design and development of new code. Eventually programmers will prefer to confine their use of their programming language to those features and structured design patterns which facilitate automatic checks of correctness [4,5].

Inspiring.   Program verification by proof is an absolute scientific ideal, like purity of materials in chemistry or accuracy of measurement in mechanics. These ideals are pursued for their own sake, in the controlled environment of the research laboratory. The practicing engineer in industry has to be content to work around the impurities and inaccuracies that are found in the real world, and often considers laboratory science as unhelpful in discharging this responsibility. The value of purity and accuracy (just like correctness) are often not appreciated until after the scientist has built the tools that make them achievable.

Understandable. All computer users have been annoyed by bugs in mass market software, and will welcome their reduction or elimination. Recent well-known viruses have been widely reported in the press, and have been estimated to cost billions of dollars. Fear of cyber-terrorism is quite widespread [6,7]. Viruses can often obtain entry into a computer system by exploiting errors like buffer overflow, which could be caught quite easily by a verifying compiler [8].

Trustworthy software is now recognised by major vendors as a primary long-term goal [9]. The interest of the press and the public in the project can be maintained, whenever dangerous anomalies are detected and removed from software that is in common use.

Useful. Unreliable software is currently estimated to cost the US some sixty billion dollars [10]. A verifying compiler would be a valued component of the proposed Infrastructure for Software Testing.

A verifying compiler may help accumulate evidence that will help to assess and reduce the risks of incorporation of commercial off-the-shelf software (COTS) into safety critical systems. The project may extend the capabilities of load-time checking of mobile proof-carrying code [11]. It will provide a secure foundation for the achievement of trustworthy software.

The main long-term benefits of the verifying compiler will be realised most strongly in the development and maintenance of new code, specified, designed and tested with its aid. Perhaps we can look forward to the day when normal commercial software will be delivered with an eighty percent chance that it never needs recall or correction by service packs, etc. within the first ten years after delivery. Then the suppliers of commercial and mass-market software will have the confidence to give the normal assurances of fitness for purpose that are now required by law for most other consumer products.

Historical. The idea of using assertions to check a large routine is due to Turing [12]. The idea of the computer checking the correctness of its own programs was put forward by McCarthy [13]. The two ideas were brought together in the verifying compiler by Floyd [14]. Early attempts to implement the idea [15] were severely inhibited by the difficulty of proof support with the machines of that day. At that time, the source code of widely used software was usually kept secret. It was generally written in assembler for a proprietary computer architecture, which was often withdrawn after a short interval on the market. The ephemeral nature and limited distribution for software written by hardware manufacturers reduced motivation for a major verification effort.

Since those days, further difficulties have arisen from the complexities of modern software practice and modern programming languages [16]. Features such as concurrent programming, object orientation and inheritance, have not been designed with the care needed to facilitate program verification. However, the relevant concepts of concurrency and objects have been explored by theoreticians in the 'clean room' conditions of new experimental programming languages [17,18]. In the implementation of a verifying compiler, the results of such pure research will have to be adapted, extended and combined; they must then be implemented and tested by application on a broad scale to legacy code expressed in legacy languages.

International. The project will require collaboration among leading researchers in America, China, India, Australasia, and many countries of Europe. Some of them are mentioned in the Acknowledgements and the References.

Revolutionary. At present, the most widely accepted means of raising trust levels of software is by massive and expensive testing. Assertions are used mainly as test oracles, to detect errors as close as possible to their place of occurrence [19]. Availability of a verifying compiler will encourage programmers to formulate assertions as specifications in advance of code, in the expectation that many of them will be verifiable by automated or semi-automated mathematical techniques. Existing experience of the verified development of safety-critical code [20,21] will be transferred to commercial software for the benefit of mass-market software products.

Research-directed. The methods of research into program verification are well established in the academic research community, though they need to be scaled up to meet the needs of modern software construction. This is unlikely to be achieved solely in industry. Commercial programming tool-sets are driven necessarily by fashionable slogans and by the politics of standardisation. Their elegant pictorial representations can have multiple semantic interpretations, available for adaptation according to the needs and preferences of the customer. The designers of the tools are constrained by compatibility with legacy practices and code, and by lack of scientific education and understanding on the part of their customers.

Challenging. Many of the analysis and verification tools essential to this project are already available, and can be applied now to legacy code [22-27]. But their use is still too laborious, and their improvement over a lengthy period will be necessary to achieve the goals of the challenge. The purpose of this grand challenge is to encourage larger groups to co-operate on the evolution of a small number of tools.

Feasible. Most of the factors which have inhibited progress on practical program verification are no longer as severe as they were.

1. Experience has been gained in specification and verification of moderately scaled systems, chiefly in the area of safety-critical and mission-critical software; but so far the proofs have been mainly manual [20,21].
2. The corpus of Open Source Software [http://sourceforge.net] is now universally available and used by millions, so justifying almost any effort expended on improvement of its quality and robustness. Although it is subject to continuous improvement, the pace of change is reasonably predictable. It is an important part of this challenge to cater for software evolution.

3. Advances in unifying theories of programming [28] suggest that many aspects of correctness of concurrent and object-oriented programs can be expressed by assertions, supplemented by automatic or machine-assisted insertion of instrumentation in the form of ghost (model) variables and assignments to them.
4. Many of the global program analyses which are needed to underpin correctness proofs for systems involving concurrency and pointer manipulation have now been developed for use in optimising compilers [29].
5. Theorem proving technology has made great strides in many directions. Model checking [30-33] is widely understood and used, particularly in hardware design. Decision procedures [34] are beginning to be applied to software. Proof search engines [35] are now well populated with libraries of application-dependent theorems and tactics. Finally, SAT checking [36] promises a step-function increase in the power of proof tools. A major remaining challenge is to find effective ways of combining this wide range of component technologies into a small number of tools, to meet the needs of program verification.
6. Program analysis tools are now available which use a variety of techniques to discover relevant invariants and abstractions [37-39]. It is hoped that that these will formalize at least the program properties relevant to its structural integrity, with a minimum of human intervention.
7. Theories relevant for the correctness of concurrency are well established [40-42]; and theories for object orientation and pointer manipulation are under development [43,44].

Incremental. The progress of the project can be assessed by the number of lines of legacy code that have been verified, and the level of annotation and verification that has been achieved. The relevant levels of annotation are: structural integrity, partial functional specification, specification of total correctness. The relevant levels of verification are: by testing, by human proof, with machine assistance, and fully automatic. Most software is now at the lowest level – structural integrity verified by massive testing. It will be interesting to record the incremental achievement of higher levels by individual modules of code, and to find out how widely the higher levels are reasonably achievable; few modules are likely to reach the highest level of full verification.

Cooperative. The work can be delegated to teams working independently on the annotation of code, on verification condition generation, and on the proof tools.

1. The existing corpus of Open Source Software can easily be parcelled out to different teams for analysis and annotation; and the assertions can be checked by massive testing in advance of availability of adequate proof tools.
2. It is now standard for a compiler to produce an abstract syntax tree from the source code, together with a data base of program properties. A compiler that exposes the syntax tree would enable many researchers to collaborate on program analysis algorithms, test harnesses, test case generators, verification condition generators, and other verification and validation tools.
3. Modern proof tools permit extension by libraries of specialized theories [34]; these can be developed by many hands to meet the needs of each application. In

particular, proof procedures can be developed that are specific to commonly used standard application programmer interfaces for legacy code [45].

Competitive.   The main source of competition is likely to be between teams that work on different programming languages. Some laboratories may prefer to concentrate on older languages, starting with C and moving on to C++. Others may prefer to concentrate on newer languages like Java or C#.

But even teams working on the same language and on the same tool may compete in achieving higher levels of verification for larger and larger modules of code. There will be competition to find errors in legacy code, and to be the first to obtain mechanical proof of the correctness of all assertions in each module of software. The annotated libraries of open source code will be good competition material for the teams constructing and applying proof tools. The proofs themselves will be subject to confirmation or refutation by rival proof tools.

Effective.   The promulgation of this challenge is intended to cause a shift in the motivations and activities of scientists and engineers in all the relevant research communities. They will be pioneers in the collaborative implementation and use of a single large experimental device, following a tradition that is well established in Astronomy and Physics but not yet in Computer science.

1. Researchers in programming theory will accept the challenge of extending proof technology for programs written in complex and uncongenial legacy languages. They will need to design program analysis algorithms to test whether actual legacy programs observe the constraints that make each theoretical proof technique valid.
2. Builders of programming tools will carry out experimental implementation of the hypotheses originated by theorists; following practice in experimental branches of science, their goal is to explore the range of application of the theory to real code.
3. Sympathetic software users will allow newly inserted assertions to be checked dynamically in production runs, even before the tools are available to verify them.
4. Empirical Computer Scientists will apply tools developed by others to the analysis and verification of representative large-scale examples of open code.
5. Compiler writers will support the proof goals by adapting and extending the program analyses currently used for optimisation of code; later they may even exploit for purposes of further optimization the additional redundant information provided with a verified program.
6. Providers of proof tools will regard the project as a fruitful source of low-level conjectures needing verification, and will evolve their algorithms and libraries of theories to meet the needs of actual legacy software and its users.
7. Teachers and students of the foundations of software engineering will be enthused to set student projects that annotate and verify a small part of a large code base, so contributing to the success of a world-wide project.

Risk-managed.   The main risks to the project arise from dissatisfaction of many academic scientists with existing legacy code and legacy languages. The low quality of existing software, and its low level of abstraction, may limit the benefit to be obtained from the annotations. Many failures of proof are not due to an error at all, but just to omission of a more or less obvious precondition. Many of the genuine errors detected may be so rare that they are not worth correcting. In other cases, preservation of an existing anomaly in legacy software may be essential to its continuing functionality. Often the details of functionality of interfaces, either with humans or with hardware devices, are not worth formalising in a total specification, because testing gives an easier but adequate assurance of serviceability.

Legacy languages add to the risks of the project. From a logical point of view, they are extremely complicated, and require sophisticated analyses to ensure that they observe the disciplines that make abstract program verification possible. Finally, one must recognize that many of the problems of present-day software use are associated with configuration and installation management, build files, etc, where techniques of program verification seem unable to contribute.

The idealistic solution to these problems is to discard legacy and start again from scratch. Ideals are (or should be) the prime motivating force for academic research, and their pursuit gives scope for many different grand challenges. One such challenge would involve design of a new programming language and compiler, especially designed to support verification; and another would involve a re-write of existing libraries and applications to the higher standards that are achievable by explicit consideration and simplification of abstract interfaces. Research on new languages and libraries is in itself desirable, and would assist and complement research based on legacy languages and software.

Finally, it must be recognized that a verifying compiler will be only part of a integrated and rational tool-set for reliable software construction and evolution, based on sound scientific principles. Much of its use may be confined to the relatively lower levels of verification. It is a common fate of grand challenges that achievement of their direct goal turns out to be less directly significant than the stimulus that its pursuit has given to the progress of science and engineering. But remember, that was the primary purpose of the whole exercise.

Acknowledgements. The content and presentation of this contribution has emerged from fruitful discussions with many colleagues. There is no implication that any member of this list actually supports the proposed challenge. Ralph Back, Andrew Black, Manfred Broy, Alan Bundy, Michael Ernst, David Evans, Chris George, Mike Gordon, Armando Haeberer, Joseph Halpern, He Jifeng, Jim Horning, Gilles Kahn, Dick Kieburtz, Butler Lampson, Rustan Leino, John McDermid, Bertrand Meyer, Jay Misra, J Moore, Oege de Moor, Greg Morrisett, Robin Milner, Peter O'Hearn, Larry Paulson, Jon Pincus, Amir Pnueli, John Reynolds, John Rushby, Natarajan Shankar, Martyn Thomas, Niklaus Wirth, Jim Woodcock, Zhou Chaochen, and many others.

This article is an extended version of a contribution [46] to the fiftieth anniversary issue of the *Journal of the ACM*, which was devoted to Grand Challenges in Computer Science. It is published here with the approval of the Editor and the kind permission of the ACM.

References

[1]   J Gray, What Next? A Dozen Information-technology Research Goals, MS-TR-50, Microsoft Research, June 1999.

[2]   KM. Leino and G Nelson. An extended static checker for Modula-3. *Compiler Construction:, CC'98*, LNCS 1383, Springer, pp 302–305., April 1998.
[3]   B Meyer, *Object-Oriented Software Construction*, 2nd edition, Prentice Hall, 1997
[4]   A Hall and R Chapman: Correctness by Construction: Developing a Commercial Secure System, IEEE Software 19(1): 18–25 (2002)
[5]   T Jim, G Morrisett, D Grossman, M Hicks, J Cheney, and Y Wang. Cyclone: A safe dialect of C. In USENIX Annual Technical Conference, Monterey, CA, June 2002.
[6]   See http://www.fbi.gov/congress/congress02/nipc072402.htm, a congressional statement presented by the director of the National Infrastructure Protection Center.
[7]   FB Schneider (ed), *Trust in Cyberspace*, Committee on Information Systems Trustworthiness, National Research Council (1999),
[8]   D Wagner, J Foster, E Brewer, and A Aiken. A first step towards automated detection of buffer overrun vulnerabilities. In Network and Distributed System Security Symposium, San Diego, CA, February 2000
[9]   WH Gates, internal communication, Microsoft Corporation, 2002
[10]   Planning Report 02-3. The Economic Impacts of Inadequate Infrastructure for Software Testing, prepared by RTI for NIST, US Department of Commerce, May 2002
[11]   G Necula. Proof-carrying code. In Proceedings of the 24th Annual ACM SIGPLAN-SIGACT Symposium on Principles of Programming Languages (POPL '97), January 1997
[12]   AM Turing, Checking a large routine, *Report on a Conference on High Speed Automatic Calculating machines,* Cambridge University Math. Lab. (1949) 67–69
[13]   J McCarthy, Towards a mathematical theory of computation, Proc. IFIP Cong. 1962, North Holland, (1963)
[14]   RW Floyd, Assigning meanings to programs, *Proc. Amer. Soc. Symp. Appl. Math.* **19,** (1967) pp 19–31
[15]   JC King, A Program Verifier, PhD thesis, Carnegie-Mellon University (1969)
[16]   B Stroustrup, *The C++ Programming Language*, Adison-Wesley, 1985
[17]   A Igarashi, B Pierce, and P Wadler. Featherweight Java: A Minimal Core Calculus for Java and GJ, OOPSLA`99, pp. 132–146, 1999.
[18]   Haskell 98 language and libraries: the Revised Report, Journal of Functional Programming 13(1) Jan 2003.
[19]   CAR Hoare, Assertions, to appear, Marktoberdorf Summer School, 2002.
[20]   S Stepney, D Cooper and JCPW Woodcock, An Electronic Purse: Specification, Refinement, and Proof, PRG-126, Oxford University Computing Laboratory, July 2000.
[21]   AJ Galloway, TJ Cockram and JA McDermid, Experiences with the application of discrete formal methods to the development of engine control software, Hise York (1998)
[22]   WR Bush, JD Pincus, and DJ Sielaff, A static analyzer for finding dynamic programming errors, Software -- Practice and Experience 2000 (30): pp. 775–802.
[23]   D Evans and D Larochelle, *Improving Security Using Extensible Lightweight Static Analysis*, IEEE Software, Jan/Feb 2002.
[24]   S Hallem, B Chelf, Y Xie, and D Engler, A System and Language for Building System-Specific Static Analyses, PLDI 2002.
[25]   GC Necula, S McPeak, and W Weimer, CCured: Type-safe retrotting of legacy code. In 29th ACM Symposium on Principles of Programming Languages, Portland, OR, Jan 2002
[26]   U Shankar, K Talwar, JS Foster, and D Wagner. Detecting format string vulnerabilities with type qualifiers, Proceedings of the 10th USENIX Security Symposium, 2001
[27]   D Evans. Static detection of dynamic memory errors, SIGPLAN Conference on Programming Languages Design and Implementation, 1996
[28]   CAR Hoare and He Jifeng. *Unifying Theories of Programming*, Prentice Hall, 1998.
[29]   E Ruf, Context-sensitive alias analysis reconsidered, Sigplan Notices, 30 (6), June 1995
[30]   GJ Holzmann, *Design and Validation of Computer Protocols*, Prentice Hall, 1991

[31] AW Roscoe, Model-Checking CSP, *A Classical Mind: Essays in Honour of C.A.R. Hoare*, Prentice-Hall International, pp 353–378, 1994

[32] M Musuvathi, DYW Park, A Chou, DR. Engler, DL Dill. CMC: A pragmatic approach to model checking real code, to appear in OSDI 2002.

[33] N Shankar, Machine-assisted verification using theorem-proving and model checking, *Mathematical Methods of Program Development,* NATO ASI Vol 138, Springer, pp 499–528 (1997)

[34] MJC Gordon, HOL: A proof generating system for Higher-Order Logic, *VLSI Specification, Verification and Synthesis*, Kluwer (1988) pp. 73–128

[35] N Shankar, PVS: Combining specification, proof checking, and model checking. FMCAD '96,LNCS 1166, Springer, pp 257–264, Nov 1996

[36] M Moskewicz, C Madigan, Y Zhao, L Zhang, S Malik, Chaff: Engineering an Efficient SAT Solver, 38th Design Automation Conference (DAC2001), Las Vegas, June 2001

[37] T Ball, SK Rajamani, Automatically Validating Temporal Safety Properties of Interfaces, *SPIN 2001,* LNCS 2057, May 2001, pp. 103–122.

[38] JW Nimmer and MD Ernst, Automatic generation of program specifications, *Proceedings of the 2002 International Symposium on Software Testing and Analysis*, 2002, pp. 232–242.

[39] C Flanagan and KRM Leini, Houdini, an annotation assistant for ESC/Java. *International Symposium of Formal Methods Europe 2001*, LNCS 2021, Springer pp 500–517, 2001

[40] R Milner, *Communicating and Mobile Systems: the pi Calculus*, CUP, 1999

[41] AW Roscoe, *Theory and Practice of Concurrency*, Prentice Hall, 1998

[42] KM Chandy and J Misra, *Parallel Program Design: a Foundation*, Adison-Wesley, 1988

[43] P O'Hearn, J Reynolds and H Yang, Local Reasoning about Programs that Alter Data Structures, Proceedings of CSL'01 Paris, LNCS 2142, Springer, pp 1–19, 2001.

[44] CAR Hoare and He Jifeng, A Trace Model for Pointers and Objects, ECOOP, LNCS 1628, Springer (1999), pp 1–17

[45] A Stepanov and Meng Lee, Standard Template Library, Hewlett Packard (1994)

[46] CAR Hoare, The Verifying Compiler: a Grand Challenge for Computer Research, JACM (50) 1, pp 63–69 (2003)

Address Register Assignment for Reducing Code Size

M. Kandemir[1], M.J. Irwin[1], G. Chen[1], and J. Ramanujam[2]

[1] CSE Department
Pennsylvania State University
University Park, PA 16802
{kandemir,mji,guilchen}@cse.psu.edu
[2] ECE Department
Louisiana State University
Baton Rouge, LA 70803
jxr@ee.lsu.edu

Abstract. In DSP processors, minimizing the amount of address calculations is critical for reducing code size and improving performance since studies of programs have shown that instructions that manipulate address registers constitute a significant portion of the overall instruction count (up to 55%). This work presents a compiler-based optimization strategy to reduce the code size in embedded systems. Our strategy maximizes the use of indirect addressing modes with post-increment and post-decrement capabilities available in DSP processors. These modes can be exploited by ensuring that successive references to variables access consecutive memory locations. To achieve this spatial locality, our approach uses both access pattern modification (program code restructuring) and memory storage reordering (data layout restructuring).

1 Introduction

Address calculations play a key role in determining code quality in DSP processors since instructions that manipulate address registers constitute a significant portion of overall instruction count. For example, it was found that for a set of codes from MediaBench suite (a popular benchmark suite for embedded systems) running on Motorola's DSP56000 processor, nearly 55% of the instructions are used to manipulate address registers through explicit loads and stores [15]. Consequently, optimizing address code generation by eliminating as many explicit address register loads as possible can result in significant improvements in code size and performance. Note that code size improvements are very important not only because code size directly determines the capacity of the customized instruction memory (hence, its cost) in an embedded system, but also because a smaller instruction memory means lower power consumption.

Address calculations in modern DSPs such as NEC 7701, Motorola DSP56000, Analog Devices ADSP21xx, and Texas Instruments TMS320C5x are done in address generation units (AGUs). An AGU contains a number of

G. Hedin (Ed.): CC 2003, LNCS 2622, pp. 273–289, 2003.

address registers, the contents of which can be incremented or decremented in parallel with the ongoing activity in the main datapath. The instruction format for such processors allows one to encode a CPU activity and a post-increment/decrement of an address register in a single instruction. Thus, using post-increment/decrement operations instead of explicit address register loads enhances on-chip parallelism (performance) and reduces code size (as no separate instruction is necessary to update the address register). Cintra and Araujo [3] report that although some of the register increment/decrement operations can be accommodated in VLIW instruction slots, modern VLIW DSP architectures also have auto-increment and auto-decrement modes; this is because exploiting these modes effectively saves one instruction slot which might be used for some other operation.

An optimizing compiler can exploit these post-increment/decrement operations by performing computation and data transformations as well as by assigning variables to address registers optimally. Consider the following scenario where three scalar variables c, a, and b are to be accessed in the order c,a,b in a given DSP code. Also assume that the AGU in question has a single address register that can be post-incremented/decremented by 1 and that these three variables are stored in memory in the order a, b, c. The code for implementing this sequence of accesses uses three steps. The first step loads the address register with the address of c (the first variable in the access sequence). To access the variable a next, the second step loads the address of a into the address register. In accessing the variable a, a post-increment operation can be used to modify the content of the address register so that it points to b which will be accessed next. In the final step, the variable b is accessed. Overall, we need to perform two explicit address register loads. In addition to being a waste of machine cycles, this increases code size and thereby the instruction memory size, which is at a premium in many embedded designs.

We can reduce this overhead of explicitly updating the address register by using a better choice of the order in which the variables are stored in data memory. Instead of the storage order a, b, c in the previous scenario, we can eliminate one of the two address register loads if we use the storage order c, a, b. In this case, first, we load the address register with the address of c and post-increment the address register to make sure that, after the execution of the statement that accesses c, it will point to the next location (which contains a). Next, we access the variable a, and use again post-increment to make the address register point to the variable b. Finally, we access the variable b. This problem of determining the most suitable storage order of variables is called the *offset assignment problem* and has been partially addressed by Bartley [1], Liao et al. [10,11], and others (e.g., [9,15]). Basically, these solutions first determine a suitable storage order for variables and then assign address registers to these variables to minimize the number of address register loads. In essence, since we are determining the contents of the address register(s) before each variable access, this problem can also be defined as the address register assignment problem.

A major limitation of the techniques proposed so far for the address register assignment problem is that they either focus only on modifying the storage order of variables (e.g., [10,11]) or only on modifying the intra-statement access pattern using commutativity and associativity transformations (e.g., [13]). In this work, we present a framework that considers both computation-based (intra-statement and inter-statement) transformations and storage-based optimizations in a unified setting for "reducing the code size of a given application;" that is, our main objective is to save the code space. More specifically, this work makes the following contributions.

(1) It presents an algorithm based on access pattern modification that makes efficient use of post-increment/decrement addressing modes in DSPs. This algorithm assumes a fixed storage order for variables and restructures the code to exploit these addressing modes. This algorithm is more general than the one proposed in [13] as it considers both intra-statement and inter-statement transformations.

(2) It gives an algorithm that modifies an access pattern (access sequences), given a partially-fixed storage order. A partially-fixed storage order is a storage order in which the memory locations of only a subset of the variables are fixed.

(3) It combines these two algorithms with the storage order-based optimization strategy (i.e., offset assignment) developed by Liao et al. [11], and presents a unified approach (which is demonstrated to be superior) to handle the offset assignment problem for a given control flow graph.

2   Review of Offset Assignment

The offset assignment problem [10] is one of assigning a frame-relative offset (i.e., storage location) to each variable in the code in order to minimize the number of address arithmetic instructions (that is, the instructions that load a new value to the address register) required to execute the code. The cost of an offset assignment is defined as the number of such instructions.

Given a code sequence, we can define a unique *access sequence* for it. In an operation a = b op c, where 'op' is some binary operator, the access sequence is given by b, c, a. The access sequence for an ordered set of operations is simply the concatenated access sequences for each operation taken in order. For example, for the code fragment

```
a = c + d
d = d + c + b + c + a
```

the access sequence is c, d, a, d, c, b, c, a, d, assuming that addition is left-associative. Let us assume that the variables in this code fragment are stored in memory in the following order: a, b, c, d. The cost of a given storage sequence (offset assignment) is the number of consecutive accesses (in the access sequence) for which the accessed variables are *not* assigned to adjacent locations in memory. Therefore, the cost of the offset assignment given above is four as there are four transitions in the access sequence between non-adjacent variables.

The objective of the offset assignment problem is to determine a storage order for variables such that the cost will be minimum. Liao [10] showed that the offset assignment problem is equivalent to the Maximum Weighted Path Cover (MWPC) problem and proved that it is NP-complete. His heuristic solution was later improved by Leupers and Marwedel [9] who presented a tie-breaking strategy for achieving better storage assignments.

3   Computation Restructuring for a Fully Fixed Storage Sequence

Code size reduction using address register assignment is achieved by making the *access sequence* (i.e., the order in which the variables are accessed) and the *storage sequence* (i.e., the storage order of the variables in memory) compatible. In practice, it is possible to do either of the following: modify the access sequence for a fixed storage sequence, or modify the storage sequence for a given fixed access sequence. In this section, we discuss a strategy that adopts the former approach as opposed to Liao's scheme [10] which takes the latter approach. In this work, we apply code transformations to a high-level intermediate representation (IR) of the code where optimizations such as conventional (e.g., graph coloring-based) register allocation and common subexpression elimination have already been performed. This IR has statements very similar to high-level source statements. In the remainder of this presentation, when we mention statement, we actually refer to this IR-level statement. However, to make the presentation clear, we use source-level (C-like) statements. Consider, a statement of the following form

```
a = b + c
```

Let us assume that the machine has a single address register and that the storage sequence is c, b, a. The access sequence in this example is b, c, a, which is different from the storage sequence. As a result of this, going from variable c to variable a incurs an explicit address register load (since c and a are not consecutive in the storage sequence, so we cannot use post-increment/decrement mode). Liao's approach [10] fixes this problem by modifying the storage sequence from c, b, a to b, c, a. Changing the storage sequence is a viable option provided that the variables have not yet been assigned to storage locations, or (if they have already been assigned to locations) the cost of transforming the storage sequence from one form to another (which may require copying resulting in additional memory requirements) does not outweigh its benefits. An access pattern-oriented approach, on the other hand, can optimize this code by transforming this statement into

```
a = c + b
```

The new access sequence is c, b, a which is the same as the storage sequence. Note that, for this example, just applying commutativity transformation (an intra-statement transformation) was sufficient to obtain the desired result.

Let us consider the following code fragment with two statements.

```
a = c + e
b = c + f
```

We assume a single address register and a storage sequence of a, b, c, d, e, f. It should be noted that each variable access in this code fragment (under the assumed storage sequence) will require a load to the address register. A storage layout-oriented scheme would change the storage sequence of the variables, but this may be too costly if the variables have already been assigned to storage locations (for example, during the optimization of a different set of statements that manipulate the same variables.) On the other hand, a commutativity transformation would lead to

```
a = c + e
b = f + c
```

Note that this code fragment (which is obtained from the previous one by applying commutativity transformation to the right-hand side of the second assignment statement) eliminates one of the explicit loads to the address register. That is, in going from c to b in the second assignment statement, we can make use of the post-decrement mode (as these two variables are consecutive in memory). An inter-statement transformation, on the other hand, can generate the following program fragment

```
b = f + c
a = c + e
```

Note that this code fragment is obtained from the original one by interchanging the order of two statements and by applying commutativity transformation to one of the statements. In this case, two variable accesses (i.e., going from c to b in the first statement, and going from b in the first statement to c in the second statement) can be satisfied using post-increment/decrement modes. This is a simple example that illustrates the benefit of inter-statement optimization. However, there are some cases where it is not possible to interchange the order of statements due to data dependency constraints. For example, in the code fragment

```
a = a + c
c = c + 1
```

interchanging two statements would give a wrong result as the value used for c in a = a + c would be different than the one in the original case. Here, a storage-oriented approach (e.g., [10]), on the other hand, could store a and c in consecutive locations in memory, thereby leading to the effective use of post-increment and decrement addressing modes.

The preceding examples show that neither storage based techniques nor access sequence (computation) based techniques (intra and inter statement transformations) dominate the other, and a unified framework that uses both the techniques may be needed for better results. In the rest of this section, we formulate the computation oriented transformations using a graph-based representation.

3.1   Terminology

We represent a program using a control flow graph (CFG) which is a directed graph in which each node denotes a basic block and an edge between two basic blocks indicates that there is a possibility that the flow of control (during execution) may be transfered from one of these basic blocks to the other. A basic block can be defined informally as a straight-line sequence of statements that can be entered only at the beginning and exited only at the end [16].

Consider a graph $G = (V, E)$ where V is the set of nodes (vertices) and E is the set of edges. A path cover (or cover) C of a given graph $G(V, E)$ is a set of paths such that every node in V is incident at some edge belonging to the chosen set of paths. In other words, we can think of a cover $C(V', E')$ as a subgraph of $G(V, E)$ where $V' = V$ and $E' \subseteq E$. The length of a path is the number of edges in the path, and the length of a cover is the sum of the number of edges of each constituent path. A path that has the maximum length (among all paths in the cover) is referred to as the longest path.

3.2   Layout Transition Graph

Given a basic block, we use a *layout transition graph* (LTG) to show the connections between elements that are stored consecutively in memory. The layout transition graph of a basic block is a directed graph $LTG(V, E)$, where each node v_i represents a variable that occurs in the basic block; and a directed edge $e = (v_i, v_j)$ from a node v_i to a node v_j indicates that the variable represented by v_i is stored (in memory) next to the variable represented by v_j. Whether v_i comes before v_j in the storage order or after v_j is not important for the purposes of this work (as long as they are consecutive in memory). An LTG also contains an edge from v_i to v_j if these two nodes represent the occurrences of the same variable. Note that the variable access pattern of a program touches all the nodes of the corresponding LTG.

For ease of exposition, we divide a given LTG into layers, each layer corresponding to a statement in the basic block. If the basic block contains K statements, each variable v_i in the jth statement from top (denoted s_j where $1 \leq j \leq K$) is assumed to belong to the variable set of s_j; we express this as $v_i \in s_j$. We will use s_j to denote both the statement and its variable set, where there is no confusion.

A given variable set s_i can also be divided into two logical subsets: one that contains the variable on the left hand side (LHS), and one that contains the variables on the right hand side (RHS). For a variable set s_i, the first subset is denoted by s_{iL} and the second subset is denoted by s_{iR}.

To illustrate these concepts, consider the LTG shown in Figure 1(i) for the statement a = b + c, assuming that the storage sequence is c, b, a. There is a bi-directional edge between c and b (i.e., we have a directed edge from c to b and one from b to c), and another bi-directional edge between b and a. Labeling this statement by s_1, we have $s_{1L} = \{a\}$ and $s_{1R} = \{b, c\}$. Note that the access sequence for this statement is b, c, a as shown in Figure 1(iii) using dashed arrows. It should also be noted that a new access sequence can be obtained by traversing the edges in the LTG in a different manner. If we start from the variable c, we can first traverse the edge (c,b) and then the edge (b,a), as depicted in Figure 1(iv). Note that this new traversal corresponds to transforming the statement from a = b + c to a = c + b (i.e., a commutativity transformation).

We need to emphasize that it may not always be possible to transform a statement based on its LTG. Further, not every traversal of the edges in the LTG is legal. For example, going from a to b using the edge (a,b) is not acceptable (see Figure 1(v)) as all the right-hand side references should be accessed before the left hand side reference. We can prevent some of the transitions such as this by eliminating edges from the LTG that would lead to unacceptable or infeasible transformations. For example, in order to prevent a transformation from a to b, we eliminate the directed edge from a to b as shown in Figure 1(ii). Obviously, given the two legal traversals in Figures 1(iii) and (iv), we prefer the one in Figure 1(iv) as all transitions between variables in this figure are between consecutive memory locations, meaning that we can use post-increment/decrement mode for these transitions. Another way of expressing this is that both the edges visited during the traversal in Figure 1(iv) belong to the LTG given in Figure 1(ii). On the other hand, one of the transitions taken during the traversal in Figure 1(iii) (the transition from c to a) does not have any corresponding edge in the LTG. Therefore, the objective of a traversal must be minimizing the number of transitions that do not correspond to an edge in the LTG. We will formalize this concept later.

Now, let us consider the LTG given in Figure 1(vi) for the following program fragment.

```
a = c + e
b = c + f
```

It is assumed here that the storage sequence is a, b, c, d, e, f. As before, a traversal of the nodes of this LTG corresponds to a specific access sequence. The default access sequence is c, e, a, c, f, b as shown in Figure 1(viii). Note that a different traversal of the nodes corresponds to a transformation of the code sequence. Here, an important point should be noted. In traversing the nodes (or edges), we have a restriction in the sense that once we are in a statement we need to finish all the nodes in the statement before moving to a node in another statement. That is, we are not allowed to go from a node in s_{kR} to a node in $s_{k'R}$ if $k \neq k'$, assuming that each statement has a left hand side variable.

The preceding discussion indicates that we need some restrictions on the traversal order of the nodes in the LTG. For this purpose, we use a modified form of the LTG called *constrained layout transition graph* (CLTG), and perform our traversal on this graph. Simply, in those cases where the compiler can detect that variable v_i in statement s_k cannot be accessed immediately after the variable v_j in statement $s_{k'}$ (s_k and $s_{k'}$ are not necessarily distinct here), the corresponding edge (if any) from v_j to v_i in the LTG should be removed when constructing the CLTG (Instead of deleting edges from the LTG to construct the CLTG, it is possible to directly construct the CLTG using the necessary edges, albeit using somewhat more complicated rules. The correctness of the algorithms is not affected by the choice of either method to construct the CLTG).

A constrained layout transition graph, written $CLTG(V', E')$, is a subgraph of the $LTG(V, E)$ such that $V' = V$ and E' contains all the edges in E *except* those that can lead to an incorrect or infeasible code transformation. The construction of the CLTG subsumes both the intra-statement constraints (i.e., evaluation rules that need to be obeyed when processing an RHS expression) and the inter-statement constraints (i.e., dependence and other constraints between statements). For example, a CLTG cannot contain an edge between the variable occurrences of the right hand sides of two different assignment statements. In mathematical terms, an edge $e = (v_i, v_j) \in E$ does not belong to E' if $v_i \in s_{kR}$ and $v_i \in s_{k'R}$, where $k \neq k'$. Figure 1(vii) depicts the CLTG for the LTG in Figure 1(vi). Note that the default traversal (access sequence) given in Figure 1(viii) does not use any of the edges in the underlying CLTG. Consequently, an explicit address register load is necessary prior to each variable access. Now consider the traversal given in Figure 1(ix). In this case, the new access sequence corresponds to a transformation in which the right hand side of the second statement is transformed using commutativity. Note that one of the transitions in this traversal (i.e., the one from c to b) has a corresponding edge in the CLTG given in Figure 1(vii). Finally, let us focus on the traversal given in Figure 1(x). The transformation corresponding to this traversal is one of interchanging the order of the two statements and applying the commutativity transformation to one of the statements. In this traversal, two transitions, one going from c to b and the other going from b to c have corresponding edges in the CLTG. These two examples in Figure 1 show that the preferred traversal must maximize the number of transitions that have corresponding edges in the underlying CLTG. In other words, it should minimize the number of transitions that do not have corresponding edges in the CLTG.

It should be noted, however, that although a given CLTG shows possible legal transitions between nodes, it is still possible to generate an illegal traversal (access sequence) on the CLTG. For example, by itself, accessing two nodes v_i and v_j consecutively may not break any dependence; however, after this modified access sequence, it may not be possible to generate legal code due to a new restriction (in the access order) resulting from the said transition between v_i and v_j.

3.3   Traversing the CLTG

We formulate the problem of modifying a given basic block code for effective use of the address register(s) as one of determining a path cover and a traversal order in the CLTG. We assume for now that the AGU has only a single address register.

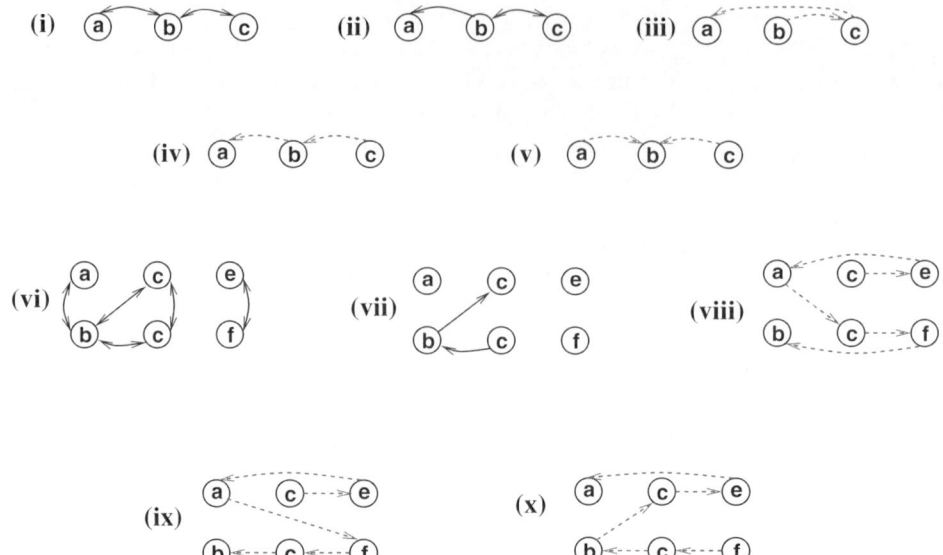

Fig. 1. (i-v) LTG, CLTG, and different traversals for an assignment statement under the storage sequence c, b, a. (vi-x) LTG, CLTG, and different traversals for a program fragment under the storage sequence a, b, c, d, e, f.

Legality. In order to generate correct code (that is, to preserve the original semantics of the basic block), we impose the following conditions on the traversal order:

(1) Each node in the LTG (i.e., a variable occurrence in the basic block) should be visited.

(2) For a given layer in the LTG corresponding to the statement s_k, all nodes in s_{kR} should be visited before any node in s_{kL}.

(3) Once the traversal reaches the layer corresponding to the statement s_k, it should finish all the variables in that layer (i.e., the set $s_{kL} \cup s_{kR}$) before moving to another layer.

(4) All the data dependences and other restrictions such as latency constraints or expression evaluation constraints should be observed.

Condition (1) indicates that each variable should be touched (by any legal execution of the code). We enforce Condition (4) by ensuring that we do not make a transition from a $v_i \in s_k$ to a $v_j \in s_{k'}$ (even if v_i and v_j are consecutive in memory) when there is a data dependence from $s_{k'}$ to s_k. To enforce Condition (2), we do not allow a transition from the node $v_i \in s_{kL}$ to a node $v_j \in s_{kR}$. To enforce Condition (3), we disallow transitions between node $v_i \in s_{kR}$ and any node $v_j \in s_{k'R}$ for $k \neq k'$. A transition from a node $v_i \in s_{kL}$ to a node $v_j \in s_{k'L}$ (where $k \neq k'$) is allowed only if $s_{k'}$ has no variables on the right hand side (i.e., $s_{k'R} = \emptyset$). Also, there cannot be a transition from a node $v_i \in s_{kR}$ to a node

$v_j \in s_{k'L}$ (where $k \neq k'$) unless $s_{k'}$ has no variable on the right hand side (i.e., $s_{k'R} = \emptyset$) and s_k has no LHS variable, which cannot occur in our framework.

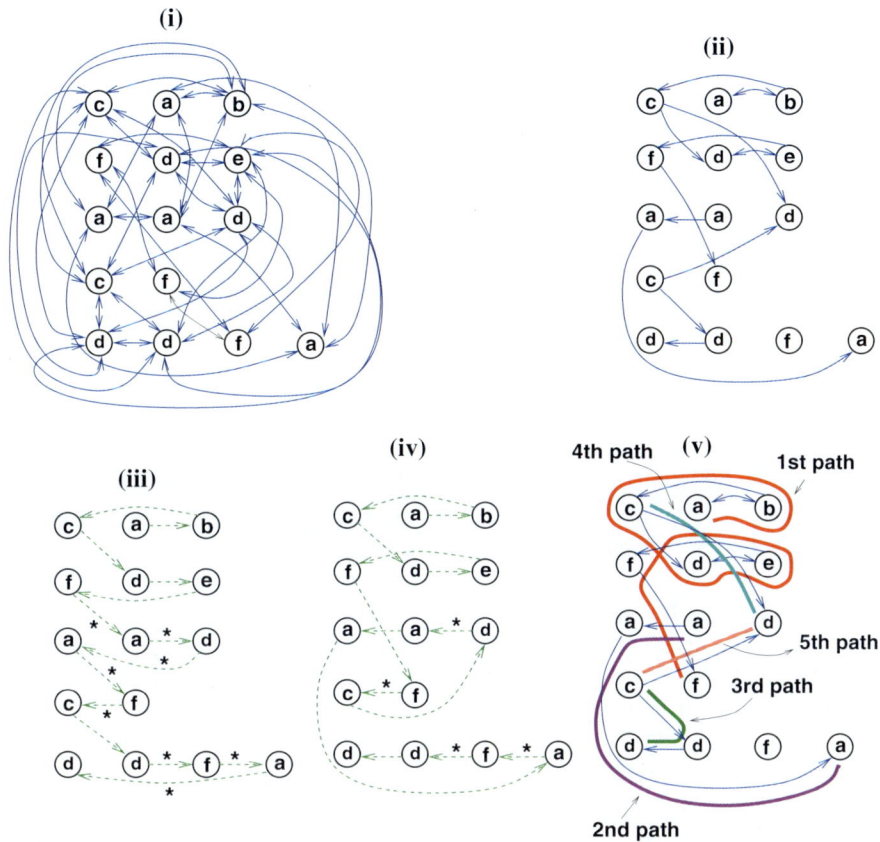

Fig. 2. (i) LTG and (ii) CLTG for a given basic block. (iii) Default access sequence. (iv) Optimized access sequence. (v) Example paths in the CLTG.

Profitability. The objective of the traversal of the nodes in the CLTG is to minimize the *cost of the traversal,* which is defined as the number of transitions from a node v_i to a node v_j such that v_i and v_j are not consecutive in the storage sequence (i.e., there is no edge (v_i, v_j) in the CLTG) for all i and j. It should be noted that a storage sequence imposes constraints on the CLTG. If a transition from v_i to v_j does not use an edge in the CLTG, this means that a post-increment or a post-decrement cannot be used for this transition; thus, new value should be loaded in the address register (using an explicit load instruction), thereby increasing the code size. As a result, the cost of a traversal can be viewed as the number of transitions in the access sequence that do *not* use an edge in the CLTG. Thus, the address register assignment problem can be re-expressed as

> *determining a traversal of the nodes in the CLTG—subject to the four legality conditions listed above—that minimizes the number of transitions that do not correspond to an edge in the CLTG.*

It can be shown that this problem is NP-complete; but, we omit the proof due to lack of space.

Let us now concentrate on the larger basic block given below assuming a storage sequence of a, b, c, d, e, f.

```
c = a + b
f = d - e - 2
a = a + 3d
c = 2f + 4
d = d + f + a
```

Figures 2(i) and (ii) show the LTG and CLTG, respectively, for this code fragment under the assumed storage sequence. Note that, in going from the LTG to the CLTG, many edges are dropped as they are not possible for any legal traversal. Figure 2(iii) shows the default access sequence (i.e., without any optimization). This access sequence has a cost of eight, and the transitions that contribute to this cost are marked using the symbol '*'. Our approach, on the other hand, results in the access sequence (traversal) given in Figure 2(iv). We see that the cost of this access sequence is four (again, the transitions that contribute to the cost are marked using the symbol '*'). In other words, we are able to eliminate four address register loads in the code. This traversal corresponds to the following transformed program:

```
c = a + b
f = d - e - 2
c = 2f + 4
a = 3d + a
d = a + f + d
```

Note that this optimized code is obtained from the original one through one statement reordering (inter-statement transformation) and a number of intra-statement transformations.

The Algorithm and Transformations. We now present an algorithm that takes as input a CLTG and generates as output a traversal (an access sequence) and all the necessary (inter-statement and intra-statement) transformations to obtain this access sequence. Given a CLTG, the algorithm first detects the longest directed path (i.e., the path that contains the maximum number of edges in the same direction).[1] It then transforms the portion of the CLTG (which contains a subset of the statements in the original basic block) in accordance with

---

[1] Note that the longest path detection problem is a hard problem in general. Here, we are employing a heuristic.

this longest path. Finding the longest path in a given directed graph is straightforward, and takes $O(N^3)$ time, where N is the number of nodes in the graph [5]. Transforming the program code in accordance with the longest path is more challenging. Consider the abstract CLTG in Figure 3 and the longest path shown. Note that each layer in the CLTG is labeled with a different statement id. The desired access sequence here is a, c, h, d, f, g, b, e. To achieve this access sequence, the following transformations need to be performed:

(1) The variable a should be made the last variable accessed on the RHS of the statement s_1;

(2) In statement s_2: (i) the variable h should be made the first variable accessed on the RHS; (ii) the variable h should be made to immediately precede the variable d;

(3) Statement s_4 should be made to immediately follow the statement s_2; and

(4) In Statement s_4: (i) the access of variable b should be made to immediately follow the variable g; (ii) the variable e should be made to immediately follow the variable b.

In addition to these transformations, the transformed program should not modify the following properties of the input code (CLTG):

(1') Statement s_2 immediately follows statement s_1.

(2') d is the last variable accessed on the RHS of Statement s_2.

(3') g is the first variable accessed on the RHS in Statement s_4.

If the compiler can find a series of transformations to satisfy all these constraints, we achieve the best possible access sequence (for this path). In many cases, however, this may not be possible due to inconsistencies between the requirements given above, or due to a situation that does not involve the variables on the longest path. An example of the former is the inconsistency between conditions (2.i), (2'), and (2.ii) above. That is, if we make the variable h the first variable on the RHS of the statement s_2 and insist on keeping the variable d as the last variable on the RHS, it is not possible to access h and d successively as there are two more variables on the RHS. We assume that these other variables are different from those labeled in the figure. An example of the second type of difficulty is the possibility that it may not be legal to access the statement s_4 immediately after the statement s_2 (as required by the condition(3)). This may occur for example if the statement s_3 writes a variable x (assumed to be a different variable from the ones shown in the figure) that is subsequently read by the statement s_4. Although it may not always be possible to achieve all of the desired transformations, our approach attempts to achieve as many of the desired transformations as possible. Note that this strategy helps to use as many edges in the CLTG as possible.

After the longest path has been determined and the portion of the CLTG that contains the longest path (that is, a subset of the statements in the original basic block) has been transformed, our approach continues by selecting the second longest path and transforming the relevant parts of the CLTG. A special attention is paid to ensure that we do not modify any parts of the basic block

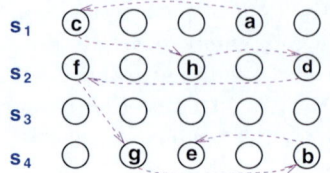

Fig. 3. An abstract CLTG and the longest path.

that have already been transformed in accordance with a longer path considered earlier. In this way, our approach selects the next longest path in each step and transforms the relevant portions of the basic block. The process stops when it is not possible to transform the basic block any further (without distorting the previous transformations). In case we have two paths of the same length, the current implementation favors the one that leads to minimal modification to the original code.

In the example in Figure 2, following the construction of the CLTG shown in Figure 2(ii), our approach determines the longest path marked as the 1st path in Figure 2(v). Based on this path, it builds an access sub-sequence a, b, c, d, e, f, f. This sub-sequence completely specifies the transformations required for three of the five statements in the code (i.e., the first, second, and fourth statements in the original code). Note also that the transformations performed along this path include an inter-statement transformation. Next, it finds the path a, a, a (marked as the 2nd path). Note that this path fixes the access sequence for the third statement in the original code completely as d, a, a. It also specifies that the variable a should be the first variable accessed in fifth statement. After that, the approach selects the path c, d, d. The (c,d) part of this path says that the fifth statement should follow the fourth statement in the transformed program, but this is not possible as the fourth statement has already been transformed, and it now (in the transformed code) comes before the third statement (in the original program). The (d,d) part of the path, on the other hand, is feasible, and indicates that d should be the last variable accessed in the fifth statement. The next path is c, d; but, the transformation implied by this is not possible. The last path is the one between c and d (marked as the 5th path in the figure). It implies that d should be the first variable accessed in the third statement, and the third and fourth statement should be interchanged. At this point, the algorithm has traversed all the paths. It next visits each statement, and fixes the access order for the variable whose order has not been fixed yet. It visits the fifth statement (in the original code) and makes f the second variable accessed on the RHS. The final access sequence is shown in Figure 2(iv).

4   Computation Restructuring: Partially Fixed Storage Sequence Case

So far, we have assumed that the storage sequence (storage pattern) of variables is fixed completely. That is, a storage location is assigned to each program variable. In this section, we describe how to optimize an access sequence when only a subset of the variables have fixed memory locations. This is called the partially fixed storage. Specifically, given a partially fixed storage pattern of a basic block, we address two subproblems:

(1) Determining the best access sequence for all variables in the basic block, and

(2) Determining the storage sequence for the variables in the basic block whose memory locations are yet to be determined.

This problem is important because the compiler employs it during procedure-wide optimization (as will be discussed in the next section). Our approach to the problem involves the following three steps:

(1) Determine the best access (possibly partial) pattern for the partial storage order given,

(2) Determine the storage sequence for the variables whose memory locations are yet to be determined, and

(3) If there is further flexibility, then determine the best access pattern for the portions of the basic block that involves the variables whose storage sequence was determined in Step (2).

Consider the following program fragment assuming a single address register and a partially fixed storage sequence of e, b, d.

```
e = e + d
a = d + c
f = 3c + b
a = (a * c) + (a * g)
```

Figure 4(i) shows the CLTG for this basic block, under the given partial storage sequence. Clearly, there is just one path in this case. Transforming the code in accordance with this path gives us:

```
e = d + e
f = b + 3c
a = d + c
a = (a * c) + (a * g)
```

Note that this transformation (which corresponds to Step (1) above) involves one statement interchange and one commutativity transformation. In the next step (which is Step (2) above), the compiler attempts to determine a storage sequence for the variables whose storage locations are yet to be determined. We achieve this using a *modified version* of Liao's heuristic [10]. Liao summarizes the access sequence using a graph called the *access graph*. In this graph, each variable is represented by a node and a weighted edge between two variables corresponds to the number of transitions between them. Liao then runs an algorithm on this graph to select a path cover, with no node having more than two selected edges incident on it.

The variables represented by the nodes connected by a selected edge are assigned to consecutive memory locations. The objective is to maximize the total weight of the edges selected (which corresponds to capturing the most frequent transitions). We modify this heuristic as follows. Let $\mathcal{L} = \{v_i\}$ be the set of all variables v_i that have already been assigned to consecutive storage locations. Let us assume for now that there is only a single such set. We use $b_{\mathcal{L}}$ to denote the first (start) node of $\mathcal{L}$, and $t_{\mathcal{L}}$ to denote the last (terminal) node. Each node in the modified access graph corresponds to either a single node v_j such that $v_j \notin \mathcal{L}$ or a block node $v_{\mathcal{L}}$ that represents $\mathcal{L}$. There exists an edge between v_j ($\notin \mathcal{L}$) and $v_{\mathcal{L}}$ if and only if there is an edge between v_j and $b_{\mathcal{L}}$ or an edge between v_j and $t_{\mathcal{L}}$. We also keep track of whether the edge between v_j and $v_{\mathcal{L}}$ is due to (incident on) $b_{\mathcal{L}}$ or $t_{\mathcal{L}}$.

Figure 4(ii) shows this modified access graph for our example. Note that this access graph is constructed by taking into account the transformations (both inter-statement and intra-statement) done in the previous step. Next, we run Liao's heuristic [10] on this access graph. Figure 4(iii) show the maximum weight cover detected by the heuristic. Afterwards, we determine the complete storage order (sequence) for the variables. In our example, this sequence is e, b, d, f, c, a, g. Although it does not occur in this example, in some cases, the compiler may have additional scope, and may apply Step (3) above to further modify the access pattern to accommodate the needs of the variables whose storage locations have been determined in Step (2). Note that although we explain this strategy assuming that there is a single block node ($\mathcal{L}$), it is straightforward to extend the approach to multiple block nodes. Note also that since our approach is essentially basic block oriented, we can expect its effectiveness to increase when it is used in conjunction with techniques that increase basic block sizes (e.g., superblocks/hyperblocks).

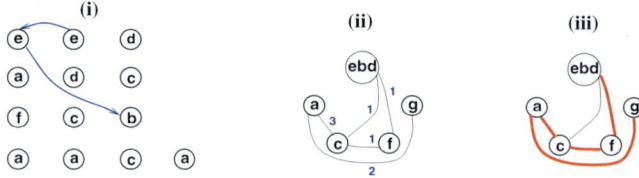

Fig. 4. (i) An example CLTG. (ii) An access graph for partially fixed storage sequence. (iii) Selected maximum weight cover.

5   Intra-procedural Optimization Strategy

We now present a unified strategy that employs both access sequence and storage sequence transformations to make effective use of address registers. The approach works on a representation called *weighted control flow graph* (WCFG), which is a CFG with weighted nodes (basic blocks). A node weight specifies the number of times the corresponding basic block is entered (dynamic execution frequency). This is typically calculated by considering the execution frequencies of edges and branch probabilities.

Our approach to this global (procedure-wide) optimization problem is as follows. After determining the execution frequencies of basic blocks and labeling them, we visit basic blocks one-by-one, and optimize a basic block completely before moving to the next one. The optimization order is determined by the weights (i.e., basic block labels).

The first (most frequently executed) basic block is optimized using Liao's heuristic (explained in Section 2). After optimizing this basic block, we determine a storage sequence for all the variables accessed by this basic block. Note that this step determines only a partial storage sequence (called the *storage subsequence*) as the variables accessed by this block form, in general, a subset of all the variables declared in the program. Then, we move to the next most frequently executed basic block, and optimize it using the approach explained in Section 3 or Section 4 depending on whether all the variables manipulated by this basic block has already fixed memory (storage) locations or not. After optimizing this basic block, new storage subsequences (for the variables accessed by this second most frequently executed basic block, but not accessed by the most frequently executed basic block) are determined. Afterwards, we move to the third most frequently executed basic block and, in optimizing it (using the techniques given in Section 3 and Section 4), we take into account all the storage sequences determined so far. In this way, our approach handles the basic blocks one-by-one, and in optimizing each of them, it considers the storage sequences found so far. If at a given point, the storage location for each variable in the code is fixed (i.e., a complete storage sequence is determined), the remaining basic blocks are optimized using the technique discussed in Section 3. At the end of the process, if the storage sequences found do not form a single connected component, they are made so using a post-processing pass.

6   Summary

In this work, we have presented a compilation framework that employs both program restructuring and storage order optimizations to reduce the size of the generated code for embedded processors by eliminating as many explicit address register loads as possible. Reducing code size is extremely important as in many embedded systems a reduction in code size means a reduction in memory size. Work in progress includes the investigation of different ways of combining storage layout and code restructuring transformations, incorporating partitioning of variables among different address registers, and studying the impact of SSA transformation on code size. We also plan to make experiments with different architectures as different instruction set architectures (ISA) can lead to different code sizes [6].

References

1. D. Bartley. Optimizing stack frame accesses for processors with restricted addressing modes. Software – Practice and Experience, 22(2):101–110, February 1992.
2. P. Briggs. Register Allocation via Graph Coloring, Ph.D. Thesis, Computer Science Department, Rice University, Houston, TX, April 1992.
3. M. Cintra and G. Araujo. Array reference allocation using SSA-form and live range growth. In Proc. ACM SIGPLAN 2000 Workshop on Languages, Compilers, and Tools for Embedded Systems (LCTES), June 2000, Vancouver B. C., Canada.
4. K. Cooper and P. Schielke. Non-local instruction scheduling with limited code growth. In Proc. Workshop on Languages, Compilers, and Tools for Embedded Systems (LCPC), pp. 193–207, June 1998.
5. T. Cormen, C. Leiserson, and R. Rivest. Introduction to Algorithms, MIT Press, Cambridge, Massachusetts, 1990.
6. J. W. Davidson and R. A. Vaughan. The effect of instruction set complexity on program size and memory performance. In Proc. International Conference on Architectural Support for Programming Languages and Operating Systems (ASPLOS), 1987, pp. 60–64.
7. M. Kandemir. A compiler technique for improving whole program locality. In Proc. 28th Annual ACM Symposium on Principles of Programming Languages (POPL), London, UK, January, 2001.
8. C. Lee, M. Potkonjak, and W. Mangione-Smith. MediaBench: A tool for evaluating and synthesizing multimedia and communications systems. In Proc. the 30th International Symposium on Microarchitecture (MICRO), pp. 330–335, 1997.
9. R. Leupers and P. Marwedel. Algorithms for address assignment in DSP code generation. In Proc. the International Conference on Computer Aided Design (ICCAD), pp. 109–112, November 1996.
10. S. Liao. Code Generation and Optimization for Embedded Digital Signal Processors, Ph.D. Thesis. MIT, June 1996.
11. S. Liao, S. Devadas, K. Keutzer, S. Tjiang, and A. Wang. Storage assignment to decrease code size. ACM Transactions on Programming Languages and Systems (TOPLAS), 18(3):235–253, 1996.
12. S. S. Muchnick. Advanced Compiler Design and Implementation. Morgan Kaufmann Publishers, 1st edition, July 1997.
13. A. Rao and S. Pande. Storage assignment optimizations to generate compact and efficient code on embedded DSPs. In Proc. ACM SIGPLAN Conference on Programming Language Design and Implementation (PLDI), May 1999.
14. R. Wilson et al. SUIF: An infrastructure for research on parallelizing and optimizing compilers. SIGPLAN Notices, 29(12):31–37, December 1994.
15. S. Udayanarayanan and C. Chakrabarti. Address code generation for DSPs. In Proc. the 38th Design Automation Conference (DAC), June 2001.
16. M. Wolfe. High Performance Compilers for Parallel Computing, Addison Wesley Publishing Company, 1996.

Offset Assignment Showdown: Evaluation of DSP Address Code Optimization Algorithms

Rainer Leupers

Institute for Integrated Signal Processing Systems (ISS)
RWTH Aachen, Germany
leupers@iss.rwth-aachen.de

Abstract. Offset assignment is a highly effective DSP address code optimization technique that has been implemented in a number of ANSI C compilers. In this paper we concentrate on a special class of offset assignment problems called "simple offset assignment" (SOA). A number of SOA algorithms have been proposed recently, but experimental results and direct comparisons are still sparse. This makes the practical selection of a suitable SOA algorithm for implementation in a compiler very difficult. This paper aims at closing this gap by providing a comprehensive benchmark suite and empirical evaluation based on real-life application programs. Our results for the first time permit a detailed assessment of all major SOA algorithms. In addition, we propose a new and superior combination of SOA heuristics.

1 Introduction

Due to the increased importance of software in embedded system design, code optimization techniques for embedded processors, particularly for *digital signal processors (DSPs)*, have gained high interest in academia and industry. As compared to general-purpose processors, DSPs show a number of special hardware features, many of which impose new challenges on compiler construction:

- Harvard architecture with separate program and data buses
- Dual memory banks for high data access bandwidth
- Hardware multiplier for fast product computation
- DSP-specific instructions like multiply-accumulate, multimedia (SIMD) instructions, and saturating arithmetic
- Limited amount of instruction-level parallelism
- Inhomogeneous register set
- Support for zero-overhead hardware loops
- Real-time capabilities
- Dedicated *address generation units* (AGUs)

This paper considers code optimization techniques aiming at maximum utilization of AGUs.

G. Hedin (Ed.): CC 2003, LNCS 2622, pp. 290–302, 2003.

1.1   Address Generation Units and Offset Assignment

Offset assignment is a central code optimization technique in many C/C++ compilers for DSPs. It exploits the fact that many standard DSPs (e.g. TI C2x/C5x, Motorola 56xxx, Analog Devices 210x, ST D950) as well as numerous application-specific DSPs comprise an AGU that is capable of performing address (or pointer) arithmetic in parallel to the main data path.

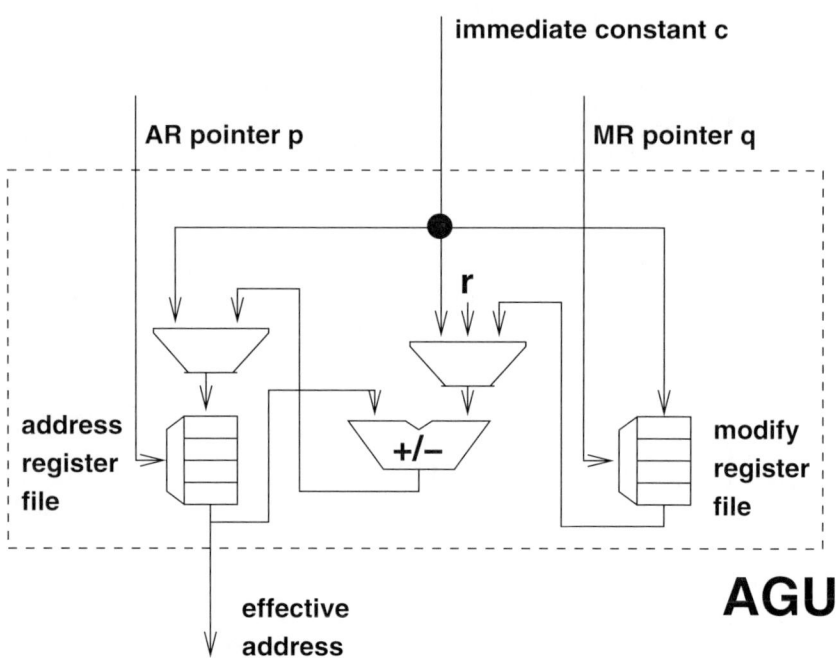

Fig. 1. Address generation unit (AGU) architecture in DSPs with address register (AR) and modify register (MR) files.

A typical DSP AGU (see fig. 1) comprises a file of address registers (ARs) that store pointers for indirect memory addressing modes. In order to optimize clock speed and to save silicon area, DSPs, in contrast to CISC and RISC machines, frequently do not support "base-plus-offset" addressing modes. Instead, in order to compute a new address $a' = a \pm c$ from a given address a stored in some AR, that AR has to be explicitly modified by adding or subtracting some constant c. The code efficiency of such AR modifications depends on the concrete value of c: if the absolute value of c is small enough such that c fits into the *auto-increment range* $R = [-r, r]$, then c can be encoded as an immediate operand into the same instruction that performs a memory access (LOAD or STORE) at address a. In that case, the AR modification can be performed within the AGU in parallel to the memory access by means of an *auto-increment* (or *auto-decrement*, dependent on

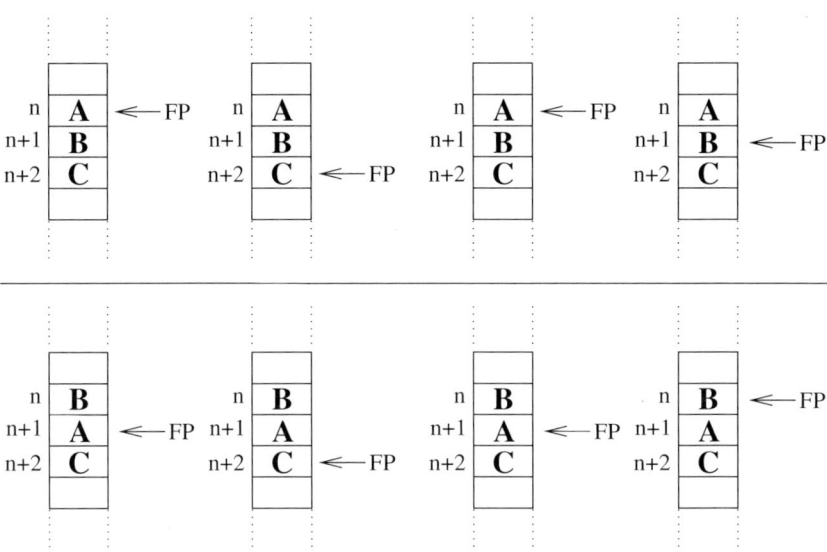

Fig. 2. Illustration of offset assignment

the sign of c) operation. Otherwise, if $|c| > r$, an extra instruction is required to compute the address $a' = a \pm c$ for the next memory access.

Hence, the auto-increment based address computation results in the highest code performance and density, and any C/C++ compiler for DSPs should aim at maximizing its use when generating code for address computations. One way to do this is *offset assignment*, where the memory layout for program variables is optimized such that the maximum number of address computations for scalar variables can be implemented by auto-increment. This is possible due to the fact that the stack layout for the local scalar variables of a C function can be freely chosen by the compiler.

1.2   Offset Assignment Example

Fig. 2 illustrates a sample stack frame layout in a DSP-specific compiler. The compiler typically allocates one of the ARs as a *frame pointer* (FP), which is used to address local variables on the stack. Suppose, we have three such variables, A, B, and C, which are accessed in the sequence $S = (A, C, A, B)$. Furthermore, suppose the auto-increment range R is restricted to $[-1, 1]$. This special case of using a single FP and $R = [-1, 1]$ is called *simple offset assignment* (SOA).

The upper part of fig. 2 illustrates the situation when the variables are assigned to stack locations (or *offsets*, relative to the stack frame boundary) n, $n + 1$, $n + 2$, in alphabetic order. Initially, FP points to variable A at address n. The next access goes to C located at $n + 2$. Due to the missing "base-plus-offset" addressing mode in DSPs, FP cannot remain constant throughout the entire function execution (as it normally holds for CISC or RISC compiled code), but needs to be implemented as a *floating* or *roving* frame pointer. Thus, in order to access the variables according to sequence S, FP needs to be modified by the values $+2, -2, +1$, in that order. Due to $R = [-1, 1]$, only the last FP modification (+1) can be implemented by auto-increment, while two extra instructions are required to implement the modifications by +2 and -2. However, as shown in the lower part of fig. 2, the situation changes drastically when the variables are assigned to memory addresses in the order $B - A - C$, in which case the access sequence S implies FP modifications by $+1, -1, -1$, all of which fall into the auto-increment range R. Hence, the latter variable layout will result in better code, and it is the goal of SOA algorithms to compute such "good" variable layouts.

1.3   Motivation

Experimental surveys indicate that it is not unusual for DSP machine code to comprise 20%–30% (sometimes even more than 50%) of instructions used for address computations [1], [2]. In terms of total code size, the effect of performing offset assignment within a C compiler is typically in the order 5%–20% [3], which is quite significant for DSPs with tight ROM size constraints. Due to their high importance for DSP code quality, offset assignment techniques have been implemented in several research (e.g. SPAM [3] or RECORD [4]) and industrial compilers (e.g. TI's C2x/C5x C compiler [5] or CHESS [6]) for DSPs.

Even though SOA is just a special case of offset assignment problems, it represents a real-world problem. This is due to the fact, that many DSPs show a relatively small instruction word length (mostly 16 bits), which allows only for a narrow auto-increment range like $[-1, 1]$. Moreover, generalized offset assignment approaches using multiple frame pointers mostly rely on SOA algorithms as subroutines.

Consequently, a number of different SOA algorithms have been proposed in the literature. In spite of this, from a scientific viewpoint, the situation is not really satisfactory, since so far there has been no comprehensive benchmarking of the different SOA algorithms for real-life problems. Some algorithms have been compared to others, but frequently the comparisons are incomplete and are based on small program fragments or even random problem instances, so that reported results are hardly reproducible. So the question of which SOA algorithm is the "best" (w.r.t. their computation time vs solution quality tradeoff) is still largely open.

Therefore, in this paper we do not just propose yet another SOA algorithm, but our main goal is to consolidate previous work by means of a comprehensive empirical study, in which we evaluate a set of different algorithms for a large suite of realistic SOA problem instances. This allows us to draw conclusions on which algorithms are most useful in practice and may be promising platforms for future offset assignment research. In more detail, the contributions of this paper are:

1. We briefly review the major existing SOA algorithms and available experimental comparisons.
2. We propose an extensible benchmark suite, called *OffsetStone*, for offset assignment algorithms together with the necessary tool support.
3. We use OffsetStone to evaluate a total of 8 SOA algorithms and give detailed experimental results about their performance in terms of computation time and (both absolute and relative) solution quality.

4. We present a new combination of two fast SOA heuristics that turns out to be superior to all previous heuristics.

The remainder of this paper is structured as follows. Section 2 discusses related work and gives a more precise description of the SOA problem. Section 3 outlines the OffsetStone benchmarking methodology and its tools. In section 4, we provide detailed experimental results. Finally, section 5 gives conclusions and mentions future work.

2   Related Work

2.1   Access Graph Model

Bartley [5] proposed the *access graph* model for the simple offset assignment (SOA) problem, which forms the baseline for most SOA algorithms. Given a variable set $V = \{v_1, \ldots, v_n\}$ and a variable access sequence $S = (s_1, \ldots, s_m)$ of a basic block with $\forall i \in [1, m] : s_i \in V$, the access graph is an undirected, complete, and edge-weighted graph $G = (V, E, k)$ with $E = \{\{v, w\} | v, w \in V\}$. The function $k : E \rightarrow \mathbf{N_0}$ assigns a weight to each edge $e = \{v, w\}$ that denotes the number of *access transitions* between v and w in S, i.e., the number of subsequences of S of the form (v, w) or (w, v). Due to the symmetry of auto-increment and auto-decrement, the ordering of v and w is irrelevant here. Likewise, self-edges of the form $\{v, v\}$ can be neglected. The left part of fig. 3 exemplifies the access graph model for $V = \{A, B, C, D\}$ and $S = (D, A, C, B, A, D, A, B, C)$.

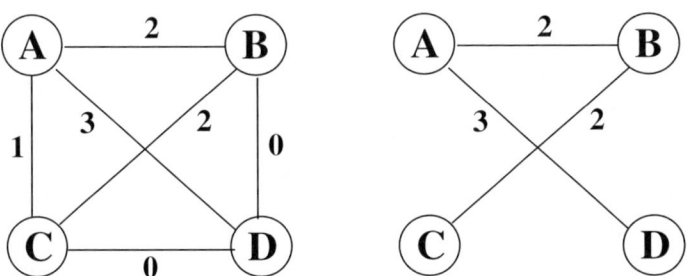

Fig. 3. Access graph model and maximum weighted Hamiltonian path

Any access transition (v, w) in S can be implemented by auto-increment, if and only if v and w are assigned neighboring stack locations, i.e. the offset difference of v and w is covered by the auto-increment range $[-1, 1]$. In order to maximize the use of auto-increment addressing, obviously those variable pairs $\{v, w\}$ should be neighbors in the stack frame, whose edge weight $k(\{v, w\})$ in G is high, since this will save many extra instructions for address computation.

2.2 Offset Assignment Heuristics

As pointed out by Liao [3], the SOA problem eventually amounts to finding a *maximum weighted Hamiltonian path* P in G, i.e. a path touching each node once with the maximum edge weight sum (see right part of fig. 3). The memory layout is derived from P by assigning those node pairs to adjacent memory locations, which are also neighboring in P (i.e. either C-B-A-D or D-A-B-C in the example from fig. 3).

The *cost* of an SOA solution P is defined as the sum of the weights of G's edges *not* covered by P. This corresponds to the number of extra address computation instructions to be inserted into the machine code. By means of a simple reduction from the classical Hamiltonian path problem [7] it can be shown that computing P is an NP-complete problem. Hence, heuristics should be used, except for small problem instances.

Bartley [5] proposed a greedy heuristic for finding path P. His algorithm iteratively picks an edge e of highest weight $k(e)$ in G and checks whether inclusion of e into a partial path P would still allow for a valid solution. This is iterated until a complete path with $|V| - 1$ edges has been selected.

Liao [3] proposed a more efficient implementation of Bartley's SOA algorithm, by temporarily neglecting edges of zero weight (which are frequent in realistic access graphs) and using an efficient Union/Find data structure for checking for cycles. Besides the implementation issues, Liao's algorithms produces the same results as Bartley's.

In his thesis [1], Liao additionally proposed a branch-and-bound (B&B) algorithm for SOA, which can be used to construct optimal solutions. The B&B algorithm is capable of effectively pruning the huge search space, but it can generally only be applied to small problem instances due to sometimes exhaustive runtime requirements.

Both Bartley's and Liao's heuristics do not include a special handling of edges with equal weight during path construction. However, same-weight edges are very common in access graphs, and the solution quality may critically depend on the order in which edges are investigated during path construction. Therefore, Leupers and Marwedel [4] proposed to extend Liao's algorithm by a *tie-break* heuristic for choosing among same-weight edges. An experimental evaluation for a set of random SOA problem instances indicated that the tie-break heuristic on average gives a slight improvement over Liao's heuristic. This has been confirmed by independent experiments in [8], [9], while other experiments on some of the DSPStone [10] benchmark programs reported in [2] did not indicate such an improvement.

A genetic algorithm (GA) based approach to SOA has been presented in [11]. In contrast to most other methods, it does not use the access graph model, but constructs offset assignments directly by a (relatively time-consuming) simulation of a natural evolution process. Actually, the GA has been mainly intended for a more general class of offset assignment problems, but it can easily be restricted to solve the SOA problem. A direct comparison to fast heuristics for the special case of SOA has not been reported, though.

Atri et al. proposed an *incremental* SOA algorithm [12]. It starts with an initial SOA solution, constructed by some heuristic, and performs an iterative improvement by a local exchange of access graph edges selected for the maximum weighted Hamiltonian path. An experimental comparison to Liao's heuristic [3] for a set of random SOA instances indicated that the initial solution can be improved in 3–8% of the cases considered, where the average improvement is about 5%. Unfortunately, no comparison to other SOA algorithms was reported.

Besides these approaches, many generalizations of SOA have been considered, including the *general offset assignment* (GOA) problem [3], [4], [17], [11] that handles multiple frame pointers, DSPs with auto-increment operations between the memory accesses [13], auto-increment ranges beyond ±1 [14], [15], [16], AGUs with modulo addressing modes [17], exploitation of scheduling freedom in the variable access sequence [9], as well as procedure-level offset assignment [18]. Other researchers have dealt with DSP-specific compiler techniques for address register assignment in case of arrays and predefined memory layouts (e.g. [2], [19], [20], [21], [22], [23]), which are not directly related to SOA.

3   Evaluation Methodology

Summarizing the discussion of SOA algorithms in section 2, many techniques have not been directly compared to each other so far, while the few comparisons that do exist are mostly based on small data bases or random problem instances. However, random instances generally do not well reflect real-world problems, since the latter tend to show higher locality in the variable access sequences.

3.1   OffsetStone Benchmarks

For sake of a more reliable and reproducible evaluation of available SOA algorithms, we have composed OffsetStone, a large suite of SOA problem instances extracted from 31 complex real-world application programs written in ANSI C. These include computation-intensive DSP applications (e.g. MPEG2, MP3, ADPCM, DSPStone, FFT, JPEG, GSM, Viterbi) but also more control-dominated standard applications (e.g. GZIP, FLEX, BISON, CPP). Altogether, the C applications chosen for OffsetStone comprise more than 300,000 lines of C source code. They are certainly representative and much broader than what has been used for SOA benchmarking in previous work.

From a benchmarking viewpoint, an interesting observation is that there are no significant differences in the behavior of the SOA algorithms for different benchmark types (i.e. DSP or general-purpose). Therefore, there was no need to restrict the evaluation to DSP applications only.

For each application program, we extracted SOA problem instances by means of the following steps:

1. The ANSI C sources for the application are translated into a three address code intermediate representation (IR) by means of the LANCE C frontend [24], in order to make the variable access sequences explicit. Additionally, this step inserts temporary variables for intermediate results, that a compiler would normally generate.
2. The IR is optimized by standard techniques used in most compilers, including common subexpression elimination, dead code elimination, constant folding, jump optimization, etc. This step ensures that the IR does not contain superfluous variables and computations, which a compiler would eliminate anyway.

3. From the optimized IR, the detailed variable access sequence is extracted from each basic block.
4. Since any offset assignment is valid throughout an entire C function, one *global* access graph is constructed per function by merging[1] the local access graphs of the basic blocks. In this way, all local access sequences are represented in a single graph. Each global access graph forms one instance of the SOA problem.

With this methodology we obtained a total of more than 3000 realistic SOA problem instances[2]. The extraction is restricted to variables fitting into a single memory word, i.e., variables that directly qualify for offset assignment. We also excluded pointer variables, since these are mostly allocated in address registers and not on the stack frame.

Our approach assumes that all variables extracted will actually be assigned to the stack. This is not necessarily true, since a compiler generally will be able to keep some of the variables in the data path registers. However, as DSPs with AGUs typically show very few data path registers, it is reasonable to assume that the extracted sequences are very close to the actual access sequences in compiled code.

3.2 SOA Algorithms Included in OffsetStone

For the extracted benchmarks, we evaluated the following 8 SOA algorithms:

1. **SOA-OFU**: A trivial offset assignment algorithm, where variables are assigned to offsets in the order of their first use in the code. This order would typically be used in non-optimizing compilers without a dedicated SOA phase, and thus serves as a baseline case for our experiments.
2. **SOA-Bartley:** Bartley's SOA heuristic [5] based on the access graph model.
3. **SOA-Liao:** Liao's SOA heuristic [3] based on the access graph model.
4. **SOA-BB**: Liao's branch-and-bound algorithm [1] for optimally solving SOA.
5. **SOA-TB**: SOA-Liao extended by the tie-break heuristic proposed in [4].
6. **SOA-GA**: The genetic algorithm for SOA from [11].
7. **SOA-INC**: The incremental SOA algorithm from [12], using SOA-Liao for constructing initial solutions.
8. **SOA-INC-TB**: A new combination of SOA algorithms, using SOA-INC in combination with SOA-TB for constructing initial solutions. As will be shown later, using SOA-TB instead of SOA-Liao in total results in a higher optimization potential for SOA-INC.

---

[1] In this formulation, SOA minimizes *code size*. For *performance* optimization, profiling information can be exploited by assigning higher edge weights to frequently executed program paths.

[2] The OffsetStone benchmark access sequences are available from the author upon request, including the corresponding tools for access sequence extraction and the C++ source code for our implementation of the 8 SOA algorithms. This allows other researchers to easily reproduce the results, to add more offset assignment algorithms to the existing infrastructure, and to extend the benchmark suite by extracting access sequences from further application programs.

4 Experimental Results

The 8 SOA algorithms have been implemented in C++ in the form of different routines within a single driver program. Naturally, high attention has been paid to uniform software engineering practices, in order to ensure a fair comparison. The algorithms have been applied to all OffsetStone benchmarks, where the costs (according to the metric defined in section 2) and the CPU times (on a 1.3 GHz Linux PC) have been measured. An exception, however, is the SOA-BB algorithm. Due to the sometimes excessive runtime requirements, we restricted its use to problem instances with at most 12 variables (this already corresponds to $12! \approx 479 \cdot 10^6$ possible solutions).

4.1 Performance Relative to SOA-OFU

We first focus on a comparison to the "naive" algorithm SOA-OFU. Table 1 gives the average percentage of the solution cost of 6 SOA algorithms (SOA-OFU set to 100%, SOA-BB not included here due to runtime limitations). SOA-Bartley and SOA-Liao are combined into a single column since they always produce identical results.

The line labeled "average" in table 1 shows the average cost values over all OffsetStone benchmarks. As can be seen, all SOA algorithms reduce the cost as compared to SOA-OFU by about 25% on average, with a relatively small difference to each other (the reason for this will become clear in table 3). The best results are produced by SOA-GA, followed by SOA-INC-TB and SOA-TB.

For sake of completeness, we also applied the algorithms to random access sequences, as it has been frequently done in previous work. The line labeled "random" in table 1 shows the average results obtained after applying the SOA algorithms to a set of 3000 random SOA problem instances with varying numbers of variables and access sequence lengths as they typically occur in practice. Even though the order of result quality does not change, the performance difference between the algorithms is smaller, and the result quality as compared to the naive algorithm SOA-OFU is much lower ($< 8\%$) than for real SOA problems. This can be explained by the fact that the edge weights in the access graph are more uniformly distributed for random sequences than for real sequences. This means that there are no big "peaks" in the objective function so that even optimal SOA solutions are not much better than naive (SOA-OFU) solutions. Hence, the optimization potential for SOA algorithms is significantly lower. This confirms our above statement that random problem instances are not the best choice for evaluating SOA algorithms.

4.2 Runtimes

Table 2 shows results on the average runtime requirements (CPU milliseconds) per SOA problem instance. SOA-OFU is not included, since it requires essentially no processing time at all. Note that SOA-Bartley in its original form can only be used for small problem sizes, due to its very high runtime requirements. However, we found that it can be easily accelerated by temporarily suppressing the zero-weight edges in the access graph. The first line in table 2, therefore, refers to this improved implementation of SOA-Bartley. Nevertheless, its "twin" algorithm SOA-Liao is still faster on average.

Table 1. Relative cost of SOA algorithms compared to SOA-OFU solutions (100%)

benchmark	Liao	TB	INC	INC-TB	GA
8051sim	83.1	79.8	80.7	79.0	79.0
adpcm	81.1	79.3	80.1	78.6	78.5
anagram	68.9	66.9	68.2	66.2	65.6
anthr	81.1	79.9	80.9	79.9	79.9
bdd	78.6	76.9	78.4	76.9	76.9
bison	78.2	77.1	78.1	77.0	77.0
cavity	85.1	82.4	84.6	82.2	82.2
cc65	78.4	76.3	77.2	76.3	76.2
codecs	81.5	80.3	81.4	80.3	80.3
cpp	77.4	76.3	77.3	76.3	76.3
dct	77.6	77.8	77.6	77.4	77.4
dspstone	76.4	74.4	76.0	74.3	74.3
eqntott	65.0	65.0	65.0	65.0	65.0
f2c	73.7	72.7	73.6	72.6	72.6
fft	92.0	92.0	92.0	92.0	92.0
flex	71.3	69.3	71.0	69.3	69.3
fuzzy	77.5	74.2	77.0	74.2	74.2
gif2asc	83.1	82.0	83.0	81.7	81.7
gsm	81.5	80.9	81.3	80.9	80.8
gzip	77.1	73.2	76.3	73.2	73.2
h263	70.3	70.0	70.0	70.0	69.6
hmm	70.5	67.4	69.8	67.3	67.3
jpeg	73.7	71.8	73.4	71.7	71.6
klt	68.2	66.1	67.6	66.1	66.0
lpsolve	78.1	77.1	77.8	77.1	77.1
motion	90.6	91.1	90.6	89.6	89.6
mp3	72.3	71.6	72.2	71.6	71.4
mpeg2	77.0	76.0	76.8	75.9	75.8
sparse	75.9	75.1	75.9	75.1	75.1
triangle	65.8	64.4	65.6	64.4	64.3
viterbi	89.3	85.0	89.1	84.9	84.9
average	76.71	75.23	76.40	75.16	75.10
random	92.74	92.24	92.62	92.17	92.13

Table 2. Average runtime per problem instance

Algorithm	CPU time (msecs)
SOA-Bartley	0.97
SOA-Liao	0.67
SOA-TB	0.68
SOA-INC	4.60
SOA-INC-TB	23.00
SOA-GA	8296.26

Table 3. Average overhead compared to optimum

Algorithm	% overhead
SOA-BB	0.00
SOA-OFU	67.09
SOA-Liao	4.34
SOA-TB	0.16
SOA-INC	2.28
SOA-INC-TB	0.11
SOA-GA	0.00

The average runtimes are mostly in the order of milliseconds or even less, with SOA-Liao and SOA-TB being the fastest algorithms. There is a big gap to SOA-GA though, which on average needs about 8.3 CPU seconds per problem instance. This leads to a clear separation of SOA algorithms into *fast* and *slow* ones, where the latter category comprises SOA-GA and SOA-BB.

4.3   Performance Relative to Optimum

For about 41% of all benchmark problems (i.e. the "small" problems with at most 12 variables), we computed optimal solutions by means of the SOA-BB algorithm. This allowed us to measure the absolute quality of computed SOA solutions. The results are given in table 3, which shows the average percentage of cost overhead compared to the optimal solutions for each algorithm. Naturally, the trivial algorithm SOA-OFU shows the highest overhead. As can be seen, all heuristics get more or less close to the optimum, which explains the small differences found in table 1. SOA-Liao yields an average overhead of 4.34%, while SOA-INC-TB is the best of the fast heuristics, with an overhead of only 0.11%. SOA-GA found the optimum in all cases. For the test cases covered by table 3, SOA-BB needed about 3.5 CPU seconds per SOA instance, while SOA-GA took 0.8 CPU seconds. The CPU times of the fast heuristics are negligible in practice.

5   Conclusions

Given that the OffsetStone benchmarks provide a good representation of real-world SOA problems, the experimental data from section 4 permit to draw the following conclusions that were not available from previous work:

- Generally, the performance difference between SOA algorithms for real problems is surprisingly small. Hence, it might appear that the concrete algorithm used in a C compiler for DSPs does not matter much. However, under the tight cost constraints of embedded systems where sometimes every program ROM word matters, the best algorithm with an acceptable runtime should certainly be chosen.
- SOA-Bartley can be easily implemented much more efficiently than in the originally proposed form, but SOA-Liao is still faster while giving the same results.

- SOA-TB achieves better average results for real-life problems than SOA-Liao/SOA-Bartley at virtually no increase in computation time, and it also achieves better solutions than SOA-INC.
- The new combination of SOA algorithms (SOA-INC-TB) proposed in this paper achieves the best results of all fast heuristics tested here. Hence, it can be recommended for fast compilers and can replace the use of SOA-Bartley/Liao, SOA-TB, and SOA-INC. At least for "small" problems it achieves an extremely low average overhead compared to optimal solutions.
- In case priority is given to highest code quality and not to high compilation speed (say, in a final compiler run with highest optimization effort to generate production code with minimal ROM size), the SOA-GA algorithm should be preferred. For "small" SOA problems, SOA-BB can be used to compute optimal solutions, but we observed that SOA-GA finds the optimum in virtually all cases (even though it is not guaranteed to do so) at less than 25% of the computation time requirements of SOA-BB. SOA-BB is frequently fast but sometimes shows extreme peaks in computation time due to its branch-and-bound nature, whereas the runtimes of SOA-GA are predictable.
- The use of random access sequences for evaluation of SOA algorithms, though quite common in previous research, does not accurately reflect the algorithm behavior for real applications. Our experimental results indicate that random sequences do allow for a coarse performance comparison between algorithms, but they definitely do not exhibit their optimization potential for real-life application code.

OffsetStone is the first effort towards fair benchmarking of offset assignment algorithms based on a huge suite of realistic problem instances. It allowed us to provide an in-depth evaluation of most state-of-the-art SOA algorithms. The results provide valuable hints both for compiler developers and researchers working on offset assignment in C compilers for DSPs. As a secondary contribution, we were able to identify a new combination of fast heuristics (SOA-INC-TB) that is superior to previous algorithms.

As a first step, in this paper we have focused only on SOA, the most basic class of offset assignment problems. In the future, the suite of algorithms included in OffsetStone will be extended to also cover generalized offset assignment problem formulations, e.g. offset assignment with variable live range information, exploitation of scheduling mobility of instructions, or general offset assignment with multiple address registers, some of which have been mentioned in section 2.

References

1. S. Liao: *Code Generation and Optimization for Embedded Digital Signal Processors*, Ph.D. thesis, Dept. of Electrical Engineering and Computer Science, Massachusetts Institute of Technology, 1996
2. S. Udayanarayanan, C. Chakrabarti: *Address Code Generation for Digital Signal Processors*, 38th Design Automation Conference (DAC), 2001
3. S. Liao, S. Devadas, K. Keutzer, S. Tjiang, A. Wang: *Storage Assignment to Decrease Code Size*, ACM SIGPLAN Conference on Programming Language Design and Implementation (PLDI), 1995

4. R. Leupers, P. Marwedel: *Algorithms for Address Assignment in DSP Code Generation*, Int. Conference on Computer-Aided Design (ICCAD), 1996
5. D.H. Bartley: *Optimizing Stack Frame Accesses for Processors with Restricted Addressing Modes*, Software – Practice and Experience, vol. 22(2), 1992
6. Target Compiler Technologies: *http://www.retarget.com*
7. M.R. Gary, D.S. Johnson: *Computers and Intractability – A Guide to the Theory of NP-Completeness*, Freemann, 1979
8. B. Wess: *Minimization of Data Address Computation Overhead in DSPs*, 3rd Int. Workshop on Code Generation for Embedded Processors (SCOPES), 1998
9. A. Rao, S. Pande: *Storage Assignment using Expression Tree Transformations to Generate Compact and Efficient DSP Code*, ACM SIGPLAN Conference on Programming Language Design and Implementation (PLDI), 1999
10. V. Zivojnovic, J.M. Velarde, C. Schläger, H. Meyr: *DSPStone – A DSP-oriented Benchmarking Methodology*, Int. Conf. on Signal Processing Applications and Technology (ICSPAT), 1994
11. R. Leupers, F. David: *A Uniform Optimization Technique for Offset Assignment Problems*, 11th Int. System Synthesis Symposium (ISSS), 1998
12. S. Atri, J. Ramanujam, M. Kandemir: *Improving Offset Assignment for Embedded Processors*, Languages and Compilers for High-Performance Computing, S. Midkiff et al. (eds.), Lecture Notes in Computer Science, Springer, 2001
13. N. Sugino, H. Miyazaki, S. Iimuro, A. Nishihara: *Improved Code Optimization Method Utilizing Memory Addressing Operations and its Application to DSP Compilers*, Int. Symp. on Circuits and Systems (ISCAS), 1996
14. B. Wess, M. Gotschlich: *Constructing Memory Layouts for Address Generation Units Supporting Offset 2 Access*, Proc. ICASSP, 1997
15. N. Kogure, N. Sugino, A. Nishihara: *Memory Address Allocation Method for a DSP with $\pm$ 2 Update Operations in Indirect Addressing*, European Conference on Circuit Theory and Design (ECCTD), 1997
16. A. Sudarsanam, S. Liao, S. Devadas: *Analysis and Evaluation of Address Arithmetic Capabilities in Custom DSP Architectures*, Design Automation Conference (DAC), 1997
17. B. Wess, M. Gotschlich: *Optimal DSP Memory Layout Generation as a Quadratic Assignment Problem*, Int. Symp. on Circuits and Systems (ISCAS), 1997
18. E. Eckstein, A. Krall: *Minimizing Cost of Local Variables Access for DSP Processors*, ACM Workshop on Languages, Compilers, and Tools for Embedded Systems (LCTES), 1999
19. C. Liem, P.Paulin, A. Jerraya: *Address Calculation for Retargetable Compilation and Exploration of Instruction-Set Architectures*, 33rd Design Automation Conference (DAC), 1996
20. C. Gebotys: *DSP Address Optimization Using a Minimum Cost Circulation Technique*, Int. Conference on Computer-Aided Design (ICCAD), 1997
21. R. Leupers, A. Basu, P. Marwedel: *Optimized Array Index Computation in DSP Programs*, Asia South Pacific Design Automation Conference (ASP-DAC), 1998
22. W.-K. Cheng, Y.-L. Lin: *Addressing Optimization for Loop Execution Targeting DSP with Auto-Increment/Decrement Architecture*, 11th Int. System Synthesis Symposium (ISSS), 1998
23. G. Ottoni, S. Rigo, G. Araujo, S. Rajagopalan, S. Malik: *Optimal Live Range Merge for Address Register Allocation in Embedded Programs*, 10th International Conference on Compiler Construction (CC), 2001
24. LANCE C Compiler: *http://LS12-www.cs.uni-dortmund.de/lance*

Integrating High-Level Optimizations in a Production Compiler: Design and Implementation Experience

Somnath Ghosh, Abhay Kanhere, Rakesh Krishnaiyer, Dattatraya Kulkarni,
Wei Li, Chu-Cheow Lim, and John Ng

Intel® Compiler Laboratory, Intel Corporation
2200 Mission College Blvd, Santa Clara, CA 95051
Telephone number: +1-408-765-0142
wei.li@intel.com

Abstract. The High-Level Optimizer (HLO) is a key part of the compiler technology that enabled Itanium™ and Itanium™2 processors deliver leading floating-point performance at their introduction. In this paper, we discuss the design and implementation experience in integrating diverse optimizations in the HLO module. In particular, we describe decisions made in the design of HLO targeting Itanium processor family. We provide empirical data to validate the design decisions. Since HLO was implemented in a production compiler, we made certain engineering trade-offs. We discuss these trade-offs and outline key learning derived from our experience.

1 Introduction

The Explicitly Parallel Instruction Computing (EPIC) technology behind the Itanium™ processor architecture provides a rich set of features [3,4], which allow the compiler to exploit instruction-level parallelism (ILP) and optimize applications in many new ways. Intel's compiler for Itanium processor family incorporates and extends the latest optimization techniques, and new techniques have been designed specifically for the Itanium architecture [3,4]. As a result, the Intel compiler helped deliver the world's best floating point performance during the introduction of the Itanium and Itanium2 processors. The High-Level Optimizer (HLO) has been a key component that helped achieve this performance. Broadly, HLO encompasses optimizations that operate on high-level program structures such as loops and arrays. In this paper, we discuss the design and implementation of HLO targeting Itanium processor family and describe key learning out of this experience.

Processor speed has been increasing much faster than memory speed over the past several generations of processor families. HLO component in the Intel compiler for the Itanium processor applies loop-based and region-based control and data transformations in order to: i) improve data access behavior with memory optimizations, ii) maximize resource usage in innermost loops, and iii) expose higher instruction-level parallelism.

G. Hedin (Ed.): CC 2003, LNCS 2622, pp. 303–319, 2003.

In HLO, we have implemented numerous well-known and new transformations, and more importantly, we combined and extended these transformations in special ways so as to exploit the Itanium™ processor architecture features for higher application performance. Fig. 1 shows the contribution of optimizations in HLO to the performance of the SPECfp2000 benchmark suite, consisting of 14 F77/F90/C programs. All experiments in this paper were conducted using version 6.0 Beta of the Intel Compiler for Microsoft Windows 2000/XP on an 800MHz Itanium processor based system with 4MB L3 cache. The graph shows the performance improvement or serial speedup over baseline. The baseline contains all optimizations excluding HLO used for SPEC base reporting. In particular, baseline includes inter-procedural optimizations and profile feedback.

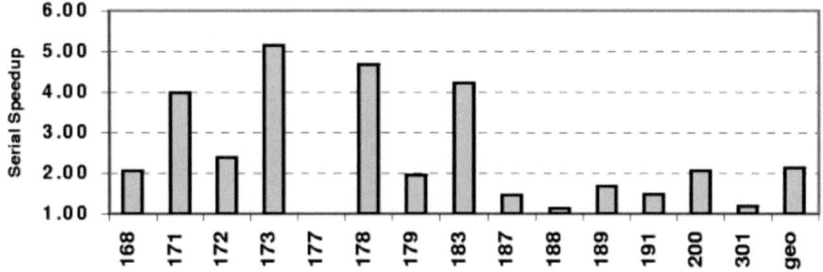

Fig. 1. Serial speedup due to optimizations in HLO. (`geo' is geomean)

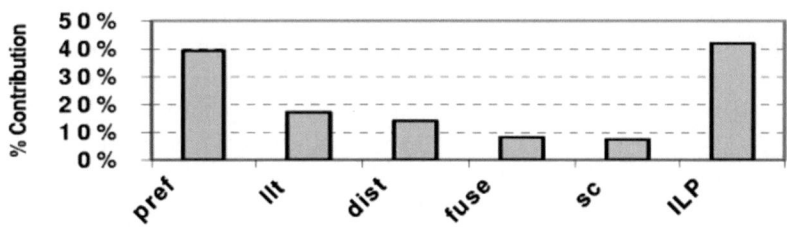

Fig. 2. Impact of individual optimizations in HLO on SPECfp2000 performance

Substantial performance gains from HLO are the result of selection of a large repertoire of transformations, design decisions that took into account the details of the Itanium architecture and careful and iterative phase-ordering decisions. This paper describes the experience in designing and implementing the HLO. The objective of this paper is to:

• Describe design decisions made during building of HLO targeting Itanium processor family.

• Present experimental results that validate the design decisions.

- Locality optimizations [1, 9]: linear loop transformations, loop fusion , loop distribution and strip-mining.
- Discuss the key learning and engineering trade-offs in a production compiler.

The rest of the paper is organized as follows. Section 2 provides design considerations for optimizations in the HLO targeting the Itanium processor family. Section 3 validates the design decisions with empirical data that show the impact of individual HLO transformations and how they interact with rest of the transformations. Key learning appears in Section 4 and concluding remarks in Section 5.

2   Design Considerations Targeting the Itanium™ Processor

In this section, we outline the design considerations for various optimizations in HLO while targeting the Itanium processor. The optimizations in HLO have been designed and implemented with a conscious effort to exploit the features in the Itanium processor architecture. In HLO, we have implemented many transformations that fall under these broad categories:

- Locality optimizations [1, 9]: linear loop transformations, loop fusion , loop distribution and strip-mining.
- ILP optimizations: unrolling, register blocking, affine-condition unswitching, and load-pair insertion.
- Maximize resource usage: Scalar replacement of memory references, affine-condition unswitching, and load-pair insertion.
- Data prefetching.
- State-of-the-art dependence and section analysis to support optimizations [1].

Fig. 2 shows the impact of individual optimizations in HLO on the performance of the SPECfp2000 benchmark suite. In the graph, x-axis shows the optimizations or groups of optimizations. Here *pref* stands for data-prefetching, *llt* for linear loop transformations, *dist* for loop distribution and strip-mining, *fuse* for fusion, *sc* for scalar replacement, and finally *ILP* stands for unroll-and-jam, affine-condition unswitching, and load-pair insertion. The y-axis is the percentage improvement because of the HLO optimizations over all other optimizations in our compiler.

This performance improvement is the result of 1) Itanium-architecture conscious design of optimizations and 2) careful orchestration of interaction between optimizations. Consequently, we are able to derive an efficient phase-ordering in our HLO which is shown in Fig. 3. (The figure does not include demand-driven calls to optimizations as a way of implementing certain other optimizations.) There exists no established technique to derive an optimal phase-ordering which is a computationally hard problem. In the subsections that follow, we describe design criteria for several optimizations targeting Itanium™ processor family. We also describe the rationale in positioning each optimization relative to other optimizations in the phase-order. These rationales together form the basis for a partial order of optimizations. The final phase order was derived from this partial order by considering other constraints such as minimizing compile time, say by minimizing updates to the dependence graph, and ease of maintenance. In Section 3, we evaluate the current phase-order by providing empirical data on the interaction among HLO optimizations – a positive interaction validates the choices and a negative interaction shows opportunity for improvement.

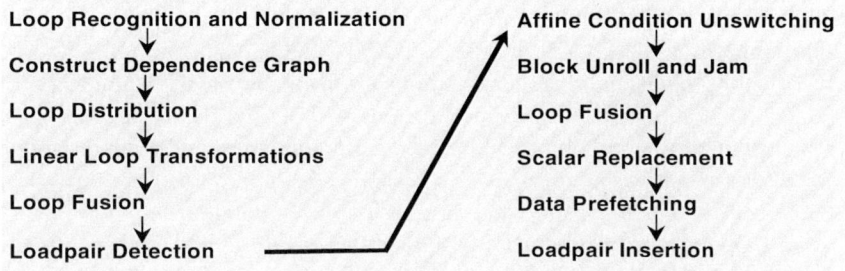

Fig. 3. Current phase-ordering of optimizations in HLO

2.1 Locality Optimizations

Caches are an important hardware means to bridge the gap between processor and memory access speeds. However, programs, as originally written, may not effectively utilize the available cache. Our design consideration was to:

- implement all loop transformations that are well-known in the community and in-dustry to improve the locality of data reference [1,2,7,9].
- account for the fact that L2 is first level at which floating-point data may reside.
- account for the benefit of data prefetching in reuse models that trigger many loop transformations.

We have implemented *linear loop transformations*, *loop fusion*, and *loop distribution* in the Intel compiler to improve data locality. As a combined effect, linear loop trans-formations [6,9] can dramatically improve memory access locality. They can also im-prove the effectiveness of other optimizations, such as scalar replacement, invariant code motion, and software pipelining. For example, a loop interchange can make ref-erences to arrays to be inner-loop invariant, besides improving the access behavior of other references. Important design considerations are:

- Make sure phase order is such that linear loop transformations occur sufficiently early to enable other transformations.
- Software pipelining [5] is important on the Itanium processor family, so use linear loop transformations to improve effectiveness by enabling parallelism in inner loops, and by interchanging, whenever possible, so that innermost loops have suf-ficiently large counts.
- Linear loop transformations have to be aware of the benefits of exposing refer-ences with spatial locality for effective data prefetching.

Loop fusion [1,8] is effective in improving cache performance, since it combines the cache context of multiple loops into a single new loop. Thus, data reuse across nested loops is within the same new nested loop. Loop fusion increases opportunities for reducing the overhead of array references by replacing them with references to compiler-generated scalar variables. Loop fusion also improves the effectiveness of data prefetching. While implementing loop fusion for the Itanium processor family, one must consider:

- 128 floating-point and 128 general registers available in the Itanium processor family. This allows aggressive loop fusions without the risk of register pressure. The design allows for loop fusion across call boundaries, and code motion to enable loop fusion.
- Trade-offs between locality and instruction level parallelism. For example, a fused loop may not be software pipelined because of dependences. In this case, the benefits of locality must outweigh the benefits of exploiting ILP across the back-edge of the fused loop.

Besides enabling other transformations, loop distribution [1,9] spreads the potentially large cache context of the original loop into different new loops, so that the new loops have manageable cache contexts and higher cache hit rates. While designing loop distribution for the Itanium processor family, the design considerations included the following:

- As in other compilers, use loop distribution to create perfect nests, enable loop interchange and loop blocking.
- Use loop distribution to partition a loop into loops with calls or non-inlined intrinsic and loops without calls. This is because, loops with calls cannot be software pipelined in the current compiler.
- Large loops may be distributed to avoid running out of rotating registers in software pipelining. This requires tradeoff between loss of locality and benefit of software pipelining.
- Ability to expose ILP across loop back-edges has sufficiently higher benefit to tilt the balance towards expansion of scalar variables to enable loop distribution.

Phase-ordering constraints: Loop distribution, linear loop transformations, and loop fusion are run in that order. Loop distribution exposes perfect nests and thus opportunities for linear loop transformations. Together, they expose opportunities for loop fusion. All three rely on the same cost model for better synergy.

2.2 ILP Optimizations

In this section we describe unrolling while the other ILP optimizations are covered in Section 2.3. The design of the Intel compiler for the Itanium processor unifies loop blocking, unroll-and-jam [1,9], and inner loop unrolling. Loop unrolling exposes parallelism across instructions in adjacent loop iterations. The large number of registers in the Itanium processor architecture enables the compiler to unroll loops by significantly larger factors without register spills than compilers for other contemporary architectures. This feature can be used to expose outer loops as new inner loops for software pipelining. While designing block-unroll-jam for the Itanium processor family, we had the following considerations:

- Unroll aggressively so as to extract greater ILP using large register file, and expose outer and larger loops to software pipelining and effective data prefetching.
- While blocking, consider the interaction of prefetching, need for a larger loop iteration count for efficient software pipelining, available bandwidth, and primarily the ability to issue 2 Fused-Multiply-Add (FMA) instructions in a cycle.
- Unroll and unroll-and-jam to maximally use machine resources and avoid *fractional II* loop body that under-utilizes machine resources.
- Use unrolling to expose more opportunities for loop fusion, insertion of load-pair instructions, and maximal resource usage.

- Pay attention to compile time since loop unrolling increases code size linearly, and the increase could adversely affect later optimizations that are quadratic or cubic in compile-time complexity.

Phase-ordering constraints: From the discussion above, it is clear that unroll-and-jam should be performed after loop distribution, interchange, and fusion, but before data prefetching and scalar replacement. We will find later that load-pair insertion has to be done after unrolling as well. However, note that there is an advantage to performing loop fusion again after loop unrolling as it exposes more conforming loop nests to loop fusion. Thus there is a second call to fusion after unroll-and-jam as shown in Fig. 3.

2.3   Maximizing Resource Usage

This category of optimizations includes scalar replacement of memory references, load-pair insertion, and affine-condition unswitching. Scalar replacement [2] is a technique to replace memory references with compiler-generated temporary scalar variables that are eventually mapped to registers. Most back-end optimization techniques map array references to registers when there is no loop-carried data dependence. However, the back-end optimizations do not have accurate dependence information to replace memory references with loop-carried dependence by scalar variables. Scalar replacement, as implemented in the Intel compiler for the Itanium^{TM} processor, also replaces loop invariant memory references with scalar variables defined at appropriate levels of the loop nesting.

The design considerations for scalar replacement on an Itanium processor based platform are:

- Map the compiler-inserted scalars directly onto rotating registers supported by the Itanium architecture [3]. The scalar moves required for scalar replacement [2,7] to preserve values across iterations are marked as MCOPY statements. The code generator maps the scalars to appropriate rotating registers so that explicit move instructions are unnecessary.

- Ensure that exact dependence information is available for the common cases. This also implies that all earlier transformations such as unrolling will have to maintain accurate dependence information.

Itanium processor architecture provides instructions that load a pair of floating-point numbers at a time [3]. Such load-pair instructions take a single memory issue slot, thus possibly reducing the initiation interval of a software pipelined loop. For example, the loop in Fig. 4(a) has three memory operations per iteration. By using load-pair operations, the number of memory references can be reduced to two per iteration after unrolling (4(b) and 4(c)). The load-pair optimization has to take into account the following requirements on the Itanium processor.

- Load-pairs can be issued only at certain alignment boundaries, for example 16-byte boundary for double precision data elements. We therefore either need to generate code to peel off aligned portions of loops, or generate multi-version code for different alignment combinations.

- The load-pair results have to be loaded into an odd-even register pair. This requirement can only be enforced during register allocation in the code-generation phase of the compiler. We however chose to implement the load-pair optimization phase in HLO because high-level information is available to identify adjacent memory loads, and because we rely on loop unrolling to expose more load-pair opportunities than what would normally be found in user code.

- There must be a utility to determine the number of load-pairs that need to be inserted to balance memory operations and computations.

Affine-condition unswitching hoists conditions out of loops. This has been used in the compiler community to mostly expose perfect nests. However, we find that it is quite useful in improving the effectiveness of software pipelining as well. The initiation interval for loops with conditions tends to be much larger than what it should be considering that only some of the branches will be taken in any iteration of the loop.

We use affine conditions to partition the loops into many loops, where in each new loop there is code corresponding to one of the paths. As a result the initiation intervals of the new loops will only correspond to the instructions that are always executed. A key design consideration was to avoid code size bloat and un-switch only the critical conditions.

Phase-ordering constraints: Scalar replacement of memory references should be one of the last few optimizations in HLO since transformations such as loop interchange and unrolling expose new opportunities for scalar replacement of memory references. Array contraction is also performed as part of scalar replacement since they use similar logic. Since, scalar replacement and array contraction need accurate dependence analysis, the dependence graphs must be rebuilt before entering scalar replacement.

The interaction between load-pair insertion and loop unrolling influenced the design of load-pair insertion technique and the phase-ordering between unroll-jam and load-pair insertion.

- Position insertion of load-pairs after unroll-jam, because the latter exposes opportunities for inserting load-pair instructions.

- However, load-pair insertion cannot call unroll-jam on demand because that would also require other optimizations such as scalar replacement, that eliminate redundant loads, to be done after unroll-jam

These two constraints influenced us to divide load-pair insertion into two stages. The first stage of load-pair optimization is therefore executed immediately before loop unrolling, so that the loop is analyzed to estimate the number of load-pairs that may be generated if the loop were to be unrolled by a factor of 2.   Loop unrolling will then factor the result into its resource usage model to determine the unroll factor.

The second stage is where the load-pairs are actually identified. Since it is run after unrolling, we are able to identify load-pairs that are either derived from user's original code or exposed by loop unrolling. Because we want to prevent load-pairs from being applied to redundant loads, this stage is placed after scalar replacement.   Scalar replacement is also run after loop unrolling because the latter may expose redundant loads to be eliminated.

Affine-condition unswitching has to be run after linear loop transformations, because that is when we know that the innermost loop will be exposed to software pipelining. It is advantageous to perform affine-condition unswitching immediately after linear transformations. We made an engineering decision to move it later in phase-order and position it after load-pair detection so as to minimize updates to dependence graph.

```
do j=1,1000
   y(j)=y(j)+a*x(j)
Enddo
            (a)
```

```
do j=1,1000,2
   t1,t2=ldfpd(x(j))
   t3,t4=ldfpd(y(j))
   y(j)=t3 + a*t1
   y(j+1)=t4 +a*t2
enddo
            (b)
```

```
.b1:
   (p25) stfd  [r42]=f64
   (p21) fma.d f55=f7,f37,f42
   (p16) add   r43=16,r44
   (p16) ldfpd f49,f32=[r44]
   (p21) fma.d f60=f7,f54,f47
         nop.i 0 ;;
   (p25) stfd  [r3]=f59,16
   (p16) add   r32=16,r33
         nop.i 0
   (p16) ldfpd f42,f37=[r33]
         nop.f 0
         br.ctop.sptk .b1 ;;
            (c)
```

Fig. 4. An example of the use of load pairs

2.4 Data Prefetching

Data prefetching is an effective technique to hide memory access latency. Prefetch instructions (named *lfetch* in the Itanium processor architecture) have one argument: the address to be prefetched. The effect of the instruction is to move the cache line containing the address to a higher level of the memory hierarchy. The address itself has no cache alignment requirement.

In the example in Fig. 5, the compiler inserts prefetches for arrays a and b making use of the support for rotating registers in the Itanium processor architecture to minimize the prefetch overheads. In this example, **incr** is a function of the cache line size, prefetch frequency, and the number of arrays that need to be prefetched within the loop. The addresses of the two arrays **a** and **b** that require prefetching are initialized before the loop (**r33** and **r34**). The design considerations for a prefetching algorithm on the Itanium processor are:

- Use data-locality analysis to selectively prefetch only those data references that are likely to suffer cache misses. References with spatial locality are selectively prefetched under a conditional of the form **(i mod L) == 0**, where **i** is the loop index and **L** denotes the cache line size. When multiple references access the same cache line, then only the leading reference needs to be prefetched.
- The cost incurred while prefetching data arises from the added overhead of executing prefetch instructions as well as instructions required for prefetch address calculation and predicate computation. The prefetch instructions will occupy memory slots, thereby increasing resource usage. *Compute-intensive* applications normally have sufficient free memory slots. Benefits from prefetching have to be weighed against the increase in resource usage in *memory-intensive* applications.
- The predication support in Itanium processor architecture provides an efficient way of adding prefetch instructions. The conditionals within the loop are converted to predicates through if-conversion, thus changing control dependency into data dependency. Indirect array references are prefetched making use of speculation support to load the index array speculatively.
- When multiple array references with spatial locality are accessed uniformly within a loop, prefetches can be issued with a single *lfetch* instruction that uses a rotating register to rotate the addresses of the different arrays that must be prefetched [4]. An example of this technique is illustrated in Fig. 5. This technique obviates the need for predicate calculations within the loop and saves memory slots that would otherwise be occupied by multiple *lfetch* instructions.
- Prefetch distance is estimated based on the memory latency, the resource requirements in the loop, and data dependence information.

The large number of registers available in the Itanium processor architecture enables prefetch addresses to be stored in registers obviating the need for register spill and fill within loops.

Phase-ordering constraints: Prefetching is run after most of the other optimizations within HLO. This is because prefetching can benefit from a lot of these other optimizations. Loop unroller will unroll all inner loops with small trip counts to expose any outer loops that may have a larger trip count. This makes the prefetches more effective. Fusion may reduce the total number of prefetches issued if the loops that are fused access the same data. Performing scalar replacement before prefetching ensures that a lot of memory references with group locality are replaced by temporary variables, thus reducing the compile time for prefetching.

As a whole, prefetching also interacts a lot with other optimizations outside HLO. For example, strength reduction is run after HLO, making sure that the addresses that are inserted by prefetching are strength-reduced. Also, there is a handshake between prefetch and the software-pipeliner that is part of the code-generator. As part of HLO, the compiler estimates the likelihood of a loop being pipelined. If a loop is predicted

to be software-pipelined, an estimate of the initiation interval of the loop based on resource requirements is computed in advance. This estimate aids in the distance calculation for the prefetches in the loop. Also when prefetch relies on register rotation, the
address copies are specially marked (shown as MCOPY in Fig. 5) for the software
pipeliner. These special copies are turned into automatic copies using register rotation
by the pipeliner.

```
for (i=1; i<n; i++)
    a(i)= b(i-1) + b(i+1)
            (a)
```

```
r33 = 80+ r16                    add    r33 = 80, r16
r34 = 80+ r18                    add    r34 = 80, r18
for(i=1; i< n;i++)               Loop:
{                                (p16)  ldfd f32 = [r8], 8
 a(i)= b(i-1) + b(i+1)           (p16)  ldfd f37 = [r3], 8
 r32 = r34 + incr                (p24)  stfd [r2] = f46, 8
 lfetch.nt1 [r34]                (p20)  fma  f42 = f36,f1,f41
 r34 = r33   //MCOPY             (p16)  add  r32 = 16, r34
 r33 = r32   //MCOPY             (p16)  lfetch.nt1 [r34]
}                                       br.ctop Loop
            (b)                                (c)
```

Fig. 5. Prefetch example illustrating the use of rotating registers: (a) original loop, (b) prefetch
for a and b using a single lfetch instruction with rotation shown as explicit assignments, and (c)
assembly code on Itanium™ processor with register rotation

3   Evaluation of Design Decisions

Certain compiler optimizations are independent in nature, in that their effect is independent of other optimizations. However, many compiler optimizations are highly in-
ter-dependent. The interaction between the optimizations tends to be complex. An interaction could be positive in that an optimization enables several other optimizations
or improves the effectiveness of other optimizations. An interaction could also be
negative in that an optimization may disable, reduce, or mask the effectiveness of
other optimizations. A chosen phase-ordering is most effective when all interactions
are positive. In this section, we present experimental data for the interaction between
optimizations in our HLO to show the effectiveness of our chosen phase ordering.

3.1   Experimental Framework

The data presented here are based on the performance of our compiler on the
SPECfp2000 benchmark suite. We used version 6.0 Beta of the Intel Compiler for Mi-
crosoft Windows 2000/XP on an 800MHz Itanium processor based system with 4MB
L3 cache. All the experiments done here are intended to show the interaction between

important optimizations in HLO. Later, we also present the interaction of some other important compiler modules with HLO.

We use the following notations in the discussion here:

- OPT: Set of all HLO optimizations under consideration.
- *opt*: one individual optimization in OPT.
- *P(X):* Represents the performance with the optimizations in *X* turned on.

In order to show the interaction among the optimizations in OPT, we measured the performance of all the benchmarks in SPECfp2000 with the following configurations:

- *P(BOTTOM):* Baseline performance where just the optimizations in OPT are disabled. BOTTOM represents all optimizations except HLO optimizations in OPT.
- *P(TOP):* Performance with all optimizations in BOTTOM and OPT turned on. This corresponds to the base compiler options for the reported SPECfp2000 performance numbers.
- *P(BOTTOM+opt):* Performance of BOTTOM with optimization *opt* turned on. This data is collected for each optimization in OPT.
- *P(TOP-opt):* Performance of TOP with optimization *opt* turned off. This data is collected for each optimization in OPT.

The intuition behind collecting the above data is to find the effect of each optimization when applied along with other optimizations as opposed to when applied on its own. This shows how an optimization performs in the absence and presence of other optimizations and thereby provides insight into interaction of this optimization with the other optimizations. We can make the following observations based on the above data:

1. *P(BOTTOM+opt) – P(BOTTOM),* say *gain_at_bottom*, gives the performance improvement or degradation when *opt* is the only HLO optimization turned on.
2. *P(TOP) – P(TOP-opt),* say *gain_at_top*, gives the performance improvement or degradation of *opt* when applied along with other optimizations.

Clearly, when the above quantities are same for an optimization *opt*, then *opt* does not interact with any other optimization in OPT. In other words, if *opt* improved (degraded) performance when applied on its own, then it would continue to improve (degrade) by the same extent when applied along with remaining optimizations in OPT. When *gain_at_top* is very large compared to *gain_at_bottom*, then most of the benefit from applying *opt* is the result of its positive interaction with other optimizations. This could happen, for instance, when another optimization in OPT that is applied earlier enables *opt* or improves its effectiveness. We can also get such a scenario if *opt* enabled a later optimization in OPT. This implies that a favorable phase-ordering was chosen.

Similarly, if *opt* interacts negatively with the remaining optimizations in OPT, *gain_at_top* is less than *gain_at_bottom*. This usually suggests room for improvement either as tuning of an optimization or change in phase ordering. It may also be the case that two optimizations in OPT target the same performance issue, and the benefits obtained from the two optimizations are not additive in nature.

The graphs presented in this section show this interaction. We explain this with respect to the graph shown in Fig. 6. We normalize all the data with respect to *P(TOP)-P(BOTTOM)*. The actual speedup of *P(TOP)* over *P(BOTTOM)* was shown in Fig. 1

and Fig. 2. For a given optimization in OPT, we provide cumulative bar graphs for each benchmark performance. As shown in the legend, for a given benchmark we show the following sections on a bar in this order:

1. *P(BOTTOM+opt) - P(BOTTOM)*: Performance gain (loss) from applying only optimization *opt* from the set of HLO optimizations in OPT.
2. *P(Top-opt) - P(BOTTOM)*: Performance gain (loss) from applying all optimizations in OPT except *opt*.
3. This is the additional gain or loss to reach *P(TOP)-P(BOTTOM)*. This is due to the interaction of *opt* with other optimizations in OPT. Positive and negative interactions are shaded differently.

Note that if *gain_at_bottom* is equal to *gain_at_top*, i.e. when there is no interaction, we can easily deduce that the first two sections in a bar should add up to *P(TOP)-P(BOTTOM)* which has the value one in our graphs. Similarly, if *gain_at_top* is more than *gain_at_bottom*, i.e. when there is positive interaction, then *P(TOP)-P(BOTTOM)* is more than the sum of the first two bar sections. On the contrary, it is less than the sum of the first two sections if the interaction is negative.

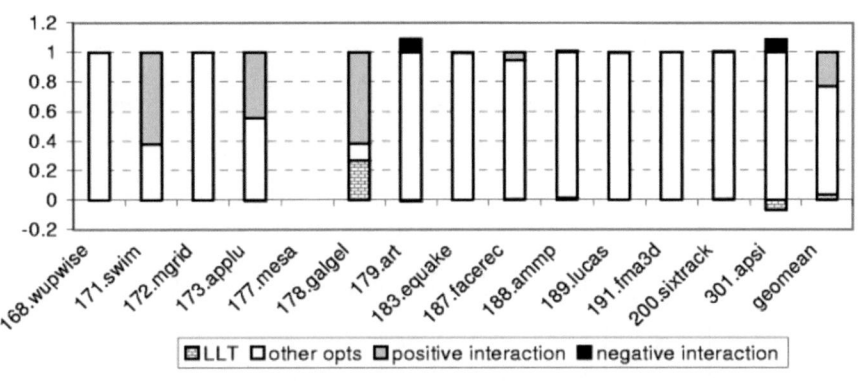

Fig. 6. Interaction graph for linear loop transformations

3.2   Analysis of Interaction Data

The graphs and analysis provided here show that HLO optimizations tend to have a high degree of interaction. They also validate our design consideration and phase-ordering and provide some useful insights to further opportunities. (The legend shown in Fig. 6 applies to all the graphs for all optimizations discussed in this section.)

3.2.1   Linear Loop Transformations

Fig. 6 shows the interactions for linear loop transformations. This shows that these transformations interact significantly with other optimizations in HLO for the benchmarks 171.swim, 173.applu, 178.galgel, and 301.apsi. In 171.swim, linear loop transformations interact with data prefetching. Loop interchange exposes array accesses with spatial locality that make data prefetching more effective. For 173.applu, there is interaction between linear loop transformations and loop fusion. In this case, two adjacent loops could be fused only after loop reversal of the second loop. Interactions in 178.galgel are described in detail in Section 4. Note that 301.apsi shows negative interaction both at bottom (below y=0 in the graph) and top (above y=1 in the graph), which is a manifestation of small performance loss due to loop interchange. The performance loss is due to differences in distances computed for data prefetching for unit stride and non-unit stride array references.

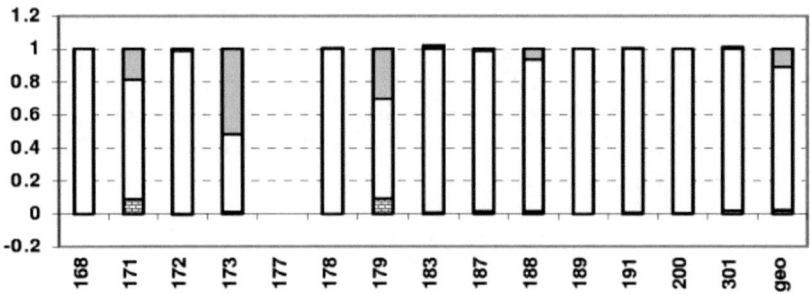

Fig. 7. Interaction graph for loop fusion

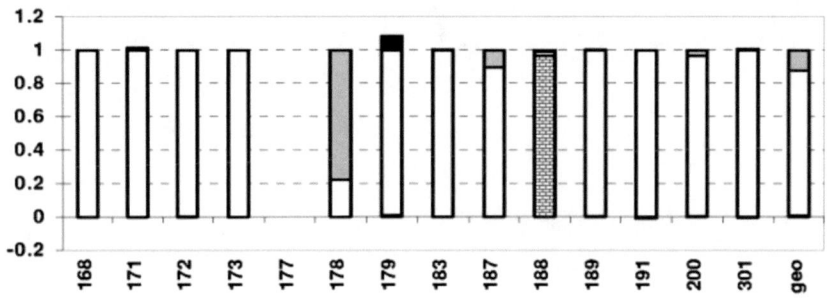

Fig. 8. Interaction graph for loop distribution

3.2.2 Loop Fusion
In order to enable effective loop fusion, transformations like code motion, loop peeling, loop reversal, and extensive array section analysis are required. Fig. 7 shows the interaction for loop fusion. We observe that interaction is high for 171.swim, 173.applu, and 179.art. There are two primary reasons for interactions in 173.applu – first, loop reversal enables more fusion as explained in the last subsection; second,

loop fusion enables many scalar replacements. Loop fusion enables scalar replacements and improves the effectiveness of data prefetching in 179.art.

3.2.3 Loop Distribution

Fig. 8 shows the interaction for loop distribution. 178.galgel has a very high interaction. As we will explain in Section 4, a combination of loop distribution, interchange, and unroll helps to considerably improve the performance of 178.galgel. But, loop distribution when applied alone, has no effect on performance. In 188.ammp, loop distribution helps software pipelining by partitioning loops into pipelineable and non-pipelineable sections. 179.art has a short run-time and the negative interaction in the graph is within experimental error.

3.2.4 Scalar Replacement

Interaction for scalar replacement of memory references (which also includes array contraction) is shown in Fig. 9. Scalar replacement of memory references, when applied alone, improves performance for 172.mgrid and 301.apsi.. In 172.mgrid, 173.applu, 178.galgel, and 200.sixtrack, other transformations help scalar replacement to be more effective. In 173.applu, a large number of scalar replacements are enabled by loop fusion. In 200.sixtrack, loop unrolling enables more opportunities for scalar replacement in key loops.

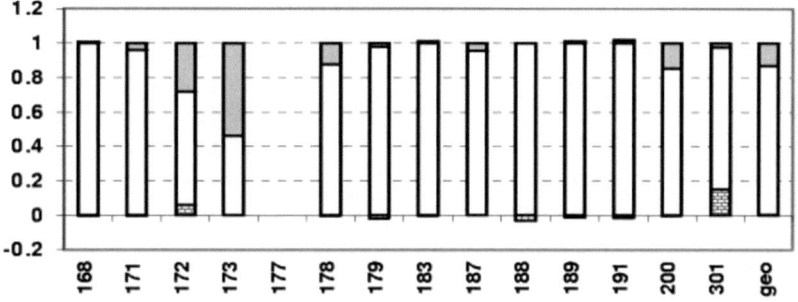

Fig. 9. Interaction graph for scalar replacement

3.2.5 ILP Enhancing Techniques

Interaction of loop unrolling, load-pair insertion and affine-condition unswitching is shown in Fig. 10. In 173.applu, loop unrolling enables loop fusion across large regions. In 183.equake loop unrolling enables loop fusion and prefetching. 200.sixtrack is a floating-point intensive code with many opportunities for extracting ILP. In this application, loop unrolling enables larger loops to be pipelined. Larger loops also help prefetching to be more effective.

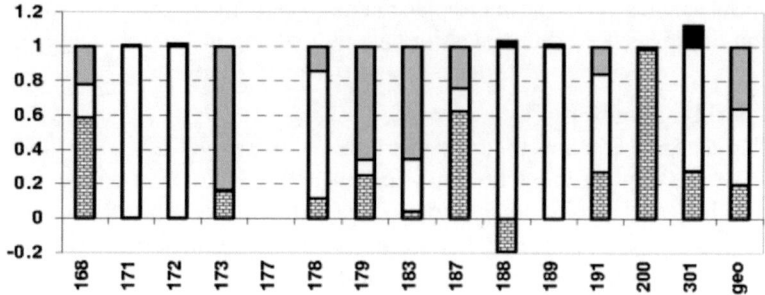

Fig. 10. Interaction graph for loop unrolling and load-pair insertion

3.2.6 Data Prefetching

Interaction for data prefetching is shown in Fig. 11. It is interesting to note that data prefetching on its own benefits nearly all applications in the graph. Data prefetching also shows significant positive interaction with other optimizations. For example, bars for 183.equake, 171.swim and 173.applu show large improvement in performance due to positive interactions with other transformations.   Loop unrolling, fusion, and blocking are key helpers. For example, unrolling of loops exposes larger inner loop to data prefetching. Note that the gains from prefetching for 173.applu are present only in the presence of other optimizations. Bar for 189.lucas is dominated by the gain from prefetch alone and does not show interactions with other HLO optimizations. 200.sixtrack does not benefit from prefetching, and there is a small degradation in performance at the bottom and at the top. This is because the data accessed fits in the cache, and prefetching only adds to the resource requirements without any noticeable benefit. The geomean for benefits from prefetching alone is close to 20%, and this increases to about 40% at the top (as shown in Fig. 2) due to significant positive interactions.

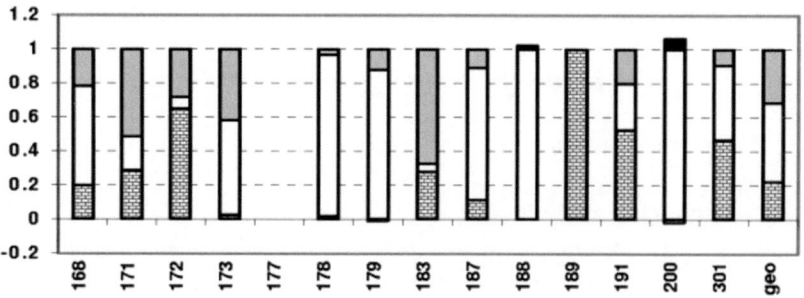

Fig. 11. Interaction graph for data prefetching

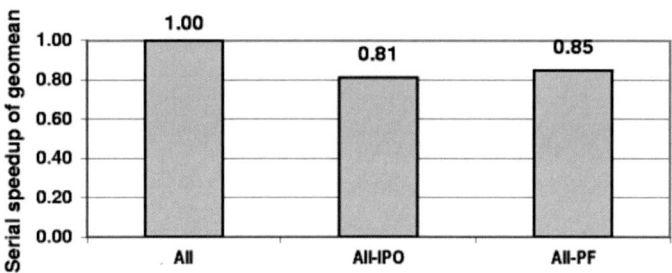

Fig. 12. Influence of IPO and Profile feedback (PF) on HLO. (All=HLO+IPO+PF)

4 Key Learning

The design decisions discussed in previous sections were all related to the fact that we were targeting HLO for Itanium processor family. However, some of our other decisions were made because we implemented HLO in a production compiler. In a production compiler, minimizing compile time, memory usage, and maintenance costs is very important. In fact, while designing a production compiler, designers tend to forego an opportunity to improve performance in order to improve compile time, memory usage or maintenance efforts. For example, positioning affine-condition unswitching early in phase-order can enable more transformations. However, unswitching causes an update on the dependence graph that is expensive. We chose to position unswitching later in the phase-order, because we viewed the compile time increase a higher penalty than potential gains of moving it earlier in the phase-order. In contrast, we chose to rebuild rather than incrementally update dependence graph after certain sequence of transformations. This decision slightly increased the compile time. However, we estimated that the increase in compile time was better than the engineering cost of maintaining an incremental dependence update mechanism.

Early in the design and implementation phase of HLO, we decided that the transformations needed only the high-level resource estimates – such as number of basic blocks. However, we learned that the transformations can be more effective with low-level resource estimates. We redesigned resource estimation to include an estimation of initiation interval of loops, number of registers, and whether a loop is likely to be software pipelined. This redesign proved to be key to many transformations including loop fusion, distribution, unrolling and insertion of load-pair instructions.

Traditional compilers tend to do a maximal loop distribution followed by a loop fusion. We learnt that for certain engineering applications this can result in sub-optimal performance. We had to overlay the loop distribution heuristics to control distributions by distributing only at heuristically determined points.

Load-pair instructions proved to be very important for certain engineering applications. However, for certain other applications, load-pair instructions did not yield significant improvements as we expected. We learnt that for these applications saving memory resources did not matter as much because the memory operations were incurring a higher latency than what was assumed at the time of scheduling.

We believe that HLO communicates more information to the code generator compared to other high-level optimizers in the industry. This helped us tightly integrate the two components for higher overall performance. We made several decisions that helped communicate only the information that would be needed to minimize memory usage and compile time. For example, dependence information that can be easily deduced from a symbolic memory disambiguator was not explicitly communicated via a dependence graph.

In this paper, we did not discuss the impact of analysis beyond HLO. Effectiveness of optimizations in HLO is enhanced by inter-procedural optimization (IPO) and profile feedback [4], that are included in the SPEC base options. Their interactions with HLO are shown in Fig. 12.

5 Concluding Remarks

In this paper, we described design decisions made while designing and implementing HLO targeting Itanium processor family. We presented experimental results that validate the design decisions. The results showed a well designed high-level optimizer can have significant impact on overall performance. Such a design must consider at least the architecture-driven design considerations discussed in this paper. From the evaluation of the design choices we made, we can conclude that implementing the entire repertoire of transformations is disproportionately more effective than a subset. Since HLO was implemented in a production compiler, we made certain engineering trade-offs. We discussed these trade-offs and outlined key learning derived from our experience.

References

[1] R. Allen and K. Kennedy, Optimizing Compilers for Modern Architectures, Morgan Kaufmann Publishers, 2002.
[2] S.Carr, "Memory-Hierarchy Management" Ph.D. Thesis, Rice University, July 1994.
[3] J. Huck, D. Morris, J. Ross, A. Knies, H. Mulder, and R. Zahir, "Introducing the IA-64 Architecture," IEEE Micro, Sept-Oct 2000, 12–23.
[4] R. Krishnaiyer, D. Kulkarni, D. Lavery, W. Li, C. Lim, J. Ng, D. Sehr, "An Advanced Optimizer for the IA-64 Architecture," IEEE Micro, Nov-Dec 2000.
[5] M.S. Lam, "Software Pipelining: An Effective Scheduling Technique for {VLIW} Machines," in Proceedings of the ACM SIGPLAN 1988 Conference on Programming Language Design and Implementation, June 1988, 318–328.
[6] W. Li and K. Pingali, "A Singular Loop Transformation Framework Based on Non-Singular Matrices," International Journal of Parallel Programming, volume 22 (2), 1994.
[7] S. Muchnik, Advanced Compiler Design Implementation, Morgan Kaufman, 1997.
[8] Singhai & McKinley, "A parameterized Loop Fusion Algorithm for Improving Parallelism and Cache Locality", by The Computer Journal, 1997"
[9] M. Wolfe, High Performance Compilers for Parallel Computing, Addison-Wesley, 1996.

Improving Data Locality by Chunking

Cédric Bastoul[1] and Paul Feautrier[2]

[1] Laboratoire PRiSM, Université de Versailles Saint Quentin
45 avenue des États-Unis, 78035 Versailles Cedex, France
`cedric.bastoul@prism.uvsq.fr`
[2] École Normale Supérieure de Lyon
46 Allée d'Italie, 60364 Lyon, France
`paul.feautrier@ens-lyon.fr`

Abstract. Cache memories were invented to decouple fast processors from slow memories. However, this decoupling is only partial, and many researchers have attempted to improve cache use by program optimization. Potential benefits are significant since both energy dissipation and performance highly depend on the traffic between memory levels. But modeling the traffic is difficult; this observation has led to the use of heuristic methods for steering program transformations. In this paper, we propose another approach: we simplify the cache model and we organize the target program in such a way that an asymptotic evaluation of the memory traffic is possible. This information is used by our optimization algorithm in order to find the best reordering of the program operations, at least in an asymptotic sense. Our method optimizes both temporal and spatial locality. It can be applied to any static control program with arbitrary dependences. The optimizer has been partially implemented and applied to non-trivial programs. We present experimental evidence that the amount of cache misses is drastically reduced with corresponding performance improvements.

1 Introduction

Technological advances in the realization of integrated chips result in faster clocks for processors, and in larger capacity for memory. In consequence, if nothing is done, processors will starve because their memory systems cannot supply data at the required speed. Memory hierarchies are a good solution to this problem: they are cheap and efficient, at least for ordinary programs and situations. Nevertheless, their efficiency decreases dramatically for scientific computing and signal processing codes, where large data sets are accessed according to highly regular patterns. Next, their temporal behavior is difficult to predict; this forbids their use in systems with hard real time constraints. Lastly, moving data from level to level uses a lot of power, which renders them unsuitable for embedded systems.

A lot of work has been devoted to improving the behavior of memory hierarchies. There are two kinds of approaches for this problem. The first approach consists in designing highly optimized libraries (LAPACK is a good example [1]) for the most common linear algebra and signal processing algorithms. This method

G. Hedin (Ed.): CC 2003, LNCS 2622, pp. 320–334, 2003.

often gives the best results, provided the source problem and the target architecture are within the scope of the available library. The second approach tries to optimize the source program at compile time. This method is not restricted to a given set of algorithms and can be adapted, with minor modifications, to any memory hierarchy architecture. The present work belongs to the later approach.

Most optimizing compilers try to transform the source program in order to improve the behavior of the memory hierarchy. The basic principle is to regroup all accesses to a given memory cell, in order to take a maximum advantage of possible reuses. This is obtained first by applying loop transformations [15,11] according to some cost model [13], then by tiling the resulting loop nest [16] with tiles having a carefully chosen size [4]. Basically, this method applies only to perfect loop nests in which dependences are non-existent or have a special form (fully permutable loop nests). Another data-centric [9] approach starts from a memory cell and tries to build the slice that accesses this cell. Here again, dependences greatly complicate the transformation process.

As said above, previous methods require most of the time severe limitations on the input program. Our work can be applied to a wide application domain since we do not lay down any requirement on dependences provided that the program has static control [5]. This program class includes a large range of problems which are discussed in depth by Xue [17]. The properties of such programs can be summarized in this way: (1) control statements are **do** loops with affine bounds and **if** conditionals with affine conditions (in fact control can be more complex, see [17]); (2) arrays are the only data structures, and their subscripts are affine; (3) affine bounds, conditions and subscripts depend only on outer loop counters and structure (or size) parameters.

All methods mentioned earlier are based on a heuristic cost model. Let us consider for instance two accesses to the same memory cell. It seems probable that the longer the time interval between these accesses is, the higher the probability of the first reference to be evicted from the cache is. Hence, loop transformations aim at moving these references to neighboring iterations of some innermost loop. Our technique is based on an estimate of the memory traffic, and tries to find the loop transformation that minimizes this estimate, under the constraint that all dependences are satisfied. This technique, which we call *chunking* is presented in section 2. Section 3 explains how to construct good chunking functions for a given program. Section 4 deals with the problem of code generation when the chunking functions are given. Section 5 describes our implementation and experimental results. Section 6 compares chunking to other approaches. We then conclude and discuss future work.

2   Chunking

The principle of our method is to partition the set of operations of a program in subsets small enough that their accessed data fit in the cache: the *chunks*. The program is then executed chunk by chunk, as if there was a cache flush between each of them. These subsets must be such that their sequential execution is

equivalent to the execution of the original program. In practice, chunks will
be numbered then executed in order of increasing numbers. A chunk number
will be assigned to each operation, i.e. to each instance of each statement. In
other words, for each statement S we seek a *chunking function* θ_S associating
a chunk number $\theta_S(x)$ to each iteration vector x. The original operations will
be rescheduled accordingly to these chunking functions. We present in figure 1
an example of chunking of a simple program. We assume as input hypothesis
that n array elements can fit in the cache, but m cannot. Such a simple code yet
exhibits several difficulties: non-perfect loop nest, dependences between different
statements, parameters and multiple references. In this example, the order of the

```
do i=1, n
   a(i) = i                    ! S1
   do j=1, m
      b(j) = b(j) + a(i)       ! S2
   enddo
enddo
```

(a) source program

$$\theta_{S1}\left(\left[i\right]\right) = \left[i\right] ; \theta_{S2}\left(\left[\begin{matrix}i\\j\end{matrix}\right]\right) = \left[j+n\right]$$

(b) chunking functions

```
do c=1, n
   a(c) = c                    ! S1
enddo
do c=n+1, n+m
   do i=1, n
      b(c-n) = b(c-n) + a(i)   ! S2
   enddo
enddo
```

(c) target program

Fig. 1. Running example

operations has been modified for a maximal use of temporal locality, according to
the chunking functions in figure 1(b). In the target program, c gives the number
of the current chunk. This example will be used for illustration throughout this
paper. It can be noticed that the code can be restructured in the same way by
conventional loop distribution, loop permutation and skewing. Chunking is set
in the framework of the polytope model and every chunking can be broken down
in a succession of well known transformations. In fact, chunking does not aim to
find *new* transformations but to find the *right* transformation automatically.

3   Computing Chunking Functions

The quality of a chunking can be assessed by using two valuations. First, the *footprint size* which is the number of memory cells accessed by the operations of a chunk. Next, the *traffic* which is the number of data movements between main and cache memories. We want to build an optimal chunk system *i.e.* where each chunk footprint fits in the cache and the traffic is minimal. To be able to generate the target code, we are looking for affine chunking functions. Subsequently, for an operation $S[x]$, instance of the statement S with the iteration vector x in the iteration domain D_S, the chunk number can be written:

$$\theta_S(x) = T_S x + k_S.$$

T_S is a matrix called the *chunking matrix*; its dimensions are $g \times \rho(S)$ with $\rho(S)$ the number of loops surrounding S. The choice of the value of g is postponed till section 3.2. k_S is a constant vector. Chunking functions are calculated in several steps which are discussed in the next sections. In section 3.1 we show how to compute an asymptotic evaluation of the traffic with respect to the chunking functions. Then we exhibit the constraints that the chunking functions must satisfy to minimize the traffic. Section 3.2 explains how to find all the functions verifying such constraints. Section 3.3 shows how to choose the functions in such a way that the transformation is legal for dependences. Lastly, section 3.4 and 3.5 gives respectively the constraints which have to be satisfied by the chunking functions in order to achieve group-locality and spatial-locality.

3.1   Asymptotic Evaluation

It is hard to find an accurate solution to the traffic evaluation problem for a particular cache type. Modeling the replacement mechanism is quite difficult, but it is bypassed by chunking. However, several difficulties remain, hence we propose the following simplifications on our cache and memory models:

- conflict misses do not change the order of magnitude of the traffic; this assumption is satisfied by fully associative caches and is close to be satisfied by modern caches with high associativity; most discrepancies can be compensated by using an effective cache size smaller than the real one;
- we will be satisfied with asymptotic evaluation of the traffic; in many cases, program transformations can change the order of magnitude of the traffic, then it would be useless to fiddle with constant factors or worse, units in the last decimal place; in some cases, *i.e.* when self-reuse has already been exploited, only the constant factors can be improved; the question of deciding if a more precise evaluation can influence the target code is left for future work.

In our model, it is possible to make estimates of footprint sizes and traffic with respect to the chunking functions. Considering a statement S, an array A

and a subscript function f, the footprint generated by this reference is the set of memory cells accessed during the chunk execution:

$$\mathcal{F}_{S,A,f}(t) = \{f(x) \mid x \in D_S, \theta_S(x) = t\}. \tag{1}$$

Let us suppose that the cache is empty at the start of a chunk and that its footprint fits in the cache. Then any cells in the footprint is copied once to the cache at some time during the execution of the chunk and stays there until the termination of the chunk. Hence the traffic can be estimated as the number of pairs ⟨data, chunk number⟩:

$$\mathcal{T}_{S,A,f} = \mathrm{Card}\ \{\langle f(x), \theta_S(x)\rangle \mid x \in D_S\}. \tag{2}$$

Since input programs have static control, subscript functions are affine and can be written $f(x) = Fx + a$, where F is the subscript matrix of dimension $\rho(A) \times \rho(S)$, with $\rho(A)$ the dimension of array A, and a a constant vector.

Theorem 1. *Let* $H = \{Ux \mid Vx = 0, x \in D\}$ *be a set where* U *and* V *are arbitrary integral matrices of the right dimension, and where* D *is a bounded full dimensional domain such that the value of each component of the vector* x *is an integer in a segment of length* m. *Then* $\mathrm{Card}\ H$ *is of the order of* m^l *with* $l = \mathrm{rank}\ \begin{pmatrix} U \\ V \end{pmatrix} - \mathrm{rank}\ V$.

Proof. Let us first study the dimension of the subspace $K = \{Ux \mid Vx = 0\}$. This corresponds to the rank of the application f from $\ker V$ to $\mathrm{Im}\ U$ that associates Ux to x. According to a well known algebraic theorem, we have $\dim \ker V = \mathrm{rank}\ f + \dim \ker f$. As $\ker f = \ker U \cap \ker V$, it follows:

$$\mathrm{rank}\ f = \dim\ \ker V - \dim\ (\ker U \cap \ker V).$$

Since D is such that the value of each component of x is an integer in a segment of length m, it follows that each component of Ux also is integral and belongs to a segment of length proportional to m. Hence, the size of H is of the order of m^l. Since $\dim \ker V + \mathrm{rank}\ V =$ number of column of V, we have finally $\mathrm{Card}\ H$ is of the order of m^l with $l = \mathrm{rank}\ \begin{pmatrix} U \\ V \end{pmatrix} - \mathrm{rank}\ V$. ∎

The orders of magnitude of the cardinals of sets describing footprints (1) and traffic (2) are directly given by theorem 1. The asymptotic size of footprints are found with V as T and U as F, and considering the traffic, with V as the null matrix and U as the block matrix $\begin{pmatrix} T \\ F \end{pmatrix}$ composed of the matrix T for its first rows and of the matrix F for the next rows. If the value of each component of x is an integer in a segment of length m, we have:

$$\mathrm{Card}\ \mathcal{F}_{S,A,f}(t) = O\left(m^l\right), \text{with } l = \mathrm{rank}\ \begin{pmatrix} T \\ F \end{pmatrix} - \mathrm{rank}\ T,$$

$$\mathcal{T}_{S,A,f} = O\left(m^k\right), \text{with } k = \mathrm{rank}\ \begin{pmatrix} T \\ F \end{pmatrix}.$$

These evaluations depend on F which can be extracted by analysis of the source code and T which is the unknown of the problem. Thus we can find the constraints that T has to satisfy in order that the footprints fit in the cache and the traffic is minimal.

Let us consider one statement with n array accesses, the subscript matrix of the ith access being F_i. All tuples $\left\langle \text{rank } T, \text{rank} \begin{pmatrix} T \\ F_i \end{pmatrix} \text{ for } 1 \leq i \leq n \right\rangle$ corresponding to the possible sets of constraints can be enumerated. We need to know the cache size C and an estimate of the size parameter m. We then determine an integer α such that $m^\alpha \leq C$. A footprint component of size $O\left(m^{l_i}\right)$ fits in the cache if $l_i \leq \alpha$. We can thus eliminate all tuples for which this condition is not satisfied, and we can rank the remaining ones in order of increasing traffic. It then remains to try building a T which satisfies the rank condition of the best tuple. If this is proved to be impossible, we start again with the next tuple.

3.2   Building Chunking Matrices

Thanks to the evaluations, we know which rank constraints must be satisfied by the chunking matrices to minimize the traffic. In this section, we show how to build such matrices, at first when the corresponding statement includes only one reference. Then, we show that there always exists a chunking matrix such that each associated footprint fits in the cache.

For a statement S with one reference, it is always possible to find a matrix T such that rank $T = v$ and rank $\begin{pmatrix} T \\ F \end{pmatrix} = w$, provided that v and w have compatible values (i.e. $\rho(S) \geq w \geq v$). The building process is described by the algorithm in figure 2. From the returned matrix T, we can generate the set of matrices with the required properties: the set of CT matrix where C is a matrix of full row rank. We will choose in this set the matrices in order to satisfy additional constraints described in section 3.3 and 3.4.

Let us demonstrate that this algorithm builds a matrix T that answers the requirements. Since the matrix T is composed of v linearly independent rows, the constraint rank $T = v$ is satisfied. These rows are those of G^{-1} from $\rho(S)-w+1$ to $\rho(S) - w + v$. Hence, the kernel of T is generated by the column vectors of G from 1 to $\rho(S) - w$ and from $\rho(S) - w + v + 1$ to $\rho(S)$. The kernel of $\begin{pmatrix} T \\ F \end{pmatrix}$ is the intersection of the kernel of T with the kernel of F, hence it is generated by the $\rho(S) - w$ first column vectors of G and the constraint rank $\begin{pmatrix} T \\ F \end{pmatrix} = w$ is satisfied. As for the choice of g, the number of rows of T, it is clear that bordering a matrix by null rows does not change its rank. Since when reordering the program it is useful to have all chunking function of the same dimension, we may take $g = \max \rho(S)$.

The generalization to n references implies the combination of n constraints: rank $\begin{pmatrix} T \\ F_i \end{pmatrix} = w_i$ for $1 \leq i \leq n$. The matrix G must have for each reference

---

Construction Algorithm: Build a matrix under rank constraints.

Input: the subscript matrix F and the rank constraints rank $T = v$ and rank $\begin{pmatrix} T \\ F \end{pmatrix} = w$.

Output: a matrix T respecting the rank constraints.

1. Compute a basis of ker F and complete it to a basis of $N^{\rho(S)}$.
2. Let G be the matrix of these vectors (vectors added to complete to a basis of $N^{\rho(S)}$ are the last columns).
3. Compute G^{-1}, inverse of G.
4. Build matrix T:
   a) For i from 1 to v:
      i^{th} row of $T = (\rho(S) - w + i)^{th}$ row of G^{-1}.
   b) Complete T with null rows.

Fig. 2. Construction Algorithm

exactly $\rho(S) - w_i$ vectors of a basis of ker F_i for a total of at most v vectors. Such a matrix does not always exist. The choice of vectors to be included in the matrix G is essential. We can guide this choice by adding for each reference as many vectors from a preceding reference as possible. If a solution does not exist for a tuple, then we try to find another one for the next more interesting tuple.

A chunking matrix such as each footprint fits in the cache always exists. The hardest constraint for the footprints is to have a size in $O\left(m^0\right)$, and the last tried possibility will be the tuple $\langle \rho(S), w_i = \rho(S)$ for $1 \leq i \leq n \rangle$. The corresponding chunking generates for the ith reference footprint sizes of $O\left(m_i^0\right)$ and the maximal traffic of $O\left(m_i^{\rho(S)}\right)$. Its solution $T = Id$ always exists and is the trivial chunking where there is one chunk per operation.

Example 1. Let us consider the source code in figure 1. We assume that a is an array of n cells which fits in the cache and b is an array of m cells which does not fit in the cache. Then, the acceptable orders of magnitude for the footprints size are $O\left(n^1\right)$ and $O\left(m^0\right)$. The program has two statements:

- the statement $S1$ has just one reference to the array a with the index matrix $F_{S1,1} = \begin{bmatrix} 1 \end{bmatrix}$; the matrix T_{S1} having the best properties corresponds to the tuple $\langle 1, 1 \rangle$, it will generate footprint sizes of $O\left(n^0\right)$ and a traffic of $O\left(n^1\right)$; the algorithm builds $T_{S1} = \begin{bmatrix} 1 \end{bmatrix}$;
- the statement $S2$ has two references, the first one to the array a with the index matrix $F_{S2,1} = \begin{bmatrix} 1 & 0 \end{bmatrix}$ and the second one to the array b with the index matrix $F_{S2,2} = \begin{bmatrix} 0 & 1 \end{bmatrix}$; the matrix T_{S2} having the best properties would correspond to the tuple $\langle 1, 2, 1 \rangle$, it would generate footprint sizes of

$O\left(m^0 + n^1\right)$ and a traffic of $O\left(m^1 + n^2\right)$; the construction is possible and gives $T_{S2} = \begin{bmatrix} 0 & 1 \\ 0 & 0 \end{bmatrix}$.

3.3   Legality

Since chunking reorders operations, it must satisfies dependences. In this section, we explain how chunking functions can be chosen in such a way that the transformation satisfies dependences. We will show that there always exists a valid solution which satisfies the constraints described in previous sections.

Chunks are numbered in the order they will be executed, and inside each of them, operations are executed in the original sequential order. Let us consider $I_{\mathcal{P}}$, the statement set of the program $\mathcal{P}$, and $\delta_{\mathcal{P}}$, the dependence relation on $\mathcal{P}$; a chunking is legal if and only if:

$$\forall S, R \in I_{\mathcal{P}}, \quad S[x] \, \delta_{\mathcal{P}} \, R[y] \Rightarrow \theta_S(x) \leq \theta_R(y). \tag{3}$$

There is no *a priori* reason for (3) to be satisfied by the chunking matrices as constructed by the algorithm in previous section. However, we are free to modify them as long as we do not change their rank properties. We are also free to adjust the constant vectors k, as they have no impact on the footprints and traffic (at least asymptotically). Thus, for any statement S, the chunking function can be written

$$\theta_S(x) = C_S T_S x + k_S,$$

where C_S is a matrix of full row rank. We use the Farkas algorithm [6] to solve (3) and to find the set of all C_S and k_S. If the problem has no solution, we declare a failure and try the next best traffic/footprint combination.

A legal solution such as the footprints fit in the cache always exists. It corresponds to the worst solution, in which all the chunking matrices are identity matrices. In this case, the original program is not modified. This possibility must always be left open, since it might happen that the source program is already optimal.

Example 2. Let us continue the example of section 3.2. The chunking functions associated to the proposed matrices are:

$$\theta_{S1}\left([i]\right) = [1][i] + [0] = [i]; \; \theta_{S2}\left(\begin{bmatrix} i \\ j \end{bmatrix}\right) = \begin{bmatrix} 0 & 1 \\ 0 & 0 \end{bmatrix}\begin{bmatrix} i \\ j \end{bmatrix} + \begin{bmatrix} 0 \\ 0 \end{bmatrix} = \begin{bmatrix} j \\ 0 \end{bmatrix}.$$

These functions do not describe a valid chunking: the dependence from $S1$ to $S2$ is not satisfied. For instance, the operation $S2\begin{bmatrix} 2 \\ 1 \end{bmatrix}$ is executed in chunk number 1 whereas the operation $S1\begin{bmatrix} 2 \end{bmatrix}$ on which it depends is executed later, in chunk number 2. Our method makes it possible to correct this chunking so that all the dependences are respected and the quality is preserved. The correction suggested by our prototype is the following one:

$$\theta_{S1}\left([i]\right) = [1][i] + [0] = [i]; \; \theta_{S2}\left(\begin{bmatrix} i \\ j \end{bmatrix}\right) = \begin{bmatrix} 0 & 1 \\ 0 & 0 \end{bmatrix}\begin{bmatrix} i \\ j \end{bmatrix} + \begin{bmatrix} n \\ 0 \end{bmatrix} = \begin{bmatrix} j+n \\ 0 \end{bmatrix}.$$

To homogenize the chunking functions, one can add null dimensions, or remove them if they are null for all the functions, since this does not change the ranks. We have finally $\theta_{S1}\left(\left[\,i\,\right]\right) = \left[\,i\,\right]$ and $\theta_{S2}\left(\left[\begin{smallmatrix} i \\ j \end{smallmatrix}\right]\right) = \left[\,j + n\,\right]$.

3.4   Group-Reuse

There is group-reuse when two statements, $S1$ and $S2$, access the same array A through indexing matrices F_1 and F_2 (for the sake of readability, we will use homogeneous coordinates in this section). There is reuse if there exists iteration vectors x_1 and x_2 such that $F_2 x_2 = F_1 x_1$, and this reuse is exploited if these two operations are in the same chunk:

$$\forall x_1 \forall x_2, F_2 x_2 - F_1 x_1 = \mathbf{0} \Rightarrow T_2 x_2 - T_1 x_1 = \mathbf{0}. \tag{4}$$

Observe that this constraint has the same shape as a dependence constraint. If $F_2 x_2 = F_1 x_1$, then $S1[x_1]$ and $S2[x_2]$ are in dependence. This dependence may be a read-read dependence, which may not be taken into account in other circumstances, but which exists nevertheless. As to the right-hand side of (4), it is similar but more restrictive than the right-hand side of (3). As a consequence, we can give a more precise result:

Theorem 2. (4) is true iff $\left(T_2 - T_1\right) = N\left(F_2 - F_1\right)$ where N is a matrix of full row rank.

Proof. Let x be the concatenation of vectors x_1 and x_2. Formula (4) can be written

$$\forall x, \left(F_2 - F_1\right) x = 0 \Rightarrow \left(T_2 - T_1\right) x = 0.$$

$\left(F_2 - F_1\right) x = 0$ and $\left(T_2 - T_1\right) x = 0$ describe two sets where one point belonging to the first one necessarily belongs to the second one too. Therefore the first one is a subset of the second one. So it can be written as the second one with b additional constraints:

$$\left(F_2 - F_1\right) x = 0 \Leftrightarrow \begin{cases} \left(T_2 - T_1\right) x = 0 \\ Q x = 0 \end{cases}$$

then $\begin{pmatrix} T_2 - T_1 \\ Q \end{pmatrix} = M\left(F_2 - F_1\right)$ with M a matrix such that $\det M \neq 0$ (the system is not modified by linear transformations). Let us write M as $\begin{pmatrix} N \\ N' \end{pmatrix}$ where N' is the matrix made with the b last lines of M. Now we have $\begin{pmatrix} T_2 - T_1 \\ Q \end{pmatrix} = \begin{pmatrix} N \\ N' \end{pmatrix}\left(F_2 - F_1\right)$ and finally $\left(T_2 - T_1\right) = N\left(F_2 - F_1\right)$. ∎

The unknowns are the entries of N, which define the linear transformations to apply to $\left(F_2 - F_1\right)$ in such a way that the chunking functions respect the dependences. This is clearly the same problem as the correction for dependences in section 3.3. We solve them at the same time, by adding the necessary constraints (a set of constraints by pairs of references in which group-reuse is detected) to the initial problem. This theory, which does not assume that group-reuse is associated to constant dependences, can even be used for "self-group-reuse", when the two accesses to A are in the same statement. Here, we deduce from (4) that the linear subspace $G = \{x_2 - x_1 | F_1 x_1 - F_2 x_2 = 0\}$ is included in the kernel of $T = T_1 = T_2$.. It is easy to find a basis for G by gaussian elimination techniques. The resulting vectors can be taken into account when building the chunking matrices. Improving group-locality do not change the order of magnitude of the traffic. It can divide the traffic generated by n references by a factor of n.

Example 3. Let us consider the source code in figure 3(a). All control centric

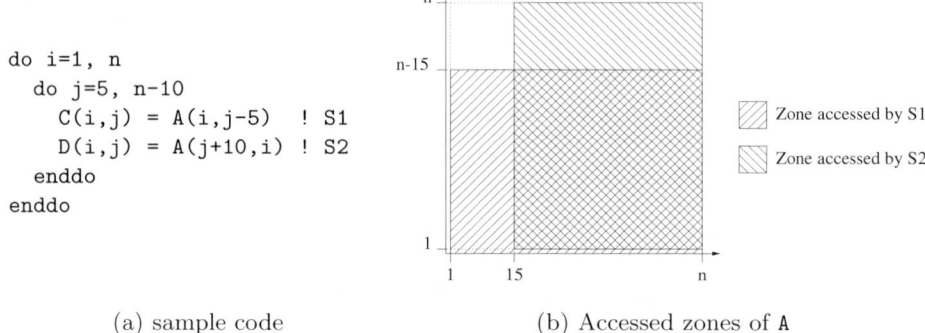

```
do i=1, n
  do j=5, n-10
    C(i,j) = A(i,j-5)   ! S1
    D(i,j) = A(j+10,i)  ! S2
  enddo
enddo
```

(a) sample code   (b) Accessed zones of A

Fig. 3. Example of group reuse

methods will estimate that there is no self reuse and no exploitable group-reuse. The reason is that they fail to consider non uniformly generated references (uniformly generated references are such as their subscript functions differ in at most the constant term [7]). In fact there is good reuse between the two statements for a part of the array A as shown by the figure 3(b). In this example, there is no dependence, then we can use the trivial solution of $(T_2 - T_1) = N(F_2 - F_1)$, that is $T_1 = F_1$ and $T_2 = F_2$. Therefore, the chunking functions will be :

$$\theta_{S1}\left(\begin{bmatrix} i \\ j \end{bmatrix}\right) = \begin{bmatrix} i \\ j - 5 \end{bmatrix} ; \theta_{S2}\left(\begin{bmatrix} i \\ j \end{bmatrix}\right) = \begin{bmatrix} j + 10 \\ i \end{bmatrix}.$$

This transformation leads to the target code below. The group-locality is now maximal: in the shared zone of A, the two statements access the same memory cell during the same iteration.

```
do c1=1, 14
  do c2=0, n-15
    C(c1,c2+5) = A(c1,c2)        ! S1
  enddo
enddo
do c1=15, n
  C(c1,5) = A(c1,0)              ! S1
```

```
      do c2=1, n-15
        C(c1,c2+5)  = A(c1,c2)        ! S1
        D(c2,c1-10) = A(c1,c2)        ! S2
      enddo
      do c2=n-14, n
        D(c2,c1-10) = A(c1,c2)        ! S2
      enddo
    enddo
```

3.5 Spatial-Reuse

There is spatial reuse for a reference if it accesses data on the same cache line during different iterations. As for group locality, improving spatial locality do not change the order of magnitude of the traffic. It can divide the traffic generated by a reference by a factor of d, where d is the cache line length in words. Spatial locality is achieved if the operations accessing the same cache line are in the same chunk. Let us consider a reference to an array A with the subscript function F. Let i be the number of the major dimension of A, i.e. the dimension with data lines ordered successively in memory. Then spatial locality is achieved for A if the operations accessing the memory cells of the major dimension are in the same chunk. In other words, spatial locality is achieved if $F_{i,.} \in \ker T$.

This constraint is added in the T construction algorithm seen in section 3.2 by asking for a more accurate choice of vectors to be included in the matrix G. If the new constraint prevents the construction of T, we can try with another line of the subscript function and suggest the corresponding data layout transformation. This result can be compared with the Kandemir et al. method [8], where both loop and data transformations are used to improve spatial locality. Chunking does not require a non-singular transformation matrix, but it can achieve spatial locality only for a given loop level. However, in practive results are often alike.

4   Code Generation

Code generation is the last step to the final program. It is often ignored in spite of its impact on the target code quality. We must ensure that a bad control management does not spoil performance, for instance by producing redundant guards or complex loop bounds. An outline of the resulting code is a loop on the number of chunks L which contains the chunk operations. If the chunk numbers are vectors, we have as many surrounding loops as chunking dimensions.

Because the input problem is a static control program, the bounds on statement iteration spaces can be specified by a set of linear inequalities defining a polyhedron [10]. In the chunking case, we change the scanning order of this polyhedron by substitution of the original dimensions by chunking dimensions. The code generation is then a well known Z-polyhedron scanning problem. At present, the best solution is the Quilleré et al. one [14]. Their method is well adapted to the chunking problem provided we generalize it somewhat. We have implemented an extended version, CLooG, which can handle sequential inner loops and imperfect loop nests. Our resulting code is quite efficient.

5   Experimental Results

We are implementing our approach in the *chunky*[1] source-to-source optimizing tool. This prototype implements at present the process from the chunking function calculation to the code generation, but without group and spatial locality improvement support. This prototype already allows us to present preliminary results for some important non-trivial problems. The experiments were conducted on a PC workstation with a Pentium III processor running at 1GHz. This processor comes with two cache levels: a split first level (L1) for instructions and data of 16KB each and an unified second level (L2) of 256KB. Figure 4 shows the evolutions of the number of cache misses observed with hardware counters for the original and target versions of the running example (see figure 1), according to the value of the parameter m.

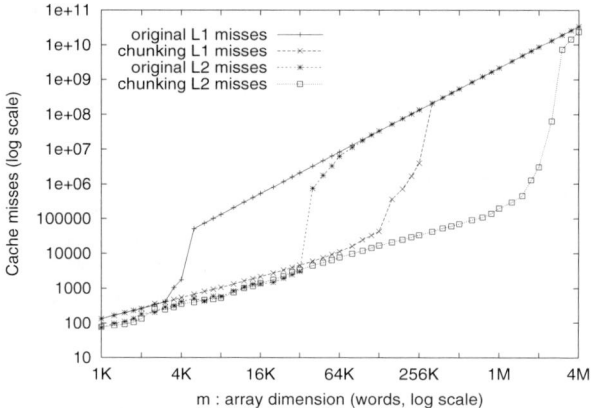

Fig. 4. Cache misses for the running example

The ratio m/n is set to 64 in order to better show the impact of our method. The number of cache misses sharply grows when the array b becomes larger than a cache level in the original program. The chunked program has a better behavior. The miss growth comes later, when the input hypothesis are no longer satisfied, *i.e.* when the array a cannot fit in the cache. We have observed the same phenomenon on most of the programs with good data reuse we have tested. Some experimental results on well known problems are shown in figure 5. The compiler option was O3 for the original programs, but O1 for the transformed programs in order to prevent any compiler optimization that can disturb the chunking. As for the running example, chunking can reduce the number of cache misses by more than one order of magnitude. This cache miss reduction can imply a significant performance improvement. The speedup is better with big problems. Since the

---

[1] Parts of Chunky are freely available at `http://www.prism.uvsq.fr/~cedb`

problem	array size (words)	missdown (%)	speedup (%)
running example	16K	99.1 (L1)	7
	1M	99.9 (L2)	427
LU decomposition	80 * 80	79.3 (L1)	2
	256 * 256	84.1 (L2)	43
Cholesky factorization	80 * 80	70.3 (L1)	2
	256 * 256	85.5 (L2)	46
Gauss-Jordan	80 * 80	70.2 (L1)	-13
	256 * 256	93.1 (L2)	26

Fig. 5. Experimental results

miss penalty for an L2 miss is of the order of 10 times an L1 miss, these results are not surprising. The situation of Gauss-Jordan for $80*80$ arrays shows how it is necessary to avoid control overheads. In this (rare) case, despite the attention given to code generation and a significant cache miss reduction, our method fails to improve performance on small problems. The point of view is quite different when the critical resource is energy, like in embedded systems. Cathoor et al. [3] show that data movements in the hierarchy is one of the main cause of energy consumption. In this case, a cache miss reduction is always a benefit.

6   Related Work

The effort of research to create effective locality optimizing compilers began with Wolf and Lam [15] and their *data locality optimizing algorithm*. This algorithm applies unimodular transformations to loop nests in order to maximize locality, according to evaluations of legal loop transformations relevance. Then it applies tiling [16] to the innermost loops. In comparison, our approach is applicable to a wider range of programs since in one hand we do not require perfect nests or nests such as they can be made perfect. And on the other hand because we do not require that dependences must have any simplified shape (Wolf and Lam algorithm needs that the dependence vectors be lexicographically positive). Moreover, to make perfect loops and to tile imply severe control overhead while we minimize it thanks to an accurate code generation method.

Li [11] generalizes the framework of unimodular matrices [2] by using linear, non-unimodular transformations to change the iteration space. We expect our algorithm will find more accurate transformations in practice since Li's transformation and dependence types are quite simple: the transformations do not handle parameters and the only case discussed is the one where dependences are represented by distance vectors.

McKinley et al. [13] propose a technique based on a detailed cost model that drives the use of loop permutation, fusion and distribution. They apply the basic transformations according to a definite order, while this strategy can be ineffective for some problems. To find which is the best application order of the transformations for a given program is known to be very hard. Chunking bypasses this difficulty because it unifies all kind of linear transformations in a single framework. For group-reuse, McKinley et al. consider the classic case of *uniformly generated references* [7], with small restrictions. We propose to go beyond this case by optimizing group-locality between non uniformly generated references when they are in different statements. In compensation, chunking processing is heavier than the McKinley et al. algorithm.

Alternatively to these control centric techniques, Kodukula et al. [9] propose a data centric approach that plans to act on data movement directly, rather than as a side-effect of control flow manipulations. Our work shares many features with [9]. Both papers are set in the framework of the polytope model, and aim at partitioning the code in pieces which are (almost) free of cache misses. Both techniques transform the code by well known transformations (loop exchange, loop skewing ...): the problem is not to invent *new* transformations, but to find the *right* transformation for a given program. There are however several important differences. Kodukula et al. start from the following intuition: once a datum has been brought into the cache, it is beneficial to execute all operations which access this datum. Our approach is different since we start from an estimate of the traffic and try to minimize it. In both cases we have to find a transformation legal for dependences. But while Kodukula et al. can just check if their transformation respects dependences, we have integrated the legality in the transformation construction. Lastly, while Kodukula et al. use an arbitrary array blocking, we show that significant improvements can be obtained without blocking. Testing whether blocking can improve our results is left for future studies.

7   Conclusion

In this article, we have presented a method based on traffic evaluations for data locality improvement. It exhibits many advantages. First of all, the computed solution always fulfills the memory requirements imposed. Next, it can be applied to any static control slice of a program. Lastly, there is no requirement on dependences and we compute the space of all legal transformations directly. The method requires nothing besides the original code but the relative sizes of the cache and data.

First results are very encouraging and make us believe that our technique is a new significant way to achieve data locality automatically for a large amount of problems. Moreover, chunking seems to be well adapted to several extensions and we plan to obtain even better theoretical and practical results. We are currently working on tiling which seems to be the natural continuation of our approach. Intuitively, tiling is a question of aggregating small chunks or splitting big ones. We are also working on a more accurate solution for spatial locality improvement. A step in that direction is the work of Loechner, Meister and Clauss [12], which is based on precise counting of memory accesses. Lastly, we must deal with programs which have static control regions but do not have static control *in toto*. Locality optimization have the nice property that there is no need of applying it to far away statements, since the hope of having reuse in this situation is very small. Hence chunking can be applied locally, i.e. to loop nests or small subroutines, and there is no danger of an excessive compilation time. Our method can be adapted to local memories (or software managed caches) at the price of more attention to footprint layout.

References

1. E. Anderson, Z. Bai, C. Bischof, S. Blackford, J. Demmel, J. Dongarra, J. D. Croz, A. Greenbaum, S. Hammarling, A. McKenney, and D. Sorensen. *LAPACK User's Guide, Third Edition*. SIAM, 1999.
2. U. Banerjee. Unimodular transformations of double loops. In *Advances in Languages and Compilers for Parallel Processing*, pages 192–219, Irvine, august 1990.
3. F. Catthoor, S. Wuytack, E. De Greef, F. Balasa, L. Nachtergaele, and A. Vandecappelle. *Custom memory managament methodology*. Kluwer Academic, 1998.
4. S. Coleman and K. McKinley. Tile size selection using cache organization and data layout. In *ACM SIGPLAN'95 Conference on Programming Language Design and Implementation*, pages 279–290, La Jolla, june 1995.
5. P. Feautrier. Dataflow analysis of scalar and array references. *International Journal of Parallel Programming*, 20(1):23–53, february 1991.
6. P. Feautrier. Some efficient solutions to the affine scheduling problem, part I: one dimensional time. *International Journal of Parallel Programming*, 21(5):313–348, october 1992.
7. D. Gannon, W. Jalby, and K. Gallivan. Strategies for cache and local memories management by global program transformation. *Journal of Parallel and Distributed Computing*, (5):587–616, 1988.
8. M. Kandemir, J. Ramanujam, and A. Choudhary. Improving cache locality by a combination of loop and data transformations. *IEEE Transactions on Computers*, 48(2):159–167, february 1999.
9. I. Kodukula, N. Ahmed, and K. Pingali. Data-centric multi-level blocking. In *ACM SIGPLAN'97 Conference on Programming Language Design and Implementation*, pages 346–357, Las Vegas, june 1997.
10. D. Kuck. *The Structure of Computers and Computations*. John Wiley & Sons, Inc., 1978.
11. W. Li. *Compiling for NUMA parallel machines*. PhD thesis, Cornell Univ., 1993.
12. V. Loechner, B. Meister, and P. Clauss. Precise data locality optimization of nested loops. *Journal of Supercomputing*, 21(1):37–76, january 2002.
13. K. McKinley, S. Carr, and C. Tseng. Improving data locality with loop transformations. *ACM Transactions on Programming Languages and Systems*, 18(4):424–453, july 1996.
14. F. Quilleré, S. Rajopadhye, and D. Wilde. Generation of efficient nested loops from polyhedra. *International Journal of Parallel Programming*, 28(5):469–498, october 2000.
15. M. Wolf and M. Lam. A data locality optimizing algorithm. In *ACM SIGPLAN'91 Conference on Programming Language Design and Implementation*, pages 30–44, New York, june 1991.
16. M. Wolfe. Iteration space tiling for memory hierarchies. In *3rd SIAM Conference on Parallel Processing for Scientific Computing*, pages 357–361, december 1987.
17. J. Xue. Transformations of nested loops with non-convex iteration spaces. *Parallel Computing*, 22(3):339–368, 1996.

Author Index